# GIFTED?

## THE SHIFT TO ENRICHMENT, CHALLENGE AND EQUITY

JOHN CATT
FROM HODDER EDUCATION

Every effort has been made to trace all copyright holders, but if any have been inadvertently overlooked, the Publishers will be pleased to make the necessary arrangements at the first opportunity.

Although every effort has been made to ensure that website addresses are correct at time of going to press, Hodder Education cannot be held responsible for the content of any website mentioned in this book. It is sometimes possible to find a relocated web page by typing in the address of the home page for a website in the URL window of your browser.

Hachette UK's policy is to use papers that are natural, renewable and recyclable products and made from wood grown in well-managed forests and other controlled sources. The logging and manufacturing processes are expected to conform to the environmental regulations of the country of origin.

Orders: please contact Hachette UK Distribution, Hely Hutchinson Centre, Milton Road, Didcot, Oxfordshire, OX11 7HH. Telephone: +44 (0)1235 827827. Email education@hachette.co.uk. Lines are open from 9 a.m. to 5 p.m., Monday to Friday.

**ISBN: 9781036003241**

© Morgan Whitfield 2024

First published in 2024 by
John Catt from Hodder Education,
An Hachette UK Company
15 Riduna Park, Station Road,
Melton, Woodbridge IP12 1QT
Telephone: +44 (0)1394 389850
www.johncatt.com

A catalogue record for this title is available from the British Library

# REVIEWS

*Gifted?: The Shift to Enrichment, Challenge and Equity isn't just another piece of academic dribble; it's a heartfelt manifesto for true inclusivity in our schools. As someone deeply invested in educational equity, I found this book resonating with the very principles I hold dear. It offers a critical yet hopeful examination of how we can stretch all minds, not just the ones we've pre-labelled as 'gifted'. This book is a clarion call to dismantle barriers and cultivate a landscape where every student can soar. If you, like me, believe in nurturing every child's potential and are seeking actionable insights to make this a reality, this book is an essential read. It's a potent reminder that enrichment isn't a privilege for the few but a right for all.*

**Leisa Grace Wilson, editorial director,
Teach Middle East and Schoolfinder.ae**

*This book is an eye-opening read, dispelling the myths of 'gifted and talented' that have been circulating schools for far too long. Morgan flips this idea of an elite few being 'gifted' and instead advocates for a 'challenge-for-all' approach, allowing children of all backgrounds to have a level playing field in a truly inclusive learning environment. This evidence-based book will provide you with the essential pedagogy to begin building opportunities in the classroom that truly embrace inclusivity. Let's stop putting that lid on education, which creates a systemic bias towards those who should be successful, and instead provide a system where all can achieve.*

**Cat Chowdhary, author of *So...
What Does an Outstanding Teacher Do?***

*This is an important book, different to anything I have ever read before, and one I can highly and wholeheartedly recommend to anyone in education who believes every child deserves to succeed and thrive.*

**Kate Jones, author of *Love to Teach*,**
***Retrieval Practice* and *Smashing Glass Ceilings***

Gifted?: The Shift to Enrichment, Challenge and Equity *delivers a powerful wake-up call to the educational community. With razor-sharp insight and genuine conviction, Morgan dismantles the outdated notion of 'gifted and talented' and champions a bold new approach to teaching and learning. Through compelling arguments and practical strategies, this book implores educators to embrace inclusivity, equity and rigorous challenge for all students. This book is a must-read for anyone committed to transforming education and creating a more equitable future for our students.*

**Stephen Moffatt, deputy head, MA, NPQH**

*As educators, it's our goal to create rigorous challenge for all students. In this book, Morgan explores the research behind the strategies that help provide teachers with practical advice and guidance on how we can empower our students so that all your students can achieve mastery. I strongly recommend this book to any new or experienced teacher seeking a research-informed guide on supporting every student.*

**Steve Oakes, author of *The Student Mindset***

*Morgan Whitfeld's excellent* Gifted?: The Shift to Enrichment, Challenge and Equity *brings fresh energy to this important area of educational thinking, presenting a vision for curriculum and pedagogy that is simultaneously challenging and inclusive. I love the extended circus metaphor that runs through the book, guiding us along a tightrope and through rings of fire as we explore the problematic 'gifted' concept, then leading us up to the Big Boom of learner autonomy. It's an engaging book full of conviction and insight, and I would highly recommend it as an addition to any CPD library.*

**Tom Sherrington**

*Morgan, in this book, joins the ever-growing number of colleagues who have moved away from provision for the gifted and instead introduced high challenge for everyone, in the evidence-informed belief that almost all students are capable of high performance. Constructing excellence in individuals, rather than responding to it in some individuals, brings us closer to the Organisation for Economic Co-operation and Development's objective of all students learning at high levels rather than just some. Morgan provides a really practical guide to help teachers work in this way.*

**Dr Deborah Eyre of High Performance Learning**

*A thought-provoking book that establishes a clear direction not only for teachers and their organisations, but more importantly, for regulators and governing bodies. Coming away from the attainment ceilings created in schools is integral to improving the socio-economic status of our children and their life chances.* Gifted?: The Shift to Enrichment, Challenge and Equity *provides a realistic and universal way to achieve this.*

**Kyle Knott, principal, Newlands School Dubai**

*In a time where the world seemingly hangs in the balance with much of what we know being challenged,* Gifted?: The Shift to Enrichment, Challenge and Equity *packs a huge punch in confronting age-old predispositions. Full of evidence-based research, inquiry and sensible solutions to move learning forward for all young people. Morgan writes with passion, enthusiasm, and a laser-focused lens on breaking barriers and building bridges so that all students can flourish where it matters most: education. I challenge any educator to read this book and not come away from it with a renewed sense of purpose; it's a must-read for all working in education!*

**Olly Lewis, author of *The EdTech Playbook***

*Dedicated to the most inspiring educators I know,
Mom and Dad.*

# FOREWORD

In the spirit of transparency, I should begin by stating I know Morgan in a personal and professional capacity. I worked alongside Morgan and we shared an office space. Now former colleagues, we have remained friends. This may appear to be a biased foreword, but I consider this to be a foreword written by someone who knows the author and has seen her interact with students, parents, carers and colleagues. I have listened to Morgan present on this topic, which she is very passionate, enthusiastic and knowledgeable about. I have now had the privilege to read her thoughts, experience and advice all captured together in this wonderful book. I can tell the reader with confidence that this author does practise what she preaches and does so with determination for all children to succeed.

My first leadership role was 'more able and talented coordinator'. This was a whole-school position that focused on supporting teachers and students to ensure the most-able learners were achieving their potential. This was a very data-driven role, as the grades and scores told me which students to target and challenge. In all honesty, I wasn't fully sure how to do this, but the aim was clear: ensure the students predicted the top grades achieve those grades.

Within my classes, I knew the students who had a passion for history and a wealth of historical knowledge, but those students weren't always on the gifted register. The data was based on cognitive ability tests, which do not include humanities-based questions but focus on aspects like spatial ability and non-verbal problem solving. I didn't challenge this approach to looking at 'more-able', 'gifted' and 'talented' children, but Morgan tackles this among many other misconceptions and mistakes that have been made in this field. The title itself – *Gifted?: The Shift to Enrichment, Challenge and Equity* – shows the need for a different approach in schools. Morgan doesn't just highlight a problem; she provides plenty of practical solutions and well-informed guidance based on evidence and experience.

This book has made me reflect on my own teaching practice and experiences, as well as provided inspiration for future curriculum design, lesson planning and delivery. As stated, my previous role focused on stretching and challenging a small percentage of students who were considered bright. The question is: how do we challenge everyone? Encouraging students to engage with historical sources, interpretations and ambitious texts is one way to stretch and extend in the subject of history, but as a whole-school coordinator I had no idea what this looked like in other subjects outside of my own teaching experience. Morgan shines a light on the importance of the teacher and their knowledge of the curriculum and the knowledge of the learners in their classes.

This book clearly shows how support and challenge are for everyone and the importance of challenging those who would otherwise go unchallenged. Morgan is very clear with her advice throughout the book. As she eloquently states, 'Teachers have an ethical responsibility to stretch all students and to recognise each pupil as a distinct individual.' I have not always done this, regrettably, but moving forwards I feel more confident and able to do so.

Challenging the term 'gifted' is refreshing and generates vital discussion for teachers and school leaders to consider, reflect on and act on. Conversations about 'ability' are essential in every school. This book can help shape the discourse on curriculum aims, quality, delivery and impact. Linked to this is pedagogy and using evidence-informed approaches to support and enhance teaching and learning, which Morgan explores in detail and depth.

I found the examples and evidence woven throughout the book to be fascinating as well as insightful. From the Bronx to Kent, from debunking learning styles and checking cognitive biases, there is a wealth of information for the teacher and leader to absorb, reflect on and learn from. This is an important book, different to anything I have ever read before, and one I can highly and wholeheartedly recommend to anyone in education who believes every child deserves to succeed and thrive.

Kate Jones

# CONTENTS

Introduction ....................................................................................... 15

    The Shift to Enrichment ...................................................... 19

    The Shift to Challenge for All ............................................. 19

    The Shift to Equity ............................................................. 20

    Reference List ..................................................................... 22

**PART 1: ENRICHMENT** ........................................................ **23**

**1. The Greatest Show on Earth** ......................................... **25**

    Bronx School of Science in New York City ........................ 27

    Bringing the Circus to Town: the Weald of Kent Grammar School Annexe ................................................................. 34

    UK Department for Education's History with Gifted and Talented .......... 39

    Reference List ..................................................................... 46

**2. Not My Circus, Not My Monkey** ................................... **49**

    The Mother of Giftedness .................................................. 51

    The Father of Testing ......................................................... 55

    The Legacy of Cognitive Ability Testing ............................ 59

    Geniuses – Just Like Us ...................................................... 65

    Reference List ..................................................................... 68

**3. Jumping Through the Rings of Fire** ............................. **71**

    Ability Grouping ................................................................. 72

    Gifted Classes .................................................................... 77

    Acceleration ....................................................................... 80

    Push-In and Pull-Out ......................................................... 88

Overall Impacts of Traditional Gifted Interventions ..................................... 91

Reference List ......................................................................................... 93

**4. Walking the Tightrope** ....................................................................... **97**

Assumption 1 – Gifts are Discovered ........................................................ 99

Assumption 2 – Cognitive or Standardised Testing is Best Practice for
Identifying Student Capacity ................................................................... 103

Assumption 3 – We Need to Have a List .................................................. 123

Reference List ...................................................................................... 135

**5. Aerial Acrobatics** ............................................................................. **139**

Aerial Acrobatics – Component 1:
Enriched Curriculum ............................................................................. 143

Aerial Acrobatics – Component 2:
Enriched Pedagogy ............................................................................... 155

Aerial Acrobatics – Component 3: Enriched Mindset ............................... 171

Conclusion ........................................................................................... 180

Reference List ...................................................................................... 182

**PART 2: CHALLENGE** ........................................................................... **189**

**6. Astonishing the Audience** ................................................................. **191**

Oracy .................................................................................................. 193

Debate-Centred Instruction and Argumentation ..................................... 196

Reference List ...................................................................................... 206

**7. Come one! Come all!** ........................................................................ **209**

Harkness Conference Method ................................................................ 210

Overcoming the Challenges of Implementing Harkness ........................... 221

Reference List ...................................................................................... 226

**8. Slow Build Up to a Big Boom** ........................................................... **229**

Project-Based Learning .......................................................................... 232

Conclusion: Learner Autonomy .............................................................. 250

Reference List ...................................................................................... 252

**9. Flying on the Trapeze? Put Up a Safety Net** .................................. **257**

The Challenges of Challenge.................................................... 259

Making Challenge Routine ...................................................... 263

Profiles of Underachieving Pupils ............................................ 266

Reference List ....................................................................... 284

**PART 3: EQUITY**.....................................................................**289**

**10. Tossing Your Hat in the Ring** ...................................... **291**

Differentiated Model of Giftedness and Talent ....................... 296

Evolving Complexity Theory..................................................... 299

'Chance' and Enrichment.......................................................... 300

Action Over Traits: The Actiotope Model.................................. 305

Design with Diversity, Equity and Inclusion ............................ 309

Reference List ....................................................................... 311

**11. The Travelling Circus** ................................................. **315**

Around the World and Back in Time ........................................317

Gifted Approaches in Broad Strokes......................................... 322

Reference List ....................................................................... 333

**12. Welcome to the Big Top**............................................... **337**

Purposes of Enrichment........................................................... 338

Case Study: Alexandra Park School,
Haringey, London, UK ............................................................. 339

Analyse Outcome, Not Intent.................................................. 356

Culturally Responsive Instruction ........................................... 359

Representation and Diversity at the Top .................................. 365

Reference List ....................................................................... 376

**Acknowledgements** ......................................................... **381**

# INTRODUCTION

*Giftedness is not a thing. It has no physical reality, no weight, no mass. It is a social construct, not a fact of nature. It is something that was invented, not discovered.*

**Dr James Borland, 2005, p. 14**

*I celebrate teaching that enables transgressions—a movement against and beyond boundaries. It is that movement which makes education the practice of freedom.*

**bell hooks, 1994, p. 12**

Luka requests a seat at the very front of my class in our first geography lesson. His back is ramrod straight as he sits poised to shoot up his hand at the first opportunity. I recognise this look, a keen expression that beams with confidence and enthusiasm. At the first volley of questions, he speaks too long and too fast. When discussing with his group he gesticulates and argues with zeal. He lingers at my desk at the end of the lesson and trails off on a wonderful tangent about tsunamis. I test him on destructive plate boundaries. He boasts he already understands tectonics because he borrowed the textbook over the summer. Then he eagerly shares that he has conquered naming all the capital cities in 10 minutes and read every article National Geographic has ever published. Luka confides that his dream is to visit the lava fields in Iceland and to someday work in sustainable energy.

Luka has taken up most of the break time and I come out of the interaction amused and smiling. I make a few mental notes about his favourite topics. Then I promptly look up his past test scores and exam results. His last set of reports noted off-task behaviour. His standardised score is middling, internal reports show an average B student and his effort grades across the board are mixed. Would he be identified as gifted? Probably not. Would he benefit from further extension? Yes.

Luka's case presents a common dilemma for teachers. Is he being stretched and challenged? Does the curriculum have the depth or breadth to captivate him? Is his passion being channelled into higher-order skills and enquiry? A student can be crying out for extension, but data analysis and structures of a school often overlook them. He won't appear to be underachieving by tests that measure his 'potential'. He is meeting age-related expectations. Yet he is being underserved. Students may be unintentionally hidden – we need to find them.

Once we see a student who needs more challenge, how do we provide it? Do we simply progress through the materials at a faster pace? As a subject teacher, I can give Luka extra exercises in my lessons, direct him to the Model United Nations after school or assign him podcasts to 'learn around' the subject. These are all valuable, but can also be narrow, unavailable or passive respectively. Luka starts with intellectual curiosity, and I should be creating opportunities for exploration, innovation and mastery. Luka's passion could easily be stamped out when it should be sparked.

Let's take a peek at how education has traditionally characterised 'gifted and talented'. Gifted commonly refers to academic subjects, arguably what are considered core subjects like English, mathematics and the sciences. Defining talent has been more subjective, done by observing excellence in practical application subjects such as physical education and dance. Note that I don't specify 'gifted' as current attainment and performance in academic subjects. Giftedness can often have a narrow definition where a single cognitive ability test score can trump all other criteria. Students may be identified with the assumption that they are universally advanced, or highlighted based on standardised assessment, as opposed to interest in the subject or characteristics of effective learning. Incomplete, limited and divisive – identification can be reductive. As a fellow teacher recently commented to me, 'G&T? Seriously? Is that still a thing?'

Provision for 'gifted and talented', 'more able' or 'high-ability' students is a hot-button issue for teachers. In any staffroom, the topic proves polarising – selective programmes can be elitist, exclusive and antiquated. Gifted and talented programmes have a profound history of racism, sexism and ableism. Streaming, ability setting, pull-out groups and gifted classes are problematic and broadly entrench social immobility. At the same time, there have been national panics about the lack of progress for more able learners (Wilshaw and Ofsted, 2016). There is an expectation that these students are provided with additional challenge. School programming for those identified varies widely, from acceleration to mentorship to special extracurricular activities. A policy may simply dictate that the 'high-aptitude' students be assigned more difficult work and take exams earlier. Identifying students who seemingly deserve a higher investment beyond the classroom is a tricky proposition. For instance, the top 2% by any measure is a simplistic way to label and divide a set of students. As Dr James Borland writes of giftedness: 'This simplistic dichotomization of humanity into two distinct, mutually exclusive groups, the gifted and the rest (the ungifted?), is so contrary to our experience in a variety of other spheres of human endeavour as to cause one to wonder how it has survived so long in this one' (Borland, 2005, p. 7).

'Gifted and talented' is a zombie. It is dead, but still walking around. There are new labels to stratify students – 'more able', 'significantly able', 'high-end learners'. New labels do not equal new thinking. The concept of 'gifted' is still stubbornly embedded in our educational structures. Semantics can take over the debate as the term 'G&T' is slowly being removed from registers and seating plans across the world, but a pedagogical focus still revolves around a classification. New language is inadequate as there are issues in identification processes that hinder engagement and motivation, or mask underachievement. 'More able' is not only a measure of academics – students can be 'more able' when they have more financial resources, more access, more visibility, more support or more cultural acceptance. Given the fraught nature of G&T provision, there has been a move towards more egalitarian and progressive implementation. This is why education is shifting towards whole-school enrichment programmes, challenge for all and equity.

This book has one simple thesis: enrichment and challenge are for everyone. This is a principle designed to ensure the accessibility of opportunities. It is not a blanket statement – students have different needs and unique barriers, so we should vary our teaching strategies. Teachers have an ethical responsibility to stretch all students and to recognise each pupil as a distinct individual. Like any other need, those students who require extension should be actively developed. The goal of effective instruction is to challenge those who would otherwise go underchallenged. I wish to explore practices to stretch all students in and out of the classroom.

## Enrichment, Challenge for All and Equity

Enrichment is providing opportunities for extension that enhance, deepen, complement and elevate learning for all students. We can enrich our curriculum, pedagogy, mindset and educational structures.

Challenge for all is an inclusive approach to instruction, whereby every student is invited, and given the tools, to reach a place of mastery.

Equity is a principle and process for fairness and social justice. The principle means acknowledging that we do not all start from the same place, so must create opportunities for all individuals and communities to thrive. The process is ongoing, requiring us to identify and overcome intentional and unintentional systemic barriers.

*Gifted?* The title of this book places a hard emphasis on the question mark to indicate an era that is ending. The word 'gifted' is uncomfortable – we should interrogate why. The word automatically creates a category of students. My argument is simply this: we don't need a category. What I suggest is that we reimagine challenge. Challenge is not reserved for a special classification of students, it is not a race to the top, nor is it guaranteed when we differentiate. The 'gifted' mindset needs more than a rebrand; it requires an overhaul and change in ethos. Educators should acknowledge the inherent privilege and invisible hurdles of gifted provision. Keep the challenge and remove the exclusivity.

There are schools and programmes that have been trailblazing – opening doors for all students. These success stories make for a fascinating study as they have put on new lenses and implemented initiatives with equity in mind. This is the transition in thinking from 'developing gifted students' to creating enriching ecosystems. We need structures that embrace diversity, and conditions wherein educators foster enquiry and cogitation. We can target those who need extension, while simultaneously opening doors for all. To reimagine giftedness, we need to embrace **enrichment, challenge and equity**.

# The Shift to Enrichment

In this first section, we will be looking at the tricky business of identification, scrutinising the messy repercussions, getting a crash course in gifted research and surveying the debates surrounding giftedness. All of this is designed to take you on a journey that ends in enrichment for everyone.

As educators, we want our instruction to continuously extend our learners. The gifted paradigm tends to court controversy, and there are deep divides about how we provide extension. Typical interventions involve acceleration, special classes or bespoke after-school activities. Cognitive ability testing, setting or tracking, and invite-only programming all have strong proponents and detractors. Dividing students into streams and selective gifted programmes has left students out – most crucially, those from historically marginalised communities. The achievement gap is an opportunity gap (Carter and Welner, 2013). Creating inclusivity begins with recognising the inequity of gifted structures and understanding why they exist. The history of gifted and talented pedagogy is telling – it exposes the obstacles that have limited (and are still limiting) students' participation in enrichment activities and the level of challenge they receive in lessons. How can educators confront the complicated origins of 'giftedness'? Are we measuring what we value? Why are the stakes so high?

An important component is overcoming the larger structural biases. As egalitarian as we hope education can be, the world is mirrored in our institutions. We are all confronting systemic barriers in our schools and recognising our weaknesses. Gifted labels can magnify existing inequity. There are issues with targeting students, as threading the needle of identification is delicate.

# The Shift to Challenge for All

We can add challenge to our curriculum (what we teach), our pedagogy (how we teach it) and our mindset (who we are including). Transforming our teaching practice begins with examining our presuppositions and then evaluating what impactful challenge for all looks like in action. There is fantastic literature on powerful knowledge, teaching to the top and personalised responsive teaching. All students should be given an overarching challenge to reach.

There are pervasive narratives that educators should prioritise extension for some students and not others. We may assume that 'more-able' students can independently get on with work. There is the myth that the trick to teaching is pitching lessons judiciously to the 'middle ability', and then differentiating up and down. When I began my career, I simply tagged an extension question onto every task for students who completed the work quickly – it ticked a box. It was only after my first year of teaching that I realised how ineffective this was. Later I developed the principles of a) challenge-first instruction, b) invite all and c) not more, but interesting. I completely changed my tactics when it came to establishing expectations. The more I taught, the more I was willing to trial new strategies. How can we upend traditional lesson formats? What tools can we give students to dive deep? How can we build autonomy in our learners? What does critical thinking and collaboration look like in action? How do we facilitate student-led learning? It is useful to put a spotlight on oracy, debate-centred argumentation, discussion-based instruction, metacognition and project-based learning. This is the optimistic and enthusiastic realisation of enrichment: it brings the curriculum to life and stimulates a lifelong love of learning.

There are the challenges of challenge. Students have capacity but may face barriers in actualising or demonstrating their skills. This could be due to neurodivergence, speaking in a second language, trauma, cultural bias, economic context, social exclusion or stereotype threat, to name a few examples. Teaching and learning is not one size fits all. Listening to students is the first step; giving them a platform for that voice is the next.

## The Shift to Equity

Diversity, equity and inclusion are the foundation of enrichment and challenge for all, and designing from this lens can uplift students from any starting point. This book looks at how teaching and learning practices are inextricably linked to equity. Whole-school policies and leadership buy-in can confront structural barriers, address student needs, empower staff and lend parity to equity-seeking groups. Culturally responsive instruction supports high levels of learning. This requires diverse leadership, ongoing continuous professional development and a reflective staff. Gifted programmes have traditionally been a place of selection and elitism. We want to establish safe and inclusive learning spaces. Enrichment requires a diversity of voices and expanded methods for feedback.

Gifted models have been underpinned by specific worldviews. How have gifted ideas been advanced, critiqued and transfigured? How has pedagogy evolved to challenge for all? Borrowing and learning from current best practice, then implementing with accessibility and inclusion in mind, is key. Launching enrichment programming in your school can be powerful, especially if tailored to the context of your pupils and community. The goal is an electric environment for students. We will examine how initiatives can be enacted while still respecting the golden rule: enrichment is for everyone.

It is important to recognise the dialogue required to tackle these issues. I write about equity as a person who has privilege. I hope to capture the nuance of these discussions but recognise that many problems of inequity are not my lived experience. My goal is to not own the conversation. There is a history of white allies dominating the research, policy creation and 'championing visions of equity and inclusion yet to be endorsed by the people of color they claim to support'. (Douglass Horsford, 2021). Whenever I think I have a perfect solution, I encounter a difficult reality. I have made policy mistakes, overlooked students and fallen into classic 'gifted and talented' traps. I've also entered into spirited debates with my colleagues and evolved my perspective.

A challenge-for-all philosophy can drive achievement and improve student outcomes in the short and long term. To that end, I've witnessed the changes in the self-regard, resilience and ambitions of young people. Building enthusiasm and engagement means welcoming all students into enrichment initiatives. I am constantly surprised by how pupils have risen far above any expectation I could have set. Students have left me awestruck, astonished and amazed. This book is a reflection of my experience establishing enrichment programmes over the past decade. My classroom practice has changed dramatically in how I extend students. A challenge-for-all approach has reinvigorated my teaching and has the power to revolutionise school ethos. The shift to enrichment, challenge and equity creates magnificent possibilities. The message to all students should be: you belong here.

# Reference List

Borland, J. H. (2005) 'Gifted education without gifted children: The case for no conception of giftedness.' In: Sternberg, R. J. and Davidson, J. E. (eds.) *Conceptions of Giftedness*, 2nd edn. Cambridge: Cambridge University Press, pp. 1–19.

Carter, P. L. and Welner, K. G. (2013) *Closing the Opportunity Gap: What America Must Do to Give Every Child an Even Chance*. New York, NY: Oxford University Press.

Douglass Horsford, S. (2021) 'Whose vision will guide racial equity in schools?' *Education Week*, 17 March, [Online]. Available at: www.edweek.org/leadership/opinion-whose-vision-will-guide-racial-equity-in-schools/2021/03 (Accessed: 1 January 2024).

Hooks, B. (1994) *Teaching to Transgress: Education as the Practice of Freedom*. New York, NY: Routledge.

Wilshaw, M. and Ofsted. (2016) *HMCI's commentary: most able pupils*. Available at: www.gov.uk/government/speeches/hmcis-monthly-commentary-june-2016 (Accessed: 16 September 2022).

# PART 1:
# ENRICHMENT

# 1. THE GREATEST SHOW ON EARTH

*What's the point in having high expectations for just some of our students? Where on earth is the sense in picking off our "most able" 10% and deciding to push this elite to scholastic excellence?*

**David Didau, 2022**

*We mistakenly believe that the education system must choose between a system focused on nurturing the elite and a system that is effective for the majority.*

**Dr Deborah Eyre, 2011, p. 54**

*Rather than continuing to produce and consume research that "discovers" the inequalities every person of color already knew existed, I wonder if we might instead envision a system of education where everyone is free.*

**Dr Sonya Douglass Horsford, 2021**

We have all been the ringmaster. Our classroom is a stage, and we insist on audience participation. The spotlight is on you to start the spectacle, and then with a wave, you bring out the fire dancers, tumblers and jugglers. They take over the show while you facilitate, observe and occasionally nudge them along. All students are high-flying acrobats – you raise the trapeze and build them a ladder. You feel the energy when you come through the doors. A constant whirl of activity where your eyes don't know where to look. There is joy in the busyness, where each performer is engaged. This is enrichment at its best.

I am a proponent of enrichment and challenge for all because it is a big tent. The framework that teachers create for students in our classrooms can be extended to whole schools. The trick is to have purposeful models that enhance learning inside and outside the classroom. Enrichment must respond to two challenges: how can schools capture that dynamism? How can we invite everyone to the show?

I was at a dinner party and sat beside an enthusiastic teacher whose school had recently decided to create an initiative for their 'high-aptitude pupils'. The plan was an after-school programme with a heavy STEAM emphasis. The students would work with science teachers and an architecture firm to design a new, environmentally sustainable cafeteria for the school. The teacher asked how this could be improved upon. The project sounded amazing, and to enhance, I suggested a pivot towards student choice, as students might prefer going beyond a science and engineering focus. I leapt into project-based learning and how students are motivated when they can choose their speciality as opposed to being heavily directed. We bounced ideas off each other for some time. Then I caught myself mid-conversation. To start at the very beginning, the programme should be open to all students, not just the high-aptitude ones. The teacher asked, 'Why?' The whole purpose was to have a special programme for their top students. Theory and history washed over me, but my immediate response was, 'Why not?'

Schools are at different junctures in their enrichment programming, and there are regular entanglements with the old systems of gifted and talented. However, gifted thinking has erected barriers to enrichment, and gifted and talented structures miss the mark. There are ways to elevate instruction and programmes with a foundation of inclusion, and rethinking our classroom 'stars' is the first step in adjusting our perspective. There are patterns in assumptions of giftedness. The 'gifted' way of thinking puts identification at the forefront.

Traditionally, the characteristics of giftedness have two common denominators: precocity and curiosity (Freeman, 2002). Precocity is the very early development of certain skills, while curiosity is the desire to expand understanding. The first characteristic, precocity, can be assessed. Testing a child to see if they are 'ahead' of others their age seems like the most obvious identification, so standardised test scores are the dominant identifier. However, while precocity may be measurable, it is also problematic. Outside the world of education, age is irrelevant. Being a 'gifted child' does not mean one will grow into a particularly 'gifted adult' (Freeman, 2002). Many incredibly successful and intelligent adults were never considered gifted children. Precocity also has the element of time. There is extreme pressure on children identified as gifted to perform and outpace others, which can result in thwarting their all-round development, both academic and emotional.

Curiosity, on the other hand, has the opposite problem. It is unmeasurable. We could count the number of questions a child asks us (there have been studies: Berger, 2014), but we could never measure inner reflection or the depth of investigation. Intellectual curiosity is subjective, and perceiving it is open to bias. It is an ineffable criterion, and yet one of the most cited when we look for 'high-aptitude' students.

The challenge posed to enrichment, then, is to develop this curiosity in all students. An enrichment focus is not identifying gifted students; it is fostering gifted behaviours (Renzulli, 1986). The journey from 'finding gifted and talented students' to 'cultivating gifted behaviours' has been contentious. Giftedness is rooted in our conceptions of education, so there is an understanding that we should seek out exceptional students and provide them with the most challenging education possible. In conception, it makes sense to find extraordinary children and lift them up. There is, however, a conundrum in selection. Where is the gifted bar? How do we decide who has access to gifted programming? 'Genius' exists across all communities regardless of class, gender or race, so ideally, this begins with a universal opportunity for all.

Enrichment aims for equity, but this is at odds with how our education systems are organised. Understandably, parents often compete for the 'best' education for their children. Political leaders are often pressured to allocate funding for G&T programmes, streaming high attainers or special schools. Gifted initiatives strive for equality, but by definition, the movement misses being inclusive. Let's take a look at an example where outstanding schools have tried to thread the needle and made a knot with student selection.

## Bronx School of Science in New York City

The Bronx School of Science is brimming with innovation. The school is esteemed for leading in STEM, with an enquiry-based approach to learning. There is an expanded curriculum in robotics, engineering and computer science. The school has produced nine Nobel Prize winners and nine Pulitzer Prize winners – more than most countries. Alumni include a former Secretary of Defence, an Oscar-winning screenwriter, an executive editor of *The New York Times* and a director of the Hayden Planetarium. The school's formidable facilities, creative programming and dynamic staff have propelled its students into the Ivy League and world-class universities. The school's IDEAS Initiative nurtures students to Imagine, Discover, Engineer and Apply Solutions in their state-of-the-art Launch Labs. There are over 120 active extracurriculars ranging from pathogenesis research to topological crochet, from game theory to ethical hacking. There are seven student publications. Most impressively, this incredible institution is a public school. Bronx Science is one of eight storied magnet schools in New York City, standing beside Stuyvesant and Brooklyn Tech as one of the most renowned and coveted high schools in the country. It promises a free education of the highest calibre – to children who make the cut. So how does a student join these illustrious ranks?

Each year in New York City about 27,000 eighth-graders take a single high-stakes test. Students have 180 minutes to prove they belong in one of the eight magnet schools. The Specialised High Schools Admissions Test (SHSAT) became enshrined in the 1970s in a push to diversify and integrate specialist schools like Bronx Science. The test is required, under state law, to gain admittance. These schools were historically white and male, and the SHSAT was meant to correct that trend. There was a powerful movement to embrace diversity and have the school's demographics reflect the cultural mosaic of New York's metropolis. Testing was seen as a panacea. A test can't see money, colour, gender or history, and the SHSAT is open to every student, designed to be a neutral arbiter. As Robert Kolker wrote of the storied New York magnet schools, they 'reflect some of the city's most prized values: achievement, brains, democracy' (Kolker, 2011).

The result doesn't feel democratic, though. Black and Latin American students comprise almost 70% of students in the NYC public school system, yet only 10% of them are offered places in specialised high schools. In 1997 the Association of Community Organisations for Reform Now (ACORN) dropped a bombshell report showing that only a fraction of middle school students had the opportunity to learn SHSAT material in their classes. There was strong evidence that race was a significant factor, compounded by geography – schools in which the majority of students were Black and Latin American were not teaching the material for the test. Further, parents, teachers and leadership in schools facing barriers were unaware of the process to apply to gifted high schools.

ACORN investigated who *wasn't* taking the test. Schools with a majority of Black and Latin American students were being denied access to instruction necessary to do well on the examination. Parents had trouble obtaining information about the entrance exam, and in many cases were unaware of the process to apply to gifted programmes or specialised high schools. There was 'not a level playing field for winning the prize of a desk at Stuyvesant, Bronx Science, or similar schools' (New York Chapter of Association of Community Organization for Reform Now, 1997). ACORN referred to the policies as a de facto Jim Crow, leading to segregation within the New York City school system.

This is not a simple story of minorities being excluded. While white students are disproportionately represented, the majority of students given places in the gifted high schools identify as Asian. The 'Asian' category encompasses a huge swathe of diversity with many different ethnicities, cultures, languages and religions. Indian, Iranian, Japanese and Filipino students fill the busy hallways of the school. You can't say Bronx Science isn't diverse. In 2021 the student body had 77.7% minority enrolment (US News and World Report, 2022), and the specialised high schools have long served as a homing beacon for first- and second-generation immigrant communities. But it is glaringly obvious who is missing from these classrooms.

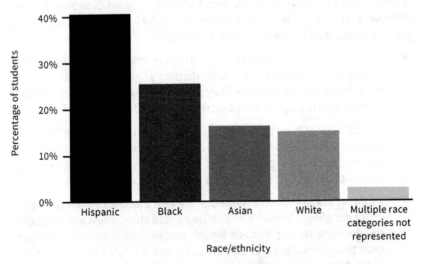

**2018–2019 School Year**
**Demographic Breakdown of New York City Public Schools**

Figure 1.1 School diversity in New York City 2018–19 (New York City Council, 2019).

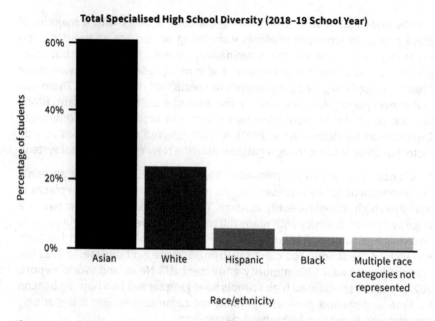

Figure 1.2 Specialised high school diversity in New York City 2018–19 (New York City Council, 2019).

Severe discrepancies exist for those given access to 'the highest level of academic achievement the New York City Department of Education has to offer' (New York City Council, 2019). Racial and ethnic identity is one of many prohibitive elements. The ACORN report on SHSAT barriers in New York begins with case studies. Here are a few examples:

- Spanish-speaking parents wish to have their child, whose first language is Spanish, in their district's gifted programme, so they apply for admission. They are informed that testing for the programme is only done in English and that there is a $50 fee.

- A child with SLCN (speech, language and communication needs) scores sufficiently high on an IQ test and qualifies for a gifted programme. He applies, but his parents are told that the school lacks the learning support and inclusion staff to provide the support he needs.

- A mother discovers midway through the year that one of the four classes in her daughter's school is a dedicated gifted class. She is informed that the deadline for applications for the programme was during the year prior to kindergarten and that the programme is full. She wasn't aware of the application process or how to get a gifted diagnosis.

Poverty is a significant factor. There are students who can afford summer camps and private tutoring to prepare for the entrance exam and others who cannot. The SHSAT was indicative of what was happening in gifted education throughout New York City. While 74% of students city-wide experience poverty, fewer than 50% of students at specialised high schools experience poverty (New York City Council, 2019). In the city's roughly 80 gifted programmes, white and Asian children make up about 70% of students. Again, these groups constitute only approximately 25% of the overall school system (Shapiro, 2021). There are students from equity-seeking backgrounds for whom these gifted programmes, and entrance to a magnet school, are a ticket to a better life. These children can get an exceptional score on the test, but a few points make all the difference, and one wrong question can leave them behind.

Words matter and inclusive language is paramount. At the same time, language is evolving and can change depending on context and discourse. Identities are not universal and experiences in those identities are not uniform. The language used may not be the preferred choice of everyone reading and it is difficult to have a one-size-fits-all approach. The language throughout this book has been carefully chosen to avoid causing harm by perpetuating problematic terminology or implicit bias. Taking into account a great deal of variation in language use across the world, I have used 'marginalised', 'equity-seeking groups', 'underserved', 'underrepresented', 'under-resourced', 'low-income' and 'people of determination/people with physical differences' as these terms tend to be the least problematic and the most inclusive. Whenever possible this book uses the term 'equity-seeking groups' to encompass people who are outside any dominant cultural group or have lower socio-economic status. I have used 'marginalised ethnic groups' where possible. This is to bridge a divide where North America favours the terms POC (people of colour) or BIPOC (Black, Indigenous and people/s of colour), while some sources in the UK still use BAME (Black, Asian and minority ethnic groups). When research is cited throughout the book that is precise in the groups studied, those groups will be specified accordingly. If we use these terms indiscriminately, we can erase differences between these communities.

I have also generally used person-first rather than disability-first language, as many prefer to be addressed as 'having' a designation or diagnosis rather than 'being' it. However, this is not always the case. For instance, some autistic people consider their autism an integral part of their identity, so prefer not to be called 'a person with autism'. This is often a personal choice, so one version of the language used is not always correct for each individual.

Policymakers have long seen these problems and tried to create a fix. Years of city-funded efforts have tried to diversify the schools without eliminating the admissions exam. This included advertising campaigns to inform families about the schools, the exam and free preparation classes available in low-income Black and Latin American communities. These campaigns have barely made a dent. New initiatives to promote diversity were introduced, such as the Discovery Programme. This offers a second chance to low-income, high-achieving students who scored a few points below the admissions cut-off. Discovery participants must attend a summer course, and if they do well there, they are admitted to one of the magnet high schools. This is wonderful in terms of offering more low-income students a place. However, it didn't make much of a difference for the Black and Latin American students who were the intended target. Discovery has disproportionately benefited Asian students, who are already over-represented in specialised high schools (Zimmerman, 2018). Arguing against an initiative like Discovery is difficult. If a low-income student can be given access to a great school through Discovery, does it matter if they are not the targeted demographic?

Should the testing be scrapped? In 2017, an education panel appointed by Mayor Bill de Blasio called for New York City to stop using academic criteria to screen applicants for admission to public magnet schools, and to phase out elementary gifted and talented programmes that required a test (Brody, 2019). Black and Latin American students had long been denied entry to these prestigious schools. The SHSAT was clearly an imperfect tool. A call for the testing system for gifted programmes and gifted schools to be dismantled seemed inevitable and sensible.

When de Blasio publicly proposed these ideas in 2019, they provoked uproar. Parents who had advocated for their children were frustrated that a lottery might take away an opportunity for those who earned it. Shouldn't hard work be rewarded? In some cases, families and friends had saved up money so that one son or daughter could take prep courses. Is a student whose parents can afford tutoring less worthy of a place? Parents with gifted neurodivergent children were upset that their programming was being threatened. Students who were in gifted programmes through elementary and middle school feared that their needs were about to be ignored. Many parents who had spent years fighting for a gifted diagnosis and championing their children feared another bureaucratic fight. Accommodations and funding for individual education plans were seen to be threatened. Parents simply wanted their children to get the very best education in a system where some schools are more well-resourced than others.

There was a backlash against the backlash. Supporters of the magnet schools erupted and there were demonstrations outside City Hall, with calls for equity appearing on protest signs held up by those on both sides of the debate. In the end, de Blasio's proposals were a political flop. Any initiatives for change failed. The SHSAT still exists. Under-resourced students and equity-seeking ethnic groups are still being left behind in admissions to gifted schools and programmes in NYC. In the meantime, inequality in New York schools has been further exacerbated due to remote learning during the COVID-19 pandemic (Domanico, 2021).

This is the tangled mess of an elite selective programme. This is the identification knot.

Failure in identification damages the larger goal of enhancing challenge for all students. This happens when we designate places in a selective school, decide who makes the cut for a gifted programme or reserve funding based on cognitive testing. In a call to reframe gifted education, a collection of pre-eminent researchers wrote in 2020:

> 'The goal of gifted and talented services is to challenge students who would otherwise go underchallenged and undereducated in school. Unfortunately, gifted education programs often use narrow and restrictive criteria to decide who can participate. As a result, they tend to focus on a tiny and homogeneous group of students, shutting out many others who would benefit from the supports and services they offer.' (Dixson et al., 2020)

This is not the first time or place that traditional identification has created inequity. Let's look across the pond, where the controversy surrounding magnet schools may feel familiar. The UK has long pushed to create social mobility through its education system. For decades the government has made equality of opportunity a priority in education, but there are still huge gaps. How were these gaps created and why do they persist?

# Bringing the Circus to Town: the Weald of Kent Grammar School Annexe

An annexe to the Weald of Kent Grammar School in Sevenoaks opened in 2017 amidst a flurry of controversy. Mary Boyle, the headteacher at a neighbouring school in Kent, called the announcement of the extension of the school 'a bad, sad day for education' (Walker, 2015). Headlines like 'Grammar school plan makes Kent a national battleground' (Benn, 2015) and 'Grammar school "annexe" in Kent is a dangerous moment' (Millar, 2015) stoked the rumbling anger. This may seem strange to an outsider. When measured by academic attainment, the Weald of Kent Grammar School had an excellent record of gaining top grades – far above national performance. The Weald is rated 'outstanding', so it was no wonder that the annexe was in high demand with 2600 citizens in Sevenoaks signing a petition for an expansion (BBC News, 2013). The proposed satellite would be co-ed, so boys could be admitted for the first time. Opening the new site 10 miles away was also logical considering 41% of students at the Weald were travelling 40 minutes every day from Sevenoaks. Grammar schools are free and all students in the area are welcome to apply for admission.

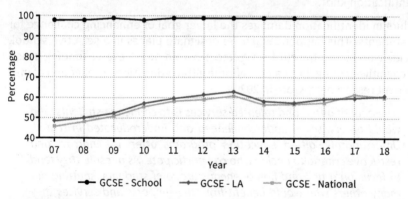

Figure 1.3 Weald of Kent attainment (KentLive, 2019).

The English system has national public examinations. Students sit 10 subject exams at the age of 16 (GCSEs). They can specialise in BTECs (vocational diplomas) or Advanced Levels (A-level) exams taken at age 18, which determine entry into university. These exam results are the quickest way to see how successful a school is. Schools will frequently have banners touting their GCSE and A-level results by the percentage of passing grades (grades 4–9 for GCSEs (previously A*–C) and A*–C for A-levels). These standardised exams make for easy comparison between schools and the results are important in how a school is judged. Schools in England are subject to inspection every 2–4 years, more frequently depending on how they are graded – 'inadequate', 'requires improvement', 'good', or 'outstanding'. Inspections are carried out by the Office for Standards in Education, Children's Services and Skills (commonly known as Ofsted).

The issue was this: under the loophole of the school being labelled an annexe, the construction of the Weald of Kent was in effect the first new grammar school to open in the UK in 50 years. Kent was testing legislation that barred any new grammar schools. Dr Nuala Burgess, the chair of Comprehensive Future, observed: 'Any new, standalone, grammar school is illegal, and the Sevenoaks annexe is tantamount to the creation of a *new selective school* [emphasis added] via the backdoor. This has to be a breach of the terms of the funding given for the satellite. I am hopping mad with anyone stupid enough to think this wouldn't happen, or deceitful enough to know it would and hope no-one would notice' (Comprehensive Future, n.d.). The divisive keyword here was 'selective'.

As Prime Minister David Cameron once put it, we 'don't want children divided into sheep and goats at the age of 11', referring to the selective 11+ exam that determines admission into grammars. The 11+ (or 11-plus) is a selective entrance exam generally taken at the beginning of Year 6. The exam is part of the admissions process for Year 7 at the UK's grammar schools, which are mostly state-funded secondary schools with a strong focus on academic achievement but include some fee-paying independent schools. The content varies between different areas of the UK but will generally have the following types of questions: English, maths, verbal reasoning and non-verbal reasoning.

The argument against grammar schools is simple. Just 2.6% of grammar pupils are from disadvantaged backgrounds. Only 3100 of the 117,000 pupils who attended grammar schools in 2015 came from families eligible for free school meals (Boffey, 2016). The pupil characteristics for the Weald of Kent Grammar paint a clear divide between the school's demographics and the national average.

| Pupils | Pupils – school | Pupils – national average |
|---|---|---|
| % English not first language | 2.6 | 16.5 |
| % Free school meals | 1.5 | 14 |
| % SEN Statement/EHC | 0.2 | 4.4 |
| % SEN | 3.4 | 10.4 |

Figure 1.4 Weald of Kent Grammar School pupil characteristics (KentLive, 2019).

The cause of this discrepancy is that some students are more prepared than others to take the test. As Francis Gilbert – one of the founders of the campaign group Local Schools Network – puts it: 'Inevitably, whatever test you use, it tends to be a test of social class, which is why you see a disproportionate number of children from wealthy backgrounds in grammar and selective schools' (Murray, 2013). There is a thriving tutoring industry, and it is easy to see why parents would make the extra investment to prepare. In 24 of Kent's 33 grammar schools, at least 96% of students achieved five or more A* to C grades at GCSE. Eight of those schools achieved 100%. In contrast, close to half of the county's 132 secondary schools scored below the national average of 59% (Murray, 2013). There is intense pressure on students to succeed when so much is on the line, and both parents and teachers point to an unhealthy tutoring and coaching culture. One mother interviewed in Kent said of the 11+: 'It utterly dominates everything. From about year 3 or 4, the reality hits home. It permeates all conversations and the children's relationships with each other. By the time you understand the system, it may be too late for your child' (Benn, 2015). Educational consultants report that some children start preparing with tutors at the age of 5.

There are 11+ preparation classes delivered by businesses like Kent's 11+ Tuition Academy, which offers weekly classes, summer intensive courses, mock exams and booster lessons (Tuition Academy, n.d.). This investment of money and time is not possible for all families. For a smaller price, 160 GBP, I found past paper bundles of Kent 11+ tests that one could purchase online, but again this is not an accessible price for all or an ideal preparation for many (Exam Papers Plus, 2024). The most expensive option is to send children to private fee-paying primary schools. Many parents see this as the best start, especially if the school's curriculum is geared towards the 11+. Independent schools have had an impact, with as many as 40% of places in

Kent grammar schools going to students from the independent sector. With all this in mind, the competition for places seems rigged. There have been attempts to create a 'tutor-proof test' in some counties, but the outcome has remained pretty much the same. As a member of parliament, Lucy Powell observed 'grammar schools have a shamefully low record when it comes to the number of children from poor backgrounds attending them' (Boffey, 2016). This is surprising given that grammar schools were conceived with the opposite outcome in mind.

The universally free grammar schools were built with post-war hopefulness. The Education Act was enacted after WWII to funnel high-achieving children into about 1600 newly formed grammar schools. These schools were designed to propel the best and brightest children into higher education and professional careers, no matter their background. The intention was to identify the limited number of 'gifted' students and give them something different to mainstream education. As Deborah Eyre noted: 'In some ways, it was a major improvement on what had gone before, as it recognised for the first time that there were large numbers of pupils capable of high levels of achievement' (Eyre, 2011, p. 6). To ensure admissions were free of any classism, it was the standardised 11+ test that determined entry. Those top 20–25% of test-takers were offered a place in a local grammar school that had a strong focus on academic achievement. Those who did not were streamed into 'regular' schools and the trades. The goal was that high achievers could be raised above their circumstances and launched into universities. In the long term, the 11+ tests were meant to result in more social equality.

Unfortunately, observers in the 1950s noted that working-class families saw shrinking household incomes if their children stayed in school longer as opposed to entering the workforce. Studies also found that the tiered system made little difference for children from lower socio-economic situations, both in gaining places in grammar schools and obtaining formal qualifications (Hart and Moro, 2016). The 1959 Crowther report for the government found that children of manual and unskilled workers were underrepresented in selective schools and over-represented in non-selective schools for a variety of reasons. I remember my nana telling me she performed impressively in her local grammar school test, but her family didn't send her because she was a girl. She spoke of her first-rate score with both pride and regret. One of my intimidatingly clever colleagues took the test cold and achieved a score of 119. The cut-off was 120 and she didn't gain entry to her local grammar. She wished she had been even a little prepared with tutors or past paper booklets in her primary school.

Grammar schools have been consistently dominated by middle-class children. It was a myth that the 'poor but bright' child was benefiting. In the 1960s the government began to shift away from grammar schools to non-selective comprehensive schools. Educational attitudes began to harden against grammars. British researcher Joan Freeman notes that in the 1970s 'greater emphasis was placed on socio-emotional concerns in teaching ... Not only were decisions on selective education found to be strongly influenced by social-class, but they even accentuated class-based opportunities because children so often conformed to what was expected of them' (Freeman, 2002, p. 13). The formal move to non-selective comprehensive schools came in 1976 (although 163 grammar schools have stubbornly remained open in some pockets of England). Grammar schools had become a cross-party issue. Margaret Thatcher as Secretary of State closed or merged most grammars and the Labour government then passed laws in 1998 banning the creation of new grammar schools. However, under-resourced students continued to leave comprehensive schools with lower grades and miss out on higher education. In the meantime, education in England continued the push for social mobility and was reinvented in 1989 with the creation of the national curriculum. The national curriculum had prescribed content and benchmark descriptors to ensure consistency across all types of schools. One of the purposes of standardisation was to ensure equity so that all students were receiving the same education. This was to create an equal playing field in the preparation and application to higher education. All students were taught the same skills and content, regardless of whether they attended a state or independent school.

Unfortunately, the problem remained. Studies repeatedly found that the national curriculum did not support high-ability pupils from comprehensive secondary schools in underserved areas. There was a move to create gifted and talented programmes in these schools to stop the leakage of high-ability pupils into the independent sector, but this faltered, and no larger shift supporting these students with specific programming was made. The national curriculum was changed in 2014 to allow teachers more flexibility in how they assessed pupil learning, but the results showed no major movement. High-ability pupils still progressed at a slower rate when they attended state-funded secondary schools and they left with lower grades than predicted. Social segregation between children of different classes and students from minority ethnic backgrounds is much higher in selective areas than in other parts of the country, as are the gaps in outcomes between children from equity-seeking backgrounds and the rest. As commentator Fiona Millar wrote, 'Grammar schools are socially divisive and anti-aspiration' (Millar, 2015).

# UK Department for Education's History with Gifted and Talented

In 1998, the UK government announced that 'gifted' and 'talented' were the terms of choice. There was a strong aversion to those terms among teachers, with their implications of fixed abilities and unearned privilege. This has produced a thesaurus of circumlocutions, with many schools using 'more able' or 'very able', or quite simply 'able' (Freeman, 2005, p. 88).

The Department for Education and Skills (DfES) defined students supported by the national programme for gifted and talented education as: 'Children and young people with one or more abilities developed to a level significantly ahead of their year group (or with the potential to develop those abilities)' (Department for Education and Skills, 2006, p. 1). In identifying gifted and talented learners, schools were encouraged to focus on:

- 'Learners who are gifted and talented relative to their peers in their own year group and school (including the top 5% nationally who are eligible for National Academy for Gifted and Talented Youth (NAGTY) membership)
- A range of abilities including talent in the arts and sport
- Ability rather than achievement, so that visible underachievers are amongst those identified.' (Department for Education and Skills, 2006, p. 1)

Guidance from the DfES's 'Identifying gifted and talented pupils: getting started' assumed a norm of around 10% of pupils per school, with schools free to determine the size of their gifted and talented population. Every school was expected to keep a register of its gifted and talented learners – the conception was that relative ability changes over time, so learners should move on and off the register when appropriate. There was an assumption that a school's gifted and talented population would be broadly representative of the whole school population in terms of gender, ethnicity and socio-economic background (although this was not the case for myriad reasons). Schools were free to use a best-fit model for identification, using quantitative and qualitative elements, with a continuous cyclical process of identification. The National Register was first announced in the 2005 White Paper 'Higher Standards: Better Schools for All' as an amalgamation of all schools' gifted and talented registers. NAGTY ran between 2002 and 2007 and provided extracurricular activities for students between 11 and 19 years of age. It introduced pupils to leading academic experts through summer schools and residential courses, as well as online material. The goal was to reach gifted students from a wide range of backgrounds while keeping them in mainstream school. Interestingly, Dr Deborah Eyre, the director of NAGTY, called out this system in her 'Room at the Top' paper, asserting that 'schools should be required to offer advanced learning opportunities as the norm and routinely expect large numbers of pupils to perform highly on them' (Eyre, 2011, p. 9). What unfolded was the realisation that the enrichment programme's successes should not have been limited to those select students alone. Dr Eyre had insight into how change for all students could be realised, which will be discussed in later chapters. NAGTY ended but this did not fundamentally change how G&T procedures were structured in schools.

In 2013, there was a pivotal government report by Ofsted's chief inspector, Sir Michael Wilshaw, devoted to how British education was failing the most able pupils in state schools (Wilshaw, 2013).[1] Two high-profile studies by Ofsted found that the brightest pupils were not given the challenge necessary to achieve high academic results upon transfer to secondary school. Thousands of pupils who achieved well at primary school, especially those from more underserved and under-resourced backgrounds, were failing to reach their full potential in secondary school. The correlation between underachievement and the state school versus independent school divide was clear. In a commentary, Sir Michael wrote:

> 'The most recent statistics paint a bleak picture of under-achievement and unfulfilled potential. ... What is most depressing is that the brightest children from disadvantaged backgrounds are the most likely not to achieve their full potential. The most able children in receipt of pupil premium funding still lag well behind their more advantaged peers.' (Wilshaw and Ofsted, 2016)

The potential is there. Take a cohort where 68% of non-selective primary school pupils achieved a level 5 or above on the 9-point scale in English and mathematics. Five years later, this cohort failed to attain A* or A grades in these subjects' secondary school examinations. In high-attaining pupils, 27% failed to achieve even the minimum expected progress of a grade B. Under-resourced students in state schools found doors closed to them due to this drop-off. In 2012, 20% of the 1649 non-selective state schools failed to produce a *single*

---

1    Ofsted covers only England; the Education and Training Inspectorate in Northern Ireland, Education Scotland (previously Her Majesty's Inspectorate of Education) in Scotland, and Estyn in Wales perform similar functions within their education systems.

*graduating student* with a grade profile of two A grades and one B grade in at least two of the facilitating subjects needed for university admission (Wilshaw, 2013). A report by the Sutton Trust identified 60,000 students who, at the ages of 11, 14 or 16, were among the top fifth of academic performers in state schools each year, but who had not subsequently entered higher education by the age of 18 (Chowdry et al., 2008).

| Measure of achievement | Advantaged students | Disadvantaged students |
|---|---|---|
| Grade B or above in secondary GCSE mathematics | 81% | 64% |
| Grade A–A* in secondary GCSE mathematics | 49% | 31% |
| Grade B or above in secondary GCSE English | 79% | 66% |
| Grade A–A* in secondary GCSE English | 39% | 26% |

Figure 1.5 Ofsted: most able students 2013 report (Wilshaw, 2013).

Simply put, those identified as the 'most able' secondary students are not doing as well as they should in the non-selective state sector where the vast majority of them are educated. Children who are not eligible for free school meals (i.e. not economically disadvantaged) are twice as likely to go to one of the top third universities (and more than twice as likely to go to one of the prestigious Russell Group universities) than children who are eligible for free school meals (Wilshaw and Ofsted, 2016). Wilshaw asserted that the whole of British society is affected when high-ability students from low-income households are not admitted into universities like their advantaged peers:

> 'This disparity risks perpetuating inequality in our society, as the elite professions continue to be disproportionately filled by graduates from these [university] institutions. As Chief Inspector, I have consistently lamented the failure of too many secondary schools to stretch our most able children, particularly the poorest. If our nation is serious about improving social mobility then our secondary schools have got to start delivering for these children. Our nation's economic prosperity depends on harnessing the talent of all our young people but especially those who have the potential to be the next generation of business leaders, wealth generators and job creators.' (Wilshaw and Ofsted, 2016)

The UK government has not been stagnant in the face of these findings. The expectation is that school policies address the needs of high-ability children.

Schools then ensure that children are identified and then demonstrably stretched and challenged. Inspectors are trained to look for evidence that a school's policy and provisions are working. The progress of high-ability pupils will usually be among the very first questions an inspector asks school leadership. When an inspector walks into a classroom, they are looking at how well the more-able children are being challenged. If the highest-ability students are stretched, it can be assumed that all students are being well served. Conversely, if the most-able pupils are not being stretched, that is an indication that things may be going wrong across all abilities.

The Ofsted report recommendations were geared towards practice in the classroom: better assessment, targeting and monitoring practices, more lesson observations to hold staff to account, imaginative homework, an improved curriculum, and boosting the use of Pupil Premium funding for all children facing social or economic barriers. A mention was made of creating a range of quality extracurricular activities, but not of 'enrichment' as a larger holistic programme. There are strong recommendations for whole-school systems of enrichment (which will be explored in the later chapters) that are yet to be popularised. With each school creating its own policy, and in the face of a data-focused inspection culture, enrichment is a big shift. As Eyre writes:

> 'In the UK we assume that only a small minority of children can achieve really high levels of academic performance and structure our system accordingly. We create a group of pupils called 'gifted children' and limit their number to 5% of the school population. ... This is a deeply flawed and old-fashioned approach. Indeed we don't stop there, we go further and presume we know who these gifted children are from an early age. We presume that a child's educational destiny can be more-or-less determined at birth by looking at a combination of their genetics and family background. Those who do well and come from disadvantaged backgrounds surprise us – we very patronisingly say they "succeed against the odds".' (Eyre, 2011, p. 12)

This British case study is fascinating because there has long been an awareness of the problem. Class differences that divide the British education system are revealed through the placement and success of high-ability students. The disparities between different types of schools translate into under-resourced students being less likely to apply and gain entry into higher education. This pattern seems long embedded in the history of British education, despite continued and earnest efforts to reverse the course. The state education system continues to exist alongside fee-paying independent schools. Around the world, we are familiar with prestigious private institutions like Harrow, Gordonstoun and Eton. To cherry-pick – 20 UK prime ministers have attended Eton, going back to the 18th century. Most recently, this includes David Cameron and Boris Johnson, who were subsequently propelled into Oxford. At the time of writing, Eton's fees sit at 49,998 GBP a year. This is not unique to the UK. Elite education across the world has traditionally propelled state leaders. Illustrious independent schools embody the privilege of those who could afford to send their children there. Grammar schools seemed to be the ticket to an equivalent education without the exorbitant fees. However, about 12% of students in grammar schools were in the private sector at age 10 and may well have stayed there had state-selection not been available. Conversely, those more affluent students who are close but missed the 11+ cut off, may exit the state sector for private schools. There are schools that have gone out of their way to balance the use of an entrance assessment with previous attainment reports, references, one-on-one interviews with teaching staff and creative writing tasks. Some schools invite students back for second interviews to give students another opportunity and emphasise that one of the most important components they consider is engagement in learning and an inquisitive mind (Royal Grammar School Guildford, 2023). Schools may use the opportunity to take a look at any disparity between performance in testing and references to provide support, with the overall goal of spotting students who can thrive in the school's environment.

Some barriers exist within the dynamics of a school. Within both selective and non-selective schools, there may be incredible enrichment and extension opportunities that less privileged students are unable to access. Then on a larger scale, there is the educational structure of non-selective comprehensive schools versus the selective independent and grammar schools. There are groups of students who have access to superb facilities, expert teachers and small class sizes that allow for easier responsive instruction. Then we have other groups of students with fewer extracurricular activities, fewer subject options and larger class sizes with overburdened teachers. It is no wonder then that there are highly capable students who are left behind because they lack the advantage. Tory education spokesman David Willetts announced in 2007 that 'we must break free from the belief that academic selection is any longer the way to transform the life chances of bright poor kids. We just have to recognise that there is overwhelming evidence that such academic selection entrenches advantage, it does not spread it' (BBC News, 2007). All of this imbues any selection-based schooling as the purview of the elite.

These case studies are not meant to be an indictment of individual schools. They are an indictment of the process of selection – how difficult it is to stratify students and the weight it carries. I wish to underline that this critique is not designed to impugn these institutions – these are incredible schools. Many of these programmes and schools have been trailblazing. As Joseph Renzulli noted:

> 'The Archilles heel of gifted education has been its inability to adequately include children who do not fall into the nice, neat stereotype of good test takers and lesson learners–ethnic minorities, underachievers, children who live in poverty, and young people who show their potential in nontraditional ways. And yet, the field of gifted education has been a true laboratory for many of the innovations that have subsequently become mainstays ... In many respects, special programs of almost any type have presented ideal opportunities for testing new ideas and experimenting with potential solutions to long-standing educational problems.' (Renzulli, 2005, p. 80)

Intentions can be good, and the work can be impactful. However, gifted thinking exists within a larger broken system. There is unequal access to: quality early childhood education (the preparation gap); unequal differences in school funding (the allocation gap); differences in how much support affluent parents can provide to their children compared to lower-income parents (the parent gap); the mindset and relations between teachers and students, which may be influenced by lower expectations and bias (the teacher–student gap); and the significant imbalance between the composition of the teaching force and student population (the culture gap) (Noguera, 2015). As Sonya Douglass Horsford rightfully asserts:

> '... the voices, experiences, and perspectives of people of color on the education of their very own children, no less, have historically been absent from the research, practice, and policy conversations that have and continue to determine their fate. Even on issues of race and equity, white allies are the experts, taking up space in the margins with what they believe the education of Black and other historically disenfranchised children should look and feel like—still determining the conditions under which children of color are to be educated.' (Douglass Horsford, 2021)

How did we get to this place? The origins of gifted and talented are complicated. We will be unearthing the tangled roots of gifted education and examining our discomfort with this history. I would like to reflect on how the echoes of giftedness are still reverberating. However, we are ready for gifted thinking to finally come to an end.

## Rethinking Ability Language

In education, there are terms used after standardised assessment to group students. This has often resulted in labelling students as 'low, middle and high ability'. Standardised terms like 'low ability' or 'more able' or 'gifted' often perpetuate inequity as educators' notions about students' 'ability' are often based upon limited evaluations of, and assumptions about, students' prior knowledge and other educational advantages. Ability thinking has a cognitive bias and can be interpreted or implemented as a set fact. While this book will use the common parlance 'ability' in some cases for easy reference or when quoting others' work, I like to move away from this vernacular whenever possible.

In place of 'ability' we can more accurately refer to a student's 'attainment' – that is, where a child is in that subject. For example, whether they are high-attaining in this topic or low-attaining. Attainment can change. This then halts limiting language about ability and potential. This framing is about knowing where our students are without pigeonholing them or putting a ceiling on their learning. While 'ability' is perceived as fixed, I like to refer to students' 'capacity' for learning, as capacity can be built.

# Reference List

BBC News. (2007) *Cameron hits back over grammars*. Available at: http://news.bbc.co.uk/2/hi/uk_news/politics/6658613.stm (Accessed: 16 September 2022).

BBC News. (2013) *Weald of Kent grammar wants to open Sevenoaks annexe*. Available at: www.bbc.com/news/uk-england-kent-22911194 (Accessed: 16 September 2022).

Benn, M. (2015) 'Grammar school plan makes Kent a national battleground', *The Guardian*, 8 September. Available at: www.theguardian.com/education/2015/sep/08/grammar-school-expansion-kent-selective-education (Accessed: 16 September 2022).

Berger, W. (2014) *A More Beautiful Question*. New York, USA: Bloomsbury Publishing.

Boffey, D. (2016) 'Just 2.6% of grammar pupils are from poor backgrounds, new figures show', *The Guardian*, 15 October. Available at: www.theguardian.com/education/2016/oct/15/very-small-percentage-of-grammar-school-pupils-from-poorer-families-new-statistics-show (Accessed: 16 September 2022).

Brody, L. (2019) 'Mayor's diversity panel recommends scrapping gifted programs at New York City schools', *The Wall Street Journal*, 26 August. Available at: www.wsj.com/articles/mayors-diversity-panel-recommends-scrapping-gifted-programs-at-new-york-city-schools-11566863093 (Accessed: 16 September 2022).

Chowdry, H., Crawford, C., Dearden, L. and Vignoles, A. (2008) *Wasted talent? Attrition rates for high-achieving pupils between school and university*. London: The Sutton Trust.

Comprehensive Future. (n.d.) *Sevenoaks 'annexe' drops integration with main school site and operates as standalone grammar school*. Available at: https://comprehensivefuture.org.uk/sevenoaks-annexe-drops-integration-main-school-site-operates-standalone-grammar-school/ (Accessed: 16 September 2022).

Department for Education and Skills. (2005) *Higher standards, better schools for all: More choice for parents and pupils*. Available at: https://education-uk.org/documents/pdfs/2005-white-paper-higher-standards.pdf (Accessed: 25 October 2023).

Department for Education and Skills. (2006) *Identifying gifted and talented pupils: getting started*. Available at: https://dera.ioe.ac.uk/id/eprint/6659/7/312_DFES_identification_document-4_Redacted.pdf (Accessed: 17 May 2024).

Didau, D. (2022) 'So, what does "gifted" mean anyway?', *David Didau*, 15 October. Available at: https://learningspy.co.uk/featured/so-what-does-gifted-mean-anyway-2/ (Accessed: 11 March 2023).

Dixson, D. D. et al. (2020) 'A call to reframe gifted education as maximizing learning', *Phi Delta Kappan*, 23 November. Available at: https://kappanonline.org/call-reframe-gifted-education-maximizing-learning-dixson-peters-makel/ (Accessed: 16 September 2022).

Domanico, R. (2021) 'Saving Gotham's students', *City Journal*. Available at: www.city-journal.org/nycr-de-blasio-and-the-collapse-of-education-in-new-york (Accessed: 16 September 2022).

Douglass Horsford, S. (2021) 'Whose vision will guide racial equity in schools?', *Education Week,* 17 March. Available at: www.edweek.org/leadership/opinion-whose-vision-will-guide-racial-equity-in-schools/2021/03 (Accessed: 1 January 2024).

Exam Papers Plus. (2024) *Kent 11+ full practice tests bundle.* Available at: https://exampapersplus.co.uk/papers/eleven-plus/kent-11-plus-full-practice-tests-bundle/ (Accessed: 24 January 2024).

Eyre, D. (2011) 'Room at the top: Inclusive education for high performance', *Policy Exchange,* 4 April. Available at: https://policyexchange.org.uk/publication/room-at-the-top-inclusive-education-for-high-performance/ (Accessed: 18 December 2023).

Freeman, J. (2002) *Out-of-school educational provision for the gifted and talented around the world: A report for the Department of Education and Skills.* London: Department of Education and Skills.

Freeman, J. (2005) 'Permission to be gifted: how conceptions of giftedness can change lives.' In: Sternberg, R. J. and Davidson, J. E. (eds.) *Conceptions of Giftedness,* 2nd edn. New York: Cambridge University Press, pp. 80–97.

Hart, R. A. and Moro, M. (2016) 'Grammar schools have a long history of being dominated by middle-class children', *The Conversation,* 8 September. Available at: https://theconversation.com/grammar-schools-have-a-long-history-of-being-dominated-by-middle-class-children-64198 (Accessed: 16 September 2022).

KentLive. (2019) 'Weald of Kent Grammar School: The real schools guide 2019', *Kent News,* 20 June. Available at: www.kentlive.news/news/kent-news/weald-of-kent-grammar-school-1703695 (Accessed: 16 September 2022).

Kolker, R. (2011) 'A Bronx science experiment', *New York Magazine,* 2 December. Available at: https://nymag.com/news/features/bronx-high-school-of-science-2011-12/ (Accessed: 16 September 2022).

Millar, F. (2015) 'Grammar school "annexe" in Kent is a dangerous moment', *The Guardian,* 10 November. Available at: www.theguardian.com/education/2015/nov/10/grammar-school-annexe-kent-academies (Accessed: 16 September 2022).

Murray, J. (2013) 'The heat is on to pass the 11-plus', *The Guardian,* 18 March. Available at: www.theguardian.com/education/2013/mar/18/children-extra-lessons-grammar-schools (Accessed: 16 September 2022).

New York Chapter of Association of Community Organizations for Reform Now. (1997) *Secret apartheid II. Race, regents, and resources.* New York: ACORN Schools Office.

New York City Council. (2019) *School diversity in NYC.* Available at: https://council.nyc.gov/data/school-diversity-in-nyc/ (Accessed: 16 September 2022).

Noguera, P. A. (2015) 'Race, education, and the pursuit of equity in the twenty-first century.' In: *Race, Equity, and Education: Sixty Years from Brown.* Noguera, P. A., Pierce, J. C. and Ahram, R. (eds.) Springer Education: pp. 3–23.

Renzulli J. S. (1986) 'The three-ring conception of giftedness: A developmental model for creative productivity.' In: Sternberg, R. J. and Davidson J. E. (eds.) *Conceptions of Giftedness*. Cambridge: Cambridge University Press, pp. 332–357.

Renzulli, J. S. (2005) 'Applying gifted education pedagogy to total talent development for all students.' *Theory Into Practice*, 44(2): pp. 80–89.

Royal Grammar School Guildford. (2023) *11+ admissions process*. Available at: www.rgsg.co.uk/11-13-admissions-process/ (Accessed: 10 October 2023).

Shapiro, E. (2021) 'How the mayor's big decision could upend N.Y.C. school admissions', *The New York Times*, 9 September. Available at: www.nytimes.com/2021/09/09/nyregion/nyc-schools-gifted-education.html (Accessed: 16 September 2022).

The Good Schools Guide UK. (n.d.) *Educating the gifted child*. Available at: www.goodschoolsguide.co.uk/choosing-a-school/educating-the-gifted-child (Accessed: 16 September 2022).

Tuition Academy. (n.d.) *11+ preparation*. Available at: https://tuitionacademy.co.uk/school-tuition/11-plus-preparation/ (Accessed: 16 September 2022).

US News and World Report. (2022) *Bronx High School of Science*. Available at: www.usnews.com/education/best-high-schools/new-york/districts/new-york-city-public-schools/bronx-high-school-of-science-13207#students_teachers_section (Accessed: 16 September 2022).

Walker, P. (2015) 'Kent grammar decision is "a bad day for education", says head of nearby school', *The Guardian*, 15 October. Available at: www.theguardian.com/education/2015/oct/15/kent-grammar-decision-bad-day-education-says-head-nearby-school (Accessed: 16 September 2022).

Wilshaw, M. (2013) *The most able students: Are they doing as well as they should in our non-selective secondary schools?* Manchester: Ofsted.

Wilshaw, M. and Ofsted. (2016) *HMCI's commentary: most able pupils*. Available at: www.gov.uk/government/speeches/hmcis-monthly-commentary-june-2016 (Accessed: 16 September 2022).

Zimmerman, A. (2018) 'NYC is expanding a program to boost diversity at its elite high schools. But it isn't making a dent', *Chalkbeat New York*, 9 April. Available at: https://ny.chalkbeat.org/2018/4/9/21104702/nyc-is-expanding-a-program-to-boost-diversity-at-its-elite-high-schools-but-it-isn-t-making-a-dent (Accessed: 16 September 2022).

# 2. NOT MY CIRCUS, NOT MY MONKEY

*It is not underrepresented. It is systematically excluded. It is institutionally oppressed. Accountability starts with accurate language.*

**Nora Rahimian, co-founder of #CultureFix**

*Not 'politically incorrect', just incorrect.*

**Catherine Speedy, principal**

'Gifted and talented' is a loaded phrase that many educators have recoiled from. 'Gifted' lists in schools are often kept confidential for a reason; parents and students would be upset thinking that they are less-than. The term is discrediting because, historically, giftedness has excluded entire communities. Fellow teachers have divulged how uncomfortable they are with the connotations of labelling some students intellectually superior. Whether we use these labels to target students in the classroom, for setting or for special programmes, there is an implied 'chosenness' that is dismissive of those who don't make the cut. Gifted and talented programmes run all over the world, schools commonly place students in advanced classes or top sets, and teachers identify high achievers to present them with challenge in lessons.

Do we simply discard the term 'gifted and talented'? Use 'more-able students' or 'enrichment programming'? It is not that simple. There have been many variations in an attempt at rebranding. The problem is not one of vocabulary, although the gifted label is problematic because of the racist, sexist and elitist roots. The issue is the gifted paradigm. What is fascinating is that many of the issues of gifted and talented come down to identification. What defines the limitations of giftedness? Who is entitled to the designation and the privilege it brings? When we endow select people with giftedness there are ethical ramifications.

Could I genuinely tell a student 'you are not gifted'? I stumble at the thought. First, these words can wound, easily interpreted as 'you are not worthy'. Second, there are a plethora of gifted definitions – the term is mutable. A common measure for teachers when we differentiate in our classes is to simply point at 'the top 10%'. In England, schools are tasked with creating their own individual policies (Attfield, 2009). In the US, the qualifiers differ from state to state, with inconsistent standards for a gifted diagnosis (Riggall, 2010). Academics have created and changed their measures. There is no way to assert 'you are not gifted' because this cannot be definitively true. Giftedness is a social construct we have created and recreated, defined and measured in myriad ways.

Claiming that children are born 'high ability' or 'low ability' negates the efforts of students and the purpose of education. The Rosenthal effect indicates that our teachers' expectations are key; that when we believe students will progress, they internalise our assumptions and can exceed beyond their assumed capabilities (Rosenthal and Jacobson, 1992). Cognitive science has proven how the learning capacity can increase; it is not a set entity. If you asked me if I believed that children are born gifted or not, my immediate reaction would be of course not – we are all born with potential. A flood of assemblies I have attended and delivered over the years on growth mindset and grit would wash over me. Then I would have that guilty admission wiggle in the back of my mind. There are pupils that have bowled me over. Children who seemed effortlessly incisive and completed work miles ahead of their peers. I would look up their standardised test scores and be unsurprised by results that put them in a top stanine of a nine-point scale. I think we have all encountered these students, and perhaps assume that they have dispositional advantages, such as patience, determination, focus, confidence or ambition. Or an adeptness for reasoning, processing and memory. There is permissive logic in characterising this as innate. It is tempting to say that one can simply be born gifted. In so much of our own schooling experience, students are stratified by ability. Giftedness is built into the structures of our systems.

There is an acknowledgement that gifted labels are uncomfortable. The next step is to interrogate why. If innate genius exists then let's underline a multitude of barriers (racism, sexism, class and homophobia to name a few) that have stopped proportional detection. High cognitive abilities obviously exist equally across the diversity of communities. In this chapter we will dip into the messy history of giftedness, then into the larger debate that has raged across disciplines – what makes a high performer? From neurologists to sociologists, philosophers to psychologists, all have questioned the nature and nurture of 'giftedness'. We will be exploring the work of many educational researchers who have evolved the traditional models, but let's start with the origin story of giftedness.

# The Mother of Giftedness

While child prodigies have long been acknowledged, and then sensationalised, it was a group of psychologists at the start of the 20th century who created the 'gifted' category. Giftedness was not discovered; it was invented. This was during a booming time for education. Schools were overflowing. In the United States, enrolment went up by a shocking 47% between 1890 and 1910 due to changes in child labour laws and migration to cities. Many older students were entering schools for the first time, resulting in overpopulated elementary schools with large classes of students at extremely different levels. In New York City, 39% of students were above the expected age for their grade in 1904 (Margolin, 1993). Given the strain on the education system and the mixed abilities of children, there were many proposals suggesting how to best group students. There were practical reasons for 'sorting' children, but the discussion was heavily shaped by the societal biases around class and ethnicity at the time.

Leading the debate on cognitive ability were psychologists Leta Stetter Hollingworth, Edward Lee Thorndike (Hollingworth's mentor) and Lewis Terman (Hollingworth's detractor). Thorndike and Hollingworth worked together in the education department of Columbia University. Terman and Hollingworth never met, but together they shaped the modern gifted movement. The debate they began continues today – the role of genetics versus the significance of the environment. Giftedness entered the nature versus nurture debate.

Hollingworth is recognised as the mother of gifted education and is credited with coining the term 'gifted child' (Held, 2010). She was a feminist pioneer who began her graduate work by researching the cognitive abilities and psychology of women. What set Leta Hollingworth apart from her peers was her perspective on the social development of children; she wanted to know what early factors could foster intellectual growth. She was in a unique position to comment on the importance of societal factors due to her uphill battle as a female academic. She was raised by a wandering and alcoholic father. She began her career as a teacher but had to give up the profession once she was married, as per policy in her school district. Looking for stimulation, in 1911 she began studying sociology and education at Columbia

(Held, 2010). At this time she still lacked the right to vote, which she actively fought for as a member of the Women's Suffrage Party (National Women's History Museum, n.d.). I would describe her as tenacious. Hollingworth's early experiments challenged the notion that men had more intellectual variation than women. Her work set out to prove that there are no innate biological differences that make men more gifted than women. Hollingworth completed her dissertation on the subject of women's mental incapacity during menstruation, a belief called 'functional periodicity'. The theory gave legitimacy and cover for institutions to refuse entry to women, whether this be a butcher's shop or a university. For three months she tested subjects of both genders in tasks challenging motor skills and cognition. The first half of the dissertation is a rigorous statistical analysis, concluding that there is no empirical evidence linking menstruation to decreased performance in women's cognitive function (Hollingworth, 1914a). The second half of the dissertation examines existing research and demolishes the fiction of female fragility. The work was a dainty step forward for women and a great leap for Hollingworth, as she was then offered a position at Columbia's Teachers College by a man whose theory she often challenged – Edward Thorndike.

Thorndike's work had set the tone for views on intellect and genetic heredity. He was one of the first prominent researchers to conclude that men's intelligence was highly variable, with males more prevalent on the extreme ends of the intelligence spectrum, both low and high (Hollingworth, 1914b). He maintained that the intelligence of men varied from 5% to 10% more than women (Seller, 1981). This supposedly explained why almost all of history's great geniuses were men while women's contributions and intelligence were huddled in 'average'. His papers pointed out that the most famous and influential people of the past had been men, celebrating their accomplishments. Thorndike acknowledged that environment contributes, but only insofar that the intellect one was born with could be exploited with opportunity. The assumption was based on a mistaken anatomical observation that men have larger brains (Shields, 1982). Thorndike saw gender variability as a very small difference with a very large effect when it came to giftedness: 'In particular, if men differ in intelligence and energy by wider extremes than do women, eminence in and leadership of the world's affairs of whatever sort will inevitably belong oftener to men. They will oftener deserve it' (Thorndike, 1910, p. 35). It's interesting that Hollingworth seemed to genuinely like Thorndike. She thanked him in her work for his mentoring (Hollingworth, 1914a). Even with that support, it must have been strange to work with colleagues so patronising of women's capacity – to be a lone voice representing her gender.

Thorndike believed very few women could become 'a great man'; it would be a rarity of genetics. So recognising that there was little chance ladies would have the potential to excel in science or statesmanship, it was best to steer them into jobs of 'average-level' thinking suited to their nature, such as nursing and teaching. Men were instinctive aggressors while women were natural caregivers. Thorndike believed it was a waste to 'overeducate' a woman when the prospect of her being gifted was so small. According to Thorndike, educators should consider the intellectual and professional limitations of ladies: 'Not only the probability and the desirability of marriage and the training of children as an essential feature of a woman's career, but also the restriction of women to the mediocre grades of ability and achievement should be reckoned with by our education systems' (Thorndike, 1906). This may first read as ancient history, but ideas about gender differences and intelligence have reverberated and repeated. There are many obstacles, including mindset, that keep us in a place where women are still under-represented in political leadership and the sciences. There is the oft-cited research that found men self-estimate their IQs significantly higher than women do theirs. Men have also judged their fathers' IQs to be significantly higher than their mothers (Hogan, 1978). Gendered preconceptions can catch us unaware, such as assuming that for high-attaining boys, physics or maths come naturally, while girls perform well because they work harder. Where did this come from? Ideas about males being biologically more able have long been disproven, but it is valuable to know where these preconceptions began (Feingold, 1992). Even in the early 1900s, Hollingworth poked holes in the incomplete and contradictory data. She used her research to dispute beliefs that linger today by underlining the cultural factors holding back women's opportunities and recognition.

I highly recommend perusing Hollingworth's papers to rejoice in her plucky smackdowns of sexist 'scientific' tropes. 'All manner of sex differences in deportment and achievements have been ascribed to alleged sex differences in variability ... men have apparently been willing to recognize as a cause of women's inferior attainment almost any factor except the most obvious and incontestable one, i.e., that they have borne and reared the young and men have not' (Montague and Hollingworth, 1914). She viewed society's enforcement of gender roles as a powerful barrier keeping women from achieving at the same level as men, noting that women were 'at present hindered by individual prejudice, poverty, and the enactment of legal measures' (Hollingworth, 1914b). Hollingworth knew that girls have gifts. She had seen it in her students. The ingrained sexism at the time ran the gauntlet from condescending to openly misogynistic. The trick was using an abundance of data to overcome decades of sloppy research.

It is no coincidence that the roots of sexism in this field were being unearthed by a person lacking gender privilege. Privilege has been a constant tension in gifted education. Despite her inclusion of girls, Hollingworth felt that tension herself. The gifted school she founded garnered the same criticism that gifted programmes receive today – it was exclusive. However, she spent much of her career concentrating on children with specific learning difficulties, and how education could grant them the opportunity to grow. Leta Hollingworth is an imperfect hero. For all the groundbreaking work she did, her writing is part of a larger eugenics conversation, particularly the links she makes between class and intelligence. Intersectional feminism did not exist as a movement; however, she was not quite a 'product of the time' either. She was a founding member of the Heterodoxy Club, a society of influential feminists established in 1912 to debate liberal ideas and reform (Held, 2010). Despite this, she made flawed assertions. In 1938 she wrote in *The Literary Digest* that 'mediocre or dull parents can no more produce a brilliant child than a tomato plant can produce a plum' (Held, 2010). She argued that children do not become gifted because they have better environments or access to learning opportunities, but rather because gifted people earn and select superior environments. From her perspective, this explains why gifted children were less likely to emerge from the lower classes. She supported women's right to choose to be pregnant, but not in the case of being 'mentally defective'. At best her arguments about the role of the environment are not as progressive as we would like to interpret. At her worst, she endorsed sterilisation for those with low cognitive functioning (Klein, 2002).

Hollingworth remains renowned for her work on the social and emotional development of children and for creating the first gifted curricula. She wrote the first textbook on gifted pedagogy and taught the first university course devoted to the subject. She used classrooms as her laboratory. During this time, most extraordinary children were often left alone with the assumption that they were fine to sort themselves out. She published two books on how to identify and support them: *Gifted Children* (1926) and *Children Above IQ 180* (1942). In the end, the good I take away is that she established:

1. There are no innate differences that make one gender more gifted than others.

2. Education and environment matter. Factors such as culture, social psychology, status and family background have a key role in developing capacity.

3. We require an education system that supports the individual needs of students. The requirements of unique students are not adequately met.

With Hollingworth as the mother of giftedness, we could conclude that her early work makes for a great start to the field; however, identifying a problem is not the same as solving it. The messy history of giftedness is then made even messier by the racism, classism and sexism built into identification. Time to probe the beliefs of Dr Lewis Terman.

# The Father of Testing

About 100 years ago, a select group of bright students was tapped on the shoulder and asked, 'Would you like to take a test?' Based on the result, a chosen few were rechristened – burdened and blessed with the title of child genius. Since then, every few years a new article or an extension of the study has come out, allowing the public to catch up on the lives of these gifted children. Lewis Terman's Stanford Genetic Study of Genius is the oldest and longest longitudinal study in psychology (Leslie, 2000). The children, lovingly referred to as Termites, were followed for over 80 years. During this time Terman was more than a distant lab coat: 'He crashed through the glass that is supposed to separate scientists from subjects, undermining his own data. But Terman saw no conflict in nudging his protégés toward success, and many of them later reflected that being a "Terman kid" had indeed shaped their self-images and changed the course of their lives' (Leslie, 2000). Terman eventually had 1528 subjects. He was truly invested in these participants; the larger purpose of his work was to show that these children were 'born leaders who ought to be identified early and cultivated for their rightful roles in society' (Leslie, 2000). While the results of his longitudinal study have been fascinating, Terman wanted to prove that geniuses would achieve a higher place in society and that their exalted status would be deserved.

Terman put forward education schemes in ability grouping, acceleration and curriculum. He advocated for universal testing so that struggling students could get the support they needed (Warne, 2018). However, his earnestness to help gifted students is all muddled up in his prejudice. Terman didn't look far for his geniuses. They tended to live near him in California, and most had been referred by their teachers to take his intelligence test. They were 99.41%

white, 56% male, mostly lived in urban areas and grew up middle class (Leslie, 2000). The lily-whiteness could have been put down to teacher bias, school bias, scholarly bias or societal bias at the time, but the sampling method was discrediting. I underline Terman as a problematic leader in the field because his work is inextricably tangled in gifted and talented programmes today. His legacy leaves us with debates about 1) the necessity of identifying gifted students and 2) what we use to measure giftedness. Terman is described as growing from a small, bookish, nervous child to an ambitious and astute man. He was an affable mentor to children who mirrored his own experience. Terman established giftedness as a specialism within education and 'ability' as a set definition. The gifted legacy must reckon with the residue of Terman being an open eugenicist.

In 1916, Lewis Terman perfected the Stanford-Binet intelligence tests (a modification of Alfred Binet's test in France). These appraised five factors of cognitive ability: fluid reasoning, knowledge, quantitative reasoning, visual-spatial reasoning and working memory (Roid, 2003)[2]. Terman trialled his test with the children of people he considered high-ability professionals, like college professors and bank presidents. He concluded that the impressive results of these children were demonstrative proof of mental abilities being hereditary, a powerful argument still cited in debates about race and education (Taylor, 1981). Terman's test was considered the best standard assessment, so it was soon used in schools and colleges as a basis for college admissions (Grodsky, Warren and Felts, 2008). It spawned modern aptitude tests like the SATs and ACTs. In preparation for WWI the US Army administered the test to over a million recruits, expanding and legitimising notions of intelligence and giftedness. Terman was also the creator of modern IQ (intelligence quotient), bringing the academic term into our everyday lexicon and changing our conception of intelligence – it can be measured in 120 minutes.

As a hereditarian, Terman believed that intelligence was innate. Your 'intelligence quotient' was constant and no amount of effort, education or environment could change the result. Terman called this the 'original endowment' because genetics determined mental ability. One might have opportunities or obstacles in life that could propel you forward or hold you back, but intelligence was like your height – measurable, unchangeable and out of your control. Terman's beliefs extended to a hereditary interpretation of results; IQ was passed down, and a parent's class and ethnic background

---

2    They can be accessed here: https://stanfordbinettest.com/

mattered. Terman was propagating eugenics and using his research to do so. In *The Measurement of Intelligence*, Terman used his IQ tests to present an argument of deficiency in Indigenous, Latin American and Black communities, supporting theories of racial intelligence popular in eugenicist circles (Maldonado, 2019). In 1916 Terman wrote:

> *'High-grade or border-line deficiency ... is very, very common among Spanish-Indian and Mexican families of the Southwest and also among Negroes. Their dullness seems to be racial, or at least inherent in the family stocks from which they come ... Children of this group should be segregated into separate classes ... They cannot master abstractions, but they can often be made efficient workers ... from a eugenic point of view they constitute a grave problem because of their unusually prolific breeding.' (Terman, 1916, pp. 91–92)*

Terman claimed his findings on racial differences in IQ scores were impartial, and that evidence of any 'soft' environmental hypothesis for learning and behaviour should be dismissed. The Genetic Study of Genius is a lauded fixture of education research. This disturbing reality sits at odds with the fact that Terman's study excluded entire groups, with no Black children despite the availability of eligible subjects (Ladson-Billings, 2021). Terman's work became the basis for gifted and talented programmes throughout the US, with the bias being eerily replicated. There have been countless studies pointing out the exclusion of Indigenous, Black and Latin American communities. One early groundbreaking study was published in 1936 by Black American academic Dr Martin Jenkins ('A socio-psychological study of Negro children of superior intelligence') where he studied high-ability Black students in Chicago. He immediately points out how neglected Black students were, and how methods of selection shut them out of gifted programmes. Gifted Black children identified through IQ tests (scoring 129–175) were not an anomaly. He writes that 'the data presented here concerning Negro children of superior intelligence add weight to the already abundant evidence that intelligence and educability are matters of individual difference rather than of racial differences' (Jenkins, 1936, p. 190). Nevertheless, these students remained systematically excluded from gifted programmes both before and after segregation – a trend that continues today.

Terman's agenda promoted the heteronormative family, where a stable marriage was of paramount importance. Another angle of Terman's project was the study of gender and sexual orientation. In a 1936 book, Terman investigated sexual 'deviancy', using tests and questionnaires under a veil of science to determine if an individual was sexually promiscuous, non-conforming to gender roles or a 'potential homosexual' (Maldonado, 2019). Over the years the Termites were also questioned about their sex lives. Terman saw IQ identification as valuable for the good of society; those who were intellectually superior should be procreating and raising families. Terman later argued that marriages could only be successful when both parents exhibited traditional gender roles – this environment would allow natural genius to flourish. There is an implicit conclusion that intelligence was linked to a heteronormative identity – one can't be gifted and gay, and one had a responsibility if gifted to be straight and reproduce.

Terman wasn't shy about his beliefs or about lobbying to have them put into action through law, whether this was through restrictions on non-white immigration, racial segregation in schools, sterilisation programmes for the 'mentally feeble' or blocking interracial marriage. IQ testing and tracking students in streams swam alongside these eugenic proposals. Apolitical Terman was not. He joined and served as a high-ranking member of many eugenic organisations, some with euphemistic names like the Human Betterment Foundation, and some with the name on the tin, like the American Eugenics Society and the Eugenics Research Association. These organisations had an impact. In 1927, an infamous ruling by the US Supreme Court legalised forced sterilisation of citizens with developmental disabilities and the 'feebleminded', who were frequently identified by low IQ scores. The ruling, known as Buck v. Bell, resulted in over 65,000 coerced sterilisations of individuals labelled with 'low intelligence'. Those in the US who were forcibly sterilised in the aftermath of Buck vs. Bell were disproportionately people of colour and people with low incomes. Compulsory sterilisation in the United States based on IQ continued until the mid-1970s when organisations like the Southern Poverty Law Center began filing lawsuits on behalf of people who had been sterilised (Martschenko, 2017). Eugenics is not simply discrimination. Eugenics has institutional goals – it is racism cloaked in science, and bigotry masked as social reform.

As researcher Daphne Martschenko wrote, 'IQ tests became a powerful way to exclude and control marginalised communities using empirical and scientific language' (Martschenko, 2017). Based on these tests, a 'meritocracy' developed that undervalued people of colour, individuals with low incomes and anyone not conforming to traditional gender roles. This research was couched in the prominent eugenics movement in the 20th century. However, like Hollingworth, Terman was not a 'product of his time'. He promulgated these theories before and after the Nazi horrors of WWII and understood the arguments against his work. So much so that he did not apply for membership of the American Psychological Association, acknowledging the scorn other psychologists had for his beliefs (Terman, 1930). There were objections to both his methodologies and the ramifications of his conclusions. These conclusions still have sway today.

## The Legacy of Cognitive Ability Testing

Cognitive ability testing has a twisted legacy because of how the results have been wielded. IQ and its variants have been widely criticised as being an overly simplistic measure but remain ubiquitous. High-stakes testing has reigned supreme. SAT or ACT results are given incredible weight in college admissions. Low GRE (graduate record examinations) scores can keep students with otherwise exceptional records from attending top graduate schools. A similar test, the Armed Services Vocational Aptitude Battery, is used when joining the armed services. An IQ cut-off is even used when deciding the eligibility of inmates for death row.

IQ tests are incomplete as a reflection of human intelligence. They are not complete measures of a person's aptitudes. IQ measures a narrow band of ability and intellectual behaviour, despite being widely viewed to be holistic. The test does not distinguish between the processes of learning and thinking, and multiple studies have pointed to IQ as being unable to measure creativity (Flynn, 1987). The test is not predictive either; studies have found that drive and energy are relatively more predictive of life success (Freeman, 2001). As researcher James C. Kaufman noted in regards to IQ: 'We wouldn't expect one blood test to yield a diagnosis for all possible diseases. Yet in common perception and often in practice, we allow a handful of scores to determine virtually everything about a person' (Kaufman, 2015, p. 60).

Despite this, cognitive ability testing has been woven into the everyday aspects of our society, codified in law and education. 'Standardized tests are used from the cradle to the grave, to select, reject, stratify, classify, and sort people,' said Gerda Steele of the NAACP, 'and they are used in ways that keep certain segments of the population from realizing their aspirations' (Fallows, 1980). Do you know the colour of a sapphire? Or the location of Cornell University? The SAT in particular has long been criticised for measuring class more than college preparedness.

Take this unfortunate SAT question:

RUNNER : MARATHON

A) envoy : embassy

B) martyr : massacre

C) oarsman : regatta

D) referee : tournament

E) horse : stable

The answer was C.

It was immediately observed that some segments of the population were more familiar with the sport of crew than others. Robert Schaeffer of the National Center for Fair and Open Testing said in relation to this question, 'You don't see a regatta in center-city L.A., you don't see it in Appalachia, you don't see it in New Mexico.' There are questions from the past that say the quiet part out loud, as a sample question from the Lorge-Thorndike IQ test illustrates:

When a dove begins to associate with crows, its feathers remain _____ but its heart grows black.

A) Black

B) White

C) Dirty

D) Spread

E) Good

The answer was B (Fallows, 1980).

This coded stereotype is hard to swallow. These early questions of IQ tests have changed over the years but remain imperfect – this is problematic given the long-term impact cognitive ability testing has and the scope of implementation.

College Board data has long noted the relationship between economic standing and SAT performance, with studies pointing out the correlation even in 1974 (Fallows, 1980) and continuing today.

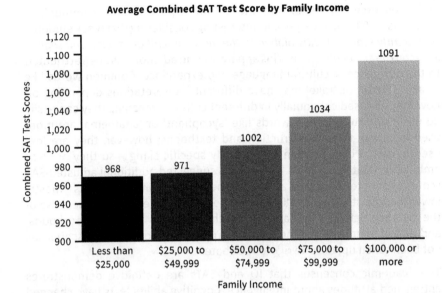

Figure 2.1 Average combined SAT test score by family income (Kantrowitz, 2021).

When looking at SAT test scores from 2017 to 2020, research found that:

- Students with family incomes of $100,000 or more are more than twice as likely as students with family incomes under $50,000 to have combined SAT test scores of 1400 to 1600.

- White students are three times more likely than Black students and twice as likely as Hispanic or Latin American students to have combined SAT test scores of 1400 to 1600.

- Male students are 42% more likely than female students to have combined SAT test scores in the 1400 to 1600 range, possibly due to differences in performance on maths exams. (Kantrowitz, 2021)

While the economic impact is connected to under-resourced and equity-seeking communities (for instance, schools in these communities are underfunded and families are less able to afford test prep tutoring), there is also the implicit bias of the test itself. It can be argued that success on the test is not based on intelligence, but rather on one's ability to comprehend and practise the values of the dominant culture. As researcher Roy O. Freedle has noted regarding the verbal section of the SAT, there is persistent evidence of an unintended cultural and statistical bias that adversely affects under-resourced students and those from equity-seeking communities (Mathews, 2003). This is especially interesting considering that Black students *consistently scored slightly higher on the more difficult questions, and slightly lower on the easier questions.* This apparent contradiction has been attributed to the difference in cultural language and experience. Common words like 'snake', 'horse' or 'rake' may have different interpretations depending on how they are used colloquially in different cultures, meaning they can easily be misinterpreted. Harder words like 'sycophant' or 'anathema' are more used in school-related instruction and textbooks; however, they are less used in casual conversation or culturally specific slang – so they are less ambiguous (Mathews, 2003). Freedle has suggested additional adjusted SAT scores be sent to colleges as a bonus, to help them identify students – mostly lower-income students of all races – whose SAT scores suffered because of the distance between the language of their families and neighbourhoods, and that of middle-class America. The proposal for adjusted SAT scores has not been taken up, despite rigorous debate.

The academic consensus that IQ and SATs are definitive demonstrates entrenched attitudes about intelligence. Cognitive ability tests have changed the trajectory of generations of students applying to higher education, but the unerring faith in these tests has also driven political projects. A classic example is the publication of *The Bell Curve: Intelligence and Class Structure in American Life.* This controversial book was written by psychologist Richard J. Herrnstein and political scientist Charles Murray. Murray has the distinction of being an eminently respected conservative scholar at the American Enterprise Institute, while also having a dangerous extremist profile page on the Southern Poverty Law Center website (n.d.). He is a statistically minded sociologist by training and spent decades working to rehabilitate long-discredited theories of IQ and heredity, turning them into a foundation on which to build a conservative policy (Southern Poverty Law Center, n.d.). His pop science bestseller put forth that IQ tests are the best and most accurate measure of intelligence; that properly administered IQ tests are not demonstrably biased against any groups, and that cognitive ability is substantially heritable (claiming no less than 40% and no more than 80%) (Murray, 2017). *The Bell Curve* asserts that heredity plays a role equal to or greater than the environment in explaining differences among ethnic groups. Critics were resistant to, and alarmed by, research conducted on race and IQ. There was a swift backlash concerning a lack of evidence, weak statistical analyses and a basis in race science (Lane, 1994). Murray is a person who still gets protested on college campuses more than 20 years later.

Debating conclusions about the validity of these tests misses the larger point – make your way to the end of *The Bell Curve* and the authors use IQ data to recommend larger public policy. In regard to Murray's work, journalist Ezra Klein has commented:

> 'My view is that contemporary IQ results are inseparable from both the past and present of racism in America, and to conduct this conversation without voices who are expert on that subject, and who hail from the affected communities, is to miss the point from the outset ... These hypotheses about biological racial difference are now, and have always been, used to advance clear political agendas – in Murray's case, an end to programs meant to redress racial inequality.'
> (Klein, 2018)

Murray writes in *The Bell Curve* that social welfare 'subsidizes births among poor women, who are also disproportionately at the low end of the intelligence distribution. We urge generally that these policies, represented by the extensive network of cash and services for low-income women who have babies, be ended' (Yglesias, 2018). The argument is that the government programmes that aim to improve the living standards of under-resourced and underserved children incentivise women with low incomes to have more babies.

In the same vein, *The Bell Curve* argues that immigration from Latin America and Africa should be curtailed as there was 'evidence that recent waves of immigrants are, on the average, less successful and probably less able, than earlier waves ... An immigrant population with low cognitive ability will – again, on the average – have trouble not only in finding good work but have trouble in school, at home, and with the law' (Yglesias, 2018). IQ scores are still part of a race science revival. In 2014, Nicholas Wade, a former *New York Times* science correspondent, wrote *A Troublesome Inheritance,* asserting that human brains evolved differently from race to race resulting in profound biological differences, and that this is supported by different racial averages in IQ scores. Wade's book prompted 139 of the world's leading population geneticists and evolutionary theorists to sign a letter published in *The New York Times* accusing Wade of misappropriating research from their field, and several academics offered more detailed critiques (Evans, 2018). The use of IQ in identity politics and social engineering makes it a fraught measurement.

At the same time, IQ has been wielded to expose inequality. Research has found that US school districts that have implemented universal screening measures for all children using IQ tests have been able to identify more children from historically under-represented groups for acceptance into gifted education. IQ tests have also helped reveal structural inequalities that have affected child development. These could include the impacts of environmental exposure to harmful substances such as lead and arsenic or the effects of malnutrition on brain health (Martschenko, 2017). All of these have been shown to have a negative impact on an individual's mental functioning and disproportionately affect low-income and equity-seeking groups. Researchers have also used IQ tests as a baseline measurement to see if interventions are working. IQ has been used to discover whether training could improve the concentration and executive functioning of children with ADHD – and found that it did. Even more fascinating, one study focusing on students with generalised anxiety saw improvements in their IQ tests when exposed to the incremental theory of intelligence, a concept of a growth mindset where intelligence is introduced as a malleable quality that can be increased through effort (Da Fonseca et al., 2008). This contributes to the argument that while IQ is useful, it is also not stagnant.

IQ itself is not evil; it is a test with limitations and a hard history we should recognise. I find myself asking – what is the difference between these IQ tests and the aptitude tests we give today? Cognitive ability assessments are what educators use to measure potential versus current achievement (or underachievement). We justify our merit as teachers and the effectiveness of schools by the value-add we deliver. Cognitive ability testing (CAT) is prevalent, but in execution the limitations are often not acknowledged in our progress tracking. I have been asked in my reporting to use cognitive ability scores to ensure that my grades are on point and in line with expectations. Which is a bit like the tail wagging the dog. I am accustomed to seeing students sit at computer screens for a few hours at the beginning of each year, squinting at spatial awareness questions and then choosing the best of four options. These assessments are imperfect, but we use them as a baseline. I remember one school leader joking that it was best to have students sit the tests on the last period of a Friday, perhaps after a gruelling physical education lesson. Our exhausted students' lower CAT scores set against their final exam results made for excellent value-add. I laughed at the time, but noted that indeed, our annual CAT tests were always booked at the end of the day.

# Geniuses – Just Like Us

I set much store in IQ tests when I was young. My Opa scored high and was a proud member of Mensa. He had a certificate posted proudly on his office wall. I saw him as one of the most intelligent human beings I've ever met, and I assumed he was born that way. When I look back and reflect on my impressions I see that, more than anything, Opa was busy. He was always tinkering, puzzling and inventing. He was creating stained-glass windows, or designing baby cradles, then learning to paint in watercolours, and writing a book on how to build a camper-trailer. His IQ score was not a defining characteristic; the certificate was merely evidence of another puzzle solved. He was driven by curiosity. He embraced challenge and enjoyed learning. Now I believe that my grandfather did not have genius, he had ingenuity.

The various versions of the Genius Study are worth reading. For the most part, Termites were people who led their lives with kids, marriage, divorce, tribulations and work.[3] Termites were more educated than 'ordinary people' (especially the women, as they were encouraged to pursue higher education). Names were kept confidential, but we know that there were 97 PhDs, 57 MDs and 92 lawyers. There were also two Hollywood moguls (Leslie, 2000). We will never know the strings Terman pulled and his full impact on the study; recommendation letters and mentoring were frequent. Early in World War II, Terman saved one Japanese child and their family from internment camps. This has been cited as a clear example that Terman saw beyond race, but I disagree that this act of protection negates the bias in his entire body of work.

We also know of two children who were tested by Terman but didn't make the cut – William Shockley and Luis Alvarez went on to win the Nobel Prize in physics. No Terman kids ever won a Nobel or Pulitzer. Just saying.

Can we function without the crutch of a test score? In recent years, universities have softened their approach to be more holistic with test-optional admissions. Harvard University announced that it will allow students to apply for admission without requiring ACT or SAT test results. It has stressed that accomplishments in and out of the classroom are valuable, whether this be community involvement or employment. Students are 'encouraged to send whatever materials they believe would convey their accomplishments in secondary school and their promise for the future. Applicants may choose to submit official test scores or self-report test scores if they so wish' (Harvard College, 2022). Harvard is one of many universities

---

3    Most famously in Malcolm Gladwell's book *Outliers*, which is a fun way to follow the findings.

that are focusing more on transcripts, letters of recommendation and student essays.

Wonderful and strange impacts of recent pandemic life include changes to university admissions. The lack of in-person exams has upended the reliance that institutions have on traditional standardised tests. Nearly 600 colleges and universities eliminated ACT and SAT requirements during the pandemic. The result has opened up more doors by emboldening students who were once reduced to a number on a standardised test. Consequently, more students set their sights on schools that would normally only accept applicants from the highest tiers of ACT and SAT scorers. Common App, the online application portal for more than 900 US institutions, reported in March 2021 that high school students were submitting applications to a greater number of schools than in the past. Common App reported an increase of 11% in application volume, with more selective institutions experiencing the greatest growth in student interest, especially from under-represented groups (O'Malley and Bohanon, 2021). Large, highly selective, private institutions experienced a 20% rise in applications from first-generation students and a 24% increase from racially and ethnically under-represented students. Experts attribute this trend in part to the fact that these colleges and universities eliminated ACT and SAT requirements during the pandemic. In 2021 it was reported that 46% of applications submitted through the Common App portal included entrance exam results, compared with 77% pre-pandemic. First-generation, low-income, and racially and ethnically under-represented students were more likely than other applicants to omit these scores. By removing the SAT/ACT scores, universities have had the opportunity to truly diversify their student bodies.

High-stakes testing should be interrogated because there is an impact in terms of equity. A similar pattern was seen in the UK when standardised exams were removed in favour of teacher- or centre-assessed work during COVID. More students overall entered higher education, with the UK 18-year-old entry rate rising to a record 37.0% in 2020, from 34.1% in 2019 (The Universities and Colleges Admissions Service, 2020). The primary admissions portal, UCAS, noted that students from more under-resourced and underserved backgrounds across the UK entered higher education in 2020 than ever before. This was reflected even in the most selective universities and courses. A report by UCAS points to the fact that more students met the terms of their offers on 'centre assessment grades' ('estimations' in Scotland) than on their original exam results. The UCAS report noted the social justice impact in terms of the multiple equality measure (MEM), which brings together information on equality dimensions (this includes sex, ethnic group, location by the index of multiple deprivation, secondary education school type and income background by free school meals). The MEM equality gap narrowed impressively in 2020, with the most advantaged pupils 4.23 times more likely to enter higher education than the most under-resourced pupils, compared to 4.40 times in 2019. Regarding race, the overall entry rate for Black students reached 47.5%. Entry to the most selective universities (referred to as higher tariff providers), which has historically been low, also reached a record level with 10.2% of Black students gaining entrance. A record number of students declaring disabilities, mental health conditions or specific learning difficulties were accepted into higher education, with a 10.4% increase from 2019 to 2020. Higher tariff providers and the highly competitive medicine courses accepted more under-resourced students than ever before. In total, the removal of standardised exams resulted in increased diversity, increased access for under-resourced students and an increase in students entering higher education in total.

A strategy of terminal testing, as opposed to cumulative triangulated assessment, can narrow opportunities for students. These outcomes demonstrate that removing heavily weighted exams can increase diversity. The lesson is that we should adapt our education system to improve accessibility. It is a shame that this lesson was so quickly discarded.

This brings us back to enrichment. This chapter is designed to underline the roots of inequity in gifted education. These have worked purposely and unwittingly to suppress the potential of generations of students. I have singled out the early leaders of the gifted movement, but they were not alone in the marginalisation of certain groups. So what is the solution? We can alter our perceptions about giftedness and ability. Our structures and institutions can change their reliance on one set test in favour of a more holistic assessment. We can reckon with the past by reframing our future. We make our programmes and classrooms inclusive, which involves actively removing barriers. We can know our students without confining them to a grouping or label.

# Reference List

Attfield, R. (2009) *Developing a Gifted and Talented Strategy: Lessons from the UK Experience*. Berkshire: CfBT Education Trust.

Da Fonseca, D., Cury, F., Fakra, E., Rufo, M., Poinso, F., Bounoua, L. and Huguet, P. (2008) 'Implicit theories of intelligence and IQ test performance in adolescents with Generalized Anxiety Disorder.' *Behaviour Research and Therapy*, 46(4): pp. 529–536.

Evans, G. (2018) 'The unwelcome revival of "race science"', *The Guardian*, 2 March. Available at: www.theguardian.com/news/2018/mar/02/the-unwelcome-revival-of-race-science (Accessed: 16 September 2022).

Fallows, J. (1980) 'The tests and the "brightest": How fair are the college boards?' *The Atlantic*, February, [Online]. Available at: www.theatlantic.com/past/docs/issues/95sep/ets/fall.htm (Accessed: 16 September 2022).

Feingold, A. (1992) 'Sex differences in variability in intellectual abilities: A new look at an old controversy.' *Review of Educational Research*, 62(1): pp. 61–84.

Flynn, J. R. (1987) 'Massive IQ gains in 14 nations: What IQ tests really measure.' *Psychological Bulletin*, 101(2): pp. 171–191.

Freeman, J. (2001) 'Mentoring gifted pupils: An international view.' *Educating Able Children*, 5: pp. 6–12.

Grodsky, E., Warren, J. R. and Felts, E. (2008) 'Testing and social stratification in American education.' *Annual Review of Sociology*, 34: pp. 385–404.

Harvard College. (2022) *Admissions update for the 2021-2022 application cycle*. Available at: https://college.harvard.edu/about/news-announcements/admissions-update-2021-2022-application-cycle (Accessed: 11 September 2022).

Held, L. (2010) *Profile of Leta Hollingworth*. Available at: https://feministvoices.com/profiles/leta-hollingworth (Accessed: 16 September 2022). Updated in 2020 by A. Rutherford.

Herrnstein, R. J. and Murray, C. (1994) *The Bell Curve: Intelligence and Class Structure in American Life*. New York, NY: Free Press.

Hogan, H. W. (1978) 'IQ self-estimates of males and females.' *The Journal of Social Psychology*, 106(1): pp. 137–138.

Hollingworth, L. S. (1914a) *Functional periodicity: An experimental study of the mental and motor abilities of women during menstruation*. New York: Teachers College, Columbia University.

Hollingworth, L. S. (1914b) 'Variability as related to sex differences in achievement: A critique.' *American Journal of Sociology*, 19(4): pp. 510–530.

Jenkins, M. D. (1936) 'A socio-psychological study of Negro children of superior intelligence.' *Journal of Negro Education*, 5(2): pp. 175–190.

Kantrowitz, M. (2021) *Admissions tests discriminate against college admission of minority and low-income students at selective colleges.* Available at: http://studentaidpolicy.com/sat-and-selectivity/How-Admissions-Test-Scores-Discriminate-Against-Minority-and-Low-Income-Students-at-Selective-Colleges.pdf (Accessed: 16 September 2022).

Kaufman, J. C. (2015) 'Why creativity isn't in IQ tests, why it matters, and why it won't change anytime soon probably.' *Journal of Intelligence*, 3(3): pp. 59–72.

Klein, A. G. (2002) *A Forgotten Voice: A Biography of Leta Stetter Hollingworth.* Scottsdale, AZ: Great Potential Press.

Klein, E. (2018) *The Sam Harris debate.* Available at: www.vox.com/2018/4/9/17210248/sam-harris-ezra-klein-charles-murray-transcript-podcast (Accessed: 16 September 2022).

Ladson-Billings, G. (2021) *Critical Race Theory in Education: A Scholar's Journey.* Banks, J. A. (ed.) New York, NY: Teacher's College Press.

Lane, C. (1994) 'The tainted source of "The Bell Curve"', *The New York Review*, 1 December, [Online]. Available at: www.nybooks.com/articles/1994/12/01/the-tainted-sources-of-the-bell-curve/ (Accessed: 16 September 2022).

Leslie, M. (2000) 'The vexing legacy of Lewis Terman', *Stanford Magazine*, July/August, [Online]. Available at: https://stanfordmag.org/contents/the-vexing-legacy-of-lewis-terman (Accessed: 16 September 2022).

Maldonado, B. (2019) 'Eugenics on the farm: Lewis Terman', *The Stanford Daily*, 6 November, [Online]. Available at: https://stanforddaily.com/2019/11/06/eugenics-on-the-farm-lewis-terman/ (Accessed: 16 September 2022).

Margolin, L. (1993) 'Goodness personified: The emergence of gifted children.' *Social Problems*, 40(4): pp. 510–532.

Martschenko, D. (2017) 'The IQ test wars: Why screening for intelligence is still so controversial', *The Conversation*, 10 October, [Online]. Available at: https://theconversation.com/the-iq-test-wars-why-screening-for-intelligence-is-still-so-controversial-81428 (Accessed: 16 September 2022).

Mathews, J. (2003) 'The bias question', *The Atlantic*, November, [Online]. Available at: www.theatlantic.com/magazine/archive/2003/11/the-bias-question/302825/ (Accessed: 16 September 2022).

Montague, H. and Hollingworth, L. S. (1914) 'The comparative variability of the sexes at birth.' *American Journal of Sociology*, 20(3): pp. 335–370.

Murray, C. (2017) *'The Bell Curve', explained: Introduction.* Available at: www.aei.org/society-and-culture/the-bell-curve-explained-introduction/ (Accessed: 16 September 2022).

National Women's History Museum. (n.d.) *Leta Stetter Hollingsworth*. Available at: www.womenshistory.org/leta-stetter-hollingsworth (Accessed: 16 September 2022).

O'Malley, L. and Bohanon, M. (2021) 'Pandemic has surprising effects on diversity in elite college admissions', *Insight Into Diversity*, 17 May, [Online]. Available at: www.insightintodiversity.com/pandemic-has-surprising-effects-on-diversity-in-elite-college-admissions (Accessed: 16 September 2022).

Rahimian, N. (2021) [Twitter/X] 06 December. Available at: https://twitter.com/norarahimian/status/1467706893015547908 (Accessed: 16 September 2022).

Riggall, A. (2010) *Young Gifted and Talented: Journeys Through Australia, China, South Africa and the United States of America*. Berkshire: CfBT Education Trust.

Roid, G. H. (2003) *Stanford Binet Intelligence Scales*. Itasca, IL: Riverside Publishing.

Rosenthal, R. and Jacobson, L. (1992) *Pygmalion in the Classroom: Expanded Edition*. New York: Irvington.

Seller, M. (1981) 'G. Stanley Hall and Edward Thorndike on the education of women: Theory and policy in the progressive era.' *Educational Studies*, 11(4): pp. 365–374.

Shields, S. A. (1982) 'The variability hypothesis: The history of a biological model of sex differences in intelligence.' *Signs: Journal of Women in Culture and Society*, 7(4): pp. 769–797.

Southern Poverty Law Center (n.d.) *Charles Murray*. Available at: www.splcenter.org/fighting-hate/extremist-files/individual/charles-murray (Accessed: 16 September 2022).

Taylor, C. M. (1981) 'W.E.B. DuBois's challenge to scientific racism.' *Journal of Black Studies*, 11(4): pp. 449–460.

Terman, L. (1916) *The Measurement of Intelligence*. Boston, MA: Houghton, Mifflin and Company.

Terman, L. (1930) 'Autobiography of Lewis M. Terman.' In: Murchison, C (ed.) *History of Psychology in Autobiography, Volume 2*. Worcester, MA: Clark University Press.

The Universities and Colleges Admissions Service. (2020) *What happened to the COVID cohort?* Cheltenham, UK: UCAS.

Thorndike, E. L. (1906) 'Sex in education', *The Bookman v. 23*, March–August, pp. 211–214.

Thorndike, E. L. (1910) *Educational Psychology*, 2nd edn. New York: Teachers College, Columbia University.

Wade, N. (2014) *A Troublesome Inheritance*. Westminster: Penguin Books.

Warne, R. T. (2018) 'An evaluation (and vindication?) of Lewis Terman: What the father of gifted education can teach the 21st century.' *Gifted Child Quarterly*, 63(1): pp. 3–21.

Yglesias, M. (2018) *The Bell Curve is about policy. And it's wrong*. Available at: www.vox.com/2018/4/10/17182692/bell-curve-charles-murray-policy-wrong (Accessed: 16 September 2022).

# 3. JUMPING THROUGH THE RINGS OF FIRE

*People are trapped in history and history is trapped in them.*

**James Baldwin, 2012**

*There is always a well-known solution to every human problem – neat, plausible, and wrong.*

**H. L. Mencken, 1920**

Jumping through the rings of fire means tackling some of the trickiest and most polemic gifted and talented approaches. These tend to be the go-to interventions for students identified as high ability or diagnosed as 'gifted'. They are widely practised, while also being widely polarising. By their nature these strategies are selective, creating inevitable controversy and inequity. There are ongoing debates about ability grouping, gifted classes, acceleration and pull-out and push-in programmes. Are they necessary? Do they work? The gist is this:

- When it comes to ability setting, overall, it hurts.

- Gifted classes or 'between class ability groupings' are problematic and perfect examples of the identification knot (see Chapter 1).

- Acceleration can be a great option. However, acceleration or 'grade skipping' tends to concentrate on identifying students who are extreme 'exceptions to the rules'. This doesn't address core issues in how schools track, stream or bind students into rigid structures.

- Pull-out and push-in programmes are both difficult to execute. However, they can be done inclusively. Whether they are impactful depends on implementation.

The purpose of this book is to provide alternatives to typical models. Conventional gifted structures have worked to exclude and separate. There are cases where a student needs to 'skip a grade' or receive advanced instruction in a subject. At the same time, gifted programmes have consequences for entire cohorts – the power to leave behind certain groups and reinforce mindsets about giftedness and fixed ability. The argument is that we need to look outside of a traditionally gifted framework. There is high variability in how programmes select students and in how they are funded, staffed, timetabled and delivered. Therefore it is difficult to judge the efficacy or comprehend every context. It is important to recognise that there are incredible initiatives that exist within these school systems. My critiques serve to underline that there are options for inclusive extension and enrichment.

# Ability Grouping

Cards on the table, in my personal experience I have loathed having classes set by ability. When I had my geography classes determined by science sets (a fluke of my school's timetable) I was frustrated by how progress and engagement shifted. The dynamics of my classroom seemed to change for the worse. But my experience is hardly universal. Classes with students at extreme ends of comprehension and large attainment gaps complicate instruction. I have observed many a maths lesson where disparate understanding of the material derailed the class, and one or two students monopolised the teacher's attention. I've seen language lessons where students with near fluency waited patiently for beginners to bravely read a few sentences. There are valid arguments that, in certain cases, ability grouping makes sense. The issue is that such grouping can have both positive and negative impacts, often simultaneously. Research in this area continues to highlight the effects on children's academic and social learning experiences. On a micro-scale, 'grouping' within a classroom is the practice of dividing students into small instructional groups; it can be part of regular seating and scaffolding of learning material, or it can be performed ad hoc for a specific task and quickly dissolved. Ability grouping is on a larger scale, where students are assigned to separate classes, sets or tracks.

I'd like to reiterate that the word 'ability' is a social and cultural construct used to classify students. Grouping by ability places students in neat categories, which can erase their individual needs and aptitudes. This is why I prefer an adaptive teaching approach. Too frequently, schools rely on cognitive test scores in streaming or setting. Notions about students' 'ability' are often based upon evaluations of, and assumptions about, students' prior knowledge and educational advantages (Johnston and Taylor, 2023). Ireson and Hallam's (1999) review of ability grouping, mostly in the UK context, found that standardised tests of general cognitive or verbal ability were the most frequently used to allocate pupils to schools or streams. The use of such tests in grouping implies that general intelligence is a single entity that predicts achievement at school. While still common, there has been a movement towards more holistic multifaceted identification.

'Setting' was once a staple of the UK school system. It involves separating pupils by ability into gradient sets (top set to bottom set). Typically this would be done in maths, science and English. Due to the structure of school timetables, there can be a knock-on effect where this setting was replicated in other subjects. Indeed, this stratification has been found to profoundly impact curriculum, student pathways and resource allocation (Delany, 1991). Setting is usually done within subjects, while 'streaming' or 'tracking' refers to allocating groups across many or all subjects. Creating 'tracks' for homogenous grouping has become more common in the US school system. The scope of separation varies in different educational systems. In some places, once students are placed, the grouping is perpetual with little possibility of moving to a higher or lower track. Systems can divide children into ability groups at very young ages – for example, identifying children for gifted classes in kindergarten or tracking pupils into separate schools at the age of 9. Some schools remain comprehensive until the end of secondary school. In some cases, grouping entails students being completely assigned to different schools, leading to little 'mixed-ability' learning or social interaction. There are studies that tout the benefits of grouping for high-ability learners, both in self-esteem and educational attainment. However, an inherent problem with the research is a lack of consistency in defining who 'gifted and talented' or 'top-set' students are. Indeed, identification changes from country to country, and school to school (Johnston and Taylor, 2023). There is a complex intertwining of dynamics that ability grouping has on curriculum exposure, pedagogy, teacher practices and perceptions, and children's own expectations of themselves as learners (Ireson and Hallam, 1999). Higher and lower tracks within a system may have the same syllabus and pedagogical aims, but a different pace of progress. Other instances of ability grouping can involve completely different curricula and educational goals, wherein students acquire different skills and capacities (Carmel and Ben-Shahar, 2017).

The negative effects of ability grouping are that it has been found to widen the achievement gap, especially for equity-seeking groups. McGillicuddy and Devine (2018) found that this had particular implications for learners assigned to the 'weaker' groups, specifically boys in primary schools, children from minority ethnic groups/migrant children and those with additional support needs. A serious consideration is the effect of ability grouping on the long-term educational trajectory of a student. This is not surprising given that the practice emerged from the idea that students have relatively fixed levels of ability. Extensive research in the US has consistently found that the net effects on achievement are small, with students in high-ability groups having slight gains at the expense of significant losses to students in low-ability groups (Boaler, Wiliam and Brown, 2000). There is substantial literature that indicates how instruction in low-set groups is of different quality to that provided for high-set groups. For lower groups, there is a slower pace, conceptually simplified curriculum and more structured written work. Teachers underestimated the range of needs and were less likely to correct misconceptions. Both teachers and students had lowered expectations. Their review found that in low-set groups 'there is a concentration on basic skills, worksheets and repetition with fewer opportunities for independent learning, discussion and activities that promote critique, analysis and creativity' (Ireson and Hallam, 1999).

Study after study on ability grouping has pointed to entrenched cycles of social immobility (as noted throughout this book). A UK survey of junior schools in the mid-1960s found that 96% of teachers taught to streamed ability groups (Boaler, Wiliam and Brown, 2000). The same study also revealed the over-representation of 'working-class' students in lower streams and the tendency of schools to allocate teachers with less experience and fewer qualifications to these groups. Again, UK studies also find that students who are lower grouped make substantially less progress, while higher-grouped students make slightly more progress compared to students who are in classrooms that do not practise grouping (Lleras and Rangel, 2009). The emotional response to setting is profound, with students reporting shame and disengagement when placed in low-ability groups (McGillicuddy and Devine, 2020).

Self-concept as it relates to ability setting has also been found to impact attainment (Ireson and Hallam, 1999). Students' intentions to learn in future were also found to be more strongly affected by self-concept than by achievement (Ireson and Hallam, 2009). At the same time, students in high-ability groups can experience anxiety and intense pressure to succeed and 'keep up'. There are other studies that look specifically at academic self-concept. Ireson and Hallam defined this as the cognitive, affective and behavioural aspects of self-esteem. They performed a longitudinal study involving students in 23 mixed secondary comprehensive schools in England and described the extent to which schools 'set' students in low-, medium- and high-ability groups. The study examined self-concept for students in English, maths and science at the age of 14–15 and followed up two years later. Students in high-ability groups had significantly higher self-concepts in all three subjects than students in low-ability groups (McGillicuddy and Devine, 2020). The conclusions held true; students' determination to learn in future was more strongly affected by self-concept than by achievement. As John Hattie writes in his rigorous book on self-concept, 'Human beings have always been interested in the interpretation of themselves' (Hattie, 1992, p. 1). There is also the argument that academic self-concept is formed through processes of social comparison, which come into play as students compare their ability with those of others in their classes or school, deemed the 'big-fish-little-pond effect' (Marsh and Parker, 1984).

One of the most illuminating pieces of research is the work of Boaler, Wiliam and Brown (2000). This was a four-year longitudinal study of mathematical learning in six UK schools. Here are the summarised findings:

- Approximately one-third of the students taught in the highest ability groups were disadvantaged by their placement in these groups because of high expectations, fast-paced lessons and pressure to succeed. This particularly affected the most able girls.

- Students from a range of groups were severely disaffected by the limits placed upon their attainment. Students reported that they gave up on mathematics when they discovered their teachers had been preparing them to simply pass with the lowest grade.

- Social class had influenced setting decisions, resulting in disproportionate numbers of working-class students being allocated to low sets (even after 'ability' was taken into account).

- Significant numbers of students experienced difficulties working at the pace of the particular set in which they were placed. For some students the pace was too slow, resulting in disaffection, while for others it was too fast, resulting in anxiety. Both responses led to lower levels of achievement than would have been expected, given the students' attainment on entry to the school (Boaler, Wiliam and Brown, 2000, pp. 6–7).

The implications of these findings are damning – there is severe and long-lasting harm done. It is no wonder that there has been a lobby for ability grouping to be phased out. However, despite all this, the practice persists. International survey data from PISA and TALIS suggest that 89% to 98% of secondary schools used some form of ability grouping within their school contexts between 2015 and 2018 (Johnston and Taylor, 2023). There is a convincing argument that pressure to meet international benchmarks (i.e. PISA and TALIS) continues to promote ability grouping as a pedagogic tool for meeting the needs of children, especially in the areas of numeracy and literacy (McGillicuddy and Devine, 2020). These country-wide scores concentrate on a limited number of subjects, and a country's so-called 'good performance' can mask massive domestic inequalities. In the UK system there is a tension between the purported aim of school autonomy and a narrow view of school success (Coulter, Iosad and Scales, 2022). Schools are given choice, but only within the narrowly defined curriculum where students are heavily assessed in high-stakes exams.

Political pressure is intense, and there have been threats to take the power to 'set' or 'not set' away from schools. In the UK, David Cameron stated in 2006 that 'I want to see setting in every single school. … I want no child held back, so my priority is not selection by ability between schools but setting by ability within schools, because every parent knows that a high-quality education means engaging children at the right level' (Wintour, 2014a). Sir Michael Wilshaw, a previous Ofsted chief inspector, has been a supporter of setting, asserting that bright teenagers fail to achieve top grades in some comprehensives because in mixed-ability classes teachers concentrate on weaker students (Wintour, 2014b). However, using this premise, ability grouping as the 'best answer' is a strange conclusion to reach. A report by the UK Education Endowment Foundation found that:

> 'Ability grouping appears to benefit higher-attaining pupils and be detrimental to the learning of mid-range and lower-attaining learners. On average, ability grouping does not appear to be an effective strategy for raising the attainment of disadvantaged pupils, who are more likely to be assigned to lower groups. Summer-born pupils and students from ethnic minority backgrounds are also likely to be adversely affected by ability grouping.' (Wintour, 2014a)

There is also evidence that pupils from disadvantaged backgrounds are more likely to be misallocated to lower sets (Education Endowment Foundation, 2023). There can be a self-fulfilling prophecy for underserved pupils, with their chances of improving attainment impeded by the combination of lower expectations and between-class stratification.

The way schools use data and judge the effectiveness of teachers can further incentivise ability grouping. Research data drawn from Australian schools where achievement data were used to group students showed that although there were no formal directives to group by ability, a cascade of performance management policies induced schools and teachers to adopt the practice (Spina, 2019). This use of data was normalised, ability grouping was viewed as evidence-informed and the grouping was evident from the early years of schooling onwards. Another pernicious problem is that parents often pressure schools for 'top sets' or special classes for the 'more able'. This feeds into Tomlinson's explanation for why England, despite the professed preference for egalitarianism in education, is still accepting of selection and segregation of students regarded as more-able in better-resourced schools and programmes. Tomlinson places this in the context of late-stage capitalism, writing: 'There is an irrational one-dimensional view of the world economy which leads to a competitive scramble to acquire élite qualifications, abandoning notions of equality and meritocracy, and deploying ruthless strategies which require economic, cultural and social capital. Parents and students in this one-dimensional world are subject to a permanent oppressive educational competition' (Tomlinson, 2008, p. 59). This resonates with me, as I have felt insistence from parents to propel their children into elite education. There is a traditional and familiar pathway to perceived success; getting your child into the 'top set' is seen as a win in the zero-sum game.

All of this is to say that ability grouping is entrenched. A subset of grouping that has become a staple of gifted models has been the creation of the gifted class for the most 'significantly able' and 'exceptional' students.

# Gifted Classes

A 'gifted' or 'special opportunity' class is a qualitatively differentiated class for identified students. This is a common US and Australian model. For example, a school could have four multi-ability Grade 7 classes and one Grade 7 gifted class for all the 'top' students in that cohort, or a gifted class of mixed ages for all the 'top' students throughout the school to be enriched and accelerated through a separate curriculum. A selection of students being placed into a discrete class within a school can also be called 'between-class ability grouping'. A systematic literature review across 2012–22 by Johnson and Taylor (2023) found that this practice has persisted in Australia despite evidence that it contributes to high levels of educational inequity and does not improve academic outcomes. In US middle and secondary schools, the predominant model still comprises special classes, usually in mathematics and English, that are targeted at 'gifted' and above-average learners in those subject areas. There are variations and combinations of streaming and acceleration options such as 'honours classes' at the secondary level, leading to Advanced Placement course options, entry into the International Baccalaureate programme or dual enrolment in college courses (VanTassel-Baska and Reis, 2004).

One of the most illuminating US studies was completed by the National Bureau of Economic Research, which looked at the selection of students for gifted classes in a large school district across 140 schools. It turned out that high-attaining children who didn't score as 'gifted' at all on an IQ test were the students who benefited the most academically from being in a gifted classroom. The positive impacts of learning in a gifted classroom environment were systematically larger for high achievers from marginalised or low-income backgrounds – groups that are the least likely to meet the traditional criteria for gifted programme participation. The study used data from three distinct groups of fourth-grade students: a) non-disadvantaged students with IQ scores ≥130, b) subsidised lunch participants and English language learners with IQ scores ≥116 and c) students who missed the IQ thresholds but scored highest among their school/grade cohort in state-wide achievement tests in the previous year. The findings indicated that separate gifted classes were more effective for students selected on past achievement (not IQ) – particularly underserved students who are often excluded from gifted and talented programmes. This third group of students had significant gains in reading and maths, concentrated among lower-income, Black and Latin American students. The maths gains persisted into fifth grade and were also reflected in fifth-grade science scores. This is a particularly pointed study given that a third of US states still mandate the use of IQ scores to identify gifted students (Card and Giuliano, 2014).

It comes back to the identification knot – as journalist Libby Nelson commented regarding the study: 'The gifted program ended up providing the biggest test score boost to kids who weren't really supposed to be there in the first place' (Nelson, 2014). When a school offers separate classes for gifted students, the most difficult questions are 'who should be allowed in?' and 'who can benefit?' Given that cognitive ability scores fluctuate and correlate heavily with family income, gifted classes on that basis are a complicated proposition. The main issue with gifted classes is that by definition they are for 'gifted students'. Exclusive gifted classes perpetuate inequity.

## Alternative to Tracking or Streaming

There are many wonderful success stories of schools moving away from 'streaming' models. Removing grouping and embracing mixed-ability teaching requires big, coordinated moves and horizon scanning the needs of students. The Hechinger Report, a non-profit, independent news organisation focused on inequality and innovation in education, outlines one such example:

> 'It was 1989, and as a new Spanish teacher in Lawrence, New York, Carol Burris was assigned an eighth grade class called Language for Travelers. Its students weren't fooled by the elegant name. All had taken a foreign language the previous year and failed, and they knew that ending up in Burris' class meant expectations had been lowered. "There was a real culture that 'We hate school and we hate language,'" Burris said.' (Blustain, 2020a)

It was notable that most of the students were Black and Latin American boys from low-income backgrounds. When Burris became a principal she made dismantling tracking a priority. Under Burris' leadership, the Rockville school district began the hard work of removing the 'tracks' that set students apart by their perceived abilities. The district began by replacing highly selective gifted classes in elementary school with project-based learning classes for all students. The report notes that these individual projects allowed students to do their own research and enquiry, and they proved to be immensely popular. This set the stage for a more accessible system: 'Once parents bought into the idea that there didn't have to be winners and losers, it was easier to move academic integration into higher grade levels' (Blustain, 2020b). Changing tracking in secondary schools was a large project and the team took years to lay the groundwork. The Rockville school district had to plan how it would help students with weaker skills manage advanced classes before they entered higher grades – no easy feat in subjects like maths. The strategies included additional maths support classes in middle school, so that all students graduated to the eighth grade having completed algebra, a prerequisite for Grades 9 and 10 advanced curriculum. 'At each step, the district used outcome data to guide its reforms and convince the community that the efforts were working' (Blustain, 2020b). The long-term project was a systematic approach to shrinking the achievement gap, and it worked.

It's become increasingly clear that ending setting and tracking in favour of more egalitarian educational approaches is a prudent move for holistic student development. Rigid tracking systems have perpetuated socio-economic, racial and ethnic divides, limiting possibilities for students based on early assessments of their abilities. In contrast, egalitarian practices promote an environment where all students are exposed to a rich and diverse curriculum, student pathways are increased, and outcomes are improved. An inclusive approach not only acknowledges the fluidity of intellectual growth and potential, but also paves the way for a more equitable educational landscape, ensuring that every student has opportunity.

# Acceleration

Acceleration traditionally refers to a student 'skipping a grade' or 'moving up a year group'. This could be subject-specific – for instance, an eighth-grader taking a tenth-grade physics class then returning to their regular lessons. It could be a student taking an early exam qualification in Spanish. It could be a student doing independent online learning in a college course while the teacher instructs other students in the regular curriculum. Or it could be a complete move, where a student goes ahead of their age range in all their lessons. This is on the assumption that the student has a grasp of the material and skills, and that they have hit a ceiling on the learning possible in their current classes. Accelerating a student is done on an individual basis, and I'm betting that all teachers have seen students who are more than capable of handling work at the next level. I've recently had one student take the SATs three years early and score in the 99th percentile. He is more than ready for university maths.

The advice to educators is to be thoughtful in making long-term decisions regarding acceleration, with special attention to the holistic growth of a child. The meta-analyses on acceleration are difficult to parse, with studies having vastly different accelerative programmes, comparison groups and outcome measures. As accelerative methods differ, there has been inconsistent impact found in terms of students' education pathways, liking for the subject or school, effect on participation in school activities, self-acceptance and personal adjustment (Kulik, 2004). When well-planned, individualised acceleration can alleviate underachievement problems; it allows students to progress to mastery stages more efficiently. The disadvantages of acceleration are that students may miss out on some learning processes, creating gaps in learning. Long-held concerns for accelerated students include: feelings of isolation if they are removed from a well-established peer group; real or imagined academic pressure from parents or teachers to succeed; and issues in emotional maturation. However, with guardrails applied, there are students who can benefit from acceleration. When it comes to decisions about acceleration, there needs to be a consideration based on many data points, input from all stakeholders and deliberation in how it is implemented. If acceleration simply means moving into a higher level with little or no adjustments made to teaching methods, it does not adequately address individual strengths or fully stretch students. It is also worth noting that one of the pitfalls is failing to notice a student's emotional fragility if pushed into a higher age group. With the right support, this can be done well – there are policies and templates to borrow from. The process entails good transition planning in combination with reflection on the socio-emotional needs of a pupil.

## The Argument for Acceleration

There is a large gifted camp in favour of acceleration for high-ability pupils. In the US, this emerged as a massive push through the publication of *A Nation Deceived: How Schools Hold Back America's Brightest Students* in 2004 (Colangelo, Assouline and Gross), followed up by *A Nation Empowered: Evidence Trumps the Excuses Holding Back America's Brightest Students* in 2015 (Assouline et al.). These reports looked specifically at whole-grade acceleration as the go-to intervention for high-ability students, touting that this better matched a student's ability to the curriculum. They also show that acceleration is research-supported and low-cost, and that accelerated students do well academically and socially. Proponents of acceleration argue that it is a tool for equity, noting:

> *'While some have criticized academic acceleration as an intervention for children of wealth, nothing could be further from the truth. In fact, it is parents of economic means who can afford to provide for acceleration if a school doesn't. They can move their child to a private school, pay for mentoring, or pay for accelerative summer classes and extra-curricular resources. Poor children, though, often have no hope of experiencing a challenging curriculum if a school says no.'*
> *(Assouline et al., 2015, p. xi)*

There is the argument that acceleration is a virtually cost-free way to level the playing field for a student from an underfunded school.

The *Nation Deceived* and *Nation Empowered* reports came out of research by the Belin-Blank Center at the University of Iowa, which provides policymakers, educators and parents with tools for acceleration. The *Iowa*

*Acceleration Scale* (IAS) is probably the most widely known manual on grade skipping and is used throughout the entire US, as well as in Australia, Canada and New Zealand. The emphasis is on systemising the decision-making procedure in order to improve outcomes and ensure objective judgements are made. The procedure provides a template for schools and parents to follow, with a point system to make a definitive recommendation. The IAS outlines the major factors in the decision for whole-grade acceleration. This includes sections on: 1) academic ability, aptitude and achievement (requires cognitive ability testing like Wechsler Intelligence Scale for Children, Stanford-Binet Intelligence Scale, SAT, ACT or CAT); 2) school and academic factors (e.g. attendance, motivation, academic self-concept and extracurricular activities); 3) developmental factors (e.g. age, physical size and motor coordination); 4) interpersonal skills (e.g. emotional development, behaviour and relationship with teachers); and 5) attitude and support (e.g. student attitude to acceleration, parent attitude to acceleration and school system attitude to acceleration). Finally, a cumulative score from all of these factors is calculated.

My contention is that this approach a) relies heavily on cognitive ability testing in selection, b) does not fix the core problem of children being underchallenged in their regular classrooms, and c) does not address systemic inequities. All students can benefit from access to advanced material, so how can we make this possible? **Creating procedures for accelerating individual pupils is not as important as building systems that give choice and flexibility to all students.**

There is more difficulty in justifying and implementing acceleration when a school system has rigid age restrictions. When schools have built-in flexibility, this is not as much of an issue. The argument that 'age trumps everything else' is inelastic – it makes more sense to reframe placement as readiness. If a student is selected to accelerate in one or more subjects, it must be approached with care, especially if we are taking the normally rigid school system and making an exemption. Is acceleration selective? Well, yes and no. In conception, all students may be considered. However, in reality, it depends on *who* gets assessed, considered and overlooked. Subjective referral systems underpromote equity-seeking groups. How we test for acceleration can have weaknesses that even universal screening cannot rectify completely. As with most issues in gifted education, an inordinate amount of time and energy is devoted to who is deserving of intervention.

I'd like to focus on these points:

- Instead of focusing on *who* should accelerate, we should instead develop *more flexible curriculum pathways*. Modular school systems can make acceleration a more accessible and viable option for students.

- Acceleration works best in conjunction with enrichment opportunities.

- Overarching challenge, with opportunities for depth and complexity, should be at the foundation of all teaching and learning. If acceleration simply means moving into a higher level with little or no adjustments made to teaching methods, the strategy will not adequately address individual strengths or fully stretch students.

- Advanced Placement or early college courses are wonderful exposure to undergraduate work. However, they are not available in all schools or to all students, especially to those from equity-seeking groups or in rural areas.

## Open and Flexible Curriculum Pathways as an Alternative to Acceleration

In terms of an enriched curriculum, I'd like to take a look at flexible and open pathways and the implications in terms of acceleration. When we design curricular systems, we should be creating freedom and opportunity for students to accelerate, with multiple entry and exit points. This allows students to enter a course or subject at their level of competence and exit once they've achieved their goals, ensuring no student feels 'trapped' in a particular educational pathway. It allows students to progress through a pathway non-linearly, rather than by age or grade. This can be facilitated through continuous assessments that are competency based, enabling students to move forward once they've demonstrated understanding. Students always have the capacity to reach mastery, ensuring they aren't prematurely moved forward or held back. There is less emphasis on whole-year acceleration when advanced units are more easily accessible. More diverse classes with students from different age groups are regular occurrences. The socio-emotional transition is not as abrupt because focus is on readiness and student choice as opposed to age. It is also easier for students with a subject-specific strength to accelerate.

Learning priorities are established by long-term performance goals – what it is we want students, in the end, to be able to do with what they have learned. The bottom-line goal of education is not to memorise a set of facts or procedural knowledge; the point is to be able to transfer understanding to new situations and apply it. Despite modular courses generally being shorter, they have long-term goals and are great examples of interleaving. Modularisation is based on the principle of dividing the curriculum into small discrete modules or units that are independent, can be nonsequential and are short in duration (e.g. over one term as opposed to two years). Students can accumulate credits for modules, which can lead to a qualification. Modular education partitions courses into smaller, Lego-like building blocks of learning and skills outcomes.

There is scope in a modular system for students to step forward and 'skip' ahead if they are already competent in a particular area of curriculum, and they can sequence learning in a more self-directed or tailored way. In these systems a student can 'fast track' because they are offered the choice to take the prerequisite courses early or compact their learning. They also can 'step back' with less stigma if they need to consolidate their learning. It is possible to have a more diverse offering of units; the modules can be self-contained and the emphasis is on skill building. Students can study topics that are of particular interest to them while building these skills – perhaps they want to specialise in a specific period of history. This also goes for educators; a teacher may have their MA research in the Zhou dynasty but never have the opportunity to teach the topic in a pathway that is heavily prescribed. Students can mix and match skills – Anant Agarwal notes in *Forbes* that this allows pupils 'to combine humanities skills with tech skills, communication skills with coding skills, analytical skills with design skills. Students will essentially be able to synthesize their own education with the customized skill set they need to advance their careers, making for a truly unique job candidate' (Agarwal, 2019). Wondifraw Dejene makes an enticing argument for modular systems, writing: '... modularization requires continuous follow-up and assessment of students' progress throughout the module/course. The practice of effective continuous assessment allows instructors making adjustments to teaching and learning in response to assessment evidence' (Dejene and Chen, 2019). The introduction of modularisation is a viable option that opens up individualised education for all pupils.

### Case Study: Cambridge School of Weston, Massachusetts, United States

A fascinating example of an open and flexible modular system is at the Cambridge School of Weston in New England. Their academic year is divided into six marking periods called 'mods' that are each six-weeks long. Each day consists of three 90-minute blocks, and for each block of instruction, students are awarded one credit. Many of the courses are offered as single blocks throughout the year, allowing for incredible depth into a specific theme or subject area. Subjects that call for more sequential or cumulative learning, such as maths or languages, are taught in blocks that span consecutive mods, with opportunities to accelerate.

As the Cambridge School of Weston explains:

> 'The Module System, also known as the Mod Plan, has been the cornerstone of our distinctive academic approach since 1973. The Mod Plan has always been innovative and continues to evolve in dynamic ways to meet the needs of our students and their education. The module plan offers students the opportunity to take an active part in shaping their educational experience, to experience broadly, and to learn deeply. ... The module system works because of its versatility. With more than 250 courses to choose from, students have countless ways to structure their studies to suit their interests, while taking the foundational courses necessary to prepare for college and beyond' (The Cambridge School of Weston, n.d.a).

Each student's schedule is curated and unique, with incredible choice in how they reach the graduation requirement. Courses use interleaving and interdisciplinary approaches – examples include food, justice and power, studies of flight and issues in sustainability. The school promotes a progressive pedagogy that 'is rooted in the student-centered philosophy of John Dewey, who advocated active, experiential learning within a curriculum designed to accommodate the interests of individual students' (The Cambridge School of Weston, n.d.b). Each curriculum pathway created through the 'Mod System' is designed to balance the specific needs and interests of students with required foundation courses.

This does have an appeal based on my own experience. My sister and I both 'skipped' ahead in some subjects. However, I was in a more modular system and she was not. When I went to secondary school, multi-grade classrooms were quite common. Courses would typically have students from three different cohorts due to the modular design; it didn't feel unusual to have students a year younger or older than myself in a lesson. When my sister went to secondary school six years later, there was a switch to streaming students, modular courses were phased out and students were placed into tiered curricular pathways. Sitting a class in the year group ahead was rarely done. She felt like the 'odd one out' socially when she went into a Grade 11 class as a Grade 10 student. For one year she had to travel to a neighbouring high school for certain lessons because her own school was unable to accommodate her timetable. Spending her lunches driving to another school made her schedule complicated, but she was lucky this option was made available to her. Unfortunately, a modular curriculum is not currently possible in many school systems. Rigid structures create constraints.

## Advanced Placement or College Courses

One of the most common accelerative options is Advanced Placement (AP) courses. AP courses offer undergraduate university-level curricula and examinations for US and Canadian high school students. Some institutions use AP test scores for college credit, to exempt students from introductory coursework, or to place students in higher designated courses in university. AP courses were originally limited to a few elite schools but have since expanded. AP courses are an incredible option with diverse, rich curricula. The issue is one of access.

Advanced Placement courses have been lauded for their ability to challenge students and provide them with a competitive advantage in college admissions. However, while these courses offer many benefits, they have also been critiqued for inadvertently contributing to educational inequity. The proliferation of advanced courses has not been uniform: 'While U.S. schools have become more diverse today than at any other point in our nation's history, students of colour in general, African American and Hispanic students in particular, continue to be concentrated in racially and economically homogenous schools where access and opportunity to gifted education, Advanced Placement (AP), and International Baccalaureate (IB) courses are limited and virtually nonexistent' (Wright, Ford and Young, 2017, p. 45). Not all schools offer AP courses, and among those that do, not all offer a full range of course options. Schools in rural or low-income areas, in particular, might lack the resources or faculty expertise to provide these classes. As a result, students in these areas may miss out on the benefits that AP courses offer. Even in schools where AP courses are available, not all students have equal access to them. Prerequisite courses, teacher recommendations or selective cumulative tracking can gatekeep which students are deemed 'ready' or 'worthy' of the challenge.

Colleges and universities tend to look favourably upon AP coursework when considering applications. So students who don't have access to AP courses are at a comparative disadvantage, as they lack this 'boost' on their applications. The admissions disparity is concerning given that the College Board has found that about 31% of colleges and universities look at AP experience when making scholarship decisions (College Board, 2012). Affluent families can invest in tutoring or test prep to help their children succeed in AP exams, further widening the socio-economic gap between advantaged and disadvantaged students in terms of scores and subsequent college admissions. AP courses often assume a certain level of background knowledge or cultural capital. For students from equity-seeking backgrounds, this might mean that even if they have access to the course, they might feel out of place or struggle more than their peers due to these unspoken assumptions. It's important to note, however, that many educators and institutions are aware of these challenges and are working to make AP more accessible and equitable. For example, some schools and districts are working to waive AP exam fees, provide more support and resources to students, and actively recruit a more diverse range of students into AP programmes.

Acceleration does not have to be within the confines of these qualifications. Students have more freedom than ever before – there are massive open online courses (MOOCs) from universities across the world, or the Khan Academy where they can accelerate both inside and outside the classroom. These can be accessible to all students with internet connections and are a wonderful option for enrichment.

## Acceleration Works Best Alongside Enrichment

As an educational strategy, acceleration is best viewed through Dr Jonathan Wai's conception of an enrichment 'dosage'. For each specific intervention we must find the right amount, mix and intensity. Wai notes that: 'What matters for each student is a consistent and sufficient educational dose across a long span of time, what we think of as life-long learning, or learning at a pace and intensity that matches a student's individual needs' (Wai, 2015, p. 73). *There is a pairing between acceleration and enrichment to make a more effective dose.*

It is more impactful to have a student take an early college physics course (acceleration) alongside entering the National Science Fair with a project they have developed (enrichment). This means that their 'educational dose' will have a density of advanced material and stimulating challenge. Whether they are taking an Advanced Placement class, opting to sit an early exam or skipping a whole grade, this is done better when skills and engagement are applied to any advanced material. Enrichment is where independent enquiry, creativity, mastery, emotional maturity and/or collaboration are layered over the individual accelerative option. Acceleration works when it is combined with enrichment opportunities and students self-regulate their 'dosage'.

# Push-In and Pull-Out

Pull-out refers to instruction provided by gifted specialists by removing select students from their regular classes. Pull-out programmes can be focused (advanced reading groups) or broad (complementing and elevating the curriculum) (University of Connecticut, 2023). Most pull-out programmes have yet to be tied to significant academic progress since they tend not to be standardised and stray from the curriculum that students' other classes are following.

A push-in approach typically refers to instruction provided by gifted specialists by routinely coming into a regular lesson and working with individual students or a select small group. Push-in can refer to 'shadowing' a particular student and providing them with assistance or higher-level curriculum materials (Shanahan, 2019). It can also refer to a gifted specialist coming into a lesson for parallel teaching, co-teaching or project work for the whole class. The push-in model tends to focus on advanced content in core subjects (e.g. maths, reading) (University of Connecticut, 2023). In the following table, you can see the pros and cons. Keep in mind that these programmes can be implemented quite differently from school to school. Some schools have implemented inclusive push-in models – this is simply an enrichment class for all students timetabled in the school day.

## Pull-Out Programmes:

| Pros | Cons |
|---|---|
| Allows a teacher to give concentrated attention to selected students and deliver more challenging or advanced activities and resources for them (Taylor, 2018). | When these identified students are pulled from classes they often then have to 'catch up' on that lesson material in addition to having the pull-out work. |
| When pull-out programmes are subject-specific and in an area of strength, those students have increased progress (for instance, there is some research that has found reading outcomes improved (Shanahan, 2019). Specialised instruction can offer more targeted and advanced curriculum challenges, mitigating the risk of under-stimulation. | Selecting students is difficult – it often means meeting a diagnosis, which can depend on parental advocacy and cost of testing. There are borderline students who don't meet the cut-off. |
| Students can work at a faster pace. | Emotional repercussions – both for students left out who may feel disappointed or disaffected (Ireson and Hallam, 1999) and selected students who feel pressured to satisfy real or perceived expectations. |
| Students still have the social benefits of regular mixed-ability classes. | Cost of employing or training specialist teachers for small-group instruction. |
| Parents and governments have a tangible way to see that students on G&T registers have accommodations; this holds schools accountable in terms of providing provision. | Timetabling and scheduling limitations can lead to infrequent implementation. |
|  | When pull-out programmes are general extension as opposed to subject-specific there can be high variability in value. The work can be disconnected from the regular curriculum. |
|  | Whole classes have less exposure to advanced curriculum materials or resources. |
|  | Subject-specific pull-out programmes tend to be for 'core' subjects, so there is potential for an uneven education (e.g. students are consistently taken out of arts or humanities lessons for additional maths). |
|  | Can perpetuate a culture of elitism where some students are 'chosen' and others are not. |

## Push-In Programmes:

| Pros | Cons |
|------|------|
| Push-in programmes where a specialist teacher comes into regular lessons to provide identified students with additional resources or instruction is equivalent to any special education accommodations. | Limited contact time with the push-in specialist teachers, so delivery is patchy and impact restricted. |
| Can be inclusive, with a specialist teacher delivering an in-depth study, STEAM unit or exploratory project for all students in the class (VanTassel-Baska and Reis, 2004). | Can have a lack of integration with regular curriculum. |
| Can provide enrichment in a familiar setting of a regular classroom, fostering peer relationships. | Takes away from regular curriculum time. |
| | Cost of employing or training specialist teachers. |
| Can be arranged as an in-class method of acceleration provision. | Frictions between regular teachers and specialists (Shanahan, 2019). |
| Can provide opportunities for collaboration between the regular teacher and a gifted specialist. | When the push-in approach is limited to select students or groups of students within a class, this can have academic and socio-emotional effects. |
| Great opportunity to introduce initiatives like project-based learning to all students. | Lack of research on impact as implementation varies widely. |
| Parents and governments have a tangible way to see that students on G&T registers have accommodations. This holds schools accountable in terms of providing provision. | |

In assessing the efficacy of push-in and pull-out programmes, it becomes evident that the success of these interventions largely hinges on the quality of implementation, the adaptability to individual student needs and the context in which they are executed. The larger question is whether push-in or pull-out programmes are the most effective interventions and a strategic deployment of resources. It is also clear that certain groups are underrepresented due to biases in identification methods. The debate revolves around how best to serve students who are underchallenged while also ensuring inclusivity, equity and the holistic wellbeing of all learners.

## Overall Impacts of Traditional Gifted Interventions

Whether ability setting, gifted classes, or push-in or pull-out, these models prioritise 'ability', with the concept of differential ability placing a ceiling of expectations over a child. In a review on raising standards, Ireson and Hallam (1999) point to a few options in contrast to ability setting:

- Create a culture of effort over ability, with additional opportunities for all students to advance and receive support. Such an approach would facilitate the broadening of access to learning with support options, remedial sessions and enrichment.

- Diversify pathways or modularise the curriculum, giving greater flexibility in the ways in which students can progress through school. Pupils, with advice and support from their teachers, take greater responsibility for their own learning, selecting modules or levels of work within modules, and evaluating their own progress. This might be done for some or all curriculum subjects while maintaining a core of compulsory subjects. This is similar to my experience coming up through the Ontario curriculum in Canada.

- Emphasis on whole-class consolidation with all students meeting similar levels of achievement before moving on. Countries like Germany, France, Switzerland and Japan have placed more importance on the development of pedagogy with the specific goal of ensuring that all pupils in a class attain a certain standard.

- Give teachers the tools, continued professional development and resources to develop high-quality mixed-ability teaching. There is often a mismatch between the underlying philosophy of mixed-ability teaching and its practice. Where a whole-class teaching-to-the-middle mode dominates instruction, the cognitive demands made on students tend to be low, as are the cognitive levels of interaction between pupils. Ireson and Hallam note that: 'The evidence to date suggests that successful mixed-ability teaching relies heavily on teacher skills. Successful teachers of mixed ability classes are flexible, use a variety of teaching modes in one lesson, vary the pace and style of approach. … They have informal relationships with their pupils, involve pupils in decision making and engage them in their learning activities' (Ireson and Hallam, 1999, pp. 351–352). This, alongside my argument of a challenge-for-all approach, provides great support for high-quality mixed-ability teaching.

This brings me to the issue of heterogenous groups and acknowledging that mixed-ability teaching is difficult. The example of a heterogenous maths class is often given as an example of where it is complicated to address the needs of all students. Catherine Finlayson Reed has a thoughtful paper that addresses the needs of 'high-end learners' in mixed-ability mathematics classrooms. She had an inclusive approach that opened up problems of depth and complexity to all students. Reed points to simple modifications with fantastic suggestions for implementation. Her discovery approach included investigations with open-ended questions, debate, conferencing, discussion to pool thoughts, self-selection of problems, opportunities for interdisciplinary connections and an 'inquiry wall' to post questions. Regarding the latter in particular: 'This wall became integral to the learning experience of the whole class. At different times during the fall semester, every member of the class contributed to the growing body of displayed information by adding questions, suggesting hypotheses, or providing answers. The wall became the foundation of self-selected, but focused, inquiry for the whole class' (Reed, 2004, p. 92). Executing mixed ability well begins with the idea of challenge for all.

Tom Sherrington has a wonderful perspective on addressing wide ability ranges in a classroom. He refers to this as 'tending the garden':

*'This metaphor suggests that teaching a mixed group is like tending a garden with a variety of specimens. You want to create strong common conditions so that everyone is thriving but you know that, over time, you have to give focused attention to individuals; you can't focus on everyone at once – it's just unrealistic. At various times you might need to provide more push and challenge to [the] most confident – checking in on their independent practice or teaching higher level concepts; at others you might get everyone working independently while you reteach material to a small group or give them more precise individual feedback.' (Sherrington, 2023)*

There is a delicate dance required of a teacher. Overarching challenge-first extension, alongside adaptive teaching, inclusive questioning, scaffolding, confidence building and an environment of high expectations all play a part in mixed-ability instruction. In terms of extension opportunities in a subject, enrichment programmes or enriched curriculum, there is going to be greater benefit when opening up and making these accessible to all students.

# Reference List

Agarwal, A. (2019) 'How modular education is revolutionizing the way we learn (and work)', *Forbes*, 25 April. Available at: www.forbes.com/sites/anantagarwal/2019/04/25/how-modular-education-is-revolutionizing-the-way-we-learn-and-work/?sh=77fd06773a26 (Accessed: 18 September 2023).

Assouline, S. G., Colangelo, N., VanTassel-Baska, J. and Lupkowski-Shoplik, A. (2015) *A Nation Empowered: Evidence Trumps the Excuses Holding Back America's Brightest Students (Volume II)*. Iowa City, Iowa: The Connie Belin & Jacqueline N. Blank International Center for Gifted Education and Talent Development.

Baldwin, J. (2012) *Notes of a Native Son*. Beacon Press: Boston, MA.

Blustain, R. (2020a) *Getting rid of gifted programs: trying to teach students at all levels together in one class*. Available at: https://hechingerreport.org/getting-rid-of-gifted-trying-to-teach-students-at-all-levels-together-in-one-class/ (Accessed: 6 March 2024).

Blustain, R. (2020b) *Gifted programs worsen inequality. Here's what happens when schools try to get rid of them*. Available at: www.nbcnews.com/news/education/gifted-programs-worsen-inequality-here-s-what-happens-when-schools-n1243147 (Accessed: 18 September 2023).

Boaler, J., Wiliam, D. and Brown, M. (2000) 'Students' experiences of ability grouping—disaffection, polarisation and the construction of failure.' *British Educational Research Journal*, 26(5): pp. 631–648.

Card, D. and Giuliano, L. (2014) *Does gifted education work? For which students?* NBER Working Paper 20453. Available at: www.nber.org/system/files/working_papers/w20453/w20453.pdf (Accessed: 18 September 2023).

Carmel, Y. H. and Ben-Shahar, T. H. (2017) 'Reshaping ability grouping through big data.' *Vanderbilt Journal of Entertainment and Technology Law*, 20(1): pp. 87–128.

Colangelo, N., Assouline, S. G. and Gross, M. U. M. (2004) *A Nation Deceived: How Schools Hold Back America's Brightest Students (Volume I)*. Iowa City, Iowa: The Connie Belin & Jacqueline N. Blank International Center for Gifted Education and Talent Development.

College Board. (2012) *AP Program*. Available at: https://web.archive.org/web/20120706134300/http://professionals.collegeboard.com/k-12/assessment/ap (Accessed: 18 September 2023).

Coulter, S., Iosad, A. and Scales, J. (2022) *Ending the big squeeze on skills: How to futureproof education in England*. Available at: www.institute.global/insights/public-services/ending-big-squeeze-skills-how-futureproof-education-england (Accessed: 6 March 2024).

Dejene, W. and Chen, D. (ed.) (2019) 'The practice of modularized curriculum in higher education institution: Active learning and continuous assessment in focus.' *Cogent Education,* 6(1).

Delany, B. (1991) 'Allocation, choice, and stratification within high schools: How the sorting machine copes.' *American Journal of Education,* 99(2): pp. 181–201.

Education Endowment Foundation. (2023) *Setting and streaming.* Available at: https://educationendowmentfoundation.org.uk/education-evidence/teaching-learning-toolkit/setting-and-streaming (Accessed: 18 September 2023).

Hattie, J. (1992) *Self-Concept.* New York, NY: Psychology Press.

Ireson, J. and Hallam, S. (1999) 'Raising standards: Is ability grouping the answer?' *Oxford Review of Education,* 25(3): pp. 343–358.

Ireson, J. and Hallam, S. (2009) 'Academic self-concepts in adolescence: Relations with achievement and ability grouping in schools.' *Learning and Instruction,* 19(3): pp. 201–213.

Johnston, O. and Taylor, B. (2023) 'A systematic literature review of between-class ability grouping in Australia: Enduring tensions, new directions.' *Issues in Educational Research,* 33(1): pp. 91–117.

Kulik, J. A. (2004) 'Chapter 2: Meta-analytic studies of acceleration.' In: Colangelo, N., Assouline, S. G. and Gross, M. U. M. (eds.) *A Nation Deceived: How Schools Hold Back America's Brightest Students (Volume II).* Iowa City, Iowa: The Connie Belin & Jacqueline N. Blank International Center for Gifted Education and Talent Development.

Lleras, C. and Rangel, C. (2009) 'Ability grouping practices in elementary school and African American/Hispanic achievement.' *American Journal of Education,* 115(2): pp. 279–304.

Marsh, H. W. and Parker, J. W. (1984) 'Determinants of student self-concept: Is it better to be a relatively large fish in a small pond even if you don't learn to swim as well?' *Journal of Personality and Social Psychology,* 47(1): pp. 213–231.

Mencken, H. L. (1920) *Prejudices: Second Series.* USA: Alfred A. Knopf, Inc.

McGillicuddy, D. and Devine, D. (2018) '"Turned off" or "ready to fly" – Ability grouping as an act of symbolic violence in primary school.' *Teaching and Teacher Education,* 70, pp. 88–99.

McGillicuddy, D. and Devine, D. (2020) '"You feel ashamed that you are not in the higher group"—Children's psychosocial response to ability grouping in primary school.' *British Educational Research Journal,* 46(3): pp. 553–573.

Nelson, L. (2014) *What makes a student 'gifted'? This study says we're getting it wrong.* Available at: www.vox.com/2014/9/24/6835643/gifted-education-classrooms-nber-study (Accessed: 18 September 2023).

Reed, C. F. (2004) 'Mathematically gifted in the heterogeneously grouped mathematics classroom: What is a teacher to do?' *Journal of Secondary Gifted Education,* 15(3): pp. 89–95.

Shanahan, T. (2019) 'Which is the best pull-out or push-in interventions?', *Reading Rockets,* 13 March. Available at: www.readingrockets.org/blogs/shanahan-literacy/which-best-pull-out-or-push-interventions (Accessed: 18 September 2023).

Sherrington, T. (2023) 'TPS3: Wide ability range!', *Teacherhead,* 10 January. Available at: https://teacherhead.com/2023/01/10/tps3-wide-ability-range/ (Accessed: 18 September 2023).

Spina, N. (2019) '"Once upon a time": Examining ability grouping and differentiation practices in cultures of evidence-based decision-making.' *Cambridge Journal of Education,* 49(3): pp. 329–348.

Taylor, A. (2018) 'Pros and cons of pull-out programs for gifted children', *HubPages,* 14 November. Available at: https://discover.hubpages.com/family/Pros-and-Cons-of-Pull-Out-Programs-for-Gifted-Children (Accessed: 18 September 2023).

The Cambridge School of Weston. (n.d.a) *The Module System.* Available at: www.csw.org/academics/the-module-system (Accessed: 18 September 2023).

The Cambridge School of Weston. (n.d.b) *We believe in the power of our approach to be transformative.* Available at: www.csw.org/about-us/who-we-are (Accessed: 18 September 2023).

Tomlinson, S. (2008) 'Gifted, talented and high ability: Selection for education in a one-dimensional world.' *Oxford Review of Education,* 34(1): pp. 59–74.

University of Connecticut. (2023) *Project BUMP UP: Rationale.* Available at: https://projectbumpup.education.uconn.edu/rationale/#:~:text=Push%2Din%20refers%20to%20instruction,%2C%20reading%2Flanguage%20arts (Accessed: 18 September 2023).

VanTassel-Baska, J. and Reis, S. (2004) 'Program delivery models for the gifted', *Gifted Today,* 27 November. Available at: https://blogs.tip.duke.edu/giftedtoday/2004/11/27/program-delivery-models-for-the-gifted/ (Accessed: 18 September 2023).

Wai, J. (2015) 'Chapter 6: Long-term effects of educational acceleration.' In: Assouline, S. G., Colangelo, N., VanTassel-Baska, J. and Lupkowski-Shoplik, A. (eds.) *A Nation Empowered: Evidence Trumps the Excuses Holding Back America's Brightest Students (Volume II).* Iowa City, Iowa: The Connie Belin & Jacqueline N. Blank International Center for Gifted Education and Talent Development.

Wintour, P. (2014a) 'Compulsory setting: schools face being forced to separate pupils by ability', *The Guardian,* 3 September, [Online]. Available at: www.theguardian.com/politics/2014/sep/03/schools-separate-pupils-ability-setting (Accessed: 18 September 2023).

Wintour, P. (2014b) 'Nicky Morgan denies she plans to back compulsory setting in schools', *The Guardian,* 3 September, [Online]. Available at: www.theguardian.com/politics/2014/sep/03/nicky-morgan-denies-plans-compulsory-setting-schools (Accessed: 18 September 2023).

Wright, B. L., Ford, D.Y. and Young, J. L. (2017) 'Ignorance or indifference? Seeking excellence and equity for under-represented students of color in gifted education.' *Global Education Review,* 4(1): pp. 45–60.

# 4. WALKING THE TIGHTROPE

*Some are born great, some achieve greatness, and some have greatness thrust upon 'em.*

**William Shakespeare, *Twelfth Night***

*I believe that the concept of the gifted child is logically, pragmatically, and—with respect to the consequences of its application in American education—morally untenable and that the aims of the field of gifted education would have a greater likelihood of being realised if we were to dispense with it altogether.*

**James Borland, 2005, p. 1**

As educators, we must hold two truths at the same time. On one hand, we know that ability is not a stagnant state; all pupils can improve and develop, and therefore labels are problematic. On the other hand, we need to challenge students effectively. Knowing where students are at allows us to target them when they need stimulating challenge. To be impactful and ethical, we must provide educational experiences that reflect individual differences in how students learn at a given time in a given subject (Borland, 2005). However, there can be a disproportionate amount of time and energy dedicated to the identification of students for the purposes of separate standalone gifted programming. Any type of identification for a selective programme misses the point. The identification debates distract from the purpose of extension and enrichment to begin with: stretch all learners.

Identifying aptitudes in students is hard. It is easy to fall back on a standardised test score, easy to presume that abilities are fixed entities, easy to devise a list. When we look at identification processes, there are some common assumptions built into systems:

- Assumption 1 – gifts are discovered.

- Assumption 2 – cognitive or standardised testing is best practice for identifying student capacity.

- Assumption 3 – we need to have a list.

We spend a lot of time searching for needles in haystacks when we could be spinning straw into gold. My argument is that we should know our students, understand different aptitudes and at the same time confront the assumptions that entrench an elitist system.

What decisions are being made using a single test score? Why do we need to have a G&T 'list'? How is 'ability' defined? If we take the time to pause and parse exactly *how* we are using information to develop students, then identification processes come into focus. The aim is not to find gifted pupils but to cultivate gifted behaviours.

Identification is walking the thinnest tightrope in front of a huge audience. This is because identification can be high stakes – setting, streaming, individual support, placement in a programme or entrance to a school are all instances where students are placed in precarious situations. It requires a lot of conscious effort to keep the balance. There is a difference between knowing our students and pigeonholing them. Let's acknowledge these key ideas:

- Knowing our students' attainment in a subject or topic makes for better progress tracking and responsive teaching.

- Compiling a gifted register can reflect social constructions of developmental potential.

- Single-criterion identification gives a snapshot of students' abilities and is limiting.

- A multifaceted continuous approach to assessment is best – when targeting extension, we can triangulate by evaluating attainment, creative productivity and task commitment.

- Creating learner profiles as opposed to gifted labels is an evolution away from giftedness and towards enrichment.

- Self-selection for enrichment programmes opens the door for all to be included. A process of nomination, validation and celebration can be used to encourage student investment.

- Learning is a process, not an event.

We will cover each of these ideas as we break down the assumptions that have made gifted identification such a fraught process.

## Assumption 1 – Gifts are Discovered

'Ability' and 'giftedness' are widely assumed to be innate, fixed and easily measured. In actuality, these are capricious terms with baked-in assumptions. The 'discovery of gifts' fallacy is part of this construction. Capacity must be developed; it is not discovered. As one of my colleagues recently stated, 'We don't use the term "ability" in our school; we use "attainment". We look at where a child is – whether they are high attaining in this topic or low attaining, we don't use a limiting language about abilities.' There is a presupposition that if there is high academic achievement, then it must be because of 'giftedness', a property some possess and others lack. So how do we counter this assumption? The myth of born giftedness is seductive and still incredibly pervasive. Students feel this as much as teachers, and I often begin my school year with students in assembly by sharing the tale of three gifted chess masters. Their gifts were not unearthed, but forged.

This story asserts that talent is nurtured and has been called one of the most amazing experiments in the history of human education. László Polgár, a Hungarian psychologist, repeatedly proclaimed that 'a genius is not born but is educated and trained' (Lundstrom, 1992). He was certain that he could turn any child into a prodigy. One just needed the right environment, encouragement and education. In 1965, Polgár conducted an epistolary courtship with a Ukrainian foreign language teacher named Klara. In his letters, he outlined a pedagogical project. He 'needed a wife willing to jump on board' (Flora, 2005), and Klara was game. The Polgárs' parenting plan was to hatch genius.

They named their firstborn daughter Susan, and as a baby, they read to her nightly in different languages. They believed that every moment was a learning opportunity, where stimulation was key. László presumed that if Susan was going to master a craft, she needed to specialise early. There were many possibilities – perhaps mathematics, piano, violin or linguistics. László believed that a child should first find joy in whichever activity, writing 'we should get the child to love what they do – to such a degree that they do it almost obsessively' (Polgár, 2017, p. 51). Susan was drawn to her father's chess set at the age of four. Her parents told her stories about each piece, teaching her how they moved across the board. She was mesmerised by the game, begging her father to play over and over. Susan had adopted her discipline. Six months later she was confidently beating regulars in Budapest chess clubs, going on to win city-wide competitions. By the time Susan was 15, she was the top-ranked female chess player in the world. She became the first woman grandmaster at the age of 21.

Her sisters Sofia and Judit followed in her footsteps, outpacing her accomplishments. They witnessed their father playing chess with Susan and clamoured to join in. Sofia is famous in the chess world for her 'Sack of Rome' in a 1989 tournament where she not only won the event, but also experts rated her performance the fifth-best ever in the history of chess (Martinez, 2021). She was 14 at the time. It was the youngest sister Judit though, who stole the show. She earned the (men's) international master chess title at the age of 12. At 15 she broke Bobby Fisher's record to become the youngest international grandmaster.

I'd like to note how unusual it was for the Polgár parents to encourage chess. Men dominated the sport for centuries. Gentle and entrenched sexism permeated chess halls. The sheer number of boys implied that girls didn't have the intelligence or strategy to compete. The Polgárs' story appeals because it takes our preconceptions about a male-dominated field and disassembles them. The Hungarian Chess Federation wanted the Polgárs to only play in women's leagues. Enraged that his girls were barred from competing, László quit the Communist Party. He put his daughters on the world stage where they were soon winning against male grandmasters twice their age. In 1989, Garry Kasparov (a chess grandmaster) told *Playboy* magazine that 'chess does not fit women properly. It's a fight, you know? Women are weaker fighters' (Cox, 2019). He pointed at Judit as a 'circus puppet'. Kasparov's stated opinion was that women chess players should stick to childbearing. This was an opinion he famously reversed when a 24-year-old Judit defeated him in 42 moves (Barden, 2002). She trounced former world chess title master Boris Spassky in a match in 1993. In 1994, she went undefeated in a chess tournament in Madrid, Spain, becoming the first woman to win a strong grandmaster tournament open to all genders.

Renowned psychologist Dr Anders Ericsson and his writing partner Robert Pool have cited the sisters as a prime example of deliberate practice.[4] Ericsson's research on the deliberate practice necessary to reach expert status has created the oft-cited and misquoted 10,000-hour rule. Distilled, the argument is that time, focus, specific goals and expert mentors are the ingredients for greatness. An Ericsson and Pool mantra I love is 'the solution is not "try harder" but rather "try differently"' (Ericsson and Pool, 2016, p. 37). It is not a certain number of hours that makes an expert; it is dedication and commitment to try new techniques and learn from failure over and over again.

The formula of deliberate practice (Ericsson and Pool, 2016):

1. Establish narrowly defined goals.

2. Be maximally focused on *improvement* during practice. This requires a state of flow and intense focus.

3. Receive and utilise immediate feedback on performance from expert teachers.

4. Consistently go out of the 'comfort zone', constantly attempt things that are just out of reach, learning from failure.

This certainly holds true of the Polgár sisters, who thoughtfully deployed metacognitive strategies to improve. These sisters were not born knowing the difference between a knight and a pawn; they were not genetically predisposed to use the two-bishop strategy. They began as novices and developed by learning from those more skilled. The girls practised for hours each day, against each other and their peers. They timed each other and played blindfolded blitz games. They profiled the competition, keeping meticulous files of tournament histories and records of previous games. Their apartment in Budapest was described as crowded and cluttered, with a library of over 4000 volumes lining the walls. The girls used historic records to play masters who had been dead for centuries. They competed, they failed, they replayed the games they lost and they undertook new tactics. They wrote for periodicals to fully clarify their approaches. They worked to discover their shortcomings or errors and how to correct them. More impressively, they also replayed games they won, looking for more elegant solutions.

---

4  I cannot recommend this book enough (*Peak* by Ericsson and Pool). The anecdotes and research are illuminating.

In a *Psychology Today* profile of Susan, she asserted, 'I had an inner drive. I think that is the difference between the very good and the best.' It has been argued in gifted circles that some people are born with ambition (a depositional trait), but László Polgár believed that we can methodically develop determination and moxie, writing that success lies on one basic principle: 'Great success is not achievable without motivation. ... If the activity is sufficiently interesting, success can also function as a strong incentive. Stimulation, encouragement, and instilling passion and trust are very important. ... If we say that [children] are clever and skilful, they will believe that as well. They often truly believe that, and try harder to actually become so' (Polgár, 2017, p. 53). This would certainly be key to overcoming the gendered expectations the Polgár sisters faced. For the latter point of deliberate practice, I would quote Susan again: 'My father believes that innate talent is nothing, that [success] is 99 percent hard work. I agree with him.' The Polgár sisters fit nicely into the narrative of hard work and resilience through failure. It has been estimated that they reached mastery through over 50,000 hours of practice (Gladwell, 2013).

Were the Polgár sisters happy with the strenuous training? All three girls look back fondly on their upbringing, recalling their early passion. They speak of being grateful to their parents. Chess was one aspect of their lives; they had many opportunities to explore beyond the black and white squares. They were far from one-trick ponies who were limited by their speciality. The girls were not instructed by László alone. Klara is often overlooked in their triumphs. However, she quietly manoeuvred the girls' success by expanding their education. She taught them high-level mathematics and languages (Susan speaks seven). She was also the parent arranging their places in tournaments across 40 countries. Klara has said, 'I am always part of the realisation. The thread follows the needle. I am the thread' (Flora, 2005). As László wrote in his book *Bringing Up Genius*: 'If we considered our daughters as manipulable figures, merely as objects and not as subjects of education, would we have been able to attain such a result? Without the active collaboration of their open, freely-chosen, independent agency and personhood, we could have achieved nothing. In this kind of education, the active participation of the child is almost as important as that of the educator' (Polgár, 2017). Children cannot be drilled into little geniuses; they must be challenged and invited. This 'experiment' is isolated; however, it neatly makes the point that no one is born knowing end-game chess strategy – we all have universal potential.

With all this in mind, I'd now like to walk the tightrope – how to know where our students are at while recognising that everyone can develop. 'Identification' should tell us how students can grow. It can be the basis for grouping, scaffolding and adaptive teaching strategies in the classroom. Carol Ann Tomlinson notes that we need 'classroom practice that looks eyeball to eyeball with the reality that kids differ, and the most effective teachers do whatever it takes to hook the whole range of kids on learning' (Tomlinson, 2014). It is necessary to *understand and know* our students' individual requirements, strengths and areas for development. Ideally, we would like a model that is proactive and locally focused on students' current needs in specific domains (Dixson et al., 2020). We need approaches that give us utility and help improve our instruction.

## Assumption 2 – Cognitive or Standardised Testing is Best Practice for Identifying Student Capacity

As Deborah Eyre has written, 'a hundred years of gifted education has shown up the various flaws in an approach based on identifying the gifted – it hasn't worked and it can't work' (Eyre, 2011, p. 11). Contradictions are rife in G&T identification. It is not unusual for the register of gifted and talented children to be taken directly from a cognitive ability test score. I've been in systems where the top 2% of scorers in each year group were put on the list. Some students had made the cut-off percentage, but they were not near the top stanine. When placed on a national scale their scores would be considered above average but not particularly notable. Some of the scores were intimidatingly high. I taught one girl who was off the charts, and this was reflected in her grades. When I set the results against internal assessments, it appeared that one or two of the children were underachieving to an embarrassing degree – was this an issue with the students or an issue in our assessments? The method had contradictions; high-achieving cohorts had children not on the list despite garnering higher scores than the students in the cohort above them. When new admissions arrived, they could bump existing students off. There is 'geographic giftedness', where students would be 'gifted' in their previous school, only to move to a new school and be labelled 'not gifted' according to different measures. These are not unusual methods. 'We put quotas on the numbers of students we think can be cognitively able. The gifted are the top 5-10%. Selective schools are the top 20-25%' (Eyre, 2011, p. 53). As one student asked when policy changed in England, 'Are we being de-gifted, miss?' (Koshy and Pinheiro-Torres, 2013, p. 2). In many places, giftedness has a financial fee attached because 'giftedness' must be diagnosed. The cost of being assessed by a practitioner and passing the requisite tests, like the WISC-V (Wechsler Intelligence Scale for Children), can often be a barrier. Parents must act as advocates to prepare their children, arranging and paying for the testing to meet entry requirements into a programme – and not all tests are free or universally delivered.

Schools tend to inherit gifted brackets from above. Overriding government policy may prescribe that 'gifted and talented' or 'more able' lists consist of the top 5% from cognitive ability testing. Government bodies may create the classifications for schools, perhaps as a tickbox for inspection or a headcount for funding special gifted programming. Hidden beneath these yardstick measurements is the absolutist assumption that some students are gifted and others are not. There is also a glibness in describing students as 'mildly', 'moderately', or 'significantly' gifted. Identification methods should not be used to exclude students from accessing extension or enrichment opportunities. It is important to note that definitions of 'high ability' or 'gifted' exist because of the structure of schools and how data is used. These are ways to view trends across groups and guide interventions. Using a single criterion is a limited way to identify students and ignores the basis of good assessment – triangulation. When understanding students, it is pivotal to look beyond one dimension. It is best practice to use many different pieces of evidence to triangulate attainment. An old debate was whether we should conservatively concentrate on the top 3% or be generous and include the top 7%. This debate misses the point. Confining identification to a single criterion like a cognitive ability test or exam result misses so many students out.

This is not to say that looking for aptitudes through a test is evil. I recently sat down with a friend who characterised himself as 'a proper diamond in the rough' whose journey was pivoted on a test. He described a childhood where he was in bottom sets and spending his day 'colouring in'. It was a high score on a standardised test that forced his teachers to look at him in a new light, move him up from bottom sets and challenge him.

> *'I was placed in bottom sets in primary school because my behaviour wasn't great, and I had very average progress tests. I was 11 and we did the test on one of the first days of school. I moved up about a month after they got the results. We all knew our numbers. I was always compared to a girl named Clara who had the same score as me. "How come Clara is doing X and you are still on Y?" It was odd in retrospect. I don't remember if every teacher referenced the number, but lots did. I moved up sets every year after that, – made top set in four years.'*

He framed this test as a defining point in his education; this was where his potential was found. It is also the beginning of his capacity being championed.

## Single-Criterion Identification

For decades, the norm for identifying giftedness has been a single-criterion cut-off score for entrance into special programmes and/or targeting extension. The most commonly used assessments are *diagnostic* or *prognostic*. In diagnostic assessments, the aim is to find out what the student knows at the moment. These are snapshots and are commonly progress or achievement tests. They assess pupils' knowledge, understanding and application, usually in what are considered core subjects like maths, English and science. These tests are useful in discovering gaps in learning and are great at tracking progress on a cohort level. As teachers, we can make our learning visible and gain feedback on the effectiveness of our instruction. They allow the educator and student to get a baseline, and when taken at regular intervals, they can monitor learning and whether it has slowed or stalled.

Prognostic tests are used to measure potential and set targets and are usually cognitive ability tests. These are tests of general intelligence, often with the aim to measure a person's capacity to problem solve, use abstract thinking and demonstrate logical thinking. There are variations of an IQ test, like the Wechsler Intelligence Scale for Children (WISC-V), that can yield 'factor scores' including verbal comprehension, visual-spatial reasoning, fluid reasoning, processing speed and working memory. There is an entire industry of testing for children under age 5, even though IQ stability is poor. A child who has begun to read and has early access to educational materials will obviously have their score inflated. Emotional maturity impacts whether children comply with direction. The score is changeable under who is delivering the test and how they engage the child, or the time of day can lead to a child being more distractable or bored. There can be an emphasis on early years determinism; however, research in neural plasticity demonstrates that significant changes occur through early childhood. 'When children are tested at a young age and retested over time there is substantial regression to the mean. In other words, a child performing at a high level at six years old may well not be at 16' (Eyre, 2011, p. 6).

I have taught for years in a system where schools commonly use cognitive ability tests (GL CAT4), which have four batteries in verbal reasoning, quantitative reasoning, nonverbal reasoning and spatial ability.[5] At this point, it is easy to be mired in the 'IQ' or standardised testing debate. Cognitive tests can be incredibly useful. They are also *one component*. I refer to CAT scores all the time. It is human nature to use these lovely, neat scores as baselines or for target setting. However, as a first and primary point of reference, they miss the larger picture of a student. It is easy to become dependent on a reductive number.

We tend to view diagnostic and prognostic assessments in schools with the assumption that they are comprehensive. Cognitive ability tests (CAT) measure overall 'aptitudes', while measures of academic performance (MAP) are progress tests that quantify the test-taker's performance in a particular subject area at that time. MAP is useful for teachers to 'pitch' their challenge at the right level and set appropriate targets. CAT can indicate a student's potential, which can tell us if a child is underachieving and needs support or intervention. Both of these indicators have been used to identify gifted children, but they are not complete or holistic, especially in isolation. Many students fly under the radar of these tests and in data tracking – no test is perfectly universal, reliable, valid, objective and easily usable. MAP tends to be used for only a handful of 'core' subjects, while cognitive ability tests with batteries cast a wider net.

I'd argue that the most valuable aspect of these tests is when we see the contrast between batteries; when something is uncovered that perhaps we didn't see before. Batteries are most useful in identifying biases. For instance, if a student's verbal reasoning score is markedly lower, we can offer suitable scaffolding in the classroom or investigate a language barrier. When we can see the first signs of disconnect, we can make referrals, investigate and look at personalised support. This ties in with an argument for universal screening for learning differences like dyslexia, which requires a more sensitive and longer assessment. A colleague who specialised in dyslexia once told me that the reductive CAT numbers were off-putting and useless. It is only when you look closely at the individual results of a student broken down by battery that these tests can reveal the first clues to solving a mystery.

---

[5]   While CAT4 and the series of Wechsler Intelligence Scale for Children are most common, there are many more. The Woodcock-Johnson Cognitive Abilities Test for general intellectual ability. MidYIS is an adaptive baseline assessment that measures aptitude, potential and progress. Kaufman Test of Educational Achievement can be a standalone screener of basic academic skills by testing reading, written language, oral language and mathematics. Raven's Progressive Matrices is a test of non-verbal intelligence and has been used to remove any cultural bias in measuring general fluid intelligence.

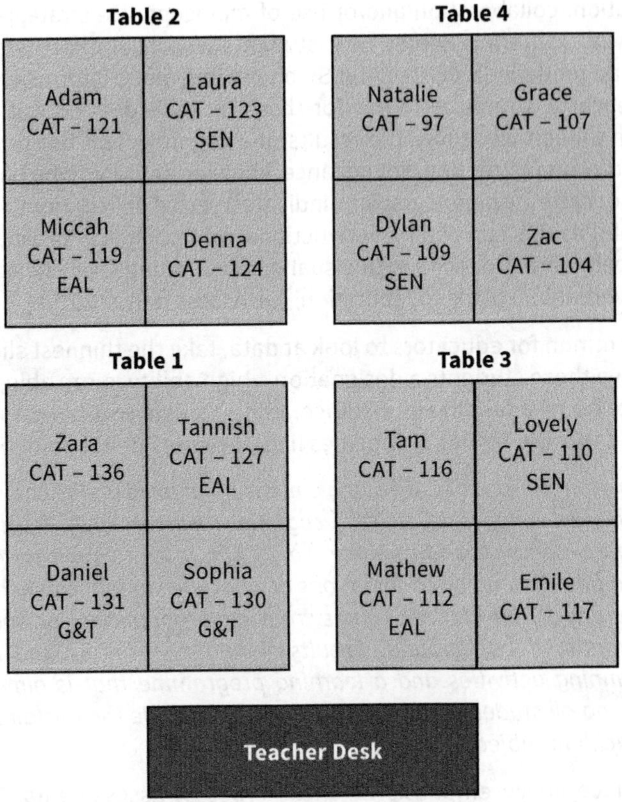

**Table 2**

| | |
|---|---|
| Adam<br>CAT – 121 | Laura<br>CAT – 123<br>SEN |
| Miccah<br>CAT – 119<br>EAL | Denna<br>CAT – 124 |

**Table 4**

| | |
|---|---|
| Natalie<br>CAT – 97 | Grace<br>CAT – 107 |
| Dylan<br>CAT – 109<br>SEN | Zac<br>CAT – 104 |

**Table 1**

| | |
|---|---|
| Zara<br>CAT – 136 | Tannish<br>CAT – 127<br>EAL |
| Daniel<br>CAT – 131<br>G&T | Sophia<br>CAT – 130<br>G&T |

**Table 3**

| | |
|---|---|
| Tam<br>CAT – 116 | Lovely<br>CAT – 110<br>SEN |
| Mathew<br>CAT – 112<br>EAL | Emile<br>CAT – 117 |

**Teacher Desk**

Figure 4.1 Cognitive bias in our planning – example seating plan. CAT is the cognitive ability test score.

We give privilege to some data points over others. I recently had a discussion with a colleague about seating plans and putting students' overall cognitive ability test score into plans. A similar tact is to then identify children above a certain score as G&T. The issue with both is that they don't represent the current reality of how that student is progressing in that subject, and this affects an educator's impression of a student. This does not reflect current attainment in that subject, so it not useful for adaptive and responsive teaching. There are also assumptions about the level of work that should then be assigned to certain students. There is inconsistency in identifying G&T students, as the 'cut-off' is not the same across all schools. There are also better options for seating plans that reflect the particular dynamics of a classroom. 'Effort' or 'attitude to learning' is a useful indicator in seating – it encompasses self-regulation, collaboration and/or use of metacognitive strategies (e.g. sit students with low effort scores near students with high effort where these skills can be modelled). SEND/EAL/ESL on seating plans informs teachers of specific teaching strategies to use for those on individual education plans. This doesn't mean we ignore the results of a cognitive test but use *the best data* that informs instruction. For instance, knowing students who have a mild, moderate or extreme bias (e.g. scores indicate a verbal deficit) from a cognitive test is useful as this can change instructional approach (e.g. providing those students with verbal deficits with visual cues or sitting them near students with high verbal scores for collaboration) (GL Assessments, 2020).

It is still common for educators to look at data, take the thinnest slice off the top and give those students a designation – high ability, more able, gifted or scholars, to name a few. In any instance, using a single criterion can miss out on pupils' capacity. Testing companies like GL Assessments point out that:

> '*Any misconceptions of CAT4 being a measure of fixed ability should be challenged. Like physical abilities, cognitive abilities can be developed through experience and practice. Low CAT4 scores should never be used to put a ceiling on expectations of what the student can achieve, particularly if the student comes from an economically or socially disadvantaged background. Results should be used as the basis for planning activities and a learning programme that is aimed at improving all students' reasoning abilities alongside their attainment in curriculum subjects.*' (GL Education, 2023)

Schools place heavy emphasis on these types of assessments. They can underpin whole-school improvement. An example is MidYIS assessment for 11–14-year-olds (from Cambridge's Centre for Evaluation and Monitoring). This is an adaptive, curriculum independent, baseline test to predict (I)GCSE aptitudes, potential and progress. The online 50-minute assessment is used in 109 countries, with over 481,000 students aged 11–14 taking a CEM MidYIS assessment in the 2023–2024 academic year (Cambridge University Press and Assessment, 2023). The test can be used to identify gifted students, set student targets, determine progress and calculate value-add, and it is often the foundational data for a school's self-evaluation. This is a basis for data-informed decision making; however, it can erase nuance and create an over-reliance on one indicator, with teaching and learning implications for how students are perceived.

I recently had a conversation with a friend who pointed out that as teachers we were constantly collecting data – thousands of data points through hundreds of interactions all day and every day with students. He asked my position on cognitive ability testing on a scale of one (it's nothing) to 10 (it's the only thing). My answer was that a cognitive test was a data point, and I don't want to negate that, but at the same time I have massive worries about the disproportionate weight we give that one data point. The repercussions one test score can have on the trajectory of a child's education, and the social immobility it perpetuates, are scary. Cognitive testing is a useful tool, but I'm uncomfortable with how this tool is often crudely and bluntly wielded.

## Single-Criterion Identification

**Cognitive ability tests:** prognostic tests used to measure potential; usually tests of general intelligence (e.g. WISC-V, CAT4, MidYIS).

**Progress tests:** diagnostic assessment of current performance, usually delivered in highlighted subjects like maths, English and science (e.g. measures of academic performance tests and GL progress tests).

**Summative tests:** assessment of learning. For instance, departments use end-of-year exam results from the previous year to identify their high-ability students.

**Baseline assessments:** useful for pitching curriculum and measuring progress, and frequently the basis for grouping or setting students (baselines can vary – they can be a teacher-created assessment to identify prior knowledge and understanding in the classroom, or a universal CAT test that determines targets and value-add).

**Competition:** although infrequent, gifted identification can come in the form of competition, like the Olympiad competitions in Russia. This can favour more confident pupils or overlook those with inclusion needs.

There are many issues with a high-stakes test on which a major educational decision is made, even when there is a reasonable degree of validity. Using one test to permanently stream students is fundamentally unethical. When year-group-level testing is 'too easy' for high-performing students, there is a 'ceiling effect' among those who could demonstrate greater learning beyond the level of the assessment. There are decisions regarding the norming sample, standard score and percentiles when a standardised test represents a student's relative standing. Small statistical issues can have massive repercussions. The SAT and ACT use the normal distribution. Researchers like Mark Kantrowitz, who studied admissions at selective colleges, have found that statistical artefacts in the way SATs are scored have outcomes that discriminate against under-resourced and equity-seeking students (Kantrowitz, 2021). Problems are more likely to occur at two or more standard deviations beyond the mean and can also occur to a lesser extent at lower test scores. When the location of the bell curve is shifted due to changes in the average test scores, small differences in test scores at the mean can be magnified at the highest and lowest test scores. Kantrowitz found that 280 selective colleges, especially the 24 colleges with 25th percentile combined SAT test scores of 1400 to 1600, had a significantly below average enrolment of Black and Latin American students (Kantrowitz, 2021). Differences in the percentage of students with high test scores when test-takers are aggregated by income, race and gender have consistently been acute. Assumptions about validity should also be interrogated. For years the analogies and antonym sections of the verbal SATs were criticised for creating generations of students who studied massive lists of 'SAT words'. As Jeff Rubenstein of test prep company Princeton Review notes, 'The idea that kids would be memorizing "lummox" and "clumsy" instead of reading Dickens is absurd' (Pringle, 2003). Antonyms were nixed in 1994, and analogies in 2005. The SAT has changed to include more reading comprehension questions and an optional essay section, and has expanded the maths portion.

We have all experienced overconfidence in our tests. An important measure is construct validity; the degree to which any test can be said to measure the construct it proclaims. This is one of the largest issues with SAT/ACT and IQ. A 2019 article in the *Journal of Applied Research in Memory and Cognition* found that what is typically touted as 'general intelligence' is little more than a statistical artefact resulting from the same brain regions being activated for similar tasks on cognitive ability tests. The article looks at how our understanding of working memory has progressed and notes that 'cognitive ability testing has focused on application, often without providing a sound theoretical basis for the tests' (Kovacs and Conway, 2019). There is also correlational validity, with some social scientists arguing that cognitive ability scores correlate highly with other constructs, like socio-economic status (or 'life success') (Lazine, 2022). The correlation between the status of a person's family income at the time of the test has consistently been found to be the greater influence.

Dr Donna Y. Ford of Ohio State University notes that the divides in race and ethnicity scores seen in widespread cognitive ability testing can be explained thusly: 'If these tests were not biased, we wouldn't have different IQ scores along racial and ethnic lines – but we do. It's an indication that there is something wrong with these tests, not with us' (Whitten, 2020). Mistakes or unconscious biases happen; even things we consider the most trustworthy are susceptible. Testing bias can be invisible. Dr Roy O. Freedle spent years analysing the test of English as a foreign language (TOEFL) – an exam for students from abroad who want to qualify for places at English-speaking schools. He found that various linguistic aspects of the questions, like word order, repetition, word placement or interrogative style, can have an impact on the success of different language learners (Mathews, 2003). Culture and language frame our construction of the world in ways tests cannot easily account for. One study found just that while doing cognitive ability testing on the Tsimane people, an Indigenous group living in Bolivia. Many Tsimane do not use labels for shapes, which affects their scores on a measure that requires the tester to think about and manipulate shapes. Dr Steven Piantadosi of the University of California, Berkeley commented: 'People without words for shapes probably do this type of task differently than we do, just as if the Tsimane gave us an IQ test with a bunch of leaf shapes that we didn't know the names for, but they did' (Whitten, 2020).

## Assessment Weaknesses

**Validity assumptions:** that the test measures what it is intended to measure and does so consistently.

**Clarity:** length or breadth of the test, unclear or ambiguous direction, use of unfamiliar language or format, etc.

**Pertinence:** the assumption that a test is timely, addressing present needs.

**Domain-specific:** the test is tailored to a particular subject or skill but used as a universal indicator.

**Ceiling effect:** the test is too easy for high-performing students.

**Second language learners:** the test presents barriers in phrasing and terminology.

## Neurodivergence and Processing Barriers

**Cultural bias and cues in questions:** assuming equal familiarity and fluency with the dominant culture.

**Test conditions:** the environment and state in which a student undergoes the assessment (e.g. Muslim students taking exams while fasting during Ramadan).

**Accessibility issues and students of determination:** for example, colourblind students unable to analyse charts or maps.

**Referral bias:** students are referred by a teacher or administrator to take a test as opposed to universal testing.

**Stereotype threats:** for example, assumptions that girls are not good at maths or sciences.

**Emotional variables:** for example, test-taking anxiety or student motivation.

**Norming sample, standard score and percentiles:** can be misleading when a standardised test represents a student's relative standing with age equivalency. When the location of the bell curve is shifted, small differences in test scores at the mean can be magnified at the highest and lowest test scores. Norm-referenced versus criteria-referenced assessments can change the interpretation of results.

**Objectivity assumptions:** assumptions of equitability – that a test is free from bias and subjectivity.

We have all seen the above-mentioned issues affect our students. A girl who is so wracked with anxiety that she is suddenly afflicted with a stomach bug before assessments. A second-language speaker who repeatedly raises his hand during an assessment to ask what words mean. Students who are mystified reading about frost when they have lived their whole lives in the desert. These problems render students invisible. Students' needs can be eclipsed by another identification – for example, diagnosed neurodivergence or wheelchair users who don't receive the challenge they require. Multi-exceptional children (e.g. a child with high aptitude and dyslexia) think and process information differently. It is important to note that directing students to services relies on teacher observation, access to diagnosis and family buy-in. Robust inclusion departments and counselling services are wonderful. For a student with phonophobia, being provided with noise-cancelling headphones can make all the difference in their performance. Dictionary accommodations for second-language speakers are a gamechanger. Schools can take that second look and design their assessments with the cultural context in mind. An environment that destigmatises these differences is important so that students feel they can come forward and feel empowered by their accommodations. As teachers, we know the tools necessary. The trick is to wear the lenses and see the issues in equity.

Dr Deborah Eyre speaks to the entrenched norms that keep gifted structures active in education systems:

> 'When it comes to the gifted we stubbornly hold on to the out-dated ideas of a separate sub-set of the population born with advanced inherited, definable, measurable and intellectual characteristics. Furthermore we institutionalise this belief. We put quotas on the numbers of students we think can be cognitively able. The gifted are the top 5-10%. Selective schools are the top 20-25%. ... Until we dare to believe that more people could attain highly, they never will.' (Eyre, 2011, p. 53)

Dividing students into neat categories is not the answer. Awareness of students' current attainment for purposes of responsive teaching and personalised learning in our classrooms is key. By identifying pupils who are simply high achievers we fail to reach those who are masking abilities, have underlying needs or are non-productive in school. Cognitive testing is just one data point. So let's look at how multiple criteria and continuous assessment can view students holistically.

## Multifaceted Assessment

Great assessment is continuous as it shows where a student's understanding lies in that moment and over time. Formative assessment is vital in this and also as assessment for learning. Ongoing multifaceted assessment has been popularised for a reason: triangulation uses many data sources. The use of triangulation to comprehend students' attainment and aptitudes increases the reliability of our data. We wish to capture *how* and *where* a student can be targeted for extension. Deploying different methods when gathering evidence ensures that a student exists beyond a single aptitude score. Student grades or exam results alone can overlook underachieving students, while combining formative assessment and teacher observation can help identify students whose skills and aptitudes are masked for various reasons. Written evidence is valuable, but we can observe so much *during* a task by engaging students in conversation to see their understanding and their learning process. This is key to adaptive and responsive teaching. Holistically seeing a student is vital. Teachers collect data all day, every day, in the thousands of small moments we interact with students. Multifaceted assessment and triangulation encourage educators to use observations and products in the assessment.

Assessment should support instruction, rather than just measure its outcomes. Best practice is ongoing and includes assessment of, for and as learning. All assessment tasks influence the way in which students approach their learning – students engage with feedback to improve and we use assessment to help students become reflective learners. As Black and Wiliam write, 'Teachers need to know about their pupils' progress and difficulties with learning so that they can adapt their own work to meet pupils' needs – needs that are often unpredictable and that vary from one pupil to another. Teachers can find out what they need to know in a variety of ways, including observation and discussion in the classroom and the reading of pupils' written work' (Black and Wiliam, 2010, p. 82).

Assessment for learning involves teachers using evidence about students' knowledge, understanding and skills to inform their teaching. Ongoing formative assessment occurs throughout the teaching and learning process to clarify student learning, to inform intervention and as the basis for responsive instruction. Assessment for learning is an approach to teaching and learning that creates feedback, which is then used to improve students' performance. Students are then included in the learning process and gain confidence because they are explicitly addressing the objectives, aims and expectations. In everyday teaching, this could include fun pop quizzes, retrieval practice exercises, exit tickets, mini-whiteboards to show answers and games. Formative assessment creates opportunities for students to clarify knowledge, practise application and engage with the material. It is also part of responsive teaching in that it creates cycles of feedback, prompts, guidance and new tasks.

Dylan Wiliam has been a giant in the field of embedding formative assessment. In his model, formative assessment establishes where the learner is going, where they currently are at and how to get there. Formative assessment clarifies learning intentions, elicits evidence of learning, activates students as learning resources for one another during peer assessment and instigates student ownership when there is self-assessment (Wiliam, 2020).

## Unpacking Formative Assessment

| | Where the learner is going | Where the learner is | How to get there |
|---|---|---|---|
| **Teacher** | Clarifying, sharing and understanding learning intentions | Engineering effective discussions, tasks and activities that elicit evidence of learning | Providing feedback that moves learners forward |
| **Peer** | | Activating students as learning resources for one another | |
| **Learner** | | Activating students as owners of their own learning | |

| | Where the learner is going | Where the learner is | How to get there |
|---|---|---|---|
| **Teacher** | Before you can even begin | Responsive teaching | |
| **Peer** | | The learners' role | |
| **Learner** | | | |

Figure 4.2 Dylan Wiliam's 'Unpacking Formative Assessment' (Wiliam, 2018).

Assessment as learning is reflective and occurs when students are their own assessors. Students monitor their own learning, ask questions and use a range of strategies to decide what they know and can do, and how to use assessment for new learning.

Assessment of learning is summative and usually takes place during key points in learning (e.g. at the end of a unit). It allows teachers to see how students' skills and understanding have progressed through the curriculum. Multifaceted assessment done right is a remedy to the outdated dependence on a single score for any reductive identification. There are many advantages to using a method that includes qualitative and quantitative products. Students are no longer subject to 'one shot' in a high-stakes test. Evidenced evaluation could focus on current performance, not on cognitive ability tests which indicate 'potential'.

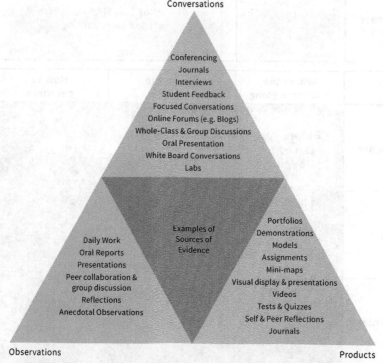

Figure 4.3 Triangulation of student learning model (Surrey Schools, 2021).

The freedom to use alternative assessment documents is powerful. As researcher Dr Ana Huerta-Macías writes, '... contrary to traditional testing, which typically provides only a set of numbers, alternative assessment documents a story for every student—and what is the ultimate goal of evaluation if not to give us the knowledge to be able to reflect on, discuss, and assist a student's journey through the learning process?' (Huerta-Macías, 2002, p. 338). Assessing ability using multiple criteria means you can highlight students who test well, impress with portfolio work and/or possess leadership skills. A system of teacher referrals can attest to a student's progress in class and socio-emotional skills.

Schools can tailor components based on cohort or subject – I highly recommend specificity. We are looking for how to set challenge in our everyday lessons. Research has found that domain-specific programmes and services are much more effective than any generalised identification and one-size-fits-all programming (Dixson et al., 2020). Empowering subjects means valuing the disciplinary nature of knowledge. Each department can highlight specific competencies instead of being beholden to a one-size-fits-all assessment – a mathematician is using different skills than an artist. To start the discussion, you can discuss:

- What evidence are we already collecting?
- What evidence of current attainment can we add that is valuable?
- What methods of evidence gathering can we use to improve personalised learning?

There are some children who are universally high achieving across all subjects. However, many more students are underchallenged or under target in just one or two domains. As Dixson et al. write: 'Schools often limit their gifted services to the few students who test at a high level in every subject, but if they focus on developing talents in specific subject areas, schools will identify many more students who would benefit from more challenging instruction' (Dixson et al., 2020). The trick is not falling into James C. Kaufman's Lucky Charms paradox of assuming one component will address all the challenge required to stretch a student. As Kaufman explains, in commercials, we see children eating Lucky Charms as part of a nutritious breakfast, alongside orange juice, scrambled eggs, yoghurt and toast. When seen this way, Lucky Charms are a good thing. But in reality, when we are in the midst of the morning rush, our children will most likely scarf down a bowl of Lucky Charms at the breakfast table by itself. Despite the best intentions,

Lucky Charms become the only source of breakfast nutrition – hardly a complete meal and definitely not ideal for our kids (Kaufman, 2015, p. 60).

The aim is that we personalise learning so that every student is challenged and reaches Vygotsky's zone of proximal development, where students productively struggle with a task (Vygotsky, 1978). Therefore our assessment design should be meaningful and actionable. Educators can select the knowledge and skills important to them by using different types of evidence. A structure that is useful is Renzulli's Three-Ring Conception of Giftedness.

## The Three-Ring Circus

In 2019, a pioneer in gifted education stood beside Mayor De Blasio in New York and told the world to please stop labelling children 'gifted'. In advocating for school reforms Dr Joseph Renzulli explained, 'I talk about the development of gifted behaviours, rather than "you're gifted and the kid next to you is not."' Many in education have used 'gifted' as a noun, referring to individuals or groups as 'the gifted'. Renzulli has consistently used the word 'gifted' to describe *a place of mastery* – a gifted musician, a gifted mathematician or a gifted writer (Renzulli, 2016). His work has the expressed goal of applying gifted pedagogy to all students as part of total talent development. As Renzulli notes, 'The term gifted is used in our lexicon only as an adjective, and even then, it is used as a developmental perspective. Thus, for example, we speak and write about the development of gifted behaviors in specific areas of learning and human expression rather than giftedness as a state of being. If we use the g-word, it is to label the service rather than the student' (Renzulli, 2005, p. 81).

Renzulli is in his 80s now, and when presenting his work he sprinkles each argument with real-life examples and stories of children's inventiveness. When he took part in De Blasio's diversity panel on education, he unnerved New Yorkers with his recommendations, like his call for districts to end standardised tests for 4-year-olds to enter gifted programmes and abolish the SHSATs. The reasoning was simple: 'Give more kids the chance to throw the ball around and we'll find out which one should be quarterback' (Brody, 2019).

Renzulli and his research partner Dr Sally Reis have been trailblazers in gifted education – most notably because their work has evolved and changed, with each iteration pushing for more inclusivity. They do not shy away from identifying aptitudes, while at the same time maintaining that schools can provide meaningful enrichment opportunities for all. One of the first key contributions Renzulli made was the Three-Ring Conception of Giftedness.

This model was a game-changer because it redefined identification. By looking beyond a single criterion, which was often a cognitive ability test, teachers could design a meaningful multifaceted approach. This didn't mean that cognitive ability tests were necessarily excluded from the equation, but wielded as a precision tool to inform teacher instruction. The aim was balance; to initiate a shift in our perception of giftedness. The three-ring model was introduced in 1976 and at the time had a backlash in gifted circles; it was 'soft' in relation to the sharpness of an IQ test. The appeal grows when you have a classroom of students in front of you as opposed to a spreadsheet of numbers. The three-ring model considers *above average ability* (in my adapted model I have changed this to *current attainment* as a strength in that subject or domain), *creativity* (out-of-the-box thinking in any subject) and *task commitment* (a cluster of traits like resilience, organisation and perseverance). The centre of the model is 'gifted behaviours'. I have adapted this to *capacity to excel*, the implication being that the three elements can be cultivated in all students.

### Adapted Version of Renzulli's Triad Model

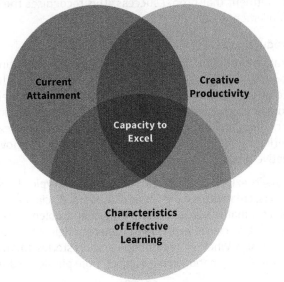

Figure 4.4 Adapted triad model (Renzulli, 2016, p. 145).

## Current Attainment

- In the moment, how is the student progressing through new content? Formative assessment is key in this adaptive approach. Cumulatively, high attainment in a subject or field can be measured through continuous assessment and a portfolio of work.

- Domain-specific competencies. This goes beyond the traditional conception of 'ability' as a purely academic measure. Within this could be the automation of information processing; rapid, accurate and selective retrieval of content.

- This component can also include strengths in leadership, collaboration, oracy, artistry and other fields not easily assessed through standardised testing.

- Renzulli specified that this strength be viewed as 'above average' performance as opposed to 'exceptional'. Research suggests that, beyond a certain level, real-world achievement is less dependent on ever-increasing performance. Rather it is factors like task commitment that propel success. This recognises the limitations of achievement tests.

## Creative Productivity

- Creative productivity means that a student is creating an original product – writing a collection of short stories, drafting a UN resolution, building a Raspberry Pi, coding an AI model or designing a sustainable fashion line. These can be pursued outside the regular curriculum in students' own time or in guided extracurricular offerings. Inventiveness, experimentation and innovation are all creative productivity in action.

- Creativity exists across all fields of study. While typically associated with the arts, creativity is a high-level skill across disciplines. A student may look at a maths task and use an unusual problem-solving approach. Designing a science experiment requires originality and the ability to hypothesise. Whether writing code or short stories, this trait recognises the use of imagination in any subject, from physics to drama.

- This element encompasses enquiry, ingenuity, out-of-the-box thinking and bravery to explore or go off-piste. Student questioning, critique, dialogue and debate can be encouraged and are evidence of critical thinking. This can also be seen when students make cross-curricular linkages, demonstrate far-thinking or relate the material to real-world application.

### Characteristics of Effective Learning

- Task commitment, grit, resilience and perseverance are part of what Renzulli considered a cluster of dispositional traits. However, I have adapted this further to encompass characteristics of effective learning – not traits one possesses but as motivations to learn and skills to practise. These behaviours can be developed and fostered in a nurturing environment, where students feel driven to work through obstacles and engage in deep practice.

- Use of metacognitive strategies to improve. Knowing how to engage with declarative knowledge (facts, information), procedural knowledge (problem-solving processes, concepts) and conditional knowledge (understanding the how, when and why of using a strategy or skill).

- Self-regulation techniques deployed for task management – goal setting, self-monitoring (planning, time management, emotional regulation), self-instruction and self-reinforcement.

- This is often observed in effort, behaviour and attitude to learning.

The three rings work together and can be viewed as a spectrum of development so that all students can reach the overlapping centre. Teachers can cultivate these components in all pupils. Giftedness is not innate or fixed – rather the interaction between these three rings allows educators *to create capacity* within students. It is the right set of conditions that foster mastery.

When using the three-ring model we can improve our approaches in each area. For *creative productivity* we can devote time in the curriculum for exploration and extension projects. To improve *current attainment* we can deploy an enriched and adaptive pedagogical approach. For *characteristics of effective learning* we can model and deliver explicit instruction for self-regulation, metacognition and deep practice.

## Schoolhouse Versus Creative-Productive Giftedness

Multifaceted identification allows us to spot those students who need challenge and may previously have been overlooked. The three-ring model is a useful tool in making 'gifted behaviours' visible. Renzulli and Reis defined two types of giftedness – schoolhouse and creative-productive. The conventional *schoolhouse giftedness* is one that we are most familiar with, while *creative-productive giftedness* is easily overlooked. They are not mutually exclusive. Schoolhouse giftedness is the child we typically associate with having gifts, and teachers can spot them fairly easily in their classrooms. These students are conscientious in lessons and clearly high attaining as evidenced by their assessments. They achieve in the traditional school environment and know how to 'navigate' school. They understand the steps to performing well. Creative-productive giftedness, on the other hand, may not correlate to impressive test results. Instead, this is a child producing original substance. Renzulli refers 'to the traits that inventors, designers, authors, artists, and others apply to selected areas of economic, cultural, and social capital' (Renzulli, 2016, p. 143). These are the students who give you their collection of poems, build electric cars or show off their detailed Minecraft worlds. What is useful in Figure 4.5 is that we can identify Student A, who Renzulli would classify as a classic 'schoolhouse' high achiever, alongside Student D, a 'creative-productive' high achiever. The distinction between schoolhouse and creative-productive giftedness matters because it determines how we develop productive behaviours.

Putting the three-ring model into action is not simple. What are the pertinent components of our reporting? Are these categories equally weighted? What skills are key to our subject? Which skills best equip our high-performing students?

| Components | Above average ability | | Task commitment | | | Creativity | | |
|---|---|---|---|---|---|---|---|---|
| | Exam performance top 10% | Leadership qualities/ ECAs | High-effort grades | High-quality homework (self-regulation) | Evidence of deep practice | Portfolio work | Questioning and outside investigation | Approach to tasks (meta-cognition) |
| Student A (School-house) | ☑ | | ☑ | ☑ | ☑ | | | |
| Student B | | | | ☑ | | ☑ | | |
| Student C | ☑ | | ☑ | | | | | |
| Student D (Creative-productive) | | ☑ | | ☑ | | ☑ | ☑ | ☑ |

Figure 4.5 Targeted extension checklist.

This example was one I have actually used in my departments. It was comprehensive, but this particular example is not one I recommend. An overly complicated exercise can be laborious. This mechanical process also did not feel like an authentic assessment, but it did turn into a reflective exercise. The process of creating these categories of measurement prompted a worthy debate. For instance, how can we spark a student's 'creative approach to tasks' if this is the quality they lack? Is our curriculum providing space for exploration? If it is rare that we find evidence of 'deep practice' then we should provide scaffolding and opportunity to develop this skill. A team can argue internally over 'how many check marks' designate high ability, then question why the check marks are necessary. Can we create extension that targets students in a new way? Can we use our framework to change our practice? How can we meaningfully measure the more subjective qualities? We should not make lists for the sake of making lists. Identifying students' abilities should be useful and give teachers clear direction. We must contemplate what is the most useful, simple and purposeful way to deploy triangulation. The important thing is that triangulation is used – it does not have to be complicated or inflexible. It just has to suit your students and your subject, and remind us that 'gifts' are strengths that appear in different ways.

## Assumption 3 – We Need to Have a List

Identification and the creation of gifted registers is a process that has traditionally resulted in labelling selected students as 'the gifted', thereby relegating all others to a non-gifted category. In recent years, however, a large body of research has argued forcefully against such a broad-stroke labelling process. Dr James Borland has a knack for writing critical commentary on giftedness while being a steadfast defender of gifted programmes. His recommendations have been to do away with any labelling altogether; that *we conceive of gifted education without gifted children* (Borland, 2005).

Let's recognise that teachers are navigating systems that reinforce giftedness, as Sapon-Shevin writes:

> *'Recognising giftedness as a social construct means acknowledging that without school rules and policies, legal and educational practices designed to provide services to gifted students, this category, per se, would not exist. This is not to say that we would not have tremendous variation in the ways in which children present themselves in schools or even in the rates and ways they learn, but the characteristic of*

*giftedness, possessed exclusively by an identifiable group of students, only exists within a system that, for a variety of reasons, wishes to measure, select and sort students in this manner.' (Sapon-Shevin, 1994, pp. 17–18)*

I was recently in a meeting where the senior leader hesitated at saying 'more able'. A few of us laughed because he needed a title for a list! We had fallen back on labels that referred to a category of students – more able or high ability. Grappling with the inherent framing was frustrating. It is strange that we use 'ability' as the orientation from which we decide who should be extended further. Consider this: do our 'lists' need to revolve around ability? Our identification systems could revolve around interests – which students need extension because they wish to pursue this subject in higher education? Or demonstrate they are intellectually curious about the subject far beyond the topics covered in the curriculum? Or exhibit characteristics of effective learning? Default expectations are that we base our planning around ability grouping as opposed to fostering the development of all students.

As Dr James Borland (2004) writes: 'I would suggest that worrying less about who is "truly gifted" and more about making curriculum and instruction truly differentiated for all students would do more to meet the goals of the gifted child movement.' Instead we can categorise what we as teachers are providing: types of extension. Who is accessing and benefiting from project-based learning as opposed to curriculum compacting? *We can change the focus by looking at how students engage with provision and how it impacts progress.* Which techniques are extending and engaging students? This comes back to holistically seeing a pupil, adapting our instruction and empowering them with choice.

## Student Profiles – Identification Without Labelling

Knowing our students and using adaptive teaching strategies is a powerful mindset to start from. Student profiles are tools for adaptive teaching that document student strengths and useful strategies (Callahan et al., 2017). One-size-fits-all scaffolding can have little connection to the specific learning of students. A better route is tailoring instruction to individual students. This is both in and out of the classroom. When there is a lack of connection between services and student needs, it is no surprise that the impact of gifted programming on achievement varies widely from school to school (Dixson et al., 2020). A strength-based profile can be used for making more personalised decisions about the types of resources and activities for development. The main goal of a profile is to foster creative productivity and stimulate the use and application of information. This emphasises the development of original materials and products. Adaptive teaching allows us to be responsive in our instruction and build rapport.

It is important to point out the *myth of learning styles* that have traditionally been a staple of learner profiles. A generation of educators was encouraged to design activities based on 'learning styles'. These 'styles' have been widely debunked (most notably by Riener and Willingham, 2010), yet stubbornly remain one of the biggest trends and myths in education. As the Early Career Framework summarises: 'There is a common misconception that pupils have distinct and identifiable learning styles. This is not supported by evidence and attempting to tailor lessons to learning styles is unlikely to be beneficial' (Department for Education, 2019, pp. 17–18). Students may have preferences about how they learn; some will report that they prefer to study visually and others through an auditory channel. However, when these tendencies are put to the test under controlled conditions, they make no difference – learning is equivalent, whether students learn in the preferred mode or not. The instinct for this type of differentiation makes sense, but a penchant for kinaesthetic, visual or auditory style categories does not provide for better or faster learning, and it does not go far enough to account for larger context and enquiry beyond a preference. As Riener and Willingham point out about the myth of learning styles:

*'Learners do differ from one another. But many who believe in the myth do not consider the critical differences between styles and abilities. Teachers should take into account the differences in learners' abilities. And adjusting a lesson not just to be appropriately pitched at the students' level of ability but to take into account their background knowledge and interests is surely an important first step in fostering learning.' (Riener and Willingham, 2010, p. 33)*

We can learn about students without pandering to, simplifying for or categorising them.

| Profile component | Examples | Purpose |
|---|---|---|
| Exploration and interest areas | Subject areas (e.g. history, biology) Topic areas (e.g. archaeology, botany) Lens for social justice/philosophy/morality | To give a vehicle for learning through a self-selected interest. Allows students to acquire an advanced level understanding of the knowledge (content) and methodology (process) that are used within particular disciplines. |
| Think-hard strategies | Discussion/debate Simulation Experimentation Investigation Peer mentoring Independent research and study Inter/intrapersonal – self-oriented, peer-oriented, teacher-oriented | To improve teaching for learning and student-centered instruction. Teachers design and provide options for activities that cater for students' learning tendencies of asking what (analytical intelligence), how (practical intelligence), and why questions (creative intelligence) (Sternberg, 2020). |
| Creative productivity | Thesis Presentation or lecture (e.g. TedTalk, classroom takeover) Audio or visual display (e.g. podcast, dramatisation, artistic, graphic, performance, sculpture, website) Service (volunteering, campaign, leadership initiative) | This allows creative productivity to flourish and advances task commitment, self-confidence and creative accomplishment. Develops self-directed learning skills in planning, organisation, resource utilisation, time management, decision making and self-evaluation. Empowers students with choice in approach to high-order thinking, ie. create, design, invent, hypothesise or judge. |

| Assessed strengths | Self-assessment | This allows students to set goals and have tangible measures to see improvement from beginning to end. Assessing using a baseline to ascertain prior knowledge and progress is incredibly valuable. This can give direction if a student requires further intervention like acceleration or curriculum compacting. We can balance creative productivity with the need for advanced content. |
| --- | --- | --- |
| | Peer assessment | |
| | Teacher assessment – exam results/grades | |
| | Effort/attitude to learning | |
| | Metacognitive Awareness Inventory (MAI) | |
| | Product evaluation (project, independent study) | |
| | | We can also use these indicators to capture underachievement. The MAI can identify and measure metacognitive approaches to tasks and allow students to track changes in their learning over time. |
| Wellbeing | Growth mindset evaluation | Wellbeing and emotional awareness to access the supports available to help. |
| | EPOCH tests to measure adolescent wellbeing (Kerns) | |
| | Pupil attitudes to self and school to identify fragile learners and uncover barriers to learning | |

Figure 4.6 Example of learner profile.

Traditional 'learner profiles' would include a subject/topic of interest, giving a vehicle for learning through a self-selected interest. I highly recommend using the Metacognitive Awareness Inventory as a component of the profile. This is a great way for students to tangibly reflect on their fundamental approach to learning. The development of specific metacognitive and self-regulation strategies can have a profound impact. It is possible to add additional behavioural traits to a profile as these are also incredibly valuable for students to gain self-awareness of how their actions shape learning. In addition, this allows a school the opportunity to cultivate positive habits in targeted students. In terms of interest, it makes sense that students would be more motivated when selecting topics that excite them and perhaps that they do not get to pursue within the regular curriculum. Research suggests that students who complete in-depth, self-selected project experiences develop strong interests and will continue to seek additional creative and productive experiences. Reis and Peters observe that 'students who experience the joys, challenges, and intensities of creative productivity in elementary, secondary school, and college are more likely to pursue creative work and challenges in their adult lives, regardless of the field, major, domain, or career they choose' (Reis and Peters, 2020). We can also reimagine learner profiles as a framework for successful behaviours, rather than a preference list for students.

An effective approach to building student profiles can be found in Dr Deborah Eyre's high performance learning model (HPL). HPL systematically teaches students the language and practices of high performance. There are set cognitive behaviours, values, attributes and attitudes that shape teaching and learning in the school. These competencies are developed and mastered over time in order to perform at a high standard. The behaviours are developed as part of normal lessons because students need frequent and regular practice in order to master them, so there is a progressive toolbox for students to embrace and teachers to deploy. As Dr Eyre writes:

> *'Despite the romantic myths of effortless cognitive superiority, the reality is that no-one reaches advanced cognitive performance in adult life without having or developing these characteristics and no-one gets there just by doing the compulsory set work. Individuals must develop a love of the subject and a desire to learn more. Yet our current approach to labelling children (including choosing gifted cohorts) does not encourage this. It suggests to them that they have a predetermined, finite ceiling to their level of achievement. An elite few think they can be "stars", but many conclude, at a relatively early age, that high attainment is not within their grasp. They see themselves as powerless. This limits the percentage of pupils who will go on to achieve high performance.' (Eyre, 2011, p. 30)*

HPL is a powerful framework because it assumes excellence from any starting point. Dr Eyre has an inclusive conception of high performance because of her role as director of the National Academy for Gifted and Talented Youth (NAGTY). She saw that NAGTY's main achievements were not for the cohort it served (the top 5% of identified 'gifted' in England's schools who for a few years received programming and guidance), but rather the development of a much better understanding of the routes to high performance and the creation of structural models that could be implemented for all students.

HPL – advanced cognitive performance characteristics (Eyre, n.d.):

| Creating | Meta-thinking | Linking | Analysing | Realising |
|---|---|---|---|---|
| Intellectual playfulness | Metacognition | Connection finding | Critical or logical thinking | Automaticity |
| Fluent thinking | Self-regulation | Generalisation | Precision | Speed and accuracy |
| Originality | Strategy planning | Imagination | Complex problem solving | |
| Evolutionary or revolutionary thinking | Intellectual confidence | 'Big picture' thinking | | |
| | | Abstraction | | |

HPL – values, attitudes and attributes (Eyre, n.d.):

| Hard working | Agile | Empathetic |
|---|---|---|
| Practice | Enquiring | Collaborative |
| Perseverance | Creative and enterprising | Concerned for society |
| Resilience | Open-minded | Confident |
| | Risk-taking | |

This conception includes a step-by-step levelling system to show where each student lies in these competencies, so the focus is on developing these characteristics.

Understanding students is a key part of our job, and we can usually spot those who need extension, but tracking their progress against all these markers is another story. The priority is that we can assess for learning and ensure that students are acquiring learning skills. The trick is recognising that these qualities can be fostered in all students. *'Identification' is simply the good practice of understanding where a pupil stands with their prior knowledge and closing any gaps in learning.* Multifaceted and continuous assessment of strengths and student profiles is useful to reflect on which students sitting in our classrooms have the capacity to be encouraged. This comes back to Renzulli's argument that 'ability' is not a static trait – it is grown. Student profiles can be used outside of the classroom – for instance, in referring students to extracurricular activities. Enrichment can be enhanced through the use of learner profiles. Teaching is dynamic and students should not be rigidly locked into a category. Enrichment programming outside the classroom should always remain open to all, and this can be accomplished through self-selection.

## Self-Identification

Selective programmes are more common than we imagine, and I've experienced the impact first-hand. This happened at an outstanding school that I admire greatly. When looking through the school's extracurricular catalogue, I saw a maths extension club that was listed as 'invite only'. My son loves maths, and playing mental maths games engages him. Unfortunately, he was not invited. The school reasoned that they were making a data-informed decision using results from the latest progress test, and that this was a provision for more-able students only. My son hadn't made the cut. When I queried the school, they responded that his GL progress test score was just below the cut-off (he scored 117 and the cut-off was 120). An exception was made after I requested a follow-up meeting and my little boy was admitted to the maths extension club. My son loved his Wednesday club and over the next term his maths progress improved immensely. However, the larger point was missed – the school's club remained invite only. Not all parents were as insistent in demanding that their child be considered for a place. This meant that other students who could have enjoyed and benefited from additional maths were not given that opportunity. *We need to challenge the assumptions that data-informed processes result in equity.*

The growing movement is to offer gifted learning opportunities to all who wish to gain entry. No child should be turned away – a fundamental pillar of enrichment. This conception of provision means an end to selective clubs or a gifted programme for a select group of students.[6] Every enrichment initiative I've run has been open, and I'm always surprised by the students who opt in.

By providing extension for all, students can identify themselves. Self-identifying is often used as a way to promote equity for marginalised communities. Australia uses self-identification and opportunity classes as a tool to promote the inclusion of Indigenous Australians and Torres Strait Islander people in gifted education programmes. China is an example of how this can be done on a national scale. The Children's Palaces of China provide a nonselective, high-level, out-of-school enrichment, which is considered 'a thriving and integral part of the Chinese education scene' (Freeman, 2005, p. 90). These learning centres focus on discovery activities, with clusters for

6　It has often been pointed out that sports trials and auditions for performing arts are selective. I would put forth that schools offer intramural sports clubs or ensemble roles within school plays so that students can practice, hone their skills and take part. All students should have the opportunity to learn, grow and reach a place of mastery.

the arts, sciences and technology. The only requirement is that students be willing to put in the effort. Keeping programmes open creates a world of possibilities for students. While multifaceted assessment is a useful tool for subject teachers for responsive instruction in the classroom, a conception for whole-school programming is part of the enrichment shift. Making any enrichment programmes self-selective means that all students are welcome to take part. I suggest a process of nomination, validation and celebration – a self-selective process that looks like this:

### Nomination

1. Students nominate themselves – a learner profile/student portfolio can be included.

2. Teachers and parents can also nominate students – this is to ensure outreach to students in need of confidence building. In the case of teacher referrals, I would send the student an invitation to participate and complete a student profile, whenever possible delivering in person.

### Validation

3. Individual interviews – students identify their strengths and targets for improvement. These targets are based on a self-assessment of skills. This can build on a learner profile of their interests and preferred learning products or focus on skills like in HPL. These interviews are important for students to feel invested and create buy-in. It also validates those who need confidence and who are referred by teachers or parents.

### Celebration

4. Students are invited to submit a meaningful piece of work they are proud of. This is optional and meant to give them a chance to show off. These could be displayed or presented at the induction of the enrichment programme.

5. Celebrating their entrance into the enrichment programme – this can be in a formal letter to parents, an evening launch or a marquee event.

I love using this approach because it builds rapport with students. In end-of-year student evaluations, students have divulged that the interview process, in particular, made them *feel* chosen and special. Even though it was a completely open inclusive programme. Interestingly, they felt selected when they had put themselves forward – I think this tapped into a very human need to be *seen*. The skills assessment and target setting had invested them in the programme. Students I surveyed had strong opinions about self-selection, one writing 'I believe that if a student has the intellectual curiosity and the motivation to attend an enrichment programme, then they should be considered as a part of the programme.'

Parent referrals are also a great way to garner support for enrichment programmes and bring in a key stakeholder. Parents see their children at home and their input creates a fuller picture. They witness their child reading precociously on the weekend or writing code in their spare time. After a parent referral, we must ensure that the child is invested and motivated. It is important that students identify themselves as possessing capacity that can be developed. Parents and teachers can work as a team to encourage their engagement in enrichment.

More broadly, rethinking identification is a movement whose time has come. Renzulli and Reis were part of a multitude of voices that asked educators to look at ability differently. I take the following away from Reis and Renzulli's (2009) work:

- Ability is not a static trait – it is a set of behaviours in combination with a nurturing environment. I would call this capacity.

- All children have capacity that can be developed. We can recognise that some students need different learning opportunities and support in their education. Building characteristics of effective learning and metacognitive strategies is paramount for all learners.

- The traditional divide between 'gifted' and 'talented' is artificial. Creativity, task commitment and domain-specific competencies are evident across all disciplines.

- An integrated schoolwide model is necessary for widespread enrichment opportunities and smaller group initiatives, all in conjunction with individualised curriculum modification for learners through overarching challenge and adaptive instruction in the classroom.

There are many critiques of the three-ring model as 'above average ability' is usually interpreted with standardised tests that are inherently limited, while task commitment and creativity are necessarily subjective and can be culturally specific in interpretation (Borland, 2004, p. 18). I have adapted this model. However, the process still has limitations. It assumes every teacher has an equal relationship with every student. It assumes that each type of assessment is equally valid and reliable. Any exercise with multiple criteria can be laborious. When looking at the demands of teachers, creating these detailed lists is a big ask if they don't buy in – but lists are not the approach a school has to take. Lists by design are limiting.

We can throw out the gifted registers. It is the process of identifying effective *strategies and behaviours* that is good practice. This is the argument of universal potential; that the right conditions lead to outstanding accomplishment. The Polgár sisters were able to harness this capacity and succeed in their chosen field. However, recognising universal potential is only the beginning. We need to track whether students from all populations are best served by our approach, then ask if we can supplement with any other strategy to embed equity. As Dr James Borland comments, 'I believe that there are individual differences in elementary and secondary students' school performance that probably derive from a complex of ability and motivational, social, cultural, sociopolitical, and other factors and that these have important educational implications' (Borland, 2005, p. 1).

Education needs to stop referring to levels of ability and put emphasis on levels of performance. Generalisations about student abilities based on standardised tests, early identification, streaming or setting are staples of our school systems. Underlying all this is the idea that it is our job to 'discover' giftedness. Instead of expending a lot of energy on a list of students, we can target certain behaviours to be developed, skills to hone, areas for growth and strategies to practise. This is key to responsive teaching.

*'What is needed is a culture of success, backed by a belief that all pupils can achieve. For assessment to function formatively, the results have to be used to adjust teaching and learning; thus a significant aspect of any program will be the ways in which teachers make these adjustments. The ways in which assessment can affect the motivation and self-esteem of pupils and the benefits of engaging pupils in self-assessment deserve careful attention.' (Black and Wiliam, 2010, p. 83)*

We can tailor our teaching methods – adaptive teaching allows us to adjust and guide all students. Challenge-first environments make extension visible and accessible to all – and raise the roof on achievement. A challenge-for-all approach within the classroom, and enrichment programming outside of it, is purposely inclusive.

This is also the fun part – enrichment can shake off the shackles of 'giftedness'. Tracking participation and outcomes in enrichment provision can tell us not only about the impact these interventions have as a whole, but also who is being impacted. Looking at the distribution and understanding how equity-seeking groups access and respond to enrichment offerings can then inform how we invite and include students. It can also take us towards a more culturally responsive instruction. These are at the heart of an enrichment philosophy. All students can be stretched, and it is our job to invite them. With this in mind, let's look at how to best deliver challenge-for-all every day in our lessons.

# Reference List

Barden, L. (2002) 'Sweet revenge for Kasparov's opponent', *The Guardian*, 11 September, [Online]. Available at: www.theguardian.com/world/2002/sep/11/3 (Accessed: 16 September 2022).

Black, P. and Wiliam, D. (2010) 'Inside the black box: Raising standards through classroom assessment.' *Phi Delta Kappan*, 92(1): pp. 81–90.

Borland, J. H. (2004) *Issues and practices in the identification and education of gifted students from under-represented groups*. New York, NY: Teachers College, Columbia University.

Borland, J. H. (2005) 'Gifted education without gifted children: The case for no conception of giftedness.' In: Sternberg, R. J. and Davidson, J. E. (eds.) *Conceptions of Giftedness*, 2nd edn. Cambridge: Cambridge University Press, pp. 1–19.

Brody, L. (2019) 'In debate over New York's gifted-students program, an expert gets spotlight', *The Wall Street Journal*, 2 September, [Online]. Available at: www.wsj.com/articles/in-debate-over-new-yorks-gifted-students-program-an-expert-held-sway-11567448445 (Accessed: 16 September 2022).

Callahan, C. M., Hertberg-Davis, H. L., Renzulli, J. S. and Delcourt, M. A. B. (2017) 'Considerations for the identification of gifted and talented students.' In: Callahan, C. M. and Hertberg-Davis, H. L. (eds.) *Fundamentals of Gifted Education: Considering Multiple Perspectives*, 2nd edn. New York, NY: Routledge, pp. 85–102.

Cambridge University Press and Assessment. (2023) *MidYIS for ages 11-14*. Available at: www.cem.org/midyis (Accessed: 25 October 2023).

Cox, D. (2019) *Judit Polgar interview: 'I had to prove myself more than a boy.'* Available at: www.chess.com/article/view/judit-polgar-interview-chess (Accessed: 16 September 2022).

Department for Education. (2019) *Early Career Framework*. Available at: www.gov.uk/government/publications/early-career-framework#full-publication-update-history (Accessed: 29 March 2023).

Dixson, D. D. et al. (2020) 'A call to reframe gifted education as maximizing learning', *Phi Delta Kappan*, 23 November. Available at: https://kappanonline.org/call-reframe-gifted-education-maximizing-learning-dixson-peters-makel/ (Accessed: 16 September 2022).

Eyre, D. (2011) *Room at the top: Inclusive education for high performance*. Available at: https://policyexchange.org.uk/publication/room-at-the-top-inclusive-education-for-high-performance/ (Accessed: 18 December 2023).

Eyre, D. (n.d.) *High Performance Learning*. Available at: www.cobis.org.uk/uploaded/COBIS_-_Our_Schools/School_Logos/COBIS_High_Performance_Learning_workshop.pdf (Accessed: 13 February 2024).

Ericsson, A. and Pool, R. (2016) *Peak: Secrets from the New Science of Expertise.* Boston, MA: Houghton Mifflin Harcourt.

Flora, C. (2005) 'The grandmaster experiment', *Psychology Today*, 1 July, [Online]. Available at: www.psychologytoday.com/intl/articles/200507/the-grandmaster-experiment (Accessed: 16 September 2022).

Freeman, J. (2005) 'Permission to be gifted: How conceptions of giftedness can change lives.' In: Sternberg, R. J. and Davidson, J. E. (eds.) *Conceptions of Giftedness*, 2nd edn. Cambridge: Cambridge University Press, pp. 80–97.

Gladwell, M. (2013) 'Complexity and the ten-thousand-hour rule', *The New Yorker*, 21 August, [Online]. Available at: www.newyorker.com/sports/sporting-scene/complexity-and-the-ten-thousand-hour-rule (Accessed: 16 September 2022).

GL Assessments. (2020) *CAT4 and strategies for learning: Cognitive abilities test.* Available at: https://support.gl-education.com/media/2783/cat4-and-strategies-for-learning.pdf (Accessed: 12 December 2023).

GL Education. (2023) *Communicating the results.* Available at: https://support.gl-education.com/knowledge-base/assessments/cat4-support/after-the-test/communicating-the-results/ (Accessed: 10 October 2023).

Huerta-Macías, A. (2002) 'Alternative assessment: Responses to commonly asked questions.' In: Richards, J. and Renandya, W. (eds.) *Methodology in Language Teaching: An Anthology of Current Practice*. Cambridge: Cambridge University Press, pp. 338–343.

Kantrowitz, M. (2021) *Admissions tests discriminate against college admission of minority and low-income students at selective colleges.* Available at: http://studentaidpolicy.com/sat-and-selectivity/How-Admissions-Test-Scores-Discriminate-Against-Minority-and-Low-Income-Students-at-Selective-Colleges.pdf (Accessed: 16 September 2022).

Kaufman, J. C. (2015) 'Why creativity isn't in IQ tests, why it matters, and why it won't change anytime soon probably.' *Journal of Intelligence*, 3(3): pp. 59–72.

Koshy, V. and Pinheiro-Torres, C. (2013) '"Are we being de-gifted, Miss?" Primary school gifted and talented co-ordinators' responses to the Gifted and Talented Education Policy in England.' *British Educational Research Journal*, 39(6): pp. 953–978.

Kovacs, K. and Conway, A. R. A. (2019) 'A unified cognitive/differential approach to human intelligence: Implications for IQ testing.' *Journal of Applied Research in Memory and Cognition*, 8(3): pp. 255–272.

Lazine, M. (2022) 'Understanding the flaws behind the IQ test', *Discover Magazine*, 3 June, [Online]. Available at: www.discovermagazine.com/mind/understanding-the-flaws-behind-the-iq-test (Accessed: 16 September 2022).

Lundstrom, H. (1992) 'Father of 3 prodigies says chess genius can be taught', *Deseret News*, 25 December, [Online]. Available at: www.deseret.com/1992/12/25/19023258/ father-of-3-prodigies-says-chess-genius-can-be-taught (Accessed: 16 September 2022).

Martinez, D. (2021) 'The sack of Rome. Magistrale di Roma, 1989', *Chess.com*, 11 March. Available at: www.chess.com/blog/damafe/the-sack-of-rome-magistrale-di-roma-1989#:~:text=The%20Sack%20of%20Rome%20is,With%20only%2014%20years%20old (Accessed: 18 March 2024).

Mathews, J. (2003) 'The bias question', *The Atlantic*, November, [Online]. Available at: www.theatlantic.com/magazine/archive/2003/11/the-bias-question/302825/ (Accessed: 16 September 2022).

Polgár, L. (2017) *Raise a Genius!* Translated by Gordon Tisher. Vancouver.

Pringle, P. (2003) 'College board scores with critics of SAT analogies', *Los Angeles Times*, 27 July. Available at: www.latimes.com/archives/la-xpm-2003-jul-27-me-sat27-story.html (Accessed: 16 September 2022).

Riener, C. and Willingham, D. (2010) 'The myth of learning styles.' *Change: The Magazine of Higher Learning*, 42(5): pp. 32–35.

Reis, S. M. and Peters, P. M. (2020) 'Research on the schoolwide enrichment model: Four decades of insights, innovation, and evolution.' *Gifted Education International*, 37(2): pp. 109–141.

Reis, S. M. and Renzulli, J. S. (2009) 'The schoolwide enrichment model: A focus on student strengths & interests.' In: Renzulli, J. S., Gubbins, J., McMillen, K. S., Eckert, R. D. and Little, C. A. (eds.) *Systems & Models for Developing Programs for the Gifted & Talented*, 2nd end. New York, NY: Routledge, pp. 323–352.

Renzulli, J. S. (2005) 'Applying gifted education pedagogy to total talent development for all students.' *Theory into Practice*, 44(2): pp. 80–89.

Renzulli, J. (2016) 'Reexamining the role of gifted education and talent development for the 21st century: A four-part theoretical approach.' *Journal for Talent Development and Creativity*, 4(1) and 4(2).

Sapon-Shevin, M. (1994) *Playing Favorites: Gifted Education and the Disruption of Community*. Albany: State University of New York Press.

Shakespeare, W. (1928) *Twelfth Night*. Boston, MA: Houghton Mifflin.

Surrey Schools. (2021) *Teacher resources: Communicating student learning to parents.*' Available at: https://surreyschoolsone.ca/quality-assessment-and-csl/resources/ Triangulating-%20Evidence-of-Learning.pdf (Accessed: 16 September 2022).

Sternberg, R. J. (2020) 'Rethinking what we mean by intelligence.' *Phi Delta Kappan*, 102(3): pp. 36–41.

Tomlinson, C. A. (2014) *The Differentiated Classroom: Responding to the Needs of All Learners*, 2nd edn. Alexandria, VA: ASCD.

Vygotsky, L. S. (1978) *Mind in Society*. Cambridge, MA: Harvard University Press.

Whitten, A. (2020) 'Do IQ tests actually measure intelligence?', *Discover Magazine*, 1 July, [Online]. Available at: www.discovermagazine.com/mind/do-iq-tests-actually-measure-intelligence (Accessed: 16 September 2022).

Wiliam, D. (2018) [Twitter/X] 25 March. Available at: https://x.com/dylanwiliam/status/977723425698361345 (Accessed: 16 September 2022).

Wiliam, D. (2020) *Formative assessment: What it is and what it's not.* Available at: www.youtube.com/watch?v=fZI4rO2ntQo (Accessed: 28 March 2024).

# 5. AERIAL ACROBATICS

*The complexity of things—the things within things—just seems to be endless. I mean nothing is easy, nothing is simple.*

**Alice Munro, 2001**

*Liberating education consists in acts of cognition, not transferrals of information.*

**Paulo Freire, 1993**

*Knowledge is 'powerful' if it predicts, if it explains, if it enables you to envisage alternatives.*

**Michael Young, 2014a, p. 74**

Extension is not for the chosen few high attainers. Nor is challenge a discrete task within a lesson. The gifted and talented paradigm tends to demand more differentiation at the top end as a mechanism for challenge. Instead, let's begin with this premise: differentiated learning outcomes must be removed from classrooms for stretch and challenge to be embedded in everyday practice (Light, 2017). There are decades of learning strategies that unintentionally send the message that 'challenge' is designed for select students, with implied expectations in how we deliver extension. There is a temptation to box in 'extension' as an add-on task – a common technique is to create extension menus where students choose a task that can run from 'mild' to 'spicy' to 'red hot chilli' in its difficulty. Does this raise the bar for all students? There may be an incentive to choose the less demanding skill. The standard expected of each task can be open to interpretation. While a task menu can provide students with choices in product or content, it does not necessarily provide complexity or change motivation.

Students can be busy but not stretched. We can give students 'one-pagers' assigning a separate task or worksheet for the lesson. We can provide additional homework, extra past papers and prep exams, study guides to follow, independent reading, go-ahead checklists, ongoing journaling and any manner of alternative activities. These all depend on the disposition of a student: how independently can they work? How much scaffolding do they need? Is there sufficient motivation? There are issues in the ceiling of a task: have we set the challenge high enough? Is it too broad or too narrow in scope? There are issues in feedback: as teachers with limited time, can we realistically provide effective feedback for all these disparate activities? There are issues in passivity: are these activities demanding interaction with learning and critical thinking? Are students engaged in productive struggle? There are issues in cognitive load: are we giving too many simultaneous tasks? Are we creating opportunities for lasting learning? Are extraneous materials and assignments leading to distraction or confusion? There are issues in recognition: are we celebrating and acknowledging those who take on extension?

Increased stratification of students, or the tasks we assign them, is not the answer. Instead, let's follow three rules for challenge:

1. Enrich our curriculum – not more, but interesting.

2. Enrich our pedagogy – challenge-first instruction.

3. Enrich our mindset – invite all.

The curriculum encompasses the learning goals set, pedagogy is the method a teacher uses to instruct, and mindset is the perspective we have about the nature of learning. These three principles work in conjunction with one another. An enriched curriculum is one that enhances the content we teach with depth and complexity. Enriched pedagogy is how we dynamically engage students through our everyday practice. An enriched mindset is one where we as educators become more aware of gifted structures and work to purposely dismantle them to ensure an inclusive approach. When reflecting on these complementary elements, a few anecdotes came to mind.

The first is the story of Abdullah. One of my colleagues, Stephen, shared this example years ago and it always stuck with me. When he was a new teacher being observed, he planned a multiplication lesson for his Year 2 students where they were drawing dots in rows and columns. Abdullah was an exuberant boy, and minutes after being assigned the task he proudly ran up to Stephen and showed off his page with three columns and four rows equalling 12 dots. 'Wonderful! The challenge question is on the board. Can you do 6 × 7?' Abdullah ran off. He returned a little bit later with a page of 42 dots. Stephen was now wary that an observer's eyes were on him, and he decided to pitch high. 'Wow, Abdullah! Can you now draw 12 × 18?' Immediately Abdullah looked at him exasperated, 'You want me to draw 216 dots, sir?' Stephen glanced around the room, saw three other students who needed attention and hurriedly replied to Abdullah, 'Yes, that would be impressive,' and left Abdullah to draw 216 dots. Stephen later said that was when he truly understood challenge. It is not more of the same skill or an additional challenge question added to every task in every lesson; true challenge must have an element of novelty and exploration. **Not more, but interesting.** He needed a strategy that was larger than a small add-on task. It also required a change in mindset – adapting instruction for individuals, while still making a high-end goal visible and accessible for all students.

The next story was the epiphany moment I had during a learning walk in a lower primary school. The pedagogy was one of learning through play with continuous provision – every room was an environment of exploration. Children moved from area to area interacting with different stations of resources. The purpose of continuous provision is to encourage children to be active learners, creatively interacting with learning materials. Each station had resource sheets, cards, exemplars, keywords, scaffolded tasks and prompts for them to use, as well as a 'challenge' task that required all the skills. I asked our head of primary how many students complete the challenge element and she looked at me with a smile and said, 'Oh they all do the challenge first! You can't hold them back – it's the fun part. They figure out everything else to succeed in that challenge.'

This was the key: **the experience for students was 'challenge first'.** They would jump to the most difficult and complicated assignment, and then use resources to meet and go beyond any assumed expectations. For instance, children would go straight to the challenge of designing a motte-and-bailey castle, seeing what worked and didn't work, using pictures to depict it realistically, categorising types, taking the initiative to label the features, and then fetching a dictionary to be more specific. The model would have a realism and historical accuracy that I typically expected of my Year 7s. Yet these children were in Year 2!

My third anecdote is an element we often observe in a great lesson, and when we try to put our finger on it, we discover that it has to do with a combination of curriculum intent and mindset. I attended a school play where Year 5 and

Year 6 pupils tackled Shakespeare's *Midsummer Night's Dream* with aplomb. They adroitly handled the intricacy of the plot and were veracious in their use of sophisticated vocabulary. Students had moved the setting from Athens to our school, explaining and making comparisons to our staff and their peers, playing and teasing out the themes. There was trust that students could thrive under the source material. It made the case that we don't need to pander, simplify or be linear in our approach. This is how I view teaching to the top; having high expectations for every student. This means **inviting all students** to engage with think-hard material.

We've all had experiences where a student surprised us by going far beyond what we assumed their ability to be. I'm sure we have also had lessons where students' questions veered into advanced territory – all of a sudden you can find yourself teaching a topic from a university course to 13-year-olds. Tom Sherrington has repeatedly asserted that we should give students layers of complexity – they crave it – so teach to the top (Didau, 2013). This can be described as scaling up – fill your Year 7 curriculum with Year 10 content and skills, exposing students to knowledge outside their age or level. We can also scale out – going beyond a state-prescribed curriculum to topics that will enrich their understanding, or construct cross-curricular connections or real-world applications. There are many ways to do this. The other day I observed a teacher who incorporated ethical dimensions to a task – we don't explicitly teach Aristotle's golden mean, but she asked students to apply it while studying geopolitics by asking how a state can act virtuously. Complexity is delicious, and the goal is to make it part of the regular diet in our classrooms. Extension should be routine and embedded, simple for students to access and teachers to plan.

One of my favourite distinctions between curriculum and pedagogy was made by Joshua Vallance, who explains that:

> 'We can take curriculum to be the *what* of teaching. The subjects, topics, people and places that end up populating lessons. In this sense, it is distinct from the pedagogic *how* of teaching. Distinct, but interrelated. If we are to strip things back to their core components, then pedagogy is the means of communicating the curriculum. Direct instruction, retrieval practice, and the myriad activities that populate Twitter on a daily basis are all modes of pedagogy.' (Vallance, 2021)

Along these lines, I'd add that mindset is the *who* of teaching – that we interrogate our practice and reflect on who we are reaching and who we are missing, because the aim is to challenge everyone.

# Aerial Acrobatics – Component 1: Enriched Curriculum

Designing a curriculum that meets diverse student needs, while ensuring equitable opportunities for learning and progression, is a complex endeavour. An enriched curriculum is one that puts deep knowledge at the forefront; it is the bedrock from which students build comprehension. We can imagine depth as having a T-shape, with a broad knowledge-rich curriculum on top allowing students to then dive deep. T-shaped depth allows for comprehension to construct a knowledge-rich curriculum. This is the productive hinterland that nurtures and sustains the core. There is a prominence given in Bloom's taxonomy to higher-order thinking skills, like analysis and evaluation, but there is a reason knowledge is the base of Bloom's pyramid. For students to apply these skills, there must first be a wide and deep schema. As Clare Sealy comments, 'Synthesis and evaluation – what we might call creativity and critical thinking – are only possible once vast amounts of knowledge have been understood. Far from being "lower order", knowledge is our precious cognitive capital, with critical thinking its dividend' (Sealy, 2018).

We know from cognitive load theory that simply flooding students with excess information and superfluous content will not lead to learning. What could be interpreted as 'reading around the subject' can be a trap where there are many resources but little cogitation. In fact, it can overload students to the point where they may concentrate on irrelevant material or only fleetingly grasp a concept before it quickly fades. Passive consumption of resources is not going to develop a deeper understanding. It is through reflection that students create linkages, so students must interact meaningfully with their learning to enable that depth of knowledge to stick. So how do we set the bar high, complicate our resources and at the same time embed them in long-term memory so students can engage with new ideas? How do we decide what is 'important' in our curriculum? What are we enhancing?

To achieve an inclusive curriculum that builds in representation, student choice and elements that stretch learners, we can consider the following principles of enriched curriculum design:

- Reflective of powerful knowledge
- Facilitates connective thinking
- Flexible and open pathways for students to progress.

## Enriched Curriculum Design is Reflective of Powerful Knowledge

Michael Young developed and popularised the concept of 'powerful knowledge', shaping the conversation on curriculum for the past decade. Powerful knowledge is a response to 'knowledge of the powerful'; the concept that 'elite' knowledge that has been included in traditional formal educational curricula often reflects the interests, values and perspectives of dominant groups in society – those with power and influence. Such knowledge has cultural capital and is viewed as the 'official' or 'legitimate' knowledge, often sidelining other perspectives. A white, heteronormative, Western curriculum is then given more legitimacy. Suppose we create a curriculum centred on knowledge of the powerful, in the hopes that all students have equal access to the 'elite knowledge' regardless of their background. In that case, we end up perpetuating inequities, neglecting or invalidating the experiences, histories and cultures of marginalised groups. As Young comments, 'The school, for all its tendencies to reproduce the inequalities of an unequal society, is the only institution we have that can, at least in principle, provide every student with access to knowledge' (Young, 2014b, p. 13). As curriculum makers, we have the opportunity to equip our students with knowledge to navigate the future.

In contrast, 'powerful knowledge' is not arguing for one piece of information to be more important; it is a democratic conception of curriculum as an entitlement for all students of all backgrounds. In summary, powerful knowledge: a) is specialised and systematically conceptualised, often the product of academic disciplines; b) provides learners with ways of explaining, analysing and understanding the world beyond their immediate experiences; and c) most importantly, equips learners with the intellectual tools to respond to complexity and challenge assumptions.

This first component gives students the basic building blocks to interact with concepts within a subject. Specialised knowledge by nature is disciplinary knowledge. Systematically layering vocabulary allows students to speak the language of a discipline. It can be fun to watch a geyser erupt from a bottle of soda when we add a candy – this is not science. The understanding of hypotheses, ability to create variables (temperature of soda, type of soda) and making observations (height of geyser) is the knowledge that makes the experiment meaningful. Doing an experiment does not make a student a scientist – they are not yet creating new knowledge or investigating a gap in knowledge. However, it gives them the tools to apply the foundations of scientific enquiry. As Daniel Willingham notes, 'The ability to think critically depends on having adequate content knowledge; you can't think critically about topics you know little about or solve problems that you don't know well enough to recognize and execute the type of solutions they call for' (Willingham, 2007, p. 12). Critical thinking requires domain-specific knowledge; it is only then that students can enact knowledge to solve a problem. This 'knowledge-in-use' is the capacity that learners need to apply knowledge and evaluate when and how to get more information when necessary (Miller and Krajcik, 2019).

This leads into the next element of powerful knowledge: a reliable map of the way the world is. What is beyond immediate perception? Powerful knowledge allows students to engage with knowledge that is distanced from their everyday experience – Young and Muller (2014) use the example of quantum theory. It has reliable predictions even if it is at odds with our lived reality; it is a framework outside our opinions and experience. It is underlined that knowledge is powerful when it goes beyond the recognisable. 'We must respect and value the experience of pupils, but we can never allow them to depend on their experience alone' (Young, 2014b, p. 13). Curriculum that relies solely on a person's own practical experience would serve to only recycle knowledge. A skilled teacher uses instruction as a bridge between the familiar and the novel.

This last component empowers students to develop their own knowledge. The mission calls for learners to actively participate in accumulating this. Students aren't expected to make scientific discoveries in their schools' labs, but to understand how to obtain new knowledge independently. Alaric Maude explains that 'to have some power over your own knowledge is knowing how to acquire knowledge and be critical of it. This does not mean the ability to undertake an academic research project to study something that has not been investigated before, but the skills to find information already available, and make sense of it. This enables young people to be independent of the dominant sources of information in our society' (Maude, 2015, p. 22). In the Australian curriculum, we could find this in the 'Inquiry and Skills Strand' for secondary students. In the International Baccalaureate Diploma, there is the 'Theory of Knowledge', considered the crowning jewel of the diploma programme. These types of initiatives ask students to explore the nature of knowledge and then complete a research project. Learning *how* to undertake an investigation requires knowledge to play both a proximal role (cumulative to make the next piece of learning possible) and ultimate role (enduring understanding to underpin larger concepts) (Vallance, n.d.). I love this component. A key purpose of powerful knowledge is to enable curiosity in learners. These fundamentals can act as a blueprint for an enriched curriculum.

## Degree of Difficulty

Start with the assumption that no text is 'too hard' for your students to access. Instead of providing one facile resource, concentrate on providing many different and difficult entry points for a topic. You can do this slowly, adding one more resource to your collection each week so that students can give the source their full attention. In terms of building an ambitious curriculum, Mary Myatt writes that 'what underpins this is ensuring that pupils with lower starting points are not offered a diminished diet, but rather are supported to access demanding work, through appropriate scaffolding and support' (Myatt, n.d.a). We must think carefully about how a task is scaffolded while at the same time curate the most challenging learning intention. Original texts, journal articles and academic studies are a useful place to start. Creating an ecosystem of complexity means providing think-hard materials. To break the intimidation factor with academic studies, you can begin by having students read the abstracts and conclusions, or break the texts into sections. It can be as easy as students highlighting the thesis, main arguments and evidence. Scaffolding 'up' is important. Difficult materials can be presented with worked examples or a graphic organiser. The main goal of a graphic organiser is to take complex information and present it in a visual format that aids understanding and recall. The danger with graphic organisers is that this can lead to simplification. Instead of making these organisers the hierarchy of knowledge, create them with logical prompts and symbols for students to further investigate and expand. Shift the intellectual responsibility by asking students to construct their own visual representations.

Inspection and reflection are necessary when evaluating evidence, as are the exercises for students to strengthen their decision-making skills. It is not easy to titrate the resources, engagement and skills students need for critical thinking. In Willingham's review on the matter, he concluded that:

> *'First, critical thinking (as well as scientific thinking and other domain-based thinking) is not a skill. There is not a set of critical thinking skills that can be acquired and deployed regardless of context. Second, there are metacognitive strategies that, once learned, make critical thinking more likely. Third, the ability to think critically (to actually do what the metacognitive strategies call for) depends on domain knowledge and practice. For teachers, the situation is not hopeless, but no one should underestimate the difficulty of teaching students to think critically.' (Willingham, 2007, p. 17)*

The trick is to create systems and routines to access and interact with rich resources, so they can map the knowledge contextually. We wish to create space for deeper thinking and extension instead of students waiting on further instruction, especially if they have already consolidated content.

Overarching challenges in the curriculum ask the 'the big question' and should be presented alongside those difficult 'think-hard' materials. For example, in Early Years continuous provision, each station provides a stimulating challenge. In my schools we have had each department create subject-specific enrichment projects, which are posted in every classroom with a focused challenge, framework and list of resources. There can be an 'innovation' or 'investigation' corner with a broad problem-based query, design endeavour, real-world application or dilemma to be resolved. Teachers can have self-access areas, sitting at an 'extension' table in the room or at a virtual site – in any case, there is a static space where students routinely visit. This also sets the stage for depth studies. Making this easily obtainable digitally, or as a classroom installation, gives students a view of where the curriculum sits and immerses them in a messy world where connections can be made. Extension is a think-hard reading list with a big challenge posted for the whole unit as opposed to an 'add-on' question in every class. This is simpler for teachers to plan and allows students to dip in and out, with a consistent place to a broader schema of knowledge. There can be links to podcasts, videos and articles that take the in-class content to a more sophisticated level. With this approach, we can set up our classroom extension to support student growth and agency. It is through creating a contextual 'lay of the land' that students can then interact with their learning and practise cogitation. Ambitious learning intention is part of a challenge-for-all curriculum.

### Technical Language – Specific Language of the Discipline

By presenting subject-specific vocabulary, students can truly articulate what they are learning in a topic. Technical language and correct terminology can help us organise information and connect ideas with rigour and clarity (Smith, 2020). Applicable in every subject, precise terminology is essential for effective communication. 'Speaking like a disciplinarian' is an invitation to specialised expertise. Research has found that fostering subject-specific language skills is a core prerequisite to supporting mathematical skill acquisition (Ufer and Bochnik, 2020). Elaboration is a great technique to develop advanced language – the student uses elements of the definition and expands the target information. This could be creating a phrase or making an analogy (The University of Kansas, n.d.). The Education Endowment Foundation has great recommendations on vocabulary in action – this includes:

- Bespoke definitions to connect words as a bridge to everyday language
- Purposeful variation to provide several contexts
- Engaging students in immediate interaction with the word meanings
- Deep processing that asks students to identify and explain
- Providing examples, situations and questions to prompt discussion (Reynolds, 2023).

Technical language equips students for a high level of engagement and enables them to secure mastery in a topic.

## Abstraction

Concepts learned through abstraction can often be more easily remembered because they are distilled into their most essential and general forms. Associative memory can then link specific details or examples to these abstracted concepts. The Depth and Complexity Model developed by Sandra Kaplan asks that students examine a subject 1) from the concrete to the abstract and from the abstract to the concrete, 2) from the familiar to the unfamiliar and from the unfamiliar to the familiar and 3) from the known to the unknown and from the unknown to the known. As students move from different modes of thinking, they will be in a position to form important conceptual foundations related to the subject matter (Kaplan, McComas and Manzone, 2016). A learner can start with a high-level overview and then explore more detailed layers as their interest or needs dictate. Rather than getting lost in minutiae, learners are encouraged to see patterns, make connections and consider broader implications. Once learners grasp an abstract concept, they can apply it across multiple specific instances without needing to relearn the underlying principles each time. Students are then better placed to take on challenge-first projects that embody the learning intention. Depth and complexity also demand that we create opportunities for interdisciplinary linkages in our curriculum design. Abstraction allows us to apply principles in a new context with transferability. This results in layered structures of reinforced knowledge.

## Enriched Curriculum Design Facilitates Connective Thinking

There can be demand that we march through the curriculum, so how do we create opportunities to pause and make linkages? Often we think of curriculum as a mountain to climb; with each step, we get progressively closer to the top. The route up is clear, with markers and signposts. Some students stall, dip in a crevasse, but they can step up again. They are moving on the same passage to the peak. While this metaphor is useful, it implies a straight line that culminates in graduation. How can they explore beyond the one mountain? How prescribed is the course?

I prefer to think of curriculum as an ocean. There are myriad destinations a school can sail towards. We can explore in many directions, with departments setting out on different journeys. Along the way, there are opportunities to pause for deep dives. These foreign territories beneath the waves are just below us, hidden and beyond our everyday experience. We learn more about the ocean of knowledge when we don't just stick to the shallow harbours or map coastlines; we probe the workings underneath the surface. Curriculum can allow us to investigate new worlds.

So let's look at how we can deliberately design a curriculum that promotes connective thinking by diversifying, incorporating interdisciplinary reflection and pausing for depth.

### Diversify and Decolonise the Curriculum

In line with powerful knowledge, there is a massive movement to decolonise the curriculum and explicitly build up narratives that include voices outside the dominant culture. This also means that curriculum is developed by a diverse range of educators. In Lola Olufemi's call to decolonise the curriculum at Cambridge University, she wrote that:

> 'After three long years as a Cambridge English student, the thing that is most memorable about my degree and the thing that has caused me the most frustration is just how unbearably white the curriculum is. Myself and countless others have written at length about the ways in which a white curriculum is nothing more than the maintenance of structural and epistemological power. Decolonising the curriculum is a process– a process that requires thought and consideration. It means rethinking what we learn and how what we learn it; critically analysing whose voices are given priority in our education and for what reason. It is not an easy process and why should it be?' (Olufemi, 2017)

Equity-seeking groups deserve to see themselves represented in curriculum, and students within a dominant culture should be exposed to knowledge outside their experience.

Diversifying curriculum means having a range of texts on reading lists, from writers of various cultures, genders, sexual orientations and socio-economic backgrounds. Texts written by and about marginalised communities should be placed at the centre, not be treated as peripheral or as an aside. There is a need in a global society for students of the dominant culture to understand a multiplicity of experience. We do a disservice to students who feel rightfully underrepresented and a disservice to those students who could grow their understanding of the world when we aren't representative or culturally responsive in our curriculum. We should be investigating the relationship between the location and identity of the writer, what they write and how they write about it. In English this means unmasking the colonial context and influence of many canonical works and literary theories. Engage with more perspectives of that work – not just taking sources from the West and establishing a Eurocentric view but listening to marginalised voices (Iqbal, 2020). Decolonisation also means acknowledging historical injustices. In my own experience in Canada, the curriculum explicitly valued Indigenous history (pre-colonial and colonial), art and oral traditions. History teachers have been especially active in decolonising and diversifying curriculum. 'By examining primary documents, students can unearth historically marginalised voices that are not usually taught in mainstream curricula, such as those of LGBTIQ+ and minority ethnic groups. Archives that provide access to a wide variety of voices and cultures are critical to preventing history being told through a narrow lens and helping diverse student groups see themselves represented in the past' (Cayley, 2021).[7] We are preparing students for a globalised world where an inclusive curriculum makes their education more relevant.

There is also the important point that the dominant culture should not monopolise the creation of a curriculum. As Sonya Douglass Horsford rightfully asserts, 'To truly transform education, we must first deepen our understanding of the great battle that we are in. This begins with actually asking people of color what they want and need and then listening to what they say. The voices, concerns, ideas, and vision for what students, parents, and educators of color want and need is the evidentiary basis upon which any agenda for educational equity must be developed, if that is, in fact, what we truly seek to do' (Douglass Horsford, 2021).

---

7   More on culturally responsive teaching, curriculum decolonisation and inclusive models for instructional design can be found in Chapter 12: Welcome to the Big Top.

## Interleaving

Interleaving is based on principles from cognitive science suggesting that varying the order of topics can make learning slightly harder in the short term but significantly enhances long-term retention. Firth, Rivers and Boyle's systematic review defined thusly: 'Interleaving means varying the order of a set of examples, whereby each item is immediately followed and preceded by an example of a different category/concept rather than appearing in blocks of the same type of item repeatedly (which is termed a 'blocked' arrangement)' (Firth, Rivers and Boyle 2021, p. 642). This might involve practising maths problems on fractions, decimals and percentages in a single session rather than dedicating one session entirely to fractions, the next to decimals and so on. In terms of curriculum design, interleaving works most effectively when it is over short spans – similar ideas in a topic requiring subtle discrimination. When students must learn to distinguish among similar concepts (or terms or principles or kinds of problems), the findings suggest that the exposures to each of the concepts are better interleaved rather than blocked (Rohrer, 2012). Firth, Rivers and Boyle's (2021) review noted that interleaving was found to be of greatest use when differences between items are nuanced, and this benefit extended across subjects. Its strength stems from helping learners to contrast similar items that would otherwise be easily confused, and as such it should be applied where teachers believe common misconceptions lie. Interleaving of a concept with contrasting examples will inevitably lead to a degree of spacing, where readdressing a concept leads to it being better remembered. However, the main goal of interleaving is to boost retention and transfer of skills. As a hybrid model, initial exposures to a concept could be blocked, and subsequent exposures could appear within interleaved assignments. By revisiting topics periodically and in varied orders, students can strengthen their memory and create linkages between concepts – this is depth. This connective thinking of interleaving can be applied on a macro level through an interdisciplinary approach to curriculum design.

## Interdisciplinary

I first taught an interdisciplinary curriculum in Birmingham, UK, and I was amazed at how adept the students were at making larger connections. This curriculum invites students to study related concepts and theories, across subjects. The approach was used in Year 7 to help students transition into secondary school – a move from one classroom teacher to 12 different subjects. The goal was for students to grapple with real-world issues that transcended the disciplines. The danger was that some subjects would offer a weaker interpretation (for example, an art project done in black and white as opposed to colour, which didn't add a critical thinking lens to the overall theme of racial injustice). This type of delivery is more 'multidisciplinary', where a topic is covered but students receive a tepid or isolated experience within each subject. Doing a full interdisciplinary model well requires an investment into cross-curricular planning. Most schools work to embed connections across topics (for instance history, English, geography and art coordinating to enhance study of WWII). The trick is doing this thoughtfully by layering themes and building out the knowledge schema. A truly interdisciplinary curriculum presents content across the disciplines by blending teachers' methodology and students' enquiry. Students examine the topic or issue through one of many complex reasoning processes, with each subject or teacher contributing a new entry point (Grady, 1994).

A case study of the interdisciplinary curriculum model can be found at the London Interdisciplinary School (LIS), where it is described as 'interleaving multiple subjects to form learning activities, inviting fresh perspectives and enhanced comprehension' (Morrison McGill, 2023). The aim is that students will be able to make connections across their learning when tackling complex problems. The faculty, staff and educators involved in designing the LIS interdisciplinary enrichment programme have worked in academic institutions including Harvard, the London School of Economics and secondary schools in both the UK and US. Each term begins with a broad challenge to explore topics such as inequality, the ethics of AI or climate change (LIS, 2023). In two-week cycles, student simultaneously engage with multiple disciplines across the arts, humanities and science fields. For example, when exploring the topic of inequality, the curriculum examines it through the lenses of subjects such as neuroscience, network science, political economy and linguistics. The London Interdisciplinary School's aim is a 'comprehensive approach [that] equips you with a range of skills, including epistemology (theory of knowledge), problem-framing, pitching, and public speaking, all of which are crucial for understanding and addressing these challenges effectively' (LIS, 2023).

We can bring connections from other disciplines into subject-specific planning. The idea is to go further than a token nod to numeracy. This means fully engaging with our colleagues to augment and enrich our planning, assessment and design.

## Depth Studies

It may seem contradictory to argue for a more diverse curriculum on one page and then insist on depth on the next. It is not an argument of depth over breadth. Instead, I would say that depth is an entry point for the many delightful tangents of breadth. This definition summarises the sentiment: depth is the opportunity to explore, to take the time for students to delve deeper and reflect after being given the lay of the land. Pausing for depth in the curriculum can be difficult when it feels we must march on through prescribed content.

Depth studies can be implemented as project-based learning – students have an opportunity to investigate a single topic or concept in greater detail by examining a range of sources. Research has shown that depth studies are more effective when there is a 'driving question' that fosters focused enquiry (Barron et al., 1998). Students should understand the *why* of the project with a clear learning goal and have frequent opportunities for formative self-assessment. The aim is a robust, knowledge-building experience. A 'knowledge-rich' curriculum is imbued with substantive and disciplinary knowledge. Instead of drilling past paper techniques, we can give students autonomy in investigation. Pursuing a depth study is a platform for complex thinking capacity. Later chapters will explore types of project-based learning, their various approaches and their efficacy.[8]

## Enriched Curriculum Design has Open and Flexible Curriculum Pathways

Designing a curriculum that meets diverse student needs, and ensures equitable opportunities for learning and progression, is a complex endeavour. The aim is an inclusive curriculum that builds in student choice and stretches learners. The repeated theme throughout this book is equity, and flexible pathways can demolish curriculum hierarchies. When we stream, set or track students into different curricula, there is a danger of limiting exposure, delaying progression and possibly narrowing future opportunities. One group is receiving knowledge and proficiency that the other is not. Research has repeatedly found that when we track students into differentiated pathways, we disproportionately impact equity-seeking groups. Curriculum plays the long game; we don't want to cut off avenues for students to advance. Creating open pathways is part of a larger discussion on dismantling the systemic inequity playing out through our educational structures.

---

8    For more on project-based, problem-based and enquiry-based learning, please to go Chapter 8: Slow Build Up to a Big Boom.

Flexible and open pathways look like:

- Removing restrictive tracks or streams that can close off pathways for students.

- Opportunities for students to accelerate, pause or consolidate. Great systems make it possible for a student to improve a particular skill or revisit an option. There is flexible pacing. Some might accelerate through content they're familiar with, while others might need more time or even need to revisit previous units/courses. Bridging units can be offered to help transition students who are accelerating to more advanced content or those who are revisiting earlier content to fill gaps. The emphasis is on mastery-based learning, not just age or grade level.

- Curriculum compacting for students to accelerate to the 'higher ends' of a course: streamlining practice or instructional time for students who have met objectives, providing scope for students who work at a faster pace, or organising and recommending enrichment options.

- Grade telescoping: taking two courses concurrently or completing two years in one.

- Focusing on comprehensive assessment as opposed to high-stakes exams.

- Introducing modularisation. This is a viable option that opens up individualised education for all pupils. Chunking content, interleaving or self-contained units can increase the granularity of curriculum (e.g. small and specific units where students can pursue the African diaspora or the Weimer Republic (or both) in their studies).

- Diversifying and personalising curriculum offering. Curriculum diversity enables the learner to have increased control over their pathway and fosters authentically student-centred learning.

  - Curriculum can be culturally responsive to a school's demographics, celebrating groups that may have traditionally been left out of the curriculum. Audit the curriculum to build a representative and decolonised curriculum.

  - Give students choice and voice in curriculum development and selection.

- Cross-curricular options, thematic units, independent study options and tech integration/platforms all create possibilities to diversify curriculum and increase student autonomy.

Implementing such a flexible curriculum requires robust systems, training and resources. However, it can provide a more personalised education, catering to individual student needs and interests, ultimately leading to better engagement and outcomes. Mary Myatt points out that 'we need to beware the "curse of content coverage". It can feel as though there is an awful amount to be taught. But if our plans are not underpinned by concepts and big ideas, it is hard for our pupils to make connections' (Myatt, n.d.b). Curriculum development is a continuous process that involves establishing clear intent for outcomes and adherence to national standards. The way schools spiral and sequence curriculum is purposeful. Curriculum expert Christine Counsell likens curriculum to a novel – we could summarise the plot in a list of bullet points in chronological order. However, the depth comes with the narrative structure, layered character development, a textured use of vocabulary, recurring themes, linkages and connections, all of which bring the story to life with a profound understanding and perspective (Counsell, 2018). Thoughtful curriculum design builds to a similar crescendo – with small pieces of knowledge illuminating a larger schema. Interdisciplinary units and depth studies can create a rich hinterland of knowledge that enriches the core.

The principles of enriched curriculum design demand that we interrogate using powerful knowledge, deploy depth and keep pathways open. Behind all of this, curriculum development works best when it is part of collective teacher efficacy. Time with other teachers for reflection and data-informed decisions can make for a more responsive and thoughtful curriculum. Curriculum development is continuous and part of long conversations and dialogues with students. With these approaches to curriculum in mind, let's look at the *how* of teaching: enriched pedagogy.

# Aerial Acrobatics – Component 2: Enriched Pedagogy

The UK House of Common's Children, Schools and Families Committee met in February 2010 to discuss the state of gifted and talented programming. When questioned about the hallmarks of good in-school provision, Joy Blaker commented: 'It is about opening up that whole opportunity for children—to give them challenge, open-ended opportunity and mixed ability working, where they can build from each other and develop a community of inquiry and where they can build their knowledge one upon another, facilitated by a teacher' (House of Commons Children, Schools and Families Committee, 2010, p. 4). The entire transcript is a fascinating read, but a few points stood out to me – the focus was not identifying outstanding students; it was about outstanding teaching for learning. This is the shift from G&T to enrichment.

I recently met with a teacher who told me about his lightbulb challenge-for-all moment. He had been assigning students 'low-ability' work in his lowest set class, without really interrogating what kept individual pupils from progressing. After reflecting on the level of challenge, he consciously decided to become more attuned to his students' productive struggle in the classroom. He assigned the 'high-ability' challenging task to all, then walked around. He observed one girl frozen while attempting to write the first sentence and sat down beside her. After a minute she tentatively asked him how to spell 'significant'. The need to spell correctly derailed her from the actual task. He asked her to go through her reasoning for the task verbally. After prompting, he then smiled and said, 'That is brilliant, work through that solution, make a hundred spelling mistakes.' He returned later and found that she had flown, giving insight and showing problem-solving skills that went far beyond her 'level'. The previous scaffolding was ill-suited to her individual requirements; the differentiated learning objective didn't address the emotional blockage or give him tools to build rapport. She was a fragile learner and had consistently given up halfway through tasks due to frustration or a lack of confidence. He hadn't seen the root cause of her stagnation. The low-ability resources had underestimated her and didn't capture the nuance of her needs.

This teacher, like so many, had thrown off the shackles of differentiation for a more inclusive and responsive pedagogical approach. In advocating for a move to adaptive teaching, Matt Bromley points out the issue of equity: 'Unlike traditional forms of differentiation which can perpetuate attainment gaps by capping opportunities and aspirations, adaptive teaching promotes high achievement for all. ... Put simply, if we dumb down or reduce the curriculum for some students, we only serve to double their existing disadvantages, rather than help them overcome those challenges to achieve in line with their peers' (Bromley, 2021). The aim of adaptive learning is to meet diverse student needs and allow students with different barriers to achieve optimal learning outcomes (Umamah et al., 2020).

UK-based Alex Quigley has made the argument that differentiation is dead, and that the nail in the coffin came from the 2021 Department for Education's

Early Career Framework (Quigley, 2023). It was here that we finally saw that differentiation has lost its usefulness as a concept, despite being so ingrained as a core component of teaching. Instead, there is now a move towards adaptive teaching. Adaptive teaching does not insist that teachers artificially create distinct tasks for different groups of pupils or set lower expectations for particular pupils. We can meet individual needs – and provide opportunities for all students to experience success – while maintaining high expectations. The foundational belief is that all pupils should have the freedom and inducement to meet high expectations (EEF, 2019). As Quigley writes: 'Adaptive teaching, then, offers a language for existing practices that were previously tricky to explain: flexible groupings, reteaching content for a struggling pupil, and generally being responsive to pupils' learning. The term describes practices that have been around for some time. Nevertheless, there seems to be consensus that adaptive teaching is a positive step forward for inclusive teaching and learning' (Quigley, 2023). Alister Talbot from the Huntington Research School notes that:

*'... it's about making those really subtle changes in the lesson to support the learning, not about using another resource for example:*

*a. Clarifying to students what good learning looks like.*

*b. Providing an intermediate goal to support the learning.*

*c. Supporting all students to work towards the same goal, but breaking the learning down, for some, into smaller steps.'*
*(Talbot, 2023)*

We can see the evolution from differentiation to adaptive instruction:

| Differentiation | Adaptive instruction |
|---|---|
| Must, Could, Should learning objectives. Some students expected to learn less, or practise less sophisticated skills, than others. | One clear learning objective with universally high expectations for all students. |
| Capped expectations for those who need the most support. | Focused support, individualised so that students have their questions answered and guidance specific to their understanding. |
| Three or more mini lessons within the lesson. Three or more types of resources for students. | One lesson for all students. |

| | |
|---|---|
| Remedial or simplified tasks so some students fall further behind learning. | Targeted catch-up, ideally with adaptive software for fast, real-time, personalised feedback. |
| Pre-planned ceiling to progress and learning. | Hinge questions and formative assessment so emergent needs are catered for by pivoting lessons in the moment. |
| Lessons planned to the middle with simplified resources for 'low ability' and extension for 'high ability'. | Observing and identifying students during the lesson who may need scaffolding 'up'. Resources maintain a degree of difficulty. |
| Planning requires a wide array of different tasks and resources. Heavy workload in teacher prep. | Teacher is fully present for students in lessons and adapts guidance and instruction instead of tasks and resources. Less teacher prep. |
| Accommodations for learners with SEN/EAL. Extension for G&T. | Universal Design for Learning – anticipating needs and removing barriers. Overarching challenge accessible to all learners. |

Figure 5.1 Differentiation versus adaptive teaching (adapted from Talbot, 2023).

Early in my career, I expended a lot of energy creating three different learning objectives (or more) and three different versions of a task (or more). In the end, I found I was generating these resources to make differentiation visible, not necessarily to meet students' real needs. There is a pressure to make resources and tasks for separate ability groups – an accountability system to demonstrate the teacher labour behind differentiation. However, when we have 'all, most, some' objectives, we naturally lower expectations. If there is an easy choice, a student may go for the bare minimum, sometimes because they think that is what a teacher expects from them. When we assign different tasks, we also send messages to students of where we think they are.

This is practical and effective, and it makes lesson planning more straightforward. As Shaun Allison and Andy Tharby write in their incredible book *Making Every Lesson Count*: 'We believe that much that is promoted as good differentiation practice is both unmanageable and counterproductive: it is not humanly possible to personalise planning for each and every child' (Allison and Tharby, 2015, p. 19). With adaptive teaching there is less room for the students to be passengers, where they simply tackle the easiest task every lesson. The aim is mastery. It is a move away from the 'bottom group' mentality of easier work and lower expectations.

Adaptive teaching is responsive and personalised – where a teacher assesses a student's mastery of a concept or skill in real-time and then dynamically adjusts. High expectations for all and a single clear learning intention is key.

Matt Bromley wrote of his experience introducing adaptive teaching: 'Most importantly perhaps, I made sure that every student in the class completed the same task – I did not differentiate tasks according to "ability" nor did I produce differentiated resources. I did not differentiate the questions I asked either – I made sure every student was required to answer questions that demanded critical thinking. Every student worked towards the same goal – and crucially that goal was the same as I'd set for my top set class' (Bromley, 2021). Adaptive teaching is not teaching 30 different lessons at once; it is providing the same ambitious curriculum and high expectations for all students. Danielson's Framework for Teaching Evaluation Instrument emphasises responsiveness in instruction (Danielson, 2013). The rubric stresses making adjustments in instruction that respond to evidence of student understanding (or lack of it). In these cases, the teacher seizes a teachable moment to enhance a lesson, conveys that a lesson isn't considered 'finished' until every student understands and goes to others in the school, and beyond, for assistance in reaching students. This may look like a teacher stopping an activity midstream and saying, 'This task isn't working, let's try another way,' or 'We will come back to this tomorrow, it's important that you understand it.' It takes bravery to be responsive when there is pressure to speed up, as opposed to pausing and going deep.

Adaptive instruction requires an incredible amount of presence and energy from a teacher. There are constraints in a busy classroom; there may be wide gaps in knowledge that must be juggled. Considering the limitations of time within a lesson, it is difficult to ensure that every student is touched and given the feedback or response they need to progress. Critiques of intense differentiation include E. D. Hirsch's oft-quoted comment: 'When a teacher is attending to the individual needs of one student in a class of 20, 19 are not receiving the teacher's attention' (Hirsch, 2016). It is easy to spend the majority of time guiding one particular student in a lesson and it cannot be rectified quickly. Great practice means immediately knowing who needs our attention through continuous assessment to identify attainment gaps, then working to close them by building out a student's schemas of knowledge.

Responsive intervention addresses pupils with inclusion needs who require a consistent cycle of adjusting, adapting and assessing in the classroom. Differentiated outcomes are not the same as differentiated support (Mould, 2021). There is still an emphasis on knowing each student's strengths and barriers – I'd point to Universal Design for Learning as a model that complements adaptive teaching. Inclusion expert Kirsten Mould underlines that 'having a full understanding of every child is extremely important in adaptive teaching. Time needs to be diverted to identifying reasons for learning struggles, not just the struggles themselves. ... The success of adapting teaching also lies in careful diagnostic assessment, in order to avoid prescriptive and inflexible delivery' (Mould, 2021). Universal Design for Learning, culturally responsive instruction and trauma-informed teaching are all extensions of responsive teaching.[9]

In terms of our everyday tactics and activities, here are a few tools to embed.

## Adaptive Teaching Strategies

We can meet individual needs without creating unnecessary workload or patronising our students. The focus is on the inclusion of the whole-class standards instead of small lessons within lessons. Intervening within lessons with individuals and small groups can be more efficient and effective than planning different tasks for different groups of pupils. We can vary instruction to be more adaptive and create routines. Here are some thoughts on adaptive teaching, many based on the recommendations from the Early Careers Framework (EEF, 2019):

- Talk less to the whole class and listen more to individual learners. Observe carefully, then intervene with individuals and small groups. Set a task with high expectations and let pupils struggle. Walk around and pause – this means waiting for pupils to ask, encouraging and prompting, so that they hit the proximal zone of development, where they productively struggle. This is more efficient and effective than planning different lessons within lessons for different groups of pupils.

- Scaffold 'up' instead of 'down'. Scaffolding down means simplifying activities, bringing content down to what students currently do, which limits progress. The emphasis tends to be remedial. Good scaffolding goes beyond simple matching or fill-in-the-box activities. Scaffolding up focuses on having students master key practices, principles and concepts that enable learner autonomy. We can divide scaffolds into those that function to communicate process, those that provide coaching and those that elicit articulation (Barron et al., 1998). In responsive teaching, this could mean live modelling in small groups, think-alouds, peer coaching or open-ended questions to activate prior knowledge.

---

9   Go to Chapter 9 for more on Universal Design for Learning, culturally responsive instruction and trauma-informed teaching.

- Keep in mind that 'unfinished learning' does not need to hold students back – instead, focus on conceptual understanding, application and procedural fluency. For example, lessons can begin with a practical scenario in which students can explore how the day's targeted skills connect to real world situations. They can then name the concept. Beginning conceptually means you can meet individual needs without creating unnecessary workload – plan by assessing pupils' existing knowledge and coach those who need additional initial support in order to access the same ambitious curriculum and high expectations. Scaffolding is gradually removed to ensure that students are working towards independence.

- Teachers can identify pupils who need new steps further broken down or information chunked, but all students deserve exposure to high-level content. We can balance the input of new content so that pupils master important concepts. We can utilise teaching assistants effectively to target support and apply technologies that build up schemas. We can anticipate barriers as students have limited working memory, different levels of prior knowledge and vocabulary, or particular SEN and EAL accommodations.

- Teachers do not need to reinvent the wheel and look for three different versions of a resource. For instance, it is tempting to rewrite a text, paraphrase it and remove the subtlety – this strips the layers of complexity. Keep the degree of difficulty: 'Whilst providing focused support to children who are not making progress is recommended, creating a multitude of differentiated resources is not' (Mould, 2021).

- Group pupils effectively and apply high expectations to all groups. Change group compositions regularly; this develops collaboration skills and also sends the message that there is no entrenched or permanent setting in the classroom.

- Teach the learning behaviour – the metacognitive strategy is not obvious but always important. If there is any peer tutoring, gear it towards modelling – have students explain the *process of how*, because the temptation is always to simply give the answer away.

- The product and outcome should be available from the start. Hinge questions at the very beginning can allow students to move forward to the larger challenge immediately.

- Constructivism asks that you recognise your students and their lived experience. It is then that you can link their existing knowledge to new abstract concepts. Have students situate their knowledge and share their perspectives. Introduce concepts via discussion. This is the jumping-off point for powerful knowledge, where concepts outside of a learner's experience can be introduced.

## Retrieval Practice

Creating a more complex world means that students need to consistently retrieve information. 'The most basic level of educational complexity – agreed on by almost all theorists – is the level of remembering and repeating' (Oxford Royale, n.d.). This allows students to transfer information from their working memory to long-term memory. When students have fluency, they can rapidly recall knowledge in their schemas. I recommend reading every Kate Jones book on retrieval practice and the cognitive science behind positioning knowledge in context. She shows that retrieval practice is a key way to enact Barak Rosenshine's Principles of Instruction: starting lessons with a short review of previous learning; presenting material in small manageable steps; asking many questions; providing models and worked examples; guiding practice; checking for understanding; and providing scaffolds and reviews (Jones, 2019). These activities, including challenge grids, revision clocks, roadmaps, thinking and linking grids, and retrieval practice pyramids, all reinforce and consolidate learning. I love the versatility of retrieval practice placemats to start discussions.

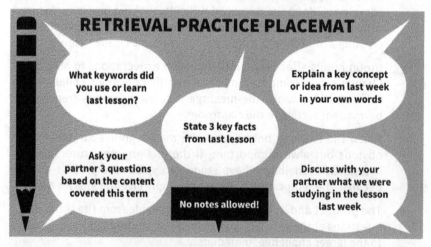

Figure 5.2 Retrieval practice placemat (Jones, 2019, p. 76).

The development of study skills such as self-quizzing and revision can be explicitly taught, first in a domain-specific way, then as transferable skills. To save you time, there are myriad online systems to chunk new knowledge and have students engage, reflect and be assessed. Online platforms like Edpuzzle have thousands of interactive video lessons with embedded questions for students to answer along the way (Edpuzzle, 2023). Using high-level content through this type of platform allows you to easily see the student engagement and track their results – it is self-paced, flexible and bite-sized. Quizlet, Nearpod, Quizizz and Plickers all allow students to test and engage with content. Mentimeter has quizzes, polls, word clouds and reflection templates. The rule is that, whenever possible, give students an opportunity to interact with your resources. We wish for information to be made 'sticky' as our long-term knowledge is made up of interconnected webs.

**Adaptive Teaching Software**

It would not be hyperbole to state that adaptive teaching software that can give specific, actionable, immediate feedback to students is a game-changer. This is real-time personalised assessment that enables students to track their progress and teachers to adjust learning strategies. What has emerged to make both retrieval practice and responsive teaching more possible is the wave of adaptive learning AI to assess, customise and consolidate. There are suites of learning platforms that use artificial intelligence and machine learning techniques to 'adapt' the learning path and pacing offered to individual students. The gap in understanding is much easier to broach if students are provided with the most efficient systems to build knowledge schemas. The pre-assessment is there to assess, sequence and customise the scaffolding. These platforms can be self-paced, give rapid feedback, save teacher time and embed low-stakes formative assessment. These platforms can collect and analyse data from various sources. In some cases data can create a detailed learner profile, which includes information about the student's current knowledge, skills development, support for diverse learners and learner progress (Silicon Valley Innovation Center, 2023).

As an added bonus, this is data-driven instruction. There are things that adaptive software captures that we may miss – for instance, some can parse the difference between performance data (pathways taken to work through material and what learners understand) and engagement data (time on task and time spent on each question). We can respond, support and motivate while wielding tools to better inform our interventions. It is important to understand how any utilised platform is working – there are systems that use advanced algorithms or decision trees, or systems that are rule-based. Teachers often have a time-consuming frictional workload (e.g. collecting and chasing down exercise books). Automation of student feedback can increase scale and immediacy, while also providing a teacher with an overview of results. Data captured by adaptive learning software can be analysed to review the needs of individual students or groups of students. Teachers can then adapt instruction to those needs and revise the curriculum accordingly. Similarly, students can use data about their skills and performance to adapt their learning practices (McGuire, 2021).

Technology can help make inequity visible. Integrated data tracking software can parse demographic differences, as it can be used to identify the progress of targeted subpopulations. This is a powerful way to identify trends and confront barriers for equity-seeking groups and under-resourced students. Holiday, O'Sullivan and Adams (2020, p. 5) note that 'having access to real-time data is also an opportunity to understand the needs of your students, especially racially minoritized, poverty-impacted, and first-generation students'.

All of this is not to say that we need software in order to be responsive. There are things that only a teacher can see and respond to. 'Socio-emotional needs' seems like an odd clinical way to frame it – simply put, teaching is a human profession. As Cavanagh et al. (2020, p. 187) note: 'One of the misconceptions that comes with the adaptive system is that the technology will replace instructors in schools. Although adaptive technology facilitates the students' learning process, the successful implementation of adaptive learning still requires human planning, interactions, monitoring, and interventions.' Adaptive teaching does not depend on technology – it depends on knowing your students. Adaptive teaching strategies have gained traction because they produce results. In fact, larger studies cite the teaching that pauses and pivots according to students' needs in the moment. According to the 2015 PISA results, 'adaptive instruction' is one of the approaches most positively correlated with student performance. Interestingly, in almost every education system that participated in PISA 2015, students who reported that their science teachers use adaptive instruction more frequently score higher on the PISA science assessment, and in every education system, these students also hold stronger epistemic beliefs that teachers adapted instruction according to their individual needs (OECD, 2016). The association with student performance was particularly strong in the Nordic countries and the Netherlands, Qatar, Singapore and the United Arab Emirates. Students who reported that their teachers adapt their instruction more frequently also held higher expectations of pursuing science-related careers (OECD, 2016). Adaptive instruction referred to teachers' flexibility with their lessons: tailoring the lessons to the students in their classes, including individual students struggling with a topic or a task.

## Concept Mapping

This deceptively simple technique is often underestimated. David Ausubel's Meaningful Learning is one of the most important expository theories for how information can be transferred from short-term memory to long-term memory (Kiliç and Çakmak, 2013). Concept mapping emerged as a strategy from the key pillars of prior knowledge, interaction and collaboration. According to this theory, meaningful learning occurs when complex ideas and knowledge are combined with students' own experiences and prior knowledge to form unique understandings. In this process, concept maps are one of our most important teaching and learning tools. There are so many mapping strategies to help students confront multifaceted information in a sophisticated manner.[10] Research underlines that the power of concept maps is magnified when conducted as a collaborative endeavour (Moreira, 2011). It can be wielded to boost communication in heterogenous groups (e.g. across year groups or mixed attainment). Visual organisation through concept mapping can be done as non-linear thinking, like brainstorming, or it can be guided within timelines, Venn diagrams and T-charts. Advanced organisers increase the chances of learning – this could be sequencing, discerning parts of the whole and building mental structures (Whitworth, n.d.).

A classic is for students to reflect and visualise complex material through conceptual spider webs.[11] They infer the 'big concept', build linkages, analyse relationships and synthesise information. We can ask students to start with nodes within their regular classwork, which facilitates the recall and processing of information. Then students can expand the web with points from additional resources, other subjects and personal experience. This externalises knowledge and the structural forms of relationships. This also allows students to see gaps or inconsistencies in understanding. From there they can prioritise some concepts over others, build hierarchies, create categories, identify patterns and discover connections. There is evidence of 'far transfer', where learners cross-link ideas in lateral, novel and unexpected ways (Victoria State Government, 2022). Moreira notes that 'we live in a world

---

10  Note that we don't wish for this mapping to be conflated with rote learning – this is not a reference to conceptual diagrams for storage of information.
11  Here is a great article with links to digital mind mapping tools: www.educatorstechnology.com/2022/12/9-great-concept-mapping-tools-for.html

of concepts. Without them we are unable to understand our world, and without conceptualization we cannot develop cognitively' (Moreira, 2011, p. 7). Concept maps can be built for each topic and then interconnected as a final project. I've had geography students build a wall of concept maps with all of our A-level topics. Concept maps make visual a learner's higher-order analysis, understanding and processing – as teachers we can tease out and prompt another conceptual world with a question.

## Contrasting Evidence

Students should wrestle with contradictions and compare multiple sources that represent differing points of view. By juxtaposing contrasting pieces of evidence, students can more readily identify gaps in their understanding or misconceptions they might have held. They must assess the strengths and weaknesses of a point and judge relevance, accuracy and credibility. In order to navigate today's information-heavy landscape, students should assume a critical lens and interrogate contemporary media, looking at the veracity of evidence and the reliability of arguments. We can have students consider the value of a study, for instance, by looking at sample size – does it have the power to draw a conclusion? When students compare and contrast, they become more active participants in their own learning. Instead of passively absorbing information, they're challenged to question, analyse and synthesise. They're encouraged to move beyond surface-level comprehension and delve into the intricacies of the evidence. Students learn to identify key points, dissect arguments and discern patterns. These skills are invaluable in academic contexts and in everyday decision making.

Contradictory case studies make for great debate. We can place students in the role of researchers. Present students with conflicting research and have them rank trustworthiness – which study informs us best? Who funded the research? What was the methodology and sample size? Does this bear on its significance? What gap in knowledge was the study designed to investigate? What is the utility of this primary, secondary or tertiary source? What is the provenance? The goal is not memorising a fact or two; the purpose is ascribing the value of the document. We can use media analysis exercises to distinguish fact from opinion. When was this published? Who created this source? Why? What cultural lens was this written from? What was the bias? How is it contestable? What wasn't included? What evidence has more weight? These are just a few questions students might grapple with when viewing new material. A close reading of a source goes beyond a summary. It allows students to draw conclusions, discover nuance and relate this evidence to other arguments. In the real world, issues are rarely black and white; we want students to see the grey. Students should be learning how to see granularity, discern integrity, and situate the work as part of a larger discussion or see the evolution of thinking. Learning to navigate and make sense of contrasting evidence prepares students for the complexities they'll encounter outside the classroom.

## Kaplan Icons

Dr Sandra Kaplan's model of depth, complexity and novelty uses icon prompts as catalysts for new lines of enquiry. Her icon-driven programme raises expectations and level of critical thinking with prompts to engage students (Winebrenner, 2018). This dual coding also allows students to remember and reframe information. These prompts are an entry point for big conceptual thinking. Depth is a process of thought for students to go from concrete to abstract – from knowing the details to distilling them down to universal principles. Depth tools include details, patterns, rules, trends, big ideas, ethical issues and unanswered questions. Then students transform these into larger themes. Students discern the nuances and discrepancies that distinguish these separate characteristics. Once these larger themes are identified, students can evaluate ethical dilemmas, injustices, inequities, biases and discrimination. Complexity is thinking about interconnection. Each petal on the flower represents the various parts that make up the whole. The tools include multiple perspectives, change over time and links across disciplines, demonstrating that links and overlap exist between topics or subjects. Students examine change and evolution and see from different perspectives (futurist, historical, ethical, economic, environmental, philosophical, political, etc.). Novelty is an invitation to explore, interpret and give original insight. The aim is to develop creative solutions to problems. Any of these icons can be added to your resources, allowing students to probe further and think differently. They provide directions to take each topic, allowing for that T-shaped approach to depth.

| Core Curriculum | Curriculum of Practice | Curriculum of Connections | Curriculum of Identity |
|---|---|---|---|
| **Rules** Define rules that define processes and procedures to accomplish a task, solve a problem, and perform an operation. | **Language of the Discipline** Specify the terminology relevant to a discipline and the multiple meanings of vocabulary across disciplines. | **Patterns** Recognize the repetition of ideas that are similar within, between, and across disciplines. | **Multiple Points of View** Identify people by their beliefs, opinions, and behaviors and appreciate individuality of thought and actions. |
| **Details** Relate the concept of details to becoming knowledgeable in an area of study; equate knowing details with scholarship. | **Ethics** Acknowledge the conflicts, dilemmas, and issues that emerge in the study and work of the 'professional'. | **Trends** Describe how events, people, and places affect each other. | |
| | **Unanswered Questions** Relate the study of unanswered questions to the work of a member of a discipline and the accumulation of knowledge in a discipline. | **Over time** Distinguish how time can and does connect ideas. | |
| | | **Big Ideas** Discern how big ideas provide the basis for linking learning across disciplines. | |
| | | **Interdisciplinarity** Describe the impact and/or influence one subject has on another. | |

Figure 5.3 Kaplan icons (Kaplan, Guzman and Tomlinson, 2009, p. 18).

## Concentric Circles of Knowledge

These different concentric circle frameworks explore layers and relationships. Starting with the core content in the middle, you can design the learning so that it radiates out using only a single element or multiple elements. The instructional design emphasises each circle as another way to analyse and understand the same standards-based content. Dr Kaplan notes that each circle invites the learner 'to venture into another way to perceive, enrich, comprehend, and evoke wonder about the content of the standard' (Kaplan, 2002, p. 21).

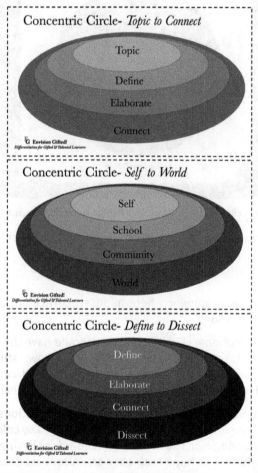

Figure 5.4 Concentric circle frameworks (Griffith, n.d.).

You can offer students choice in one or more of the rings or have them construct their own rings, so students can take ownership of their learning. Rings can be used in conjunction with Kaplan icons, and these can probe varying levels of sophistication (Kaplan, 2002).

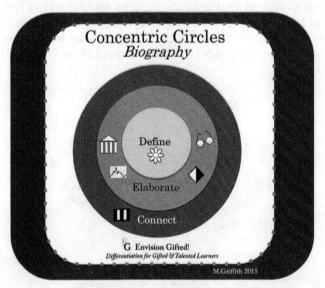

Figure 5.5 Concentric circle in conjunction with Kaplan icons (Griffith, n.d.)

All of the tools discussed in this section are great – even in isolation they are useful.

\*

Now, imagine an environment where mindset, curriculum and pedagogy work together to provide:

- A warm emotional climate. Students should have the psychological safety to take risks (Meilleur, 2020). This allows students to find nuance by expressing doubts, uncertainties and confusion. Make misunderstanding a normal and inevitable part of learning.

- Opportunities for learners to answer and ask questions and inclusive questioning is the norm. This could be achieved by cold calling using a name randomiser, use of mini-whiteboards or having students 'say it again better' to hone their answers. After cold calling, there can be a routine for the student who answered to ask the next question, before passing on to another student. Students can reflect on what makes a good question. There are prompts or topics and students generate corresponding questions. Questions are a basis for a group discussion or for students to create their own tests. Students draft 'the hardest question' and challenge each other to answer it.

- Specific feedback on performance. This could be one-on-one interview-style feedback, which is a fantastic way to establish rapport. Use whole-class feedback for students to self-assess their own work, praise students who identify and volunteer their errors, and encourage metacognitive talk – why did this error occur? What assumptions were made? How can material be revisited? What is the question asking for? What structure is required? (Sherrington and Caviglioli, 2021).

The climate sets the conditions. There are explicit and implicit ways we can embed challenge – first in our everyday instruction, which is why we should reflect on the environment we consciously and unconsciously create. Let's delve into an enriched mindset.

# Aerial Acrobatics – Component 3: Enriched Mindset

An enrichment mindset exists when we dissemble dated gifted theories and unpick the language of 'ability'. Challenge for all, teaching to the top and the anatomy of high expectations must all be viewed from the perspective that students have capability, not a set 'ability'.

## Reframe 'Ability' and Use the Language of 'Attainment'

While the common terms of high, middle and low *ability* students tend to be pervasive in education, I would like to reiterate that the framing is dangerous. It implies a fixed category and preconceived cap on a student's overall potential. What educators typically refer to as *ability* is actually a student's current level of *attainment* at that point. We collect data every day in our interactions with students and their work. We have tools to ascertain a point of mastery, prior knowledge, existing schemas or any unfinished learning – this informs how we should scaffold up our instruction. We can have learners at different stages of *attainment*, not different abilities.

## Challenge for All and Teaching to the Top

So what is teaching to the top and how can it be done effectively? Teaching to the top is promoted as a philosophical shift for both students and teachers. With teacher preconceptions affecting students' views of their capacity, educators can hinder students with low expectations, signalling through their differentiation that students should aim for the low-hanging fruit. So it becomes a self-fulfilling prophecy when both teachers and students expect the bare minimum. As Jon Eaton writes for the Education Endowment Foundation: 'The possible danger behind this is that it may lead to a lowering of expectations, particularly when in-class groupings are permanent e.g. "the bottom group" receives a different task to everyone else, regardless of the particular needs or aptitudes of the pupils in this area of learning' (Eaton, 2022).

Teaching to the top begins with assuming that there is no top. That we 'lift the lid' to learning without limits. Sherrington writes, 'I think teachers should consider the curriculum and plan activities based on the capabilities of the highest attainers as a total priority – lifting the lid ... Providing appropriate scaffolds for other students flows from this but teachers need to have the courage and confidence to challenge at the top end, relentlessly' (Sherrington, 2017). This is in opposition to the conventional practice of pitching to the middle and differentiating up and down. Conceptually the framing can be misconstrued. Teaching to the top is often read as a strategy to prioritise 'the highest-performing students' in a classroom.

David Didau points out that 'if we mean teaching to the top of the ability range then we will inevitably leave many students behind' (Didau, 2022). One of my colleagues made this astute point in a discussion:

> 'Let us just consider how students learn best. If we consider how students learn, with understanding new knowledge being fundamentally about how you can pin it onto schemas already formed from previous understanding, then, for example, teaching the finer points about how a turbo works in a car engine to a mechanic and a non-mechanic (like me) in the same classroom would be ridiculous – it would be within the mechanic's zone of proximal development, but well beyond mine ... The teacher would be left with a choice: go back to basics for me (and have the mechanic wait or do independent work – which is not the most effective way of learning), or lose me while stretching the mechanic.'

In this vein, Didau highlights that teaching to the top tends to focus on outcomes rather than children. If there is a gap between our high standards and learner outcomes, there is an assumed failure on the students' side. He suggests striving for 'gapless' instruction – taking on the responsibility of improving our practice. Didau concludes that 'because "teaching to the top" is widely misunderstood and so blandly meaningless, I've stopped recommending teachers do it' (Didau, 2022).

I take this on board, as we need to address the misinterpretation – the strategy is not prioritising high-attaining students. Aiming high means leading with challenge. As Debbie Light writes about raising the bar: 'Rather than setting a limit on what we think students can do by creating differentiated criteria, give all students the same criteria but make explicit to them how meeting the criteria becomes progressively more demanding' (Light, 2017). Andy Tharby and Shaun Allison place challenge as the first component in making every lesson count, writing, 'Put simply, challenge in education is the provision of difficult work that causes students to think deeply and engage in healthy struggle. It is unfortunate that all too often challenge is presented in the context of "challenging the most able"' (Allison and Tharby, 2015, p. 14). Their conception of challenge is one that does not neatly tick a box within differentiation. They propose that great instruction moves away from this conventional view of a teacher providing students with work that matches their 'ability profile'. Instead, have one high bar. Learning goals are elevated for all students, irrespective of their starting points. Pause and let students struggle – they will tell you what they need. When you walk around your classroom, take time to observe students, and then you can hoist them up with individual guidance, questions and strategies.

## The Power and Limitations of Growth Mindset

An enriched mindset underlines that the highest level of challenge and extension should be accessible to all. The confidence that all students can reach a high bar is in a similar vein to a growth mindset. Growth mindset has become a massive movement in education that aims to combat the dynamics of expectations for students and teachers. The principles of growth mindset have become a lodestar for school cultures. Proponent and researcher Carol Dweck has linked mindsets to achievement. Blackwell, Trzesniewski and Dweck conducted a now infamous study in 2007 with 373 seventh-graders at an inner-city NYC school. Students were divided into two groups. The control group followed entity theory and was told about the stages of memory; the other half received training in the growth mindset and incremental theory. It was predicted that when the control group of students were told that intelligence is a fixed entity, their outcomes would have a flat trajectory. The other group was taught that intelligence is malleable. They were given learning goals, had positive beliefs about effort and were taught how to apply strategies. The authors hypothesised that these students would have an upwards trajectory (Blackwell, Trzesniewski and Dweck, 2007). The results were dramatic, with the incremental group making marked progress, while the entity group performance declined over time.

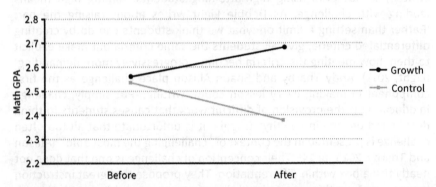

Figure 5.6 Impact of growth mindset (Blackwell, Trzesniewski and Dweck, 2007).

Dweck and her colleagues aimed to scale growth mindset interventions by moving online with the National Study of Learning Mindsets. This study followed a nationally representative sample of 12,000 ninth-grade students from 65 US schools. They participated in a 45-minute online session designed to counter the belief that intelligence is fixed and that effort or mistakes indicate a lack of ability. Students who received the intervention reported a reduction in fixed mindset beliefs, and this was accompanied by an increase in GPA for lower-achieving students (Armstrong, 2019). This has led many schools to embed a growth mindset in their institutional ethos.

It is important to note that a growth mindset is not a panacea. *There are clear critiques about how educators apply a growth mindset.* Misapplication causes learners to 'persist with ineffective learning strategies by obsessing over effort' (Papadopoulos, 2017). Then students can become frustrated when time and labour yield little or no improvement, which then can unintentionally reinforce a fixed mindset, throwing their learning off course. There needs to be metacognitive reflection to ensure that students don't simply attempt more work with the wrong strategy, leading to lots of effort with no progress. If ineffective strategies have little impact on learning goals, then we need to redirect students to try something new, rather than praise them for working hard and sticking with it. Dweck herself has revisited the temptation to praise effort. She writes, 'A growth mindset isn't just about effort. Perhaps the most common misconception is simply equating the growth mindset with effort. Certainly, effort is key for students' achievement, but it's not the only thing. Students need to try new strategies and seek input from others when they're stuck. They need this repertoire of approaches—not just sheer effort—to learn and improve' (Dweck, 2015). An enriched mindset insists that we believe in our students, have high standards and give them a toolset to advance.

## Checking Cognitive Bias

Many educators will point to the Pygmalion effect when we talk about cognitive bias in education – that student motivation, enthusiasm and subsequent achievement are driven by teacher expectations, and that when people are considered capable, they will progress and exceed beyond their assumed ability. 'One of the critical mechanisms for achieving the Pygmalion effect is the internalization, or internalization process, of the learner's perception of the teacher's sense of his or her ability to succeed' (Meilleur, 2020). In education we also refer to this as the Rosenthal effect after an experiment by Rosenthal and Jacobson in 1968. Teachers were informed at the start of the school year that a selection of their students had genius-level potential. These 'intellectual bloomers' in fact had no exceptional profile, but results showed over the course of the year that these 'bloomers' gained an average of two IQ points in verbal ability, seven points in reasoning and four points in overall IQ (Rosenthal and Jacobson, 1992). It was later noted that 'if teachers were led to expect enhanced performance from some children, then the children did indeed show that enhancement' (Chang, 2011). On the other end of the spectrum, negative expectations were explored in a 1985 study by J. E. Brophy. Negative expectations were found to be detrimental to student motivation, and the paper gave evidence of concrete behaviours of negative teacher expectations that made disadvantageous learning conditions. Examples include:

1. Giving up easily on low-expectation students.

2. Criticising them more often for failure and praising them less following success.

3. Neglecting to give any feedback following their responses.

4. Seating them in the back of the room, paying less attention and interacting with them less frequently.

5.  Less rapport, warmth and interest in them as individuals (Brophy, 1985).

There is a similar bias for students with specific learning differences. Dr Martin Bloomfield, an advocate for students with dyslexia and neurodiversity in education, speaks eloquently of his experience with his teachers as a student with dyslexia: 'It felt at the time as though it was their job to lower my expectations of myself ... If you take a child try to convince them that they cannot do something, and that child is being taught the adults know things and the child doesn't know things, then the child is likely to believe the adults. The child is likely to go through life believing he or she cannot achieve' (Letchford, 2020). This is an absolutely tragic experience, but one that is not uncommon. Research has found that students with dyslexia often experience low self-esteem and, linked with this, low academic achievement (Gibson and Kendall, 2010). There is a responsibility to address this projection and to understand learners' diverse experiences of education, learner 'intimidation', 'negative self-perception' and 'low self-esteem'.

Cognitive bias alone doesn't quite capture the whole story, and growth mindset alone will not guarantee a 'you get what you expect' phenomenon. We cannot assume that positive teaching expectations necessarily lead to high student achievement – there are too many factors. It is natural for every teacher to develop differentiated expectations. Each relationship is different, and students' emotional and intellectual needs are unique. It would be naive to think that we can be universally positive. We constantly adjust and update our impressions. In addition, students are not purely extrinsically motivated – their inner world, emotions, autonomy and independent interests play a role in their growth. A student's self-determination is not entirely within the realm of an educator's control. What we can control are the standards set and the mindset to check our assumptions.

## High Expectations in Action: Resubmission and Slow Teaching

My dad always said of teaching, 'It's hard to get harder – start with the highest expectations.' It is easier to maintain high standards if they are a set of routines built into our everyday practice, such as instruction that makes redrafting the norm. Quality is key. Having students redo work is difficult because it seems like we are 'holding still' instead of moving on with the next chunk of the curriculum. It is simpler to settle for low-quality work because it is arduous to mark multiple versions and tempting to think students are 'trying their best'. There is a lot of exertion required to hold students accountable. We must reiterate that rushed or low-quality work is not 'finished' and students are not 'done'. Once you set that standard, the expectation and insistence on excellence prepares students for rigorous instruction. It is important to consistently reinforce redrafting. If you weaken commitment to your own expectations, this undermines their value (Sherrington and Caviglioli, 2021). To set the tone, the classic example is Austin's butterfly (EL Education, 2023a). This example lets students know that redrafting is the process of improving.

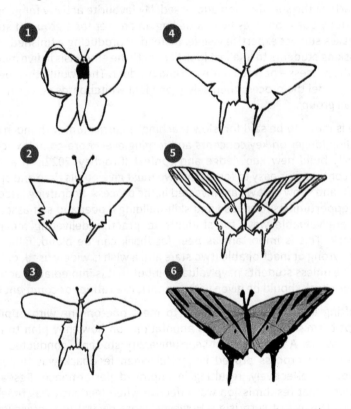

Figure 5.7 Student artwork by Austin. 'Austin's Butterfly.' Courtesy of ANSER Charter School in Boise, ID, part of the EL Education network. View online at Models of Excellence. http://modelsofexcellence.eleducation.org/projects/austinsbutterfly-drafts

Austin's butterfly drafts are an example of building excellence through multiple drafts, using self, peer and expert feedback. Ron Berger shared first-grader Austin's project on creating a scientific drawing of a butterfly to illuminate the power of critique and multiple drafts (EL Education, 2023b).

Written feedback by the teacher can be laborious with many drafts, so model answers from similar questions posted in the classrooms illustrate the expectations. Whole-class feedback done right can allow students to discover the common traps. One of the early history HODs (head of department) I worked under had amazing exemplar questions with detailed feedback posted all over her room, and it always impressed me as a dynamic environment. It really made the expectations clear and was colour coded to the parts of the specification addressed. My favourite activity for geography case study questions was live modelling an answer for a group of students – it makes subject expertise visible. Instead of producing a finished product and asking students to 'make it look like that', the emphasis in live modelling is on the process – how to create the end product. They would then be asked to live model the process themselves on giant whiteboards across the room in small groups.

There is much to be said for 'slow teaching' a curriculum with much depth, spending longer on key concepts and forging ever-more-complex schemas to easily build new knowledge and context (Bromley, 2022). In a rush to cover content, it is easy to forget that we must give pupils time and space to redraft, and show that we are invested in the process. Redrafting lessons are great opportunities for pause and skill-building – peer and self-assessment work are valuable ways for students to practise delivering meaningful feedback. This is important as peer feedback can be bland, faint praise, vague, wrong or inactionable (two stars and a wish is widely used, but rarely effective unless students have valuable input that is immediately actioned). Peer feedback should be given with support, like rubrics or comment banks.

Redrafting lessons also allow time to meet one-on-one with pupils and prompt them to make their own annotations on how they plan to redraft their answers. A study of first-year university students conducted on the resubmission process proved impactful when feedback was understood and applied effectively, resulting in improved performance. Researchers concluded that resubmission was effective when feedback was timely and specific. This is not surprising. However, most pivotal to success was the ability of the teacher to establish *rapport* (Dube, Kane and Lear, 2012). The motivation to resubmit was linked to a desire to achieve, and a constructive yet non-threatening approach by teachers propelled students to become more engaged in the process, which led to improvement.

Redrafting can be done in conjunction with non-graded feedback and works hand-in-hand with students self-reporting their grades. Predicting their performance and then comparing their response to a model answer or rubric allows students to reconcile discrepancies. This reflection can be a metacognitive exercise on how they approach questions or organisational structure. More deeply though, we wish to influence students' conception of their abilities. Teaching to the top asks students to lift their self-imposed limits. In *Visible Learning*, John Hattie gives self-reported grades an effect size of 1.33 (by comparison the average influence is 0.40). He explains that if he wrote his book again, he would rename the learning strategy 'student expectations'. The goal is not to complete a compare and contrast assignment; it is to learn where students believe they are. Hattie clarifies in an interview that 'this strategy involves the teacher finding out what are the student's expectations and pushing the learner to exceed these expectations. Once a student has performed at a level that is beyond their own expectations, he or she gains confidence in his or her learning ability' (Waack, 2013). Underpinning this is cultivating student resilience through feedback. This goes hand-in-hand with giving students tools and new strategies in how they approach learning. Moser et al. (2011) noted that 'how well people bounce back from mistakes depends on their beliefs about learning and intelligence. For individuals with a growth mind-set, who believe intelligence develops through effort, mistakes are seen as opportunities to learn and improve. For individuals with a fixed mind-set, who believe intelligence is a stable characteristic, mistakes indicate lack of ability.' To improve, we embed cognition – this includes self-regulation, planning and organisation, decision making to weigh options, memorisation techniques, ability to focus and sustain attention on a particular task, or subject-specific procedures.

If a student excels then it is time for them to dip into a larger conceptual challenge. Practice is valuable, but once there is mastery it is redundant to have a student do more of the same. We can return to a skill or piece of content through retrieval later. Challenge is not about acceleration through the curriculum or exam specification. Students don't have to race ahead on the marked mountain path. They can dive down in any direction.

# Conclusion

The principles of enriched mindset, curriculum and pedagogy create an environment of excellence and empower all pupils. There is a need to establish the standards, learning intentions and scaffolding to build skills. The principle of high expectations for all students holds true. As Willingham writes:

> 'Critical thinking is not just for advanced students. I have sometimes heard teachers and administrators suggest that critical thinking exercises make a good enrichment activity for the best students, but struggling students should just be expected to understand and master more basic material. This argument sells short the less advanced students and conflicts with what cognitive scientists know about thinking. Virtually everyone is capable of critical thinking and uses it all the time—and, as the conditional probabilities research demonstrated, has been capable of doing so since they were very young. The difficulty lies not in thinking critically, but in recognizing when to do so, and in knowing enough to do so successfully.' (Willingham, 2007, p. 18)

Challenge for all has encapsulated my approach to learning and teaching; it uplifts students from any starting point. By embedding challenge for all, we can enrich our curriculum (what we teach), our pedagogy (how we teach it) and our mindset (involving all students). Transforming our practice begins with examining our presuppositions and then evaluating what impactful 'challenge-first' instruction looks like in action. The third principle of powerful knowledge is to provide learners with ways of explaining, analysing and understanding the world beyond their immediate experience, to equip them with the intellectual tools to respond to complexity and to enable them to challenge assumptions through enquiry.

These principles demand metacognition and lifelong learning skills. A rich hinterland of knowledge fosters connective thinking, interrogation of ideas, problem solving and independent investigation. Students crave opportunities for enquiry and layers of complexity. It is through ongoing continuous professional development, and reflection on our students' agency, that we establish dynamic and inclusive learning spaces.

| Enriched curriculum design | Enriched pedagogical practice | Enriched mindset |
| --- | --- | --- |
| Reflective of powerful knowledge | Adaptive, responsive and personalised learning | Diversity, equity and inclusion |
| Challenge is inherent through layers of complexity and degree of difficulty | Inclusive challenge-first instruction | Challenge for all with universally high expectations |
| Technical disciplinary vocabulary | Clear overarching learning intentions as opposed to differentiated objectives or outcomes | Holistic development, character education and ethical global citizenship |
| Interleaving and interdisciplinary models highlighting connective thinking and abstraction | Scaffolding 'up' | Universal Design for Learning and equity |
| | Oracy, debate-centred argumentation and Harkness conference method to build intellectual risk-taking and collaboration | Models of excellence, slow teaching and resubmission |
| Diversifying and decolonising the curriculum | | Checking cognitive bias |
| Building capacity for 21st century skills and innovation | Project-based learning to foster enquiry, independent investigation and learner autonomy | Culturally responsive instruction |
| Depth as an entry point for breadth | Engagement with effective and live feedback through AI adaptive software | Trauma-informed teaching |
| Understanding by design/ backwards design | | Moral development, wellbeing and leadership growth |
| Embedded critical reflection and metacognitive strategies | Opportunities for student voice, self-regulation and agency | Enrichment programmes that extend the curriculum and student experience beyond the classroom |

Figure 5.8 Table showing components of enriched teaching.

Traditional differentiation with small extension tasks has the teacher serving small cups of water for students to sip from in every lesson. Challenge-first instruction invites students to a well, and allows them to lower the bucket and carry the weight themselves, choosing the depth and quenching their own thirst. Once we have presented students with complex information, precise vocabulary and the opportunity to interact with the material, the real fun begins! Schools can deliver initiatives that give students new ways to engage with the curriculum. In the next few chapters, we will go further into pedagogy, specifically looking at oracy, discussion-based instruction and types of project-based learning.

# Reference List

Allison, S. and Tharby, A. (2015) *Making Every Lesson Count: Six Principles to Support Great Teaching and Learning.* Carmarthen, Wales: Crown House Publishing.

Armstrong, K. (2019) *Carol Dweck on how growth mindsets can bear fruit in the classroom.* Available at: www.psychologicalscience.org/observer/dweck-growth-mindsets (Accessed: 18 April 2023).

Barron, B. J., Schwartz, D. L., Vye, N. J., Moore, A., Petrosino, A., Zech, L. and Bransford, J. D. (1998) 'Doing with understanding: Lessons from research on problem- and project-based learning.' *Journal of the Learning Sciences,* 7(3–4): pp. 271–311.

Blackwell, L. S., Trzesniewski, K. H. and Dweck, C. S. (2007) 'Implicit theories of intelligence predict achievement across an adolescent transition: A longitudinal study and an intervention.' *Child Development,* 78(1): pp. 246–263.

Bromley, M. (2021) 'Adaptive teaching explained: What, why and how?', *SecEd,* 8 December. Available at: www.sec-ed.co.uk/best-practice/adaptive-teaching-explained-what-why-and-how-pedagogy-classroom-teachers-curriculum-differentiation-teachers-standards-pisa/ (Accessed: 18 April 2023).

Bromley, M. (2022) *Slow teaching.* Available at: https://autus.group/2022/02/28/slow-teaching/ (Accessed: 18 April 2023).

Brophy, J. E. (1985) 'Teachers' expectations, motives, and goals for working with problem students.' In: Ames, C. and Ames, R. (eds.) *Research on Motivation in Education: The Classroom Milieu.* Orlando, FL: Academic Press, pp. 175–214.

Cavanagh, T., Chen, B., Lahcen, R. A. M. and Paradiso, J. R. (2020) 'Constructing a design framework and pedagogical approach for adaptive learning in higher education: A practitioner's perspective.' *International Review of Research in Open and Distributed Learning,* 21(1): pp. 173–197.

Cayley, S. (2021) 'Five reasons why primary sources should be used for teaching', *Times Higher Education,* 24 August, [Online]. Available at: www.timeshighereducation.com/campus/five-reasons-why-primary-sources-should-be-used-teaching (Accessed: 18 April 2023).

Chang, J. (2011) 'A case study of the "Pygmalion effect": Teacher expectations and student achievement.' *International Education Studies,* 4(1): pp. 198–201.

Counsell, C. (2018) 'Senior Curriculum Leadership 1: The indirect manifestation of knowledge: (A) curriculum as narrative', *The Dignity of the Thing,* 7 April. Available at: https://thedignityofthethingblog.wordpress.com/2018/04/07/senior-curriculum-leadership-1-the-indirect-manifestation-of-knowledge-a-curriculum-as-narrative/ (Accessed: 6 June 2023).

Danielson, C. (2013) *The framework for teaching evaluation instrument: 2013 edition.* Available at: www.nysed.gov/sites/default/files/danielson-teacher-rubric.pdf (Accessed: 19 May 2023).

Didau, D. (2013) 'So, what does "gifted" mean anyway?', *David Didau*, 14 June. Available at: https://learningspy.co.uk/featured/so-what-does-gifted-mean-anyway-2/ (Accessed: 18 April 2023).

Didau, D. (2022) 'Gapless instruction vs "teaching to the top"', *David Didau*, 15 October. Available at: https://learningspy.co.uk/featured/gapless-instruction-vs-teaching-to-the-top/ (Accessed: 18 April 2023).

Douglass Horsford, S. (2021) 'Whose vision will guide racial equity in schools?' *Education Week,* 17 March, [Online]. Available at: www.edweek.org/leadership/opinion-whose-vision-will-guide-racial-equity-in-schools/2021/03 (Accessed: 1 January 2024).

Dube, C., Kane, S. and Lear, M. (2012) 'The effectiveness of students redrafting continuous assessment tasks: The pivotal role of tutors and feedback.' *Perspectives in Education,* 30(3): pp. 50–59.

Dweck, C. (2015) 'Carol Dweck revisits the "growth mindset"', *Education Week*, 22 September. Available at: www.edweek.org/leadership/opinion-carol-dweck-revisits-the-growth-mindset/2015/09 (Accessed: 18 April 2023).

Eaton, J. (2022) 'EEF blog: Moving from "differentiation" to "adaptive teaching"', *Education Endowment Foundation*, 19 October. Available at: https://educationendowmentfoundation.org.uk/news/moving-from-differentiation-to-adaptive-teaching (Accessed: 18 April 2023).

Edpuzzle. (2023) *Edpuzzle.* Available at: https://edpuzzle.com/ (Accessed: 18 April 2023).

EEF. (2019) 'Early Career Framework.' Available at: https://assets.publishing.service.gov.uk/government/uploads/system/uploads/attachment_data/file/978358/Early-Career_Framework_April_2021.pdf (Accessed: 18 April 2023).

EL Education. (2023a) *Austin's butterfly: Building excellence in student work.* Available at: https://modelsofexcellence.eleducation.org/resources/austins-butterfly (Accessed: 18 April 2023).

EL Education. (2023b) *Austin's butterfly drafts.* Available at: https://modelsofexcellence.eleducation.org/projects/austins-butterfly-drafts (Accessed: 18 April 2023).

Firth, J., Rivers, I. and Boyle, J. (2021) 'A systematic review of interleaving as a concept learning strategy.' *Review of Education*, 9(2): pp. 642–684.

Freire, P. (1993) *Pedagogy of the Oppressed.* New York: Continuum Books.

Gibson, S. and Kendall, L. (2010) 'Stories from school: Dyslexia and learners' voices on factors impacting on achievement.' *British Journal of Learning Support,* (25)4: pp. 187–193.

Grady, J. B. (1994) 'Interdisciplinary curriculum development.' *Association for Supervision and Curriculum Development Annual Conference and Exhibit*, 20 March.

Griffith, M. (n.d.) *Concentric circles of knowledge*. Available at: http://envisiongifted. com/concentric-circles-knowledge/ (Accessed: 18 April 2023).

Hirsch, E. D. (2016) *Why Knowledge Matters: Rescuing Our Children from Failed Educational Theories*. Cambridge, MA: Harvard Education Press.

Holiday, T., O'Sullivan, P. and Adams, S. (2020) *Adaptive courseware implementation guide*. Available at: www.everylearnereverywhere.org/wp-content/uploads/ Adaptive-Courseware-Implementation-Guide-updated-links-by-CF-3-updated-links-included.pdf (Accessed: 18 April 2023).

House of Commons Children, Schools and Families Committee. (2010) *The gifted and talented programme: oral and written evidence*. Available at: https://publications. parliament.uk/pa/cm200910/cmselect/cmchilsch/337/337i.pdf (Accessed: 25 October 2023).

Iqbal, S. (2020) 'Decolonising and diversifying English literature', *EDI Collective*, 9 July. Available at: https://edicollectiveuom.com/2020/07/09/decolonising-and-diversifying-english-literature/ (Accessed: 11 March 2024).

Jones, K. (2019) *Retrieval Practice: Research and Resources for Every Classroom*. Suffolk, England: John Catt Educational.

Kaplan, S. (2002) 'Concentric circles of knowledge.' *Tempo,* 22(2): pp. 19–21. Available at: www.txgifted.org/files/Tempo/2002/2002-2.pdf (Accessed: 18 April 2023).

Kaplan, S. N., Guzman, I. and Tomlinson, C. A. (2009) *Using the Parallel Curriculum Model in Urban Settings: Grades K-8*. Thousand Oaks, California: SAGE Publications.

Kaplan, S. N., McComas, W. F. and Manzone, J. A. (2016) 'Teaching science and gifted students: Using depth, complexity and authentic enquiry in the discipline.' In: Taber, K. S. and Sumida, M. (eds.) *International Perspectives on Science Education for the Gifted: Key Issues and Challenges*. Oxford, England: Routledge.

Kiliç, M. and Çakmak, M. (2013) 'Concept maps as a tool for meaningful learning and teaching in chemistry education.' *International Journal on New Trends in Education and Their Implications,* 4(4): pp. 152–164.

Letchford, L. (2020) *Martin Bloomfield, Lois Letchford & Lisa McCarty 'When Learning is Trauma' and dyslexia*. Available at: www.youtube.com/watch?v=C6Rec-G2GRM (Accessed: 20 March 2024).

Light, D. (2017) *Stretch and challenge in your classroom*. Available at: www.sec-ed.co.uk/ best-practice/stretch-and-challenge-in-your-classroom/ (Accessed: 18 April 2023).

LIS. (2023) *Bachelor's degree course content*. Available at: www.lis.ac.uk/ undergraduate-degree/course-content (Accessed: 20 October 2023).

Maude, A. (2015) 'What is powerful knowledge and can it be found in the Australian geography curriculum?' *Geographical Education,* 28: pp. 18–26.

McGuire, R. (2021) *What is adaptive learning and how does it work to promote equity in higher education?* Available at: www.everylearnereverywhere.org/blog/what-is-adaptive-learning-and-how-does-it-work-to-promote-equity-in-higher-education/ (Accessed: 18 April 2023).

Meilleur, C. (2020) *Cognitive bias in education: The Pygmalion effect.* Available at: https://knowledgeone.ca/cognitive-bias-in-education-the-pygmalion-effect/ (Accessed: 18 April 2023).

Miller, E. C. and Krajcik, J. S. (2019) 'Promoting deep learning through project-based learning: A design problem.' *Disciplinary and Interdisciplinary Science Education Research,* 1(1): pp. 1–10.

Moreira, M. A. (2011) 'Why concepts, why meaningful learning, why collaborative activities and why concept maps?' *Meaningful Learning Review,* 1(3): pp. 1–11.

Morrison McGill, R. (2023) *Interleaving curriculum at London Interdisciplinary School.* Available at: www.teachertoolkit.co.uk/2023/06/15/london-interdisciplinary-school/ (Accessed: 25 April 2024).

Moser, J. S., Schroder, H. S., Heeter, C., Moran, T. P. and Lee, Y. (2011) 'Mind your errors: Evidence for a neural mechanism linking growth mind-set to adaptive posterror adjustments.' *Psychological Science,* 22(12): pp. 1484–1489.

Mould, K. (2021) 'EEF Blog: Assess, adjust, adapt – what does adaptive teaching mean to you?', *Education Endowment Foundation,* 5 July. Available at: https://educationendowmentfoundation.org.uk/news/eef-blog-assess-adjust-adapt-what-does-adaptive-teaching-mean-to-you (Accessed: 18 April 2023).

Munro, A. (2001) '"Go ask Alice", Interview by Alice Quinn', *The New Yorker,* 11 February. Available at: www.newyorker.com/magazine/2001/02/19/go-ask-alice (Accessed: April 18 2023).

Myatt, M. (n.d.a) 'Thinking about curriculum intent', *Mary Myatt.* Available at: www.marymyatt.com/blog/thinking-about-curriculum-intent (Accessed: 8 February 2024).

Myatt, M. (n.d.b) 'Five caveats for the curriculum', *Mary Myatt.* Available at: www.marymyatt.com/blog/five-caveats-for-the-curriculum (Accessed: 8 February 2024).

OECD. (2016) *PISA 2015 Results: Policies and Practices for Successful Schools (Volume II).* Paris: OECD Publishing.

Olufemi, L. (2017) 'Postcolonial writing is not an afterthought; it is British literature', *Varsity,* 21 June, [Online]. Available at: www.varsity.co.uk/comment/13261 (Accessed: 11 March 2024).

Oxford Royale. (n.d.) *The 6 levels of educational complexity and how to use them.* Available at: www.oxford-royale.com/articles/6-levels-educational-complexity/ (Accessed: 18 April 2023).

Papadopoulos, N. (2017) *How the growth mindset can harm your learning and what to do about it*. Available at: www.metalearn.net/articles/mindset-2/ (Accessed: 18 April 2023).

Quigley, A. (2023) 'Differentiation is dead, long live adaptive teaching', *Tes magazine*, 21 February. Available at: www.tes.com/magazine/teaching-learning/general/adaptive-teaching-vs-differentiation-inclusive-teaching (Accessed: 18 April 2023).

Reynolds, A. (2023) 'Vocabulary in action poster: A tool for teachers', *Education Endowment Foundation*, 28 February. Available at: https://education endowmentfoundation.org.uk/news/vocabulary-in-action-poster-a-tool-for-teachers (Accessed: 18 April 2023).

Rohrer, D. (2012) 'Interleaving helps students distinguish among similar concepts.' *Educational Psychology Review*, 24: pp. 355–367.

Rosenthal, R. and Jacobson, L. (1992) *Pygmalion in the Classroom: Teacher Expectations and Student Achievement*. New York: Irvington.

Sealy, C. (2018) 'What's all the fuss about a knowledge-rich curriculum? Part one', *Primary Timery*, 9 September. Available at: https://primarytimery.com/2018/09/09/whats-all-the-fuss-about-a-knowledge-rich-curriculum-part-one/ (Accessed: 6 June 2023).

Sherrington, T. (2017) 'Teaching to the top', *Teacherhead*, 28 May. Available at: https://teacherhead.com/2017/05/28/teaching-to-the-top-attitudes-and-strategies-for-delivering-real-challenge/ (Accessed: 18 April 2023).

Sherrington, T. and Caviglioli, O. (2021) *Teaching WalkThrus 2: Five-Step Guides to Instructional Coaching*. Woodbridge: John Catt Educational Ltd.

Silicon Valley Innovation Center. (2023) *Revolutionizing education: The power of adaptive learning platforms*. Available at: https://siliconvalley.center/blog/revolutionizing-education-the-power-of-adaptive-learning-platforms (Accessed: 15 January 2024).

Smith, R. (2020) *Five tips for teaching subject-specific vocabulary*. Available at: https://peanutbutterfishlessons.com/subject-specific-vocabulary/ (Accessed: 18 April 2023).

Talbot, A. (2023) *Adaptive teaching*. Available at: https://researchschool.org.uk/huntington/news/adaptive-teaching (Accessed: 14 February 2024).

The University of Kansas. (n.d.) *Elaboration strategies*. Available at: https://specialconnections.ku.edu/instruction/cognitive_strategies/teacher_tools/elaboration_strategies#:~:text=An%20elaboration%20strategy%20is%20where,phrase%2C%20making%20an%20analogy (Accessed: 18 April 2023).

Ufer, S. and Bochnik, K. (2020) 'The role of general and subject-specific language skills when learning mathematics in elementary school.' *Journal Für Mathematik-Didaktik*, 41: pp. 81–117.

Umamah, N., Sumardi, Marjono and Hartono, F. P. (2020) 'Teacher perspective: Innovative, adaptive, and responsive instructional design aimed at life skills.' *IOP Conference Series: Earth and Environmental Science,* 485(1): p. 012083.

Vallance, J. (2021) 'Curriculum: what are we really talking about?', *Mr Vallance Teach,* 13 March. Available at: https://mrvallanceteach.wordpress.com/2021/03/13/curriculum-what-are-we-really-talking-about/ (Accessed: 25 April 2024).

Vallance, J. (n.d.) *Curriculum intent handbook.* Available at: https://mrvallanceteach.files.wordpress.com/2021/12/curriculum-intent-handbook.pdf (Accessed: 25 April 2024).

Victoria State Government. (2022) *Adding depth and complexity.* Available at: www.education.vic.gov.au/school/teachers/teachingresources/high-ability-toolkit/Pages/adding-depth-and-complexity.aspx (Accessed: 18 April 2023).

Waack, S. (2013) *Glossary of Hattie's influences on student achievement.* Available at: https://visible-learning.org/glossary/#1_Student_Self-Reported_Grades (Accessed: 18 April 2023).

Whitworth, A. (n.d.) *One-pagers: Trying to deliberately increase the chances of learning.* Available at: www.scribd.com/document/635095003/Untitled# (Accessed: 29 April 2023).

Willingham, D. T. (2007) 'Critical thinking: Why is it so hard to teach?' *American Federation of Teachers,* Summer: pp. 8–19.

Winebrenner, S. (2018) *Teaching Gifted Kids in Today's Classroom: Strategies and Techniques Every Teacher Can Use,* 4th edn. Golden Valley, MN: Free Spirit Publishing.

Young, M. (2014a) 'Powerful knowledge as a curriculum principle.' In: Young, M., Lambert, D., Roberts, C. and Roberts, M. *Knowledge and the Future School: Curriculum and Social Justice.* London: Bloomsbury Academic, pp. 65–88.

Young, M. (2014b) 'Knowledge, curriculum and the future school.' In: Young, M., Lambert, D., Roberts, C. and Roberts, M. *Knowledge and the Future School: Curriculum and Social Justice.* London: Bloomsbury Academic, pp. 9–40.

Young, M. and Muller, J. (2014) 'On the powers of powerful knowledge.' In: Barrett, B. and Rata, E. *Knowledge and the Future of the Curriculum: International Studies in Social Realism.* London: Palgrave Macmillan, pp. 41–64.

# PART 2: CHALLENGE

# 6. ASTONISHING THE AUDIENCE

*For good ideas and true innovation, you need human interaction, conflict, argument, debate.*

Margaret Heffernan, 2012

Dynamic dialogue has repeatedly shifted the world beneath our feet. Disagreement drives change – so we should give it a stage.

What became known as 'The Great Debate' took place between 'Darwin's bulldog' Thomas Huxley and the Bishop of Oxford, Samuel Wilberforce. The annual meeting of the British Association for the Advancement of Science in 1860 began with the aim of establishing public debate and understanding of scientific matters. This was the inauguration of Oxford's University Museum, the new 'cathedral of science', and took place even before collections had been fully installed or the architectural decorations completed. In the June heat, the gentlemen engaged in a war of words, going back and forth to dispute, discuss and critique the revolutionary concept of evolution. Both sides claimed victory. The dramatic clash between science and religion captured public attention and symbolised the broader conflict between the emerging field of science and established religious institutions (Oxford University Museum of Natural History, n.d.). It was not that these discussions were not happening long before, but the platform magnified the issue in the collective consciousness. James R. Moore (1979) noted that in the Victorian era 'no battle of the nineteenth century, save Waterloo, is better known'.

Similarly, the Friedan vs. Schlafly debate remains a pivotal moment in feminist history, illustrating the ongoing struggle for women's rights and the diversity of perspectives within the movement. The debate revolved around the Equal Rights Amendment (ERA), which aimed to guarantee equal rights for women in the United States Constitution. Betty Friedan argued for the importance of the ERA in achieving gender equality and challenging the societal norms and expectations that limited women's opportunities. Phyllis Schlafly, on the other hand, opposed the ERA, claiming it was redundant, extending the reach of the federal government and undermining family values (Iaccarino, 2019). This debate helped shape subsequent activism and legislation addressing gender equality. The tensions brought forward between parenthood, work, gender roles and protections under the law are just as present today.

The format of the 1858 debate between Abraham Lincoln and Stephen A. Douglas, two senatorial candidates at the time, is still used in high school auditoriums today. The system of back and forth – point and counterpoint – was designed to set forth their divergent social values by examining questions of ethics, justice and democracy. The Lincoln–Douglas debates are regarded as a defining moment in American history and played a significant role in shaping the discourse surrounding slavery (Bordewich, 2008). The series addressed fundamental questions about the nature of slavery and human rights, and the future of a divided nation that had substantial implications. This was two white men of privilege arguing about slavery in the abstract, and it wasn't until about 100 years later that we saw a deeper discussion.

In 1965, we saw a groundbreaking debate that brought the battle for civil rights into focus. Gabrielle Bellot called it 'a debate we shouldn't need, as important as ever' (Bellot, 2017). This is one of the best examples of debate providing a platform for underrepresented voices. African-American writer James Baldwin confronted issues of racial inequality and the experiences of Black Americans in the predominantly white academic setting of the Cambridge Union. The debate proposition – 'The American Dream is at the expense of the American Negro' – gave space to what seemed like an obvious truth to Baldwin, but not to his opponent, conservative commentator William F. Buckley Jr. What soon became evident was that the two men lived in different systems of reality – Baldwin grew up poor in Harlem, while Buckley was raised with the privileges of wealth. Buckley argued that with hard work the American Dream was accessible to all. Baldwin began by highlighting the foundational divide: 'It comes as a great shock, around the age of five, or six, or seven, to discover that the flag to which you have pledged allegiance, along with everybody else, has not pledged allegiance to you.' It captured international attention, and Baldwin's eloquent words on the Black experience had a profound impact on the discourse surrounding civil rights and race relations. The weight of his words fell heavy as he spoke: 'I am stating very seriously, and this is not an overstatement. I picked the cotton, I carried it to the market, and I built the railroads under someone else's whip for nothing. For nothing … . The American soil is full of the corpses of my ancestors. Why is my freedom or my citizenship, or my right to live there, how is it conceivably a question now?' (Jones, 2020). As Bellot notes, 'It pivoted, in other words, on empathy, on rational compassion. It is a debate we keep having between an empathetic understanding of the needs of those different from oneself versus a lack of such grounded understanding; it was, *is*, a debate of a world changing versus a world staying the same' (Bellot, 2017).

All of these debates garnered global attention and were pivotal in shaping public opinion on reason, human dignity and the future of national institutions. They demonstrated the capacity of public discourse and intellectual exchange to drive social change and challenge the status quo.

Teaching our students to speak critically and empathetically is a moral imperative.

# Oracy

Creating space for student voice is powerful – oracy scaffolds linguistic, cognitive and social skills. As Medina (2020, p. 35) states, 'Studies indicate that learning diminishes when students are forced into passive roles and practices. To engage students in a more active and involved learning process, they need an opportunity to communicate verbally.' When speaking, students transform information. They make it their own by summarising and articulating into their own words. We can use rhetorical techniques like metaphor, humour and irony to elucidate and elaborate. An oracy framework can be used in formative assessment. In the UK, Voice 21, an oracy education charity, notes in its 2021–22 Impact Report that spoken language skills are one of the strongest predictors of a child's future life chances, and yet young people from low-income families miss out on opportunities to develop these vital oracy skills. Oracy increases engagement in learning, academic outcomes, confidence and wellbeing, creates better transitions as students graduate up in school, and embeds 21st century soft skills that equip students to thrive in civic life. Voice 21's research has found that:

1. Oracy boosts attainment in reading. Students' progress in reading is accelerated through high-quality oracy education. Results from standardised reading tests (New Group Reading Test) completed by

Year 6 and Year 7 students in schools participating in their Voicing Vocabulary programme revealed that 80% of students met or exceeded expected progress, with one third of students exceeding expected progress (Voice 21, 2022, p. 9). Teaching using oracy was also found to enhance early language provision.

2. Oracy education increases students' confidence and is especially crucial at transition points. Students' anxiety and nervousness about speaking in class increases significantly as they move to secondary school. Research reveals that an explicit focus on oracy fosters confidence academically, socially and emotionally. This suggests that oracy education is particularly important at transition points when students are adapting to a new social environment and academic challenge.

3. Oracy improves student outcomes across subject domains, and more subjects should take advantage. English and the humanities are the most likely to use oracy, but maths and the sciences are catching up. As Voice 21 (2022, p. 13) states, 'By empowering students to speak like specialists, we induct them into the unique ways of knowing, doing and communicating in different subject disciplines. Oracy skills are both subject-specific and generic. For example, "turn taking" is an important skill when practising oracy across a range of different subject disciplines.' Cognitively challenging classroom talk for children in Year 5 not only improves their language skills, but can also lead to gains equivalent to about two months' additional progress in English and science, and one month's additional progress in mathematics (Cambridge Primary Review Trust and York University, 2017).

Overall, oracy can improve critical thinking by encouraging learners to analyse information, construct arguments, respond to feedback and actively engage. The English-Speaking Union points to four key oracy skillsets: reasoning and evidence; listening and response; expression and delivery; and organisation and prioritisation (ESU, 2023). These skills are essential to scaffolding 'hard' academic and 'soft' social skills. Oracy engages students with complex material – when done right, it goes beyond a recitation of information. Here are some oracy activities that I love and have used in the classroom:

**Resident experts:** Students who demonstrate mastery or knowledge in a specific area are given time to prepare a short presentation or demonstration to share their expertise with their classmates, take questions from their peers, lead a discussion or create an activity (like a competition or quiz) for their classmates. I have often used this as part of curriculum compacting.

**Inner-Outer Circle:** Divide the class into two groups – the Inner Circle and the Outer Circle. The Inner Circle will sit facing each other in the centre of the room, while the Outer Circle will sit facing them around the perimeter of the room. Facilitate by posing a question or topic for discussion and give students a few minutes to reflect on their thoughts and ideas. The Inner Circle will begin the discussion, while the Outer Circle listens and takes notes (divide notes into sections: questions, insights and counterpoints). After a set amount of time the groups will switch roles, with the Outer Circle now discussing while the Inner Circle listens quietly. The Inner-Outer Circle discussion activity can be a useful tool for promoting active listening and respectful dialogue among students. By ensuring that all students have a chance to share their thoughts and ideas, this format can create a more inclusive and engaging classroom environment. A non-repeating rule is useful – only add on new thoughts. Conclude the discussion with each circle summarising key points and takeaways.

**Interviews:** Have students interview each other or community members on a particular topic, and then report back to the class. This could help them develop their questioning and listening skills, as well as their ability to summarise and synthesise information.

**Balloon debates:** A balloon debate is when students take on the roles of famous people or characters and debate a topic with the aim of persuading the audience to vote for them to be saved from a hypothetical situation, such as being stranded in a hot air balloon that is losing altitude. Typically, each participant is given a few minutes to argue their case and convince the audience that they should be saved. The audience then votes for their favourite speaker, whittling down until only one person remains, who is declared the winner.

**Presentations/speeches/role-playing/storytelling:** Many teachers abhor class presentations because they can lead to students standing up and delivering the same information on the assigned topic over and over. The audience's eyes glaze over as students dully read whatever is written on a slideshow. However, presentations can foster creativity, and teachers can encourage students to present their ideas in original ways.

With role-playing, students take on different roles and act out a scenario, such as a job interview or a news broadcast. In storytelling, students can spin a tale that applies the knowledge, either real or fictional, to their peers. We can also encourage recall by having the one-cue-card or five-bullet-point rule. We can design presentations that require students to analyse and evaluate information rather than simply recite it. Presentations are opportunities for students to identify patterns, make connections and draw conclusions from different perspectives.

These simple activities build confidence and lend students fluency when engaging with a topic. Scaffolding social skills in listening, communication and cooperation will build students up for larger exercises in debate and argumentation.

# Debate-Centred Instruction and Argumentation

Once the benefits of oracy have been explored, debating can take students further. There is a compelling theoretical basis for focusing on debate in the classroom. There can be an over-reliance on the initiation-response-feedback model where classroom discussion centres upon the teacher initiating discussion by asking a question, choosing a student to answer and then acknowledging whether the answer is correct or providing an alternative question. There are wonderful ways to get whole-class feedback (the power of mini-whiteboards!) and secure that hinge-point moment to correct misconceptions, but there are limitations in initiation-response-feedback. It can be scattershot and time intensive without necessarily encouraging a wider conversation between pupils. If it is rapid-fire or done without probing, then there is little opportunity to 'think hard'. It relies on the teacher to be the most active participant – governing and leading the class. Ideally, we should move towards dialogic teaching, which 'harnesses the power of talk to engage interest, stimulate thinking, advance understanding, expand ideas, and build and evaluate arguments, empowering students for lifelong learning and democratic engagement' (Alexander, 2019).

From the offset, debate requires learners to take centre stage, where they analyse complex arguments from multiple angles. Students must unpack the underlying assumptions, key concepts and logic – this requires analysis and appraisal. We can couch debate as a powerful method for classroom discussion. John Hattie's latest ranking of influences on student achievement places whole-class discussion as 7th of 252 interventions. Moderating a classroom discussion improves students' communication skills, so they articulate and elaborate their thoughts, while teachers benefit by seeing how students are progressing with learned concepts (Waack, 2013). Debate meets the massive push for a) student-centred learning and b) critical thinking. More teacher-centred forms of pedagogy may teach students that their voice is less valuable, that the knowledge they present is concrete and that the diverse views in the classroom are not as important as those of the educator. Debate literally places students at the forefront and on the podium.

Researchers and pedagogy experts agree that developing critical thinking skills is essential. The World Economic Forum outlines key competencies in which debate hits the nail on the head:

> '*Competencies* describe how students approach complex challenges. For example, *critical thinking* is the ability to identify, analyse and evaluate situations, ideas and information in order to formulate responses to problems. *Creativity* is the ability to imagine and devise innovative new ways of addressing problems, answering questions or expressing meaning through the application, synthesis or repurposing of knowledge. *Communication* and *collaboration involve working in coordination with others to convey information or tackle problems.*' *(World Economic Forum, 2015)*

Critical thinking has been a catch-all skill that has been thrown at any learning activity, so let's be specific. To build on the work of Robert Ennis in 1989, we can articulate that, without prompting, critical thinkers tend to:

1. Take a position or change a position based on evidence

2. Concentrate on the issue presented

3. Consider the entire situation and seek relevant information

4. Remain open-minded

5. Search for explanations

6. Seek a well-defined pronouncement of the problem

7. Manage complex problems in an orderly manner

8. Engage in reflective scepticism

9. Explore options

10. Defend reasoning with evidence

11. Demonstrate respect for other perspectives and understanding

12. Use compelling and reliable sources

13. Use metacognitive strategies to assess and make evaluative judgements.

These are all elements of debate. I would point to debate in particular as a vehicle for true critical thinking. It facilitates skill building not easily developed in a traditional didactic context and demands that students actively participate in their learning (Oros, 2007). When I think about what debate looks like in action, the components of critical thought are visible and evidenced. As a learner-centred approach, it shifts the focus from the teacher and insists on high engagement. In his dissertation on debate-across-the-curriculum pedagogy, Christopher Medina asserts that debate is a tool for changing instructional methods from 'what to think' to 'how to think'. He writes:

*'Debate is a successful method of teaching because of its inherently interactive format that requires students to engage with others and utilize higher-order thinking skills. Studies of cognitive skills have demonstrated that interactive formats are the preferred methodology for helping students to achieve critical thinking, problem-solving ability, higher-level cognitive learning, attitude change, moral development, and communication skills development.' (Medina, 2020, p. 35)*

This is an activity that imposes a structured approach to a topic and encourages students to take responsibility for their own learning. It is also tricky to do well! The following are a few powerful ways to enhance debate.

## Find the Grey

While debate is often misunderstood as establishing binary positions, in reality, it is an exercise in considering multiple ideas and evaluating different perspectives. Effective debate requires the ability to question assumptions and entertain alternative viewpoints. We should encourage students to 'find the grey' in what previously may have been black and white. We start with the premise of an open mind. Quite often, asking students to take on a position they don't immediately gravitate towards can widen their outlook. There is an epistemology to debate where students consider knowledge claims as facts (absolutist level), opinions (multiplist level), or judgements subject to scrutiny in a framework of alternatives and evidence (evaluativist level). When students reach that evaluativist level, there is a depth of understanding (Zavala, 2016). Students should be asked to seek out diverse perspectives, recognise the limits of their own experience, interrogate any assumptions and set aside personal biases – it is then that they can understand another position. After debates, it is valuable to find the gaps and ask what was missed. How were both sides right? How were both sides wrong? What is the compromise or consensus? This can be taken further by adding more perspectives and voices. For instance, traditional parliamentary debate asks parties to advocate variant positions on the same topic and to justify the positions from particular viewpoints. Imagine seeing six positions on a spectrum instead of two. You can scaffold and start with 'wearing different hats' where students run to stations across the room and give one supporting statement for each viewpoint. There is much learned in nuance, and it is important for students to see that debates are not purely pro and con or black or white.

## Evaluate in Abstract

Debate preparation quite often asks students to use research and deploy data; it is important to investigate and fact-find. However, we want students to go beyond cherry-picked statistics or simple recall of real-world examples. Debate is best when students discover the crux of the argument, so they can break the case down to a fundamental moral imperative. Evaluating in the abstract refers to the process of examining and assessing the theoretical foundations of the discourse. Can a student support a claim without relying on a real-world case study?

> *'You can assess whether you've mastered the skill of evaluating in the abstract by seeing if you can defend perspectives other than your own, or if you can transfer your analysis from one domain to another ... Can you see the points where it might be applicable, and the points where it would fall down? If so, well done – you've figured out how to evaluate a topic in the abstract, and by implication, the other levels of thinking skills as well.' (Oxford Royale Academy, n.d.)*

It requires individuals to find the underlying principles and then analyse concepts on their own merits. For example, if someone were to make the argument that democracy is the best form of government, evaluating in the abstract would involve interrogating the concept of democracy, without relying on the specific histories of real democratic governments. Quite often I ask students to use their closing arguments as an opportunity to 'answer the biggest question' that a debate poses – this often leads them to strip away the finer details and uncover the essence of an argument.

## Determine the 'Best Arguments'

Students should wrestle with the validity of arguments – what is good reasoning? It is easy to be dazzled by an impassioned speaker, but have they established a defendable position? There is much to be gained in analysing the value and logic of an argument, and seeing if the points avoid traps. There are straw man positions where a simplified summary, caricaturisation or overexaggerated point is used to make an argument easier to attack. Hollow man arguments are vague and non-specific, where speakers respond critically to issues that nobody on the opposing side made. It is useful to identify heuristic thinking, slippery slope arguments, false dilemmas, inconsistent premises, bad seed suppositions, appeals to pity and 'begging the question'. These are all great entry points to consider fallacies. Post-debate discussion is a goldmine – giving students a list of these fallacies and justifying those they think apply is a useful strategy. There is an ethical component and self-reflection – what are the inferences? For instance, students have the opportunity to point out dog whistles. Having learners judge debates and test argument validity is a powerful way to engage critical thinking.

## Know the Flow

True debate is not about regurgitating prepared arguments as statements, which results in speechifying instead of a truly engaging dialogue. Reading a prepared research statement is not debating – effective participation depends on students' reflection on the opposing viewpoint. When I first began debating, I would pick up a fragment, a specific fact or a turn of phrase and return rapid fire. I would lose track, miss whole points and not address the key arguments. I would try to write everything down as opposed to summarising and then missing key elements. The debate would go stale or simply deal with periphery issues. Instead, we wish to encourage listening to opponents' arguments and responding in the moment. To debate well requires students to discern the larger arguments that nest many pieces of evidence. Teaching students to map the debate with a template is key. This is known as 'flowing'.

A flowing framework demands that the previous arguments are summarised, and each point refuted, before bringing in new arguments to propel the discussion forward. There is a structure in a good debate that demands each point be followed up with a response. To be skilful, one must listen and appreciate what the opposition is arguing.

*'"Flowing" both enables and enforces refutation, and it makes the process of argumentation, and the unfolding of a debate, traceable and more objective. It may be the single most important way we have in argument-centred instructional work of de-mystifying – and therefore teaching – the process of academic argumentation. But flowing is a complex and difficult activity – actually series of activities – involving critical listening, summary, and refutation.' (Lynn, 2016)*

Extensive modelling is necessary for students to get the most out of debate, and flowing is an ideal tool. To model effectively, it is useful to create your own flow sheet alongside students as a debate observer. Then you reveal your flow sheet alongside the debater's flow sheets in the reflection. Flow sheets will vary depending on type of debate. A Lincoln-Douglas debate (Halvorson and Koshy, 2013) focuses on a single resolution, and the debaters present arguments for and against the resolution. In policy debate, two teams debate a specific policy proposal, such as a new law or government programme. Each team presents arguments for or against the proposal in turns. Parliamentary debate (Young Med Voices, n.d.; Azmi, n.d.) is similar to policy debate but the teams are given less time to prepare their arguments and must be able to respond quickly to their opponents' arguments, with protected time and opportunity to ask questions (points of information) to the opposing side during debate. In cross-examination debate, debaters are allowed to ask each other questions and challenge their opponents' arguments. There are many flowing templates. Whether two-person, four-person or eight-person, the flow format follows the same principles:

1. Write the resolution/position as a title.

2. In the columns across the top of the page set up the roles in speaking order.

3. In the rows the student will summarise each debater's arguments and corresponding evidence.

4. Students will move across the page to see how each debater has responded and rebutted/cross-examined. Each speaker will then add new arguments. Using arrows, short form and different coloured pens can help students keep track of the different points.

5. Conclusions should be more than a summary – they should go beyond to boil down the essence of the debate.

| Resolution: be it resolved that... (BIRT) | | | Role: proposition or opposition | |
|---|---|---|---|---|
| **Speaker 1** Proposition (Prime minister) | **Speaker 2** Opposition (Member of the opposition) | **Speaker 3** Proposition (Member of Parliament) | **Speaker 4** Opposition (Leader of the opposition) | **Speaker 5** Proposition (Prime minister closing) |
| **BIRT** State the resolution Explain the case/ theme Define the key terms | **State opposition** Ask questions about the case/ theme if needed Challenge definitions if needed | **State affirmative** Add clarity if needed | **State opposition** | **State affirmative** |
| **Constructive** Affirmative point 1 Affirmative point 2 Affirmative point 3 ⟶ | **Rebuttal** Rebut affirmative point 1 Rebut affirmative point 2 Rebut affirmative point 3 | **Constructive** Rebuild case Give examples | | |
| | **Constructive** Negative point 1 ⟶ | **Rebuttal** Rebut negative point 1 ⟶ | **Constructive** Negative point 1 – elaborate Negative point 2 Negative point 3 Negative point 4 ⟶ | **Rebuttal** Rebut negative point 2 Rebut negative point 3 Rebut negative point 4 No new arguments introduced. However, evidence or logic is allowed. |
| | | **Constructive** Affirmative point 4 ⟶ | **Rebuttal** Rebut affirmative point 4 | |
| | | | **Conclusion** Summarise position linking larger theme, offer a counter model. | **Conclusion** Summarise position linking larger theme. |

Figure 6.1 Flow sheet for debate.[12]

---

12  See these references for lots of examples: National Speech and Debate Association (n.d.), Mavaddat (n.d.) and Jacobi (2013).

Flowing creates precision and has learners divide and organise precise areas of argumentation. Learners actively critique their peers' work by finding flaws and inconsistencies in the arguments. They can anticipate arguments, develop multiple lines of argument, clarify their reasoning and create boundaries for the case in question. Debating is a high-engagement activity. Flowing gives students the tool to best undertake the challenge and increases the value of the dialogue.

## Collaboration and Negotiation

Debate requires true collaboration and teamwork. Even in a two-person debate, the volley back and forth necessitates give and take. Partnered debate teams require arguments to be divided, strengths identified and students to share the arguments with each other to reach a learning goal. Debate both rewards individual effort and mitigates the 'free rider' problem because there is no place to hide. In preparing for debate, students must decide which role they will play. They must negotiate and coordinate to present the best case possible. Within the debate, they write each other notes, whisper a key piece of information or slide a winning idea over to their partner. They must be generous with each other. Debate is not limited to the traditional structure – negotiation, cross-examination and building consensus run alongside the debate in activities like Model United Nations (MUN). MUNs encompass a rich process, which includes researching and writing position papers, preparing proposals, formal and informal caucusing, gathering signatories, collectively writing resolutions, presenting and adding amendments. Every step of the way there is deliberation, dialogue and parley. This has the hallmarks of debate with further opportunity for the development of those 21st century skills. Post-debate discussion allows students to reflect on how they worked together and how they can improve.

## Shaping the Debate

While we can provide debate topics, an additional level of active learning is for students to craft their own resolutions and debate questions. A long-term goal is for students to identify an issue and create their own cases. This could be sparked by newspaper op-eds, current events, historical controversies, ethical concerns or surprising developments in research. Resolutions can be broad and then brought into focus with a specific case study. Good cases will be specific enough to illustrate a resolution as a real-world example, while not bogging down the opponent with the expectation that they are intimately familiar with particulars (e.g. we don't have to be experts in North Korean agricultural policy to debate sanctions). Creating cases is an advanced creative skill that can be scaffolded – for example, students can set up topics with a real-world example for chat stations. They can take on the role of 'resident expert' where they research a topic in-depth, explain it in five minutes and then have the class question them on the issue. It is tempting to ask students to practise with simple debate (e.g. be it resolved that cats are better than dogs). Go in the opposite direction and look for complexity. Have students critique complex debates and break down the components of a great case that has specificity (e.g. be it resolved that public muzzling laws be instituted for pit bull breeds due to increased attacks on humans).

## Emotional Integrity

Eloquence when debating is not winning. Often, eloquence is a privilege. I often start my debates with this quote:

> *'When you debate a person about something that affects them more than it affects you, remember that it will take a much greater emotional toll on them than on you. For you it may feel like an academic exercise. For them, it feels like revealing their pain only to have you dismiss their experience and sometimes their humanity. The fact that you might remain more calm under these circumstances is a consequence of your privilege, not increased objectivity on your part. Stay humble.' (Mohapatra, 2018)*

There is a level of empathy we wish for students to gain. This means being emotionally aware of *how* we debate. As one commentator put it: 'Don't play devil's advocate when you have no skin in the game' (Digh, 2021). There is an entire hidden curriculum within debate – we are stretching and extending ourselves empathetically when the initial impulse is to judge and dismiss an issue.

The goal of a debate should not be to win at all costs, but rather to engage in a constructive dialogue. The purpose is not to prove a perfect case or completely discredit the other side's perspective. When students engage with the aim of gaining a deeper understanding of the issue, they are more likely to listen to the other person's perspective, consider their arguments and respond with thoughtful and respectful counterpoints. We can shape dissent as a brave act and disagreement as a learning opportunity. The emphasis is on the exchange of ideas.

Debate-centred instruction creates a unique opportunity for student growth:

> *'The enhancement of argumentation and presentation skills is paramount to students' ability to compete in the world beyond*

*the walls of their respective institutions. Therefore, persisting in a commitment to this groundbreaking pedagogy, building upon the lessons learned, and continuing to improve leadership skills through developing students' oral communication and critical thinking skills are essential to achieving the mission of higher education: the development of the next generation of citizen leaders.' (Medina, 2020, pp. 95–96)*

Smaller debates and oracy challenges can be built up over time to instil confidence and build skills. There can be an entire build-up over a term to a marquee debate or a tiered competition. The culmination of this instruction should literally give students the stage. A great example of integrating a long-term debate project can be seen in the Debate Across the Curriculum (DAC) model introduced into Wiley College, a historically Black college in Marshall, Texas. Beginning with entering first-year students, they are taught the basics of argumentation. These basics are reinforced through in-class debate and discussion activities. They then prepare cases to participate in an annual capstone event (Medina, 2020). Similarly, in primary and secondary schools I've seen debate built into lessons which then culminated as a house competition in front of the whole community.

The effect of embedding debate is long-lasting, the implication being that students have the confidence to speak up, question and critique. Margaret Heffernan gave an insightful talk where she illustrated the danger of echo chambers: people grow when we dare to disagree. Heffernan expounds that:

*'The University of Delft requires that its PhD students have to submit five statements that they're prepared to defend. It doesn't really matter what the statements are about, what matters is that the candidates are willing and able to stand up to authority. I think it's a fantastic system, but I think leaving it to PhD candidates is far too few people, and way too late in life. I think we need to be teaching these skills to kids and adults at every stage of their development, if we want to have thinking organizations and a thinking society.' (Heffernan, 2012)*

We live in a world where students can use AI to generate answers – their voices are best used for asking questions. Through debate, we can move towards enquiry questions to give students further opportunities to examine and scrutinise the world around them. When we take the tools of debate to the next level, we can have less-structured discussions that validate a multiplicity of student experience.

# Reference List

Alexander, R. (2019) *Dialogic teaching*. Available at: https://robinalexander.org.uk/dialogic-teaching/ (Accessed: 10 June 2023).

Azmi, M. (n.d.) *Student handout for Lincoln Douglas debate format*. Available at: www.scribd.com/document/75647597/Student-Handout-for-Lincoln-Douglas-Debate-Format (Accessed: 10 June 2023).

Bellot, G. (2017) *Baldwin vs. Buckley: A debate we shouldn't need, as important as ever*. Available at: https://lithub.com/baldwin-vs-buckley-a-debate-we-shouldnt-need-as-important-as-ever/ (Accessed: 10 June 2023).

Bordewich, F. M. (2008) 'How Lincoln bested Douglas in their famous debates', *Smithsonian Magazine,* September, [Online]. Available at: www.smithsonianmag.com/history/how-lincoln-bested-douglas-in-their-famous-debates-7558180/ (Accessed: 10 June 2023).

Cambridge Primary Review Trust and York University. (2017) *Dialogic Teaching*. Available at: https://educationendowmentfoundation.org.uk/projects-and-evaluation/projects/dialogic-teaching (Accessed: 10 June 2023).

Digh, P. (2021) *Instagram post,* 16 June. Available at: www.instagram.com/p/CQMRW6hgrX0/ (Accessed: 10 June 2023).

ESU. (2023) *Educational approach*. Available at: www.esu.org/educational-approach/ (Accessed: 10 June 2023).

Ennis, R. H. (1989) 'Critical thinking and subject specificity: Clarification and needed research.' *Educational Researcher,* 18(3): pp. 4–10.

Halvorson, S. and Koshy, C. (2013) *Lincoln-Douglas debate*. Ripon, USA: National Speech and Debate Association. Available at: www.speechanddebate.org/wp-content/uploads/Lincoln-Douglas-Debate-Textbook.pdf (Accessed: 10 June 2023).

Heffernan, M. (2012) *Dare to disagree*. Available at: www.ted.com/talks/margaret_heffernan_dare_to_disagree?language=en (Accessed: 10 June 2023).

Iaccarino, B. (2019) 'Why a woman was against her own equality: Understanding Phyllis Schlafly's opposition to the Equal Rights Amendment.' *Transformations: Research Papers*. SUNY College Cortland. 4-2020. Available at: https://digitalcommons.cortland.edu/cgi/viewcontent.cgi?article=1004&context=programs (Accessed: 10 June 2023).

Jacobi, A. (2013) *Public forum debate: Sample flow*. Available at: https://dogwoodspeechanddebate.weebly.com/uploads/5/5/7/7/55774199/pf_sample_flow.pdf (Accessed: 10 June 2023).

Jones, J. (2020) *Watch the famous James Baldwin-William F. Buckley debate in full, with restored audio (1965)*. Available at: www.openculture.com/2020/07/watch-the-famous-james-baldwin-william-f-buckley-debate-in-full-with-restored-audio-1965.html (Accessed: 10 June 2023).

Lynn, L. (2016) *Model flowing on Google Sheets*. Available at: https://argumentcenterededucation.com/2016/01/20/model-flowing-on-google-sheets/ (Accessed: 10 June 2023).

Mavaddat. (n.d.) *Flow sheet for debate*. Available at: https://quizlet.com/ca/331205827/debate-flowing-diagram/ (Accessed: 10 June 2023).

Medina, C. (2020) *The effect of debate across the curriculum pedagogy on critical thinking in higher education institutions*. PhD dissertation. University of the Cumberlands. Available at: www.proquest.com/openview/b7c1e246a2f7d3f090745d802342d0f1/1?pq-origsite=gscholar&cbl=18750&diss=y (Accessed: 10 June 2023).

Mohapatra, S. (2018) 'Inclusive logic', 6 November, *Sonalimohapatra*. Available at: https://sonalimohapatra.in/2018/11/06/inclusive-logic/ (Accessed: 10 June 2023).

Moore, J. R. (1979) *The Post-Darwinian Controversies: A Study of the Protestant Struggle to Come to Terms with Darwin in Great Britain and America 1870-1900*. Cambridge: Cambridge University Press.

National Speech and Debate Association (n.d.) *Big questions judge training: Flowing basics*. Available at: www.speechanddebate.org/wp-content/uploads/Big-Questions-Judge-Training-Intro-to-Flowing.pdf (Accessed: 10 June 2023).

Oros, A. L. (2007) 'Let's debate: Active learning encourages student participation and critical thinking.' *Journal of Political Science Education*, 3(3): pp. 293–311.

Oxford Royale Academy (n.d.) *The 6 levels of educational complexity and how to use them*. Available at: www.oxford-royale.com/articles/6-levels-educational-complexity/ (Accessed: 10 June 2023).

Oxford University Museum of Natural History. (n.d.) *The great debate*. Available at: www.oum.ox.ac.uk/learning/pdfs/debate.pdf (Accessed: 10 June 2023).

Voice 21. (2022) *Insights and impact 2021-2022*. Available at: https://voice21.org/wp-content/uploads/2023/01/Voice21-Impact-Report-2023-v21-web-1.pdf (Accessed: 10 June 2023).

Waack, S. (2013) *Glossary of Hattie's influences on student achievement: 7. Classroom discussion*. Available at: https://visible-learning.org/glossary/#7_Classroom_discussion (Accessed: 10 June 2023).

World Economic Forum. (2015) *Chapter 1: The skills needed in the 21st century*. Available at: https://widgets.weforum.org/nve-2015/chapter1.html (Accessed: 10 June 2023).

Young Med Voices. (n.d.) *Debater training manual*. Available at: www.britishcouncil.ps/sites/default/files/debater_training_manual_full_version.pdf (Accessed: 10 May 2024).

Zavala, J. (2016) *How construction of a dialog influences argumentive writing and epistemological understanding*. PhD thesis. Columbia University.

# 7. COME ONE!
# COME ALL!

*Without discussion intellectual experience is only an exercise in a private gymnasium. It has never been put to the test, never had to give an account of itself. It is some such motive that impels people to discussion; though they are too often content with the jousting of pasteboard knights. But a good discussion is not only a conflict. It is fundamentally a cooperation. It progresses towards some common understanding. This does not mean that it must end in agreement. ... A good discussion tones up your mind, concentrates its loose particles, gives form and direction.*

**Randolph Bourne, 1916**

Productive classroom talk plays a central role in student learning. Dialogic interactions stimulate and engage students. Whether teacher-to-student or student-to-student, reciprocal dialogues are sites to embed disciplinary understanding, explore issues, interrogate ideas and cooperatively engage in enquiry (Gillies, 2016). Discourse influences not only what students learn, but how they learn it. How we co-construct and reinforce meaningful discussion practices takes time and persistent, targeted scaffolding. Active listening, justification, sharing incomplete thoughts and accumulated understanding are all tricky operations that can be honed through verbal exchange (Makar and Allmond, 2018). There has been renewed interest in creating conditions for great discussion, so let's dive into an old method that is having a resurgence.

# Harkness Conference Method

The Harkness teaching method, also known as the Harkness conference, is an educational approach that emphasises student-centered, collaborative learning through small-group discussions. The approach begins with a modest but key pivot in how we frame education: let's sit at a table.

It began about 90 years ago. What started as an experiment has become the blueprint for many sixth forms, academies and prestigious universities including Yale and Harvard. The method takes its name from philanthropist Edward Harkness. Ned Harkness was the sole inheritor to his family's vast fortune. His father had invested early in Rockefeller's oil ventures, which grew exponentially when the automobile flourished. Harkness eventually grew to be one of the richest men in America. Harkness and his generous wife, Mary, spent their lives quietly and systematically giving their wealth away to social causes. Not a natural student himself, Harkness became devoted to education reform. He saw the status quo as patronising and hardly conducive to the forging of young minds. He recalled walking into classrooms and seeing pupils sitting in neat lines, with desks facing a teacher who stood at the blackboard, lecturing at bowed heads while they obediently took notes. He deplored these conditions, and later commented: 'I want to see somebody try teaching—not by recitations in a formal recitation room where the teacher is on a platform raised above the pupils and there is a class of 20 or more boys who recite lessons. ... I think the bright boys get along all right by that method, but I am thinking of a boy who isn't a bright boy—not necessarily a dull boy, but diffident, and not being equal doesn't speak up in class and admit his difficulties' (Towler, 2006). Indeed, many schools in those first few decades of the 20th century prided themselves on the practice of teachers snapping their fingers and calling on students to 'recite' rote knowledge in a sink-or-swim environment. This resulted in an alienating 'learn or leave' attitude. Harkness wished for a radical change in how to conceive learning.

It was luck that brought Dr Lewis Perry to Ned Harkness when they met by chance on a train. Upon learning Perry's position as a principal of a prestigious private school, Harkness asked Perry about the state of education and whether every child benefited. The men became fast friends while discussing how the current teaching model was ripe for change. Harkness wished to disrupt the status quo. Perry felt up to the task and returned to his post to develop a plan to enhance learning for all students. After reflection, in 1930 Perry travelled from Phillips Exeter Academy to New York with a plan for school improvement that involved a guest speaker series and a student adviser model. Lovely ideas, but ones that Harkness found tepid. He bluntly responded to Perry: 'You are thinking of improving an existing institution by building on what you have got now. I am thinking of something much more radical.' He wished for a proposition 'so different from methods prevailing here that one could see at a glance that were they adopted, the whole educational system in our secondary schools would not only be changed, but changed enormously for the better' (Towler, 2006). What he envisioned was a sweeping transformation designed to undo domineering and didactic teaching. Perry went back to the drawing board and spent six months in committee with the goal of revolutionising the traditional classroom setting. What emerged was an interactive approach to learning devised to equalise and engage.

Traditional Model          Harkness Model

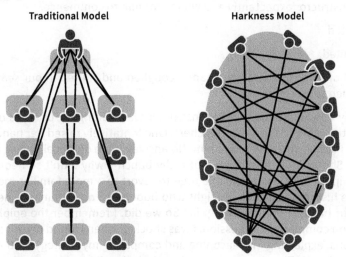

Figure 7.1 Harkness versus traditional model.

The teaching method centred around an oval table, created for an inclusive and egalitarian learning environment. To this day, the Harkness table remains a platform for intellectual risk-taking, collaborative learning and problem solving. There is no 'head' of the table where the teacher sits to command and monologue. Students gather around the table, typically in groups of 10 to 12, *alongside* their teacher. Everyone is at the same level, looking at each other eye to eye with no place to hide. The table was to serve as a springboard for open dialogue, active participation and deep engagement with the subject matter. When presented with the scheme, Harkness heartily

211

endorsed it, believing that this method would encourage independent thinking and foster a sense of self-determination among learners. Gone were the rows of desks. Headlines celebrated the largest single gift in secondary school history, with Harkness bestowing the equivalent of 105 million US dollars to Phillips Exeter for new buildings, 25 teachers to reduce class sizes and the defining collection of beautiful oak tables (Towler, 2006).

## The First Lesson

My first training session with Harkness could be best described as painfully awkward. The method in action was not what I expected. I sat in a circle with my fellow teachers and a seasoned Harkness instructor. A maths booklet had been provided, and the first problem immediately intimidated me – it had been a decade since my last proper maths lesson. We settled in and looked at the instructor expectantly and waited for him to commence.

We waited.

And waited.

Several of us scribbled on the paper, coughed and shifted in our seats. He continued to sit comfortably.

It finally dawned on us that the instructor was waiting for us. Eyes darted across the room to the maths teachers. One tentatively raised her hand. 'So, should I start?' she directed at him. No answer, but a quizzical raising of the brows. She hesitated. We were not a shy bunch – why didn't someone say something? I felt this undeniable urge to revert to a more familiar mode. It was the history teacher to my right who boomed, 'I don't think we need to raise our hands. I think we jump in.' So we did. I remember the epiphany I had upon completing the session. I was shocked when I found myself asking questions, explaining my reasoning and comparing my strategy. In the end, I felt like I won. The right answer was not elusive, it was there and we had reached it in different ways.

The lesson was effective on two levels. First, we acquired several techniques to solve the maths problem. Second, we learned how to constructively collaborate and challenge each other while undertaking the problem. Going back to Hattie's analysis, this is what powerful classroom discussion looks like at its finest. Where the Socratic method and other discussion methods may rely on teacher stimulation to reach a predetermined conclusion, Harkness revolves around student-driven action and revelation. As Kyle Botkin (2017) comments in relation to Harkness: 'Maybe teachers should not be delivering content at all. Maybe further gains are to be made from students learning from one another.' Something else happened very naturally in the training session. The maths experts in our group allowed us to struggle, they stepped back and observed, but this didn't mean they hadn't benefited. One further maths teacher commented in the debrief that she had never thought to approach this question with one of the procedures. Another laughingly commented that he was worried he might have the wrong answer and look silly. Once the tension of nervous energy and fear was pierced, we had built a higher degree of confidence and trust. We also gave space for our peers to discover their own answers.

There are a few key elements that make a truly participatory process, as follows.

## The Set Up

- Establish **discussion guidelines** from the outset, and have students contribute and shape what the standards are. You can rehearse and reiterate these in small steps to create 'routine respect'. Posting guidelines in the room or having laminated copies on the table act as constant cues. In the first sessions, students may need invitations to speak or prodding to give ground to their peers. This delicate balance requires a psychologically safe space for risk-taking. A healthy conference will have students listen with equity and empathy in mind, while also engaging with **normalised disagreement**. There are a plethora of mantras like 'collaborate, don't compete' to set the tone (Lancaster, 2020).

- The teacher has the responsibility for creating effective and thought-provoking **problem sets, prompts or reading material**. These Harkness booklets can be a lot of up-front work for teachers to curate. Using backwards design to sequence the material and cover the objectives can help. The design is **challenge first**, with the overarching prompts requiring focused reading and hard thinking before students sit down at the table. This is where **complexity** in the diet of resources we provide for students pays off – a setting for them to fully digest the material.

- **Maximal student preparation** is necessary for quality discourse. Like the Oxford tutorial style, there is an emphasis on students doing independent work and coming prepared to engage. Preparation expectations are that students arrive ready take on the central questions. They should have the shared vocabulary and entry points to the conversation. This necessitates high self-regulation on the student side and high standards on the teacher side. Holding students accountable in prep is part of the feedback.

- **Pre-Harkness goal setting** sheets that articulate a measurable goal, strategy to implement and evaluation (conquered or 'do better next time'). These can be as simple as 'ask three open-ended questions' or 'build upon a peer's points'. There can also be group goal sheets to set the targets for a session, like 'everyone cites a piece of evidence' or 'we aim to find links to our last topic'.

## The Practice

- So what does Harkness discussion look like? Jonathan Lancaster's concise Harkness guide is an invaluable resource that I can't recommend highly enough. He points out that there are four main Harkness approaches: 1) **teacher as conductor** who sets the agenda, prep and series of questions; 2) **particular-to-broad** framing with specific fact-grounded questions leading to general discussion; 3) **broad-to-particular**, which moves from establishing general principles to specific material and 4) **bubble-up** where students arrive at the table having worked through the material autonomously to have an **exploratory discussion** (Lancaster, 2020). No one approach is better than another. Some subjects or class compositions may lend themselves more naturally to a certain mode. There can be an assumption that Harkness can only work in English or humanities classrooms, when in fact the enquiry lends itself beautifully to maths and the sciences.

- One of the most common phrases about Harkness has been 'the teacher acts as facilitator'. In truth we are **training students to be the facilitators**. Teachers can structure the resources and objectives – this sits alongside the hidden curriculum of 21st century skills. Distribution of power means distribution of responsibility. Students can drive the research, create agendas, draft the questions, set the pace, moderate the exchanges and map the flow of conversation. To scaffold Harkness, you may give students roles in the discussion like 'questioner', 'researcher', 'synthesiser', etc. We model facilitation and can hand moderation to students once they are immersed in the flow of Harkness methodology. As Sam Shapiro (2024) writes, 'The moderator, and I must stress this often, is not the de facto teacher. Rather, their job is to introduce topics, organize the flow of the conversation, ask participants to specify and/or provide textual references, and generally set an intellectually engaged and stimulating tone.' We are teaching both *with* discussion and *for* discussion.

- Starters will probably change depending on how accustomed students are to Harkness and each other. This can include icebreakers to build trust and warm up. Once there are settled norms there can be a starting routine, where students reread the material, choose a thread to pick up from the last session or find consensus in setting an agenda. Activity can also vary in each class – students could spend the first few minutes formulating their own questions, summarising their thoughts in three sentences, selecting a portion of the text they wish to highlight or identifying an overarching theme. Students can use mini-whiteboards to answer a specific question to begin and then explain their thinking process. If the session is entirely student led, it is useful to give students a list of strategies to choose from to initiate the discussion.

- Discussion moves can be explicitly taught – for instance, question-asking is a low-risk way for students to enter a conversation. It is worth reiterating that confusion is a form of curiosity – it can drive learning towards definitions, provide clarity or provoke further enquiry. Honesty is often overlooked as a learning value – a student bravely admitting that they would like an explanation or example often turns the conversation. Students can be **trained in asking questions**, brainstorming reams of questions then narrowing down the ones that would be the most fruitful for discussion.

- Again, it is helpful to give students a **menu of techniques** to extend the discussion – declarative statements to open a new line of thought, reflective statements, dissenting statements or invitations to elaborate. Within agendas, there can be opportunities for co-reasoning, rational decision making, evaluation of evidence, constructive conflict, synoptic questions and exploratory talk. When students explain their ideas, we wish for them to integrate the discipline-specific vocabulary – having a list of keywords on the agenda cues students to use these terms with a high degree of precision and fluency.

- **'The pause'** is one of the greatest Harkness tools, forcing teachers to get comfortable with being silent and resist the impulse to fill the vacuum. Often, the teacher does not 'begin' the session but waits for students to initiate. One English teacher noted that in Harkness 'you subordinate your critical agenda for a belief in the process. You have to fundamentally believe that what the kids are getting at the table—out of wrestling with complexity and out of talking to each other—is more important than making sure they understand what the green light is in Gatsby' (Soutter and Clark, 2021, p. 5). At the table, the teacher must step back. Silence is golden. Unlike the Socratic method of questioning students and leading them to the pre-defined conclusion, a high-quality Harkness discussion occurs student to student (Polm, 2019).

- Teachers at the table have a responsibility to be conscious of our reactions. One counter-intuitive suggestion is the **'deny the eye'** technique, where you do not look directly at the student who is speaking. The aim is to encourage students not to direct their answers to the instructor for implicit approval, but to their peers. It's always best to explain this technique so students understand how you are stepping back. If there is a misconception in learning or a breach of discussion guidelines, then a teacher should give participants the opportunity to rectify themselves. Instead of immediately correcting them, you can wait for a peer to remedy, pose questions or redirect students back to the original prompt or text.

- Discussion should have a solid foundation, and students need to back up their thinking. **Citing evidence** shows examination, scrutiny, critique, research and grounded analysis. It is not just what a student knows, but how they prove it. Bringing independent research to the table means that students must also defend the veracity or justify its inclusion. Probing evidence and checking the impulse to cherry-pick is part of making good arguments. Part of the practice is to have students expand and explain further; encouraging students to elucidate leads to depth and sophistication.

- The **active-listening component** is often the hardest part. We are often waiting for our turn to speak as opposed to going deeper into another person's thinking. Asking students to build on and elevate previous comments is a great way to move the discussion to the next level. Listening for discussion is not an easy skill: 'There is a kind of listening unique to this pedagogy. Harkness listening, or what I will call listening for discussion, is a form of relational listening ... since it "improves" or changes the quality of relations among a group' (Backer, 2016, p. 10). Students providing each other with mutual support and treating learning as a social and communicative process are more likely to gain insight. Barbieri and Light (1992) found that the amount of talk about planning, negotiation and the joint construction of knowledge by peers correlated significantly with successful problem solving, and with successful learning outcomes in subsequent related tasks by individuals. Challenges where the group must work to find consensus or purposely disagree are equally valuable. Studies on classroom talk have found that the most productive interaction involves pupils proposing ideas and explaining their reasoning to each other. Moreover, the expression of contrasting opinions during group work was the single most important predictor of learning gain (Mercer, 2008).

## The Debrief

- Debrief at the end of the session and have students reflect on how they learned. This reflection becomes a **metacognitive plenary**. Coaching students in productive dialogue is part of Harkness – feedback at the close of a session allows students to focus on the process of learning, as much as the product. **Productive classroom talk** can be given three dimensions: accountability to the community, accountability to knowledge and accountability to accepted standards of reasoning (Michaels, O'Connor and Resnick, 2007).

- **Discussion tracking** is fantastic (I noticed that once I started tracking discussion, I was also able to shut up and listen more!). Tools for gauging discussion (in particular the bird's eye diagram of the table) allow teachers to track the exchanges. The dynamics of each class are unique, and this is a tangible way to reflect on participation and interactions. There are fantastic templates for time-speaking bar graphs, student comments forms and body language trackers for teachers to deploy (Phillips Exeter Academy, n.d.).[13] There are great digital tools for tracking as well. I'd especially recommend Equity Maps (Equity Maps iPad App, 2016). It can be useful to categorise

---

13 Phillips Exeter Academy is incredibly generous in sharing CPD and resources – these resources can all be found on their website here: www.exeter.edu/programs-educators/harkness-outreach/harkness-teaching-tools

the contributions into meaningful (citing, questioning, transitioning, sythesising, challenging) versus non-meaningful (interrupting, rambling or opining without evidence, derailing, rehearsed reading) (Lancaster, 2020; Mullgardt, 2008). It is not only the quantity of speaking (although this is a valuable indicator) but also the type and quality of interactions. What was a judgement and what was an inspection? What were the behaviours and relational skills that enhanced understanding? Who spoke the least but said the most? Parsing the contributions, the links, the conclusions and the consensus is illuminating.

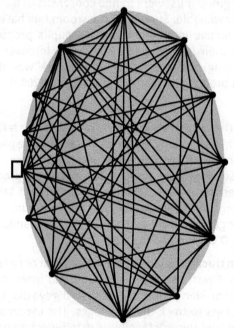

Figure 7.2 Harkness tracking map

- **Peer review and self-reflection exercises** in the debrief are great starting points. (What did I hear? Which points resonated? What do I wish I had said? Which skills can I practise? How could I describe the group dynamics?) You can create anonymous maps to show participation, with each dot representing a student in the session and the lines symbolising students' dialogue – tack the drawing on a wall and invite students to interpret (Gong, 2006). You can use individual and whole-class evaluation questions. Students can keep a mini diary of their experience with short entries on their progress after each session. Many students struggle and lose confidence with problems that differ even slightly from those they have already seen. Harkness methodology encourages students to learn from their mistakes and practise perseverance.

- So much of this book is about **equity, who gets to speak and the authority their voice is given**, hence we should be looking at discussion through this lens. Reflection is making us aware of **power dynamics** and how to resolve any inequities in who is granted a platform. Being attuned is part of culturally responsive teaching. Dr Courtney Cazden points out that: 'One of the most important influences on all talk (some say *the* most important influence) is the participants themselves–their expectations about interactions and their perceptions of each other ... All human behaviour is culturally based. Ways of talking that seem so natural to one group are experienced as culturally strange to another' (Cazden, 2001, p. 67). On one level we can be aware of cultural differences; to interrogate this further means we don't privilege one type of sociolinguistic convention over others.

- Equity Maps is an amazing app that does all the tracking and analytics of the discussion for you. This creates a powerful debrief where students get accurate feedback on how 'equitable' the discussion was. Although you are mapping discussion, it is best **not to use discussion tracking as assessment** with students performing to score 'points' or meet a quota. This can set the wrong incentives. Participation is half the story when active listening is part of the process. The goal is authentic discussion.

- A huge consideration is **creating an environment for students with learning differences**. We should examine the ways in which seminars may not be working for all students and include this in student reflection. One-on-one debriefing with a teacher can give space for students to express their needs – whether this be chunking the activity, requesting a break, varying the format or receiving affirmation. Asking the student what strategies to use is an invitation. Universal Design for Learning is an area in which to explore this further.

Harkness is a form of deliberative discourse. It is no surprise that small-group enquiry and reciprocal teaching would have an impact. Peer-reviewed studies on Harkness are limited. On the surface we can place Harkness within constructivism, deliberative discourse and 'teaching discussion', on which there is much literature. Dewey viewed reasoned discussion as the democratic foundation for education, where discourse, consultation and persuasion are a 'mode of social inquiry' (Michaels, O'Connor and Resnick, 2007). Vygotsky saw discourse as representing a qualitatively different form of communication, emphasising authentic social conditions where students try out and manipulate language to create meaning (Moll and Whitmore, 2013). There is also the function of spoken dialogue to hone social interaction and psychological development. Productive classroom discussion is not a wandering conversation, or a structured debate between opposing positions, or a competition for loudest voice in the room. Discussion activates knowledge that might otherwise remain inert – expressing thoughts can crystallise learning.

Harkness has overlap with Socratic methods, but the key difference is the assumption of authority – part of equity is acknowledging that we as educators are not the owners of all experience. Williams (2014) explains that: 'Teachers have the expertise to demand the right processes and frameworks, but the discussion does not belong to them. The pedagogical philosophy of Harkness lies in a shift in the balance of power, which even separates it from the Socratic concept of dialogue.' Reflecting on his experience as a chemistry teacher practising Harkness, Mark Hiza (2015) wrote: 'I think that my progression (my development) as a teacher is not so much linear as cyclical, ranging out from a central belief in the students' need for ownership of their learning. ... This belief is the fulcrum on which I try to maintain the balance between the self-discovery I want for my students and the leadership they want from me.' Conceptually this is described as *modulated authority*, where the teacher is not the 'authority' on content, but the 'authority' on the process of learning (Backer, 2016). Often this means privileging students' perspectives over an author's intent, respecting a divergent path when they tackle a problem and valuing multiple opinions at the same time.

Soutter and Clark's (2021) research report on building a culture of intellectual risk-taking in Harkness rings true. They point to four main precepts: 1) egalitarian and process-based philosophy, 2) safe classroom communities, 3) no single correct answer, and 4) normalised disagreement and problem solving. There is a 'good tension' in challenge, where disagreement drives a more complete understanding. There can be a creeping fear of error in schools that is propelled by examination pressures. Deep comprehension and self-efficacious learners are not bred by repetitive drilling of content. Indeed, Doug Lemov (2015) has extolled the virtues of creating a 'culture of error' to embrace any flaws and love the opportunities that mistakes present. As teachers we can model making mistakes. Appreciating vulnerability and allowing space for students to change their minds will prioritise collaboration. Asking questions and problem solving go hand-in-hand, and both are explicit Harkness goals.

# Overcoming the Challenges of Implementing Harkness

### Prep Heavy

The first challenge a teacher will note is that not all students can be relied on to do the groundwork. What if a student doesn't do the preparation work for the discussion? This soon becomes obvious if not disclosed and the immediate repercussion is usually the feeling of being lost. It is important to give students an 'out'. They can still productively add to the session by being an observer and tracking the discussion. In the debrief, the student observer can have the floor for a few minutes to report on what they saw. The student can benefit and participate, while also being given real responsibility. If this is a regular occurrence then the student's debrief and reflection should look at goals targeting preparation. If many students are unprepared, there is a massive temptation to believe that the class isn't ready or capable of discussion. Instead, trust them and hold them accountable. The routine of preparation and high expectations is one that may require 'submission of drafts'. You repeat the seminar until the preparation and quality of evidence in the session is at the standard you expect.

### Classes Sizes

The most obvious obstacle to Harkness is large class sizes that dilute the opportunity for each student to actively contribute. There is a prohibitive cost for most schools that has led to this method being the purview of elite private institutions. This is unfortunate. Harkness himself wanted to democratise the practice within education. That is not to say that the method is completely inaccessible to larger classes, but it does require creative workarounds:

- Half and half: there are a few iterations on flipped learning. You create a circle of 10–13 desks on one side of the room for a Harkness discussion, while the other half of the class work independently.

Then flip for the next lesson. In my experience, this is the least ideal option but still viable with the right classes. There is also the ability to divide groups according to extrovert/introvert, orchestrate mentoring or jigsaw the material.

- Multiple roundtables: two circles in the same room. You can move back and forth, taking turns sitting at each table to observe or moderate the discussion. Once the method is entrenched one table can be teacher-monitored while the other is student-led. There are benefits in circulating in that students have independence, while you are still able to catch gaps in student understanding.

- Inner-outer circle: this is building on the classic oracy exercise where the inner circle engages while outer circle evaluates, coaches a partner or supports by passing notes. I'd recommend a procedure for 'tapping in or out' between the circles that fits within the Harkness principles and pairing this with discussion mapping.

## School Culture

Culture eats strategy for breakfast. Brian Mullgardt (2008) explains the early challenges of implementing Harkness, writing: 'While some schools have relied on the method for many years, others, like mine, have not. In such cases, introducing this style of learning, in which no student can hide, can be difficult if students aren't used to it, and making sure it's productive also presents challenges. However, once included in a curriculum it allows students to more deeply understand material and think for themselves.'

This is a sentiment I echo deeply – Harkness is powerful, but not a method to jump into cold. When I first launched Harkness as a head of sixth form I thought we had all the foundations ready. My school had invested heavily in oval tables and small class sizes. What we didn't have were students who were ready for the pedagogy. The results in that first year were mixed at best. We observed stilted and stiff seminars. When students were unprepared to do the work beforehand the result was often a superficial chat. In some classes, students were ill-prepared to share the spotlight, overwhelming their peers. In other cases students were reticent to contribute at all. Similarly, Mullgardt (2008) acknowledged that before fully embracing Harkness he had 'come to view discussion based teaching as slow death, doled out in fifty minute blocks characterized by silence, blank stares, and lidded eyes'. Teachers automatically reverted back to dominating the conversation, or standing and expounding, or the pattern of explain-activity-assign-assess that depended on the instructor to lead.

The table is the central metaphor of Harkness, but as Guy Williams (2014) points out: 'An understanding of Harkness requires more than a furniture supplier—it requires a consideration of the educational culture or ethos where it is employed. Because I think it has value as a pragmatic approach above all else, I would also advocate that discussions move beyond simply talking about "Harkness lessons" towards inculcating a school-wide "Harkness culture".' Buy-in requires practice and willpower, so while Harkness discussion can be launched gradually, these sessions should also be frequent to be effective. One of the best pieces of advice is to not 'go at it' alone, but instead to introduce with colleagues to reinforce the format and expectations (Mullgardt, 2008). Enthusiasm is necessary for consistent application and engagement. It was following a Harkness review of our sixth form that I took stock and realised that both students and teachers required a toolbox of exercises to build up authentic Harkness lessons. I'd recommend embedding these over years and across key stages. The toolbox can commence upon entry to secondary school to layer the skills, forge the emotional maturity and set the tone.

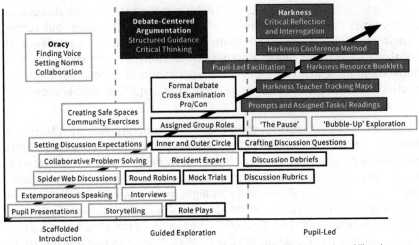

The goal is to experiment with techniques that work in the context of your school and subject, so these skills and intellectual risk-taking develop within pupils over time. These activities can be scaffolded; not every class is expected to be pure Harkness Conference Method.

**Figure 7.3 The Harkness spectrum toolbox by M. Whitfield.**

The engine of the school is in those formative years *before* high-stakes exams, so let's strengthen capacity further down the school. Purposely integrating discourse into our pedagogy can be established early on. For instance, exploratory talk in relation to a complex stimulus is at the heart of Philosophy for Children – a pedagogy that can be implemented in primary schools. Teachers use open-ended questions and there is a snowballing of student discussion in pairs, larger groups and then whole classes to gain consensus. A study of Philosophy for Children in Scotland found gains in cognition that were sustained into later stages of secondary. Alongside this, socio-emotional aspects of learning also improved (Topping and Trickey, 2014). Create a timeline with stakeholders to realise a Harkness vision. At my school we wrote a Harkness guide as an introduction – teachers gave formats of how Harkness worked in their subject areas and provided example prompts; students described their experience and offered practical advice on how to embrace the philosophy. We learned to build a Harkness atmosphere before students had Harkness conferences.

The benefits of the conference method depend on how adeptly we implement it. There was a small but interesting study that compared traditional lectures to group discussion and found no difference in total score upon assessment. However, group discussion produced significantly more learning in higher level thinking items (Garside, 1996). That is not to say that group discussion always leads to higher attainment or deeper critical thinking, but rather that in the undertaking, there is an ethos that is built – an alliance of collaborative learners. When Harkness thrives, there is increased depth in understanding, enhanced motivation, application of conceptual thinking, abstract analysis, emotional regulation, metacognitive deliberation and *community actualisation*.

I often think of the Blackfoot conception of community. Abraham Maslow's hierarchy of needs is topped with self-actualisation, where a person finds purpose and fulfilment. This psychological framing is part of motivational theory and certainly an aspiration of education. But it is also incomplete. Maslow was crucially influenced by his eight-week stay with the Blackfoot in Siksika in 1938 (Heavy Head and Blood, 2007). Cindy Blackstock of the Gitksan First Nation points out that: 'First of all, the triangle is not a triangle. It's a tipi. And the tipis in the Blackfoot (tradition) always went up and reached up to the skies.' Maslow's individualistic approach put self-actualisation at the top. For the Blackfoot people, self-actualisation was the beginning. Community actualisation and cultural perpetuity were the goals (Michel, 2014).

The intention is to create communal cooperation, collective responsibility, trust, sharing and equality over individualism and competition. Teju Ravilochan (2021a) explains that: 'In tending to our basic needs and safety, the tribe equips us to manifest our sacred purpose, designing a model of education that supports us in expressing our gifts. Community actualization describes the Blackfoot goal that each member of the tribe manifest their purpose.' Cultural perpetuity is the long view of generations, the communal wisdom enshrined and passed down as cultural care. Maslow himself critiqued self-actualisation as an end goal in 1966, writing: 'The good of other people must be invoked as well as the good for oneself. It is quite clear that purely inter-psychic individualist psychology without reference to other people and social conditions is not adequate' (Ravilochan, 2021b). We want generations that nourish each other. The Blackfoot model is inspiring.

While Harkness can empower students to speak up, I'd put forward that intrapersonal skills and an institutional ethos of collaboration should be packaged as the larger aim. A deeper, richer, nobler, kinder school is the ultimate goal. From a student perspective, Gloria Gong wrote of her experience:

> 'What are students doing at a Harkness table? Are we competitors for attention, jostling each other in a narrow field? Are we debate partners refining each other's ideas? Are we delegates at a convention striving to reach consensus? Are we actors auditioning for roles? Are we advocates of our diverse viewpoints, or mediators seeking common exchange?
>
> Are we fulfilling Edward Harkness' dream of creating a place that is safe for all who want to learn to share difficulties without fear?
>
> The amazing thing is that all these layers exist at once. One person can be drifting off into a daydream while another suddenly connects with the material in a personal and powerful way. One can be straining to meet whimsical expectations, while another undermines productive conversation. One can be listening intently to another who is struggling to speak. While we have agreed to confine ourselves to certain roles—students and teachers—and certain texts, the rest of the experience is ours to create. Harkness can be whatever we make it.' (Gong, 2006)

The intellectual freedom we give students is often constricted by curriculum and time. However, we can experiment with pedagogy that expands the sphere students inhabit. Building on this tenet, let's look at ventures that are open to all students, exploratory in nature and go beyond the taught curriculum. We can build space in the classroom to strive and thrive. Our next enrichment endeavour is long-term projects for slow learning and mastery.

# Reference List

Backer, D. (2016) 'The conference method, or Harkness pedagogy: Listening for discussion.' In: Waks, L. (ed.) *Listening to Teach: Beyond Didactic Pedagogy*. Albany, NY: State University of New York Press.

Barbieri, M. and Light, P. (1992) 'Interaction, gender, and performance on a computer-based problem solving task.' *Learning and Instruction*, 2(3): pp. 199–213.

Botkin, K. (2017) *Use of the Harkness method in the mathematics classroom*. Available at: https://capstone.extension.harvard.edu/files/capstone/files/harkness_method_capstone_paper_kyle_botkin.pdf (Accessed: 10 May 2024).

Bourne, R. (1916) 'On discussion', *The New Republic*, 27 May, [Online]. Available at: https://newrepublic.com/article/79806/discussion (Accessed: 23 July 2023).

Cazden, C. (2001) 'Variations in lesson structure.' In: *Classroom Discourse: The Language of Teaching and Learning*, 2nd ed. Portsmouth: Heinemann. Available at: https://people.wou.edu/~girodm/library/cazden.pdf (Accessed: 23 July 2023).

Equity Maps iPad App. (2016) *Equity maps*. Available at: www.youtube.com/watch?v=-oXH1vEmExk (Accessed: 23 July 2023).

Garside, C. (1996) 'Look who's talking: A comparison of lecture and group discussion teaching strategies in developing critical thinking skills.' *Communication Education*, 45(3): pp. 212–227.

Gillies, R. M. (2016) 'Dialogic interactions in the cooperative classroom.' *International Journal of Educational Research*, 76: pp. 178–189.

Gong, G. (2006) 'Power at the table', *Exeter Review*, fall issue. Available at: www.exeter.edu/sites/default/files/documents/Revolution-Power-at-table.pdf (Accessed: 23 July 2023).

Heavy Head, R. and Blood, N. (2007) 'Blackfoot influence on Abraham Maslow' [recorded presentation], University of Montana, 27 October. Available at: www.blackfootdigitallibrary.com/digital/collection/bdl/id/1296/rec/1 (Accessed: 23 July 2023).

Hiza, M. (2015) 'Reflections on teaching.' In Cadwell, J. S. and Quinn, J. (eds.) *A Classroom Revolution: Reflections on Harkness Learning and Teaching*. Exeter: Phillips Exeter Academy. Available at: www.exeter.edu/sites/default/files/documents/Revolution-Reflections-teaching.pdf (Accessed: 23 July 2023).

Lancaster, J. (2020) *The concise EHI experience guide to Harkness for high school teachers*. Available at: https://docs.google.com/document/d/1aNKUnvZKOYf8GPCcyjfmsrlI-CkkMd7v9VNZnKBUwal/edit (Accessed: 23 July 2023).

Lemov, D. (2015) *Teach Like a Champion 2.0: 62 Techniques that Put Students on the Path to College*. San Francisco, CA: Jossey-Bass.

Makar, K. and Allmond, S. (2018) 'Creating a culture of productive classroom talk.' *Australian Maths Teacher,* 74(4): pp. 19–25.

Mercer, N. (2008) 'Talk and the development of reasoning and understanding.' *Human Development,* 51(1): pp. 90–100.

Michaels, S., O'Connor, C. and Resnick, L. B. (2007) 'Deliberative discourse idealized and realized: Accountable talk in the classroom and in civic life.' *Studies in Philosophy and Education,* 27: pp. 238–297.

Michel, K. L. (2014) 'Maslow's hierarchy connected to Blackfoot beliefs', *A Digital Native American,* 19 April. Available at: https://lincolnmichel.wordpress.com/2014/04/19/maslows-hierarchy-connected-to-blackfoot-beliefs/ (Accessed: 23 July 2023).

Moll, L. C. and Whitmore, K. F. (2013) 'Vygotsky in classroom practice: Moving from individual transmission to social transaction.' In: Faulkner, D., Littleton, K., and Woodhead, M. (eds.) *Learning Relationships in the Classroom.* New York, NY: Routledge.

Mullgardt, B. (2008) 'Introducing and using the discussion (AKA Harkness) table.' *National Association of Independent Schools,* fall issue. Available at: www.nais.org/magazine/independent-teacher/fall-2008/introducing-and-using-the-discussion-(aka-harkness/ (Accessed: 23 July 2023).

Phillips Exeter Academy. (n.d.) *Harkness teaching tools.* Available at: www.exeter.edu/programs-educators/harkness-outreach/harkness-teaching-tools (Accessed: 23 July 2023).

Polm, M. (2019) *Using the Harkness method to teach the news.* Available at: www.closeup.org/using-the-harkness-method-to-teach-the-news/ (Accessed: 23 July 2023).

Ravilochan, T. (2021a) 'Maslow got it wrong', *Paces Connection,* 26 April. Available at: www.pacesconnection.com/blog/ravilochan-maslow-got-it-wrong (Accessed: 23 July 2023).

Ravillochan, T. (2021b) 'The Blackfoot wisdom that inspired Maslow's hierarchy', *Resilience,* 18 June. Available at: www.resilience.org/stories/2021-06-18/the-blackfoot-wisdom-that-inspired-maslows-hierarchy/ (Accessed: 23 July 2023).

Shapiro, S. (2024) 'The Harkness method – introduction and teaching a Harkness class', *The Learner Club,* 21 March. Available at: www.thelearnerclub.com/harkness-method (Accessed: 10 May 2024).

Soutter, M. and Clark, S. (2021) 'Building a culture of intellectual risk-taking: Isolating the pedagogical elements of the Harkness method.' *Journal of Education,* 203(3): pp. 1–12.

Topping, K. J. and Trickey, S. (2014) 'The role of dialog in philosophy for children.' *International Journal of Educational Research,* 63: pp. 69–78.

Towler, K. (2006) 'History of Harkness: The people behind the plan', *The Exeter Bulletin,* fall issue. Available at: www.exeter.edu/news/history-harkness (Accessed: 23 July 2023).

Williams, G. (2014) 'Harkness learning: Principles of a radical American pedagogy.' *Journal of Pedagogical Development,* 4(3). Available at: www.beds.ac.uk/jpd/volume-4-issue-3/harkness-learning-principles-of-a-radical-american-pedagogy/ (Accessed: 23 July 2023).

# 8. SLOW BUILD UP TO A BIG BOOM

*Creativity involves breaking out of expected patterns in order to look at things in a different way.*

**Edward De Bono, 1990**

*Learning autonomy for me is a goal of education rather than a procedure or a method.*

**Leslie Dickinson, 1994, p. 5**

*Indeed, the business of education might be defined as just such an emancipation and enlargement of experience.*

**John Dewey, 1910, p. 156**

When I saw two 12-year-old boys on stage comprehensively explaining string theory, I was gobsmacked. I didn't think they would speak so knowledgeably and extensively on the topic. They bounced ideas back and forth, used analogies to make the concepts come alive, quoted research and debated evidence that the universe is made of strings, laying bare the antagonism between general relativity and quantum mechanics. The physics teacher poked me in the ribs – did I teach them this? I asked him the same thing in return. Six months earlier I had challenged these students to do a project of their choosing. I didn't realise how ambitious they would be. Thinking back on the memory today, I Googled 'when do students learn quantum mechanics in physics British curriculum' and found that the first result was from the University of Oxford: 'Philosophy of Physics runs through the first three years of the course. In the first year, students delve into 18th-century investigations into matter and motion. In Years 2 and 3 they investigate the philosophical foundations of relativity' (University of Oxford, 2023). The next few top search results reiterated that the topic was generally explored in the first or second years of university at Stanford, MIT and the University of Manchester. While my students weren't quite quantum physicists (yet) they went far beyond any expectation I had of them.

An ecosystem of depth and complexity creates conditions for students to develop expertise. Authors Jal Mehta and Sarah Fine (2019) distil deeper learning into three domains – identity, mastery and creativity. Identity is pitched as student choice, where students wonder who they may become and what they care about. This is oft-repeated advice when designing extension and enrichment – let students' passion and interest lead. Fine describes mastery as:

> '... developing really rich conceptual knowledge and ability to execute something in some domain. Actually being able to do the work of a discipline, to think in the ways of that field or discipline ... getting how something works, not just knowing a bunch of disconnected stuff. So, for example, understanding the role of the human heart in the body is not just about being able to label where the human heart is on a diagram or being able to spit out a definition. It's actually systems knowledge that's connected to other pieces of knowledge.' (Gonzalez, 2023)

Mastery is the building of knowledge so that it can be abstracted and applied in different or larger contexts. The third domain is creativity, which is not just being a recipient of knowledge, but taking the initiative to transform it. To create something new. When I read about these interconnected domains, it hit me that this is what I had seen for years. Long-term projects require thoughtful design, the embedding of skills and an authentic audience of stakeholders – ideally some with expertise – to present to.

Similar to Fine's observation of deeper learning domains, Renzulli's Schoolwide Enrichment Triad Model is a wonderful place to start when developing a framework. This takes the theory and places it into discrete, but reinforcing, activities. The model was designed to 'encourage the creative productivity of young people by exposing them to various topics, areas of interest, and fields of study, and to further train them to *apply* advanced content, process-training skills, and methodology training to self-selected areas of interest' (University of Connecticut, n.d.). Accordingly, the three types of enrichment are interlocking, with exploration (Type I), collaboration (Type II) and investigation (Type III).

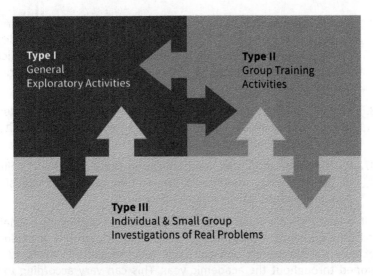

**Figure 8.1 Schoolwide Enrichment Triad Model (Renzulli, 1976).**

Renzulli's Type I (exploration) is designed to expose students to a wide variety of disciplines, topics, persons, places and events that would not ordinarily be covered in the regular curriculum. For example, an 'extension station' is set up in the classroom. This encourages students to elaborate on ideas introduced in the curriculum so that they can construct new schemas – an overriding challenge that can consolidate that knowledge or place it in situ. Exposure to new fields can be done through a lecture series, learning carousels or thematic learning, allowing students to scout different areas of scholarship. This is where we can build that environment of complexity.

Type II is collaborative endeavours pursued through group training activities. These can be carried out both in classrooms and in enrichment programmes. This is where students build skills, and critique and interact with the knowledge gained in Type I activities. Many of the strategies outlined in the previous chapter can be used in groups. These are the perfect places for students to practise 21st century competencies. These activities hone:

1. The development of creative thinking, problem solving, critical thinking and affective processes (e.g. cognitive training and analysis skills, concept mapping, backwards problem solving, brainstorming, classifying, determining cause and effect, inductive and deductive thinking, identifying pros and cons, elaborative thinking, judging credibility)

231

2. A wide variety of specific how-to-learn skills (e.g. listening, observing, perceiving, parsing what is relevant and irrelevant, noting subtleties, making inferences, logically organising and analysing, predicting outcomes, sequencing, data-gathering, field-testing, summarising) (Burns, 1994)

3. Skills in the appropriate use of advanced-level reference materials (e.g. media analysis, contrasting evidence, judging reliability or provenance, identifying human and material resources)

4. Written, oral and visual communication skills (e.g. oracy, delivery of presentations, multimedia preparation, writing of expository, persuasive, descriptive or narrated work).

Type III is where we can build structures for long arcs of challenge. Whether establishing enrichment programmes outside the classroom or extension projects in the classroom, you can have focused skillsets explored and developed throughout the academic year. This can vary according to the context of your school and students. For instance, at my current school, we focus on oracy, enquiry and creativity. This has translated into three large initiatives, one for each school term. There are many variations on these themes. I'd like to explore my favourite and most effective approaches, which require building up knowledge and skills, periods of exploration and mastery, and then independence. Let's look at the implementation, and impact, of project-based learning.

# Project-Based Learning

Project-based learning (PBL) can take many forms. It has been used in every stage of schooling from primary to university. There are many 'types' of project-based learning, with slightly different takes on the same idea – we have variations on enquiry-based learning, problem-based learning, Genius Hours and passion projects. PBL can take the shape of a personalised-learning curriculum, where in-depth studies may culminate in presentation, publication, competition, original products or solutions to real-world problems. The pedagogy of student-centred PBL has garnered significant attention in the field of education due to its potential to elevate both learning experiences and outcomes.

Tom Sherrington has perhaps summarised open-ended projects best when writing that we can begin with the instructions: 'Dazzle me' (Sherrington, 2017). Exceptional work happens when we take the lid off learning and allow students the freedom to be remarkable. David Didau extols the power of PBL as a strategy for slow learning, writing: 'The idea is that if students are given time, resources and lots of feedback they can produce beautifully presented work of breathtaking complexity' (Didau, 2012a).

There are proven educational benefits of project-based learning. Studies indicate that PBL enhances student achievement, promotes the development of essential skills, fosters engagement and improves knowledge retention. Implementing PBL in educational settings provides students with more authentic, deep and relevant learning. A literature review by Thomas (2000) analysed 222 research studies on PBL and found consistent positive effects on student achievement, knowledge retention and the development of critical thinking and adeptness in problem solving. The study also highlighted the positive impact of PBL on student motivation and engagement. A related study by the same authors examined the effects of PBL in the US context of No Child Left Behind, and there was a demonstrated positive effect on 21st century skills and academic outcomes. The same research also showed a positive correlation between PBL implementation and standardised test scores (Holmes, 2012).

There are differences that allow us to play within the structure, context and priorities of a school. How much time in the curriculum can we devote? Is PBL embedded as extension in a class or part of an extracurricular opportunity? Is PBL a major component of assessment? Is PBL evaluated through an authentic audience of external experts? Is PBL a part of the course? Is it a strand of an enrichment programme or a part of a subject's curriculum? We see PBL nested in diploma programmes (like the International Baccalaureate (International Baccalaureate Organization, 2023a)), or as a key assessment component in subject courses (Independent Study Units in the Ontario curriculum) (Centennial Collegiate Vocational Institute, n.d.), or as separate research qualifications – like the UK Extended Project Qualification (Assessment and Qualification Alliance, 2023). Students can even access PBL through external competitions – like the Regeneron Science Talent Search (Regeneron, 2023) or the MIT Think Scholars Program (MIT Think, 2022).

PBL can be individual or collaborative, where pairs, small groups or whole classes can work together. I remember doing a whole class 'news report' in Grade 7 where in small groups we reported on different eras in Canadian history. We collectively decided on the focus, divided into specialities, then recorded and pieced together the segments. The fact that this remains in my memory today is a testament to PBL's impact. The details of the history project are fuzzy but the research and communication skills made an indelible imprint on me. This is not an isolated experience. Shin's research revealed that PBL significantly enhanced students' intrinsic motivation, interest and enjoyment of learning compared to traditional instruction methods (Shin, 2018). Research in science instruction found that PBL increased knowledge retention over time (Blumenfeld et al., 1991; Blumenfeld et al., 2000). So how can project-based learning be done well?

At its heart PBL is student-centred learning. There are core principles that, when embraced, create a more engaging, meaningful and student-driven educational experience. Let's look at how these principles can be executed best. Not every component needs to be introduced – there is a reason that we parse the differences between enquiry-based learning projects and problem-based learning projects. Depending on our subjects, students, curriculum and school structures there are a plethora of ways to design PBL. While each principle is worthy of consideration, there are consistent elements as to what makes effective design.

## Sovereignty

When students have sovereignty there is a new dimension to the learning and skills developed: they are self-governing. Project-based learning consciously gives students choice in their project. At every level and at each stage the student can be put in the position of control, whether establishing the criteria, choosing the topic, setting the goals, driving the progress, mapping the timeline or deciding on the end product. The role of the teacher shifts from being the sole source of knowledge to that of a guide. Teachers provide mentorship, support and resources, fostering a learner-centred environment. Students derive power from this agency. It is also a direct route to personalisation.

It is important to note that a 'project' is not project-based learning. We assign projects all the time. In a project, the focus is on the final *product* based on directions and clear criteria. Projects tend to be assigned uniformly with the topics and structures narrowly defined. A project assignment could be an in-class presentation on the Weimer Republic, a reinterpretation of a monologue from *Hamlet* or creating a website on digital governance. The parameters are highly prescriptive in assessment and how students can demonstrate proficiency (Pearson Education Ltd, 2017). There may be an argument that PBL is evident in coursework. However, this depends on the limitations of student choice and the confines of the product. For instance, in geography fieldwork you may get the scope to choose, but it is between either glacial or coastal landscapes. While the curriculum aims to develop deeper learning and 21st century skills, it is circumscribed. There can be valuable enquiry, but it is heavily directed. These projects and coursework are great parts of our curriculum and instruction but are not exactly project-based learning.

The main difference is that in project-based learning the focus is on students' autonomy over learning. Once an essential question is chosen, teachers facilitate the process of student interrogation and experimentation. There is a line of constructivism that goes all the way back to the work of John Dewey – where students start with their foundational understanding, then construct knowledge by defining problems, creating hypotheses and using their own observations to build new schemas (Dewey, 1910). Dewey looks at how students move from concrete to abstract thinking: 'Power in action requires some largeness and imaginativeness of vision. Men must at least have enough interest in thinking for the sake of thinking to escape the limits of routine and custom. Interest in knowledge for the sake of knowledge, in thinking for the sake of the free play of thought, is necessary then to the emancipation of practical life—to make it rich and progressive' (Dewey, 1910, p. 139). Johann Friedrich Herbart, the German philosopher and educationalist, believed that the process of developing character begins with the student's interest. He viewed interest as based first on direct experiences of the natural world and second on social interactions with peers and teachers (Bybee et al., 2006). He argued that when students are personally invested in what they are learning, their curiosity and enthusiasm are naturally heightened, leading to more effective learning outcomes. Herbart emphasised the idea that education should be student-centred and tailored to individual interests and abilities. When students have the freedom to explore topics of personal interest, they develop a deeper understanding, make connections to their own experiences and are more likely to retain the knowledge and skills acquired. Additionally, Herbart argued that allowing students to pursue their interests enhances their sense of autonomy and agency, which in turn contributes to their character (Center for Teaching and Learning, n.d.).

PBL is best when students have choice. There is a difficult needle to thread, as Debbie Light notes:

> 'Setting up choice can be a tricky one to get right and, if done badly, can be detrimental to stretch and challenge if students choose less cognitively demanding tasks. Effectively incorporating choice means setting the bar high and expecting all students to produce excellent work but acknowledging the route to producing this work may be different depending on the students' needs.' (Light, 2017)

There is a feeling of risk when we, as teachers, give students free rein, whether in topic, process or end product. I have often found that when I'm not familiar with a topic a student is pursuing that counter-intuitively I want to assert control – to make sure that they keep to terrain I am confident in; that way I know they are 'on track'. However, it is when I let go that magic happens. That is when I see a student code a cryptocurrency, build hard engineering solutions in Minecraft, or design a board game that is later patented and sold to a toy company.

Student-centred learning asks that we be an advocate as opposed to an overseer – that education is a long conversation led by the learner. Giving students ownership also means giving them accountability. This brings us to the next principle of great PBL.

## Unstructured Structure

The term 'unstructured structure' may seem contradictory, as structure typically implies organisation, order and a rigid framework. However, in certain contexts, 'unstructured structure' refers to a flexible and adaptable framework that allows for freedom and creativity within a loosely defined layout. It can be seen as a balance between providing some guidelines or boundaries while also allowing room for exploration and individuality. Great PBL finds the balance. In educational settings, unstructured structure can be applied when students are given the freedom to choose their subjects, methods and products within a general set of guidelines. This can ensure the project is aligned with objectives, but it also allows students to pursue their own unique paths within those boundaries. There is research that suggests that students benefit more from unstructured projects than highly structured ones:

> '... open ended projects require students to consider assumptions and constraints, as well as to frame the problem they are trying to solve. Unstructured projects thus require students to do their own "structuring" of the problem at hand – a process that has been shown to enhance students' abilities to transfer learning to other problem solving contexts.' (Center for Teaching and Learning, n.d., p. 4)

There is much disdain for lightweight projects with a new-age feel that go on forever, keeping students busy but not learning. Making a tri-fold poster board 'pretty' can take up far more effort that could be dedicated to deeper learning. Students can go off-course and lack the media literacy to find what's truly happening beneath the surface. There is the very real danger of creating pabulum – an information dump where learners simply regurgitate facts. I remember spending hours as a kid copying notes from encyclopaedias and old National Geographic articles in the school library, then refashioning these summaries onto a neat poster board. I recall devoting an entire Saturday to dying paper into a sepia tone with tea and painstakingly using calligraphy to slightly reword a biography on Vivaldi. It looked amazing but did not reflect any deep insight.

Right before writing this chapter, I received an email from a Year 9 student that reminded me how *quality learning* can be achieved. She apologised profusely for writing on the weekend before launching a litany of questions about her upcoming exhibition project. I was thrilled; the queries were great. Half of them indicated depth, one was a tangent that needed pruning, one allowed me to challenge her assumptions and one indicated that she was spending time on a superficial aspect of the work. The trick to sovereignty is communication. The largest freedom is the open space to ask questions. Students will thrive when they have checklists (clear direction) and check-ins (personal guidance). The teacher acts as a facilitator who aids in framing, developing the plans, supplying examples and setting benchmarks. Formal and informal opportunities to interact and discuss will keep enthusiasm and expectations high. I currently spend a lot of time during my morning gate duty simply asking students how their enrichment projects are going. It is far more effective than any online nudges or emails. Sometimes you will have students who pepper you with questions. They may need to be pointed in the right direction, while at the same time, you make sure they don't become dependent on you to drive their work. You may have students who are eerily quiet, and you need to go out of your way to shine some sunlight on their progress.

Unstructured structure encourages self-directed learning while still maintaining a sense of purpose and direction. It is important to plan milestones for students, set goals with them and provide the framework. This can be achieved through anchor charts, graphic organisers or reflection journals so that students can record their progress. I like to use exemplars from the onset – a large presentation board with sections to show introduction, key questions, sub-questions, research/literature review, methodology/investigation design, implementation, analysis, implications and conclusions. Co-creating a learning intention gives students ownership. Continuous assessment and feedback are at the core of the process. Student-centred learning focuses on formative assessments, allowing for ongoing feedback and opportunities for improvement. It includes self-assessment, peer assessment and teacher feedback, providing a comprehensive view of student progress. One-on-one or small group conferences to share updates and progress are effective. The onus is on students to present their findings, share frustrations, ask questions and be active participants. PBL allows them to take a personalised path, which can help students feel seen and catered for.

A notable example of an unstructured structure is Genius Hours. Genius Hours (also called 20% time) were popularised by companies like Google, where employees were given opportunities to work on personal passion projects that existed outside of their typical work day. These projects were shown to increase productivity and creatively engage people. They have now been hyped in education as a great way for students to pursue a topic that interests them (McNair, 2022). Genius Hours are embedded into curriculum planning so that students have time to devote and space to decide. The emphasis is on empowering students by giving them choices in the topic and end product. Focus for students is autonomy, mastery and purpose. Genius Hours are by nature more open-ended – an example is the Three-Rules Genius Hour (Schneider, 2018):

1. Students must start with an essential question that cannot be answered with a simple Google search.

2. Students must research their question using reputable sources.

3. Students must create something. Their product may be digital, physical or service-oriented.

Ideally, we want scaffolding to make 'passion-based' learning manageable and meaningful. Project proposal forms, timelines and reflection journals can all be used to monitor, track progress and direct students. Andi McNair's book on Genius Hour Passion Projects provides students with a 6P map to follow as they create, design and carry out projects (McNair, 2022, p. 4).

**Passion:** What do you want to learn about? Why do you think it is interesting? What impact can it have? What can you create that is new?

**Plan:** What is the timeline? What goals have you set? Who will be your outside expert? What materials will you need to complete the project?

**Pitch:** How will you share ideas with the class? How will you get us on board?

**Project:** What do you need today to move forward? What are you creating, making or designing?

**Product:** What did you create? What can you show us to demonstrate your learning?

**Presentation:** Can you share your ideas or project with others? What tools will you use to make your presentation engaging for the audience?

Students can use designated 'hours' throughout the year to develop their personal projects. McNair notes that the emphasis is on student ownership and teacher as facilitator, writing:

> *'Genius Hour or any type of student-driven learning experience doesn't mean that students are working and we, as teachers, sit back and hope connections are made. Our role has simply changed. Instead of designing a one-size-fits-all lesson for our students, we teach by questioning and finding creative ways to weave the standards into each one of our learners' projects. We engage in conversations that help our students make connections and see the learning that might have been missed without our insight.' (McNair, 2022)*

End products are tangible evidence of creative productivity. Students can record a TED talk, bring a product to market, patent a design, write a play, build a website or app, create a sculpture or code a program. Projects can be tangentially related to the curriculum or pertinent to a specific subject. In either case, they can give T-shaped depth to your instruction. Creating space for unstructured structure opens up opportunities to go off-piste and expand the boundaries of the curriculum.

## Authenticity

Authenticity plays a massive role in project-based learning. This is underlined by Didau who notes:

> *'The main precept of PBL is that students' learning should be authentic. Most of what we get students to do in school is "pseudo-learning", that is to say, we as teachers create artificial problems for students to solve. This might be the maths problems which ask to calculate the mileage of imaginary train journeys, the production of a theatre programme for a non-existent production of a play, or the dried up twig of the speaking and listening assessment in which students are supposed to give a monkeys about something in front of a classful of their jeering peers. Either way, not good. ... (PBL) asks us, as teachers, to tap into a real issue in our community and then work out how we could get our students to interact with it in a meaningful way.' (Didau, 2012b)*

It works on several levels – ideally, the challenge should be authentic, the stakes should be authentic and the audience should be authentic. Learning experiences designed to be authentic are meaningful to students' lives. A great place to start is what is happening in the real world or what is happening right now in students' lives. They connect to real-world issues, contexts and applications, enabling them to see the relevance and purpose of their learning.

A great place to end is some type of symposium, where work is presented to the larger community, raising the stakes. This is also where external experts can be brought in to interview, interrogate, evaluate and engage with students on their work – a truly authentic audience. In my own experience, working towards a marquee event has always made PBL an extravaganza! Inviting parents and the community allows students to show off. Sarah Fine underlines this, writing: 'The difference between turning something in to your teacher and then getting a grade and performing or sharing that learning with an audience that is not just your teacher is really profound' (Gonzalez, 2023). This week I touched base with the judges for my school's upcoming annual enrichment exhibition – a diplomat, a nuclear engineer, a neurologist and a children's book author – all parents or friends of the school. In the past, I've invited professors from local universities, curators from a nearby museum, aquarium directors, sports stars, motivational speakers, founders of local charities and principals from neighbouring schools. When authenticity is embedded the expectations are kept high and the celebration of the work has weight. Problem-based learning in the form of challenges can be given an exhibition with models on display. Enquiry-based learning can be a demonstration showcase. Project-based learning can be presented at an end-of-year symposium. All are slightly different depending on how you wish to implement them.

## Jumping-Off Points

Project-based learning can be open-ended with a driving theme or 'essential' question. This is where a teacher can steer a student in a thought-provoking direction, while still empowering them to determine the research path. As mentioned, there should be clear structure, steps to follow and milestones – a framework to guide and set expectations for the quality of the finished product. Students will make the most of the agency they are given within guidelines.

Here are fundamentals for open-ended project-based learning:

1. **Organise tasks around a driving question:** Project work should start with an open-ended question that allows students to explore

and then find purpose. Students should narrow their investigation using sub-questions. An example driving question I used a few years ago was: 'As we begin to face up to the multiple economic, environmental and social challenges of our time, what innovations will offer solutions at the speed and scale required? How can we be creative? How can innovation further entrench elite power structures within society or break down these barriers?'

2. **Establish the gap in knowledge:** Once students have explored the driving question, they should investigate a gap in the research. This is the place where students can create a new approach, original technique, novel solution, practical invention or real-world application. They should engage in rigorous research where they understand the evolution of thought, develop expertise, utilise key concepts and deploy technical vocabulary.

3. **Make self-organisation explicit:** Project-based learning places the onus on students to develop project management skills. Self-regulation means that students take responsibility for planning the process, setting goals, establishing priorities, creating task checklists, mapping the deadlines, organising time, making effective use of resources, monitoring their progress and acknowledging when they need help or guidance. The Buck Institute is a fantastic place to start for PBL resources (Buck Institute for Education, n.d.).

It is important that students don't go too broad and get lost in the weeds. They should focus on a narrow gap in knowledge to investigate in-depth. Project-based learning emphasises a creative exploration. *Enquiry-based learning* and *problem-based learning* are closely related and can be integral jumping-off points for project-based learning, while PBL is a broader instructional approach. Enquiry- and problem-based learning methodologies can be employed within projects to enhance student engagement, critical thinking and deep understanding. One branch of PBL is a scientific examination through enquiry: 'If Inquiry Based Learning is about discovering an answer, Project Based Learning is about exploring an answer' (Winjigo, 2023).

## Enquiry-Based Projects

Enquiry-based learning is a student-centred process of discovery where students lead an investigation. Enquiry-based learning has been defined as 'a student-led process that begins with their own questions and wonderings. It is an approach to learning that emphasizes questions, ideas, and the natural curiosity of children. With inquiry-based learning, student questions are at the centre of their learning journey' (Victoria, 2023). Students can follow methods and practices similar to those of professional scientists in order to construct knowledge, formulate hypotheses and conduct experiments. Enquiry-based learning is a pedagogical technique that stimulates students to ask questions and explore problems on their own, rather than relying on the teacher for all the answers. What we as educators can do is provide a framework for enquiry-based learning by supplying students with relevant resources and guiding them through the problem-solving process. There are so many models of enquiry, each a little different in its approach and vocabulary. A fantastic review article by Pedaste et al. (2015) identified and summarised the core features of the enquiry learning process. This initially resulted in a list of 109 different terms and 34 sub-stages, which were then grouped into five enquiry phases: orientation, conceptualisation, investigation, conclusion and discussion. The amalgamated enquiry framework can be flexibly applied to build different pathways.

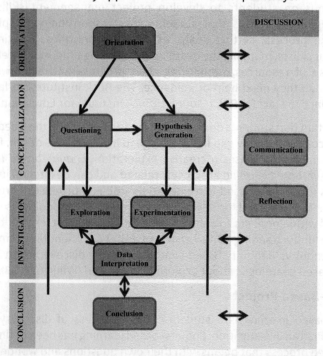

Figure 8.2 Enquiry-based learning framework (general phases, sub-phases, and their relations) (Pedaste et al., 2015).

Enquiry-based learning tends to be most associated with STEM or 'proof-based' subjects, with the aspiration to engage students in scientific discovery. However, it can be applied outside of these areas. 'The aim here is that students gain and develop their knowledge and skills through working extensively to investigate and respond in detail to an issue that's engaging and complex, rather than clear-cut' (Winjigo, 2023). Enquiry projects foster a curiosity about the world, asking students to go beyond knowledge acquisition to discover connection, meaning and resolution. Flexible and far-reaching, they ask the learner to look for links across disciplines and find causal relations. Learners can carry out a self-directed, inductive or deductive investigation, running trials to test dependent and independent variables (Pedaste et al., 2015). This is also why we need to find that sweet spot – with too broad a topic, students flounder in a sea of information.

Enquiry projects can be rooted in the curriculum. A great example is the International Baccalaureate (IB) Diploma. Enquiry-based projects take a student-centred approach where the instructor guides the students through developing an enquiry question, methodology design and data interpretation (Alper, 2018). In the IB Middle Years Programme there is a personal project for students to research their interests in a deeper and more detailed way. The project involves the enquiry cycle that 'provides an excellent opportunity for students to produce a truly personal and often creative product and to demonstrate a consolidation of their learning in the MYP while strengthening the skills they have developed' (International Baccalaureate Organization, 2022). In the secondary IB Diploma Programme there is a 'theory of knowledge' course followed by the extended essay – an independent, self-directed piece of research.

IB students are supported throughout the process of researching and writing the extended essay with advice and guidance from a mentor who is usually a teacher at the school. Students are required to have three mandatory reflection sessions. The final session, a concluding interview, is also known as viva voce – 'with living voice' they defend their work (International Baccalaureate Organization, 2023b). A Canadian study of the impact of the IB extended essay looked at undergraduate students' value of enquiry instruction and self-efficacy. Unsurprisingly, the study found a correlation between students who had the extended essay as a major academic requirement and those who rated enquiry instruction as very important (Lemay, 2013). What is fascinating is how the impact varied according to how it was implemented in individual IB schools. Where a school placed heavy emphasis on testing, it was difficult to build the trust, risk-taking and motivation necessary to engage students in enquiry units, projects or 'extended essays' that are inherently high in risk and ambiguity (Lemay, 2013). Having the extended essay in the curriculum is not the same as teachers investing in PBL. Doing enquiry projects right means giving students latitude. At the same time, enquiry as a foundation gives students a clear structure to build independent project management skills.

## Problem-Based Projects

Problem-based projects are easy to define – students are given an authentic real-world challenge and apply knowledge and skills to develop a viable solution. Using problems as a jumping-off point for project-based learning can drive innovation. While enquiry projects give structure, problem-based projects provide a defined prompt that can be taken in many directions. The goal is often for students to build a tangible, meaningful product (Victoria, 2023). Students can have wildly different takes and the diversity of solutions can demonstrate incredible ingenuity. Problem-based projects require students to analyse complex problems, think critically and develop effective solutions. Students engage in higher-order thinking processes such as analysis, evaluation and synthesis. As a pedagogical approach, the Boston University Center for Teaching and Learning uses a format that entails:

1. Identifying and defining problems in terms of given constraints or challenges.

2. Brainstorming and generating productive ideas for a given problem, devising a set of possible solutions and evaluating the best pathways and procedures.

3. Designing and prototyping the potential solutions to a problem. This is where detail is flushed out, assumptions are confronted, feedback is incorporated and challenges are overcome.

4. Testing the developed solution, products or services in a live setting or presentation.

Problem-based learning is not a 'surprise' challenge. It is effective when students have a contextual understanding of competing abstract theories that can be brought to life. The fun begins when students have an extensive knowledge base and high levels of confidence in a domain; then they have the acumen and tools to take on a problem-solving project (InnerDrive, 2022). From the offset, students should have 'too many ideas' and use a logical process to determine a strategy to solve the problem. Ideally, these problems should have many solutions or pathways to take.

We can provide case studies of actual problems where students must evaluate the roles of several players. We can encourage logical reasoning skills by posing backwards problem solving. (How did this design provide a solution? What was the original issue that needed addressing?) Engineering, coding and model building can involve trial and error. It is always fun to gamify a challenge and incentivise risk-taking. It is easy to pigeonhole problem-solving projects as a STEAM activity. However, it can be applied to creating abstract systems (e.g. design an international body that is more effective than the current United Nations; create a scheme to deliver meaningful reparations; draft a policy to address healthcare inequity within a capitalist system). These prompts can be adapted to paired or group work with a pivot towards collaboration and communication. How did the group capitalise on each other's strengths? Were there defined roles and were these effective? How did the group influence or change your perspective? Real-world relevance adds a layer of complexity. By working on pertinent and complex issues, students can see the practical applications of their work, which leads to deeper understanding and retention. Problem solving should be difficult; however, it is important that we give students a method and that we teach within a specific context (University of Waterloo, n.d.). To scaffold this, you can use guiding prompts (Figure 8.3).

| Identify and define the main problem | • What is the larger purpose of this challenge? |
| --- | --- |
| | • What are the known concepts? What do I already know or recognise about the topic? |
| | • What is the end goal? |
| | • What are the criteria for success? |
| Information needed to solve the problem | • What is unknown? What makes me wonder? |
| | • What key questions can I ask? |
| | • How does this connect to my prior knowledge? |
| | • What are the constraints? |
| | • What are the most important concepts? What are the less significant details? |
| | • What research should I conduct? |
| | • Where can I find the necessary information to answer key questions? |
| | • What are the parameters for this research so I remain on topic? |

| Devise a solution | • What would happen if …?<br>• What strategies can I use? What is the rationale for these strategies?<br>• What principles apply?<br>• What are similar problems and how have they been solved?<br>• What are the potential pitfalls or traps? What could go wrong?<br>• How can I divide this into steps? What are the sub-goals for solving the problem? |
|---|---|
| Actions to reach solution | • How do I implement? What are the steps and in which order?<br>• What is the model or procedure?<br>• How can I test and evaluate each step along the way?<br>• What is the best strategy?<br>• Am I taking the time to pause and reflect on what is working or not working? |
| Difficulties and steps to overcome | • Why is this problem difficult?<br>• What errors did I make?<br>• How can I be more elegant or efficient?<br>• What misconceptions should we correct?<br>• What are alternative methods? Are the steps I devised working?<br>• Who or where can I go for help? |
| Impact of solution and measuring effectiveness (Victoria State Government, 2019) | • How do I draw conclusions?<br>• Does this meet the success criteria I set out?<br>• Could I have approached this problem differently?<br>• What did I learn from the process?<br>• How can I apply this later or in another context? |

Figure 8.3 Self-reflective prompts for problem-based projects.

Problem and enquiry-based learning can transform entire instructional units into projects, beginning with a driving question and culminating in challenge, development of subject expertise, response, critique and reflection rolled out in phases. These questions throughout can drive the process and bring us to one of the key precepts for great project-based learning – the building of metacognitive strategies and self-regulated skills.

## Reflective Process and Metacognition

Metacognition has been hailed as the great leap forward. Embedding it brings cognitive science to life in our classrooms. It refers to the ability to reflect on one's own learning processes, and there is endless potential when students 'think about thinking'. By explicitly teaching metacognitive strategies and promoting self-regulatory behaviours, educators can empower students to become more effective learners, capable of monitoring their progress, adapting their strategies and achieving their academic goals. Metacognition is important as it asks students to be aware of procedures that enhance performance and then hone these skills. Students learn to reflect on *how* they tackled a challenge. Mark McDaniel and Gilles Einstein illustrate how the development of self-regulating learning takes more than knowledge and motivation (McDaniel and Einstein, 2020). They propose a practical theoretical framework called the knowledge, belief, commitment, and planning (KBCP) framework for guiding strategy training to promote students' successful self-regulation of effective learning strategies. The KBCP framework rests on the assumption that four essential components must be included in training to support sustained strategy self-regulation: a) acquiring knowledge about strategies, b) belief that the strategy works, c) commitment to using the strategy and d) planning of strategy implementation. In combination, this improves learners' subjective mental models of how to learn effectively, promotes conceptual change and drives behaviour.

Project-based learning places the onus on students to develop project management skills alongside self-awareness. Hattie's seminal meta-analysis revealed that metacognitive strategies, including self-regulation, self-monitoring and self-evaluation, had a substantial impact on student progress. His conclusions emphasised the importance of explicitly teaching metacognitive skills to empower students as active learners (Hattie, 2009). When gauging different types of feedback, Hattie found that focusing on metacognitive aspects, such as self-assessment, helped students develop a deeper understanding of their own learning processes and identify areas for improvement (Hattie and Timperley, 2007). Metacognition allows students to understand and control the ways they learn. A comprehensive review by Dunlosky et al. (2013) found significant positive effects of metacognitive strategies on learning outcomes. It observed that students who were taught metacognitive skills, such as goal setting, planning, monitoring and self-evaluation, consistently demonstrated improved academic performance across various subjects and age groups. Metacognition is embedded when students can use and explain specific strategies to achieve their goals, reflect on the process of learning and understand how to improve. A key component is student ownership over their own learning.

One systematic review examined studies related to learning environments for students with attention deficit hyperactivity disorder (ADHD). It emphasised the importance of incorporating metacognitive strategies and self-regulation techniques, such as goal setting and self-monitoring to support the academic success of students with ADHD and found that these strategies facilitated their engagement, self-control and learning outcomes (Byers et al., 2018). The Education Endowment Foundation (2023) has conducted extensive research on metacognition and self-regulation in education, finding that the average impact is an additional seven months' progress over the course of a year. Their analysis finds that metacognition is most effective when embedded in a school's curriculum and a specific subject lesson – the learning procedures a student uses to approach an English essay will be different to a method for solving linear equations in maths. Metacognitive strategies can also be effective when taught in collaborative groups so that learners can support each other and make their thinking explicit through discussion. The aim is for students to develop a repertoire of learning techniques, select their learning processes and seek feedback.

It is useful to also have metacognitive prompts highlighted for students to refer to throughout a project. Students should identify their thinking strategies, see areas for improvement in how they approach a problem and understand that they can find more elegant or efficient solutions.

An insightful exercise is to have students fill out a Metacognitive Awareness Inventory from the outset.[14] This can cue students to 'think about their thinking' as they embark and progress through their project. I like to use a sliding scale (1 for 'never', 5 for 'always') for the inventory as opposed to true/false, so that students can judge how often or how consciously they use metacognition. This is where the impact lies – a project is a vehicle for metacognition and self-regulation.

An effective approach to PBL places *process and reflection* at the core. There is pressure for students to feel 'correct' in academic settings. Process and reflection changes the emphasis and gives them the freedom to take risks. They don't have to be 'right' in their hypothesis; they just follow paths to a conclusion. A process-focused approach to PBL is beautifully demonstrated in British curriculum with the growing popularity of the Extended Project Qualification (EPQ). This is a standalone accreditation students can choose to showcase specialisation and research abilities. The EPQ has become increasingly relevant as a vehicle for bringing project-based learning into

---

14   The Metacognitive Awareness Inventory can be found in Schraw, G. and Dennison, R.S. (1994) 'Assessing metacognitive awareness.' *Contemporary Educational Psychology*, 19(4): pp. 460–475. It is also available at: https://advising.lafayette.edu/wp-content/uploads/sites/247/2021/10/metacognitive_awareness_inventory.pdf

mainstream schooling. Over the years in EPQ I've seen students investigate why there is a widespread belief in the conspiracy theories surrounding the JFK assassination, how we can use elephant's feet as inspiration when designing shoes and how to use game theory in university application. A recent Oxford AQA article (Drummond, 2023) expounded on 'why project-based learning is the key to university success', explaining that student-led projects nurture creativity and independent learning; 'students who participate in project-based learning qualifications alongside their A-levels are more likely to achieve better grades in their A-levels, perform better at university and experience higher levels of motivation in their studies.' Indeed, research has shown a significant correlation between completing an EPQ and higher degree performance in university (Gill, 2018). The 'Extending into the Future' report makes the connections between EPQs and future success explicit through multiple academic studies, concluding that 'the key message of this report is that the challenges of increasing competition for university places, the growing need for self-regulated and independent learners and a rapidly evolving job market, are best met by curricula containing a significant element of extended project work' (Drummond, 2023).

Most importantly, it is the process that is assessed in the end. EPQs are awarded based on how students reflect, evaluate and present their project planning, use of resources and research, development of an idea and production of an outcome (The Good Schools Guide, n.d.). Learners can write a thesis or create an artefact. It is the reflection that is assessed, so the students truly 'raise their heads above the parapet' when it comes to creative productivity. There is the opportunity for students to invent, make a guide, construct a model, film a documentary, record a podcast or create a piece of art. Throughout this pursuit, the qualification places a strong emphasis on the journey, rather than solely focusing on the final outcome. The process-oriented nature of the EPQ allows students to learn from their mistakes and make improvements. By reflecting on setbacks, receiving feedback and implementing revisions, students develop resilience.

The process is crucial because it promotes diagnostic thinking and adaptability, enhances research and information literacy, develops project management skills and allows for course correction. Students are required to assess their progress, judge the effectiveness of their research methods and identify their strengths and areas for improvement. Completing the project involves holistic ongoing self-evaluation. Self-regulation exists when students proactively take control. This involves governing one's emotions, behaviours and learning strategies to attain desired goals. When approaching an independent project there is an emotional component in controlling stress and recognising healthy boundaries. During PBL students may encounter challenges, setbacks or unexpected changes. Navigating through these situations requires agility and resilience. Celebrating the process encourages students to develop strategies for overcoming obstacles and finding alternative solutions.

## Conclusion: Learner Autonomy

My own learning was heavily influenced by project-based learning. I grew up in an age of the independent study unit (ISU). These projects were part of the Ontario curriculum and served as a pedagogical tool to promote student engagement and personalised learning. They were a core component of courses and the section of the syllabus I immediately flipped to. These embedded projects were 'challenge first' and 'not more, but interesting'. I was tackling bigger questions, specialising, creating, deciding, applying and flying all at the same time. Memories of these projects are indelibly impressed upon my mind.

Projects should encourage student choice and reading around the subject cross-curricular links. They should be pupil-driven with the freedom to choose content, pace and delivery. It is worth mentioning that the Autonomous Learner Model (ALM) by Betts and Kercher (2023) places depth studies as a core component for students' growth towards independent, self-directed learning. Fundamental to this model is a personalised curriculum, guided open-ended learning experiences for exploration and investigation, assessment of self-development and learner-created products. Completion of depth studies is integral to establishing lifelong learning skills.

The first objection to project-based learning is that there is no time to indulge in it. Time in education is a realignment of priorities, and educators are often incentivised towards test preparation over student choice in curriculum or pedagogical approaches. Ironically, the emphasis on test prep can be detrimental to results as well as whole-child development. The UChicago Consortium on School Research found in their 2008 report that teachers in the 409,000-student district would spend about one month of instructional time on ACT practice in the core classes offered during junior year. However, the ACT scores were lower in schools where 11th-grade teachers reported spending 40% of their time on test preparation, compared with schools where teachers devoted less than 20% of their class time to the ACT. The boredom factor was cited as an explanation for this seemingly counter-intuitive finding (UChicago Consortium on School Research, 2008). Learner autonomy is the ultimate goal of a project-based approach. Autonomy is essentially transforming the attitude towards learning from obedience to capacity. Students need opportunities to practise autonomy and develop individual responsibility. Learners understand this is not a licence to behave without constraint or to place them in isolation. Taking ownership of one's own learning involves 'informed autonomy', where the goal may begin as teacher-directed and then proceed as a cooperative enterprise, with learners progressively taking on more responsibility for their own learning. Leslie Dickinson has written beautifully on the topic:

> 'Those of us interested in autonomy believe that it is desirable that students ultimately become independent of teachers and teaching and become able to pursue learning projects autonomously. As teachers we do not want to be implicated in the development of teacher dependent adult students; we see the achievement of independence in learning as desirable—allowing the student to pursue his own learning objectives in ways and at times which most suit him, and so we adopt the additional teaching objective—to teach the student how to learn.'
> (Dickinson, 1994)

When students go beyond our expectations it's because we have given them the space to do so. I highly recommend that depth and complexity be shaped as long-term extension projects, building over a whole unit or even over a whole year. The issues or problems should be intricate. The skill building is done in layers, scaffolded, honed and practised, and steps are chunked. The research can then be thorough and vetted. Learners need time and space to mull, grapple and think deeply. You are not constantly adding those 'one-off' questions for extension, but instead having students persistently work towards a big multifaceted goal.

'Dazzling us' means that there are opportunities for depth and complexity to be integrated, highlighted and celebrated.

# Reference List

Alper, C. (2018) *Embacing inquiry-based instruction*. Available at: www.edutopia.org/article/embracing-inquiry-based-instruction/ (Accessed: 10 June 2023).

Assessment and Qualification Alliance. (2023) *Level 3 Extended Project Qualification*. Available at: www.aqa.org.uk/subjects/projects/project-qualifications/EPQ-7993/introduction (Accessed: 10 June 2023).

Betts, G. T. and Kercher, J. J. (2023) 'The development of the autonomous learner model for gifted and talented.' In: Renzulli, J. S., Gubbins, E. J., McMillen, K. S., Eckert, R. D. and Little, C. A. (eds.) *Systems and Models for Developing Programs for the Gifted and Talented*, 2nd edn. New York, NY: Routledge.

Blumenfeld, P. C., Soloway, E., Marx, R. W., Krajcik, J. S., Guzdial, M. and Palincsar, A. (1991) 'Motivating project-based learning: Sustaining the doing, supporting the learning.' *Educational Psychologist,* 26(3–4), pp. 369–398.

Blumenfeld, P., Fishman, B. J., Krajcik, J., Marx, R. W. and Soloway, E. (2000) 'Creating usable innovations in systemic reform: Scaling up technology-embedded project-based science in urban schools.' *Educational Psychologist,* 35(3): pp. 149–164.

Buck Institute for Education (n.d.) '*8 ways to get started with project based learning*. Available at: www.pblworks.org/get-started (Accessed: 10 June 2023).

Burns, D. E. (1994) 'Taxonomy of Type II process skills.' Available at: https://gifted.uconn.edu/schoolwide-enrichment-model/typeiips/ (Accessed: 10 June 2023).

Bybee, R. W., Taylor, J. A., Gardner, A., Van Scotter, P., Powell, J. C., Westbrook, A., Landes, N. (2006) 'BSCS 5E Instructional model: Origins, effectiveness, and applications.' *National Institutes of Health: Office of Science Education*. Colorado Springs, CO: BSCS. Available at: https://fremonths.org/ourpages/auto/2008/5/11/1210522036057/bscs5efullreport2006.pdf (Accessed: 10 June 2023).

Byers, T., Mahat, M., Liu, K., Knock, A. and Imms, W. (2018) *A systematic review of the effects of learning environments on student learning outcomes*. Melbourne: University of Melbourne. Available at: www.iletc.com.au/publications/reports/ (Accessed: 10 June 2023).

Centennial Collegiate Vocational Institute (n.d.) '2. Independent study unit (ISU).' Available at: www.ugdsb.ca/ccvi/course-websites/eng-4u1-home/units-of-study/independent-study-unit-isu/ (Accessed: 10 June 2023).

Center for Teaching and Learning (n.d.) 'Project-based learning: Teaching guide.' Available at: www.bu.edu/ctl/guides/project-based-learning/ (Accessed: 10 June 2023).

De Bono, E. (1990) *The Use of Lateral Thinking*. London, UK: Penguin UK.

Dewey, J. (1910) *How We Think*. USA: D.C. Heath & Co Publishers. Available at: https://pure.mpg.de/rest/items/item_2316308/component/file_2316307/content (Accessed: 10 June 2023).

Dickinson, L. (1994) 'Learner autonomy: what, why and how?' In: Leffa, V. J. (ed.) *Autonomy in Language Learning.* Brazil: Editora da Universidade Federal do Rio Grande do Sul, pp. 2–12.

Didau, D. (2012a) 'Slow learning – allowing students to achieve mastery', *Learning Spy,* 24 June. https://learningspy.co.uk/learning/slow-learning-allowing-students-to-achieve-mastery/ (Accessed: 10 June 2023).

Didau, D. (2012b) 'Project based learning: I did it my way', *Learning Spy,* 23 September. Available at: https://learningspy.co.uk/english-gcse/project-based-learning-i-did-it-my-way/ (Accessed: 10 June 2023).

Drummond, R. (2023) *Extending into the future.* Available at: www.oxfordaqa.com/wp-content/uploads/2023/05/OxdordAQA_Extending-into-the-Future_Digital_Singles.pdf (Accessed: 10 June 2023).

Dunlosky, J., Rawson, K. A., Marsh, E. J., Nathan, M. J. and Willingham, D. T. (2013) 'Improving students' learning with effective learning techniques: Promising directions from cognitive and educational psychology.' *Psychological Science in the Public Interest,* 14(1): pp. 4–58.

Education Endowment Foundation. (2023) *Metacognition and self-regulation.* Available at: https://educationendowmentfoundation.org.uk/education-evidence/teaching-learning-toolkit/metacognition-and-self-regulation (Accessed: 10 June 2023).

Gill, T. (2018) 'Preparing students for university study: A statistical comparison of different post-16 qualifications.' *Research Papers in Education,* 33(3): pp. 301–319.

Gonzalez, J. (2023) 'What is the secret sauce for deeper learning?' *Cult of Pedagogy,* 2 April. Available at: www.cultofpedagogy.com/deeper-learning/ (Accessed: 10 June 2023).

Hattie, J. A. C. (2009) *Visible Learning: A Synthesis of Over 800 Meta-analyses Relating to Achievement.* Abingdon, OX: Routledge.

Hattie, J. and Timperley, H. (2007) 'The power of feedback.' *Review of Educational Research,* 77(1): pp. 81–112.

Holmes, L. M. (2012) *The effects of project-based learning on 21st century skills and No Child Left Behind outcomes.* Dissertation. University of Florida.

InnerDrive. (2022) 'Cognitive load theory: A guide to the basics', *InnerDrive.* Available at: https://blog.innerdrive.co.uk/cognitive-load-theory-basics (Accessed: 10 June 2023).

International Baccalaureate Organization. (2022) 'From hair vitamins to a go-kart: One school's perspective of the MYP personal project', *The IB Community Blog,* 25 August. Available at: https://blogs.ibo.org/2022/08/25/from-hair-vitamins-to-a-go-kart-one-schools-perspective-of-the-myp-personal-project/ (Accessed: 10 June 2023).

International Baccalaureate Organization. (2023a) *CAS projects*. Available at: https://ibo.org/programmes/diploma-programme/curriculum/dp-core/creativity-activity-and-service/cas-projects/ (Accessed: 10 June 2023).

International Baccalaureate Organization. (2023b) *What is the extended essay*. Available at: www.ibo.org/programmes/diploma-programme/curriculum/dp-core/extended-essay/what-is-the-extended-essay/ (Accessed: 10 June 2023).

Lemay, D. (2013) *Exploring the learning benefits and outcomes of the IB extended essay in preparing students for university studies in Canada*. Phase I Research Report to the IBO. McGill University. Available at: https://ibo.org/globalassets/new-structure/research/pdfs/mcgillfullreportphase1final.pdf (Accessed: 10 June 2023).

Light, D. (2017) 'Stretch and challenge in your classroom', *SecEd*, 28 June. Available at: www.sec-ed.co.uk/best-practice/stretch-and-challenge-in-your-classroom/ (Accessed: 10 June 2023).

McDaniel, M. A. and Einstein, G. O. (2020) 'Training learning strategies to promote self-regulation and transfer: The knowledge, belief, commitment, and planning framework.' *Perspectives on Psychological Science,* 15(6): pp. 1363–1381.

McNair, A. (2022) *Genius Hour: Passion Projects that Ignite Innovation and Student Inquiry,* 2nd edn. New York, NY: Routledge.

Mehta, J. and Fine, S. (2019) *In Search of Deeper Learning: The Quest to Remake the American High School*. Cambridge, Massachusetts: Harvard University Press.

MIT Think. (2022) *MIT Think Scholars Program*. Available at: https://think.mit.edu/ (Accessed: 10 June 2023).

Pearson Education Ltd. (2017) *AS and A level geography – Fieldwork planner and guide*. Available at: https://qualifications.pearson.com/content/dam/pdf/A%20Level/Geography/2016/teaching-and-learning-materials/Fieldwork-Planner-and-Guide.pdf (Accessed: 10 June 2023).

Pedaste, M. et al. (2015) 'Phases of inquiry-based learning: Definitions and the inquiry cycle.' *Educational Research Review,* 14: pp. 47–61.

Regeneron. (2023) *Regeneron science talent search: Celebrating the best and brightest*. Available at: www.regeneron.com/responsibility/sts-isef#1 (Accessed: 10 June 2023).

Renzulli, J. S. (1976) 'The enrichment triad model: A guide for developing defensible programs for the gifted and talented.' *Gifted Child Quarterly*, 20(3): pp. 303–326.

Schneider, J. (2018) *How Genius Hour helps kids connect what they're learning in school to their future goals*. Available at: www.edsurge.com/news/2018-09-19-how-genius-hour-helps-kids-connect-what-they-re-learning-in-school-to-their-future-goals (Accessed: 10 June 2023).

Schraw, G. and Dennison, R. S. (1994) 'Assessing metacognitive awareness.' *Contemporary Educational Psychology* 19(4): pp. 460–475.

Sherrington, T. (2017) 'Teaching to the top: Attitudes and strategies for delivering real challenge', *Teacherhead,* 28 May. Available at: https://teacherhead.com/2017/05/28/teaching-to-the-top-attitudes-and-strategies-for-delivering-real-challenge/ (Accessed: 10 June 2023).

Shin, M. (2018) 'Effects of project-based learning on students' motivation and self-efficacy.' *English Teaching,* 73(1): pp. 95–114.

The Good Schools Guide. (n.d.) *EPQ (Extended Project Qualification).* Available at: www.goodschoolsguide.co.uk/curricula-and-exams/extended-project-qualification (Accessed: 10 June 2023).

Thomas, J. W. (2000) *A review of research on project-based learning.* Available at: https://tecfa.unige.ch/proj/eteach-net/Thomas_researchreview_PBL.pdf (Accessed: 22 May 2024).

UChicago Consortium on School Research. (2008) *From high school to the future: ACT preparation—too much, too late.* University of Chicago CCSR May 2008 Research Report, Chicago: University of Chicago.

University of Connecticut. (n.d.) *An overview of the enrichment triad model.* Available at: https://nrcgt.uconn.edu/underachievement_study/curriculum-compacting/cc_section2/ (Accessed: 10 June 2023).

University of Oxford. (2023) *Physics and Philosophy.* Available at: www.ox.ac.uk/admissions/undergraduate/courses/course-listing/physics-and-philosophy (Accessed: 10 June 2023).

University of Waterloo. (n.d.) *Teaching problem-solving skills.* Available at: https://uwaterloo.ca/centre-for-teaching-excellence/catalogs/tip-sheets/teaching-problem-solving-skills (Accessed: 10 June 2023).

Victoria State Government. (2019) *High-ability toolkit: Adding depth and complexity.* Available at: www.education.vic.gov.au/school/teachers/teachingresources/high-ability-toolkit/Pages/adding-depth-and-complexity.aspx (Accessed: 10 June 2023).

Victoria. (2023) *What the heck is the difference between IBL and PBL?* Available at: www.learningbyinquiry.com/what-the-heck-is-the-difference-between-ibl-and-pbl/ (Accessed: 10 June 2023).

Winjigo. (2023) *Inquiry based learning versus project based learning: What's the difference?* Available at: www.winjigo.com/inquiry-based-learning-versus-project-based-learning-whats-the-difference/ (Accessed: 10 June 2023).

# 9. FLYING ON THE TRAPEZE? PUT UP A SAFETY NET

*One of my core beliefs as a teacher: G&T is a total philosophy of teaching and learning. At both a pedagogical and strategic leadership level, I'd argue that cracking the issue of 'G&T' provision is the key to success - in the classroom and across the whole school. In fact, I think that if the profession could really properly address meeting the needs of the most able students in any setting, the whole system would be transformed.*

**Tom Sherrington, 2012**

*Coasting only happens when you are going downhill.*

**Kishore Borra, 2020**

*What an educator does in teaching is to make it possible for the students to become themselves.*

**Paulo Freire, 1993**

Before having my first coffee of the day, I sat down for an early morning meeting with two parents and braced for impact. I knew why they had sent an exasperated email the day before. Their daughter Jenny arrived in the country four years earlier, and she had quickly picked up English as her third language. She was reserved and self-effacing, modest about her accomplishments in both piano and clarinet. They welcomed me with smiles, but worry immediately transformed their faces when they sat down. Jenny's last report was disheartening; she was stalled. Her attainment had stayed the same, but her effort and attitude to learning had fallen. She would get her As in exams, but it looked like she didn't wish to put in the effort to reach A*s; she figured some last-minute revision could easily get her there. Jenny's teachers reported that she was withdrawn. She was detached in lessons and had seemed to erase herself from the classroom, half-engaging in tasks. Homework was on time and perfunctory. She was well-behaved, obedient and quietly underachieving. At a staff meeting two weeks before, Jenny had been highlighted on our top five hitlist of students who were underperforming in Year 11. We saw her coasting.

Jenny's mum began with trepidation. She didn't want to make any teachers feel bad but ... she looked nervously at her husband. 'Jenny is bored,' he reported, sounding sad. I enquired after Jenny's wellbeing. Her mum shook her head. 'Maybe that's part of it. Jenny used to be so proud of her schoolwork. Now she cares less, but because being good at school was so much of her identity, she is also losing confidence.' I understood that contradiction and the spiral it created. Her mum revealed that after long conversations with Jenny, it emerged that she wasn't depressed but tired of the monotony of exam preparation. Boredom had fed her apathy and eroded her sense of self. In lessons, she was waiting for something new and interesting to happen. The tasks only drilled in content that she had consolidated months ago, and reiterating it was repetitive. She retreated inwards and she wanted lessons to be over. Exams were coming up in four months, and in the meantime, she was just putting in time.

Challenge is more than progress; it is purpose. Mastering challenge strategies is one of the most valuable things we can do as educators. It is a common tactic to walk into a lesson observation, look at the objective on the board and quietly ask a student if they could do that. If they say yes and can prove it in three sentences, then challenge is lacking. Adaptive teaching is difficult because quite often we can let capable students 'get on with it'. If some students are trailing, we need to give them guidance, otherwise they would be lost and left behind. Students who already have good self-regulation and understanding often know where they are going and can get there fast, hence they don't require the same attention.

Herein lies the dilemma. Learning gaps widen for students when we don't flush out the difficulties and errors: 'the least confident students can pass from lesson to lesson, going through the motions of lesson activities, being present, caught up in the general flow, without having their individual learning issues addressed; their learning gaps go undetected at the point of instruction and often remain' (Sherrington, 2019). The best teachers pause and go from the mindset of 'does anyone know?' to 'does everyone know?' These teachers have immediate feedback and checking protocols built into the flow of the lesson, using techniques in cold calling, retrieval practice or mini-whiteboards for quick assessment. When you check for understanding in a lesson and find that 90% of students have a misconception that needs correcting, you are responsive. This is the 'hinge point' in a lesson (Didau, 2012). After routinely sampling we take the time to re-explain, reteach and refocus the material in a new way, chunking and sequencing information into small steps, explaining using analogies, modelling using visual aids, inserting guided practice, then bringing all students to a place of comprehension (Sherrington, 2019). However, while we are doing this reteaching, where are the 10% of students who have already mastered the objective? Reis and Renzulli summarise this sentiment:

> 'Just as teachers have experienced the frustration and the challenge of adjusting the curriculum for students who experience difficulty in learning, frustration also exists when we realize that for some students, a good deal of the material that is being taught has already been mastered, or could easily be mastered in a fraction of the time that may be required by other students.' (Reis and Renzulli, 1995)

These students could be doing a deep dive, tucking into a real-world debate or developing their own line of enquiry. Overarching challenge is key, and the previous chapters have gone over great strategies. However, what happens when a student isn't motivated? What are we missing?

## The Challenges of Challenge

In the UK, the publication of Sir Michael Wilshaw's 'The most able students' report in 2013 placed lack of challenge at the forefront of educational priorities. This pivotal government publication was mentioned in earlier chapters. When explaining the underachievement of 'high-ability' pupils in English non-selective state schools, there is a digression into school culture. Wilshaw invoked an ethos of determination for the creation of scholastic excellence – that students need to do the hard work and develop the resilience necessary to take on high-level academic challenge. The Ofsted report cites that state schools often have an environment of low expectations, where teachers, parents, carers and students accept a lower level of performance. Low expectations can appear as lack of quality homework, lack of extension activities, lack of challenging task work and lack of acceleration for the identified more-able students. There is a certain amount of naivety when Sir

Michael Wilshaw writes that 'many non-selective schools fail to imbue their most able students with the confidence and high ambition that characterise many students in the selective or independent sector. Why should the most able students in the non-selective sector not have the same belief that they, too, can reach the top?' (Ofsted, 2013). This implies individual failures as opposed to structural issues, such as pitting non-selective schools against selective schools. It is not self-belief that stops students. If you want to have a deep dive into why this 'culture of low expectations' is a state school issue, the argument is problematic. I highly recommend reading Geoff Barton's critique. He quite rightfully points out that:

> 'Those parents wavering between sending a child to their local state or independent school today will have heard that we, the comprehensives, are all complacent and complicit in low expectations. In reality, we spend all our time neurotically fretting about how we can help our students – all our students – to do better. That's what we do, endlessly. ... And that's why – catastrophically – some of the very parents we most need to help us keep levering standards upwards in the state system will be thinking tonight that they should play safe and send their child to the local private school – an institution where, truth-be-told, expectations, teaching quality and ambition may be no higher than in the local comprehensive.' (Barton, 2013)

Comprehensive schools have not failed students – systems have.

What is interesting is that immediately after the diversion about school culture, Wilshaw then articulates more pointed reasons that the 'more-able pupils' were not progressing. The reasoning could apply to a classroom in a selective or non-selective school. Schools can open the castle gates, but they can't expect students to swim through a swampy moat.

1.  **Emphasis on getting pupils over the grade C/D borderline.** There is much attention given to those advertised exam results. This places incredible pressure on schools, departments and individual teachers to impress with these headline results. The percentage of students getting A*–C incentivises schools to concentrate resources on getting lower-achieving students over the C/D hump. The importance of 'teaching to the test' leads to inflexibility in the curriculum for students to creatively explore and extend. In addition, when inspectors look at the value-add schools give, there is far more to be gained in having a student who has been predicted an E move up to a C grade, than a predicted A student move to an A*. Deborah

Eyre notes the preoccupation with floor-level targets and bluntly points out 'we have created a system that requires that most pupils reach mediocrity and which asks schools to arrange their structures with this as the primary expectation' (Eyre, 2011, p. 8). Note that this pressure to get students over the hump of a test boundary can be found in standardised test systems across the world. It is especially lamented in the US with an increase in state and federal tests over the past two decades.

2. **There are lost years – Years 7, 8 and 9.** Between primary school and the GCSE exams, there sits a no man's land of students aged 12–14. This tends to be where most able pupils lose progress and don't catch up to their potential. Those students identified as more able who were surveyed reported boring, repetitive, easy work during these three years of their education. As one Year 7 student put it: 'We get asked to design a lot of posters. All abilities get set the same homework. Sometimes we just have to finish what we have started in lessons' (Ofsted, 2013). It was found that in mixed-ability groups differentiation was aimed at low-attaining students or pitched to the middle. Once this ground is lost, 'more-able' students lose the motivation and foundation for their exam years.

3. **Transitions are insufficient.** Parents and students are not supported in the moves from primary to secondary or from secondary to higher education. Primary national test results are often not used to inform setting or class groups upon entry to secondary. Teachers are not made aware of the most able students in order to maintain academic momentum. On the other end of the journey, relevant expertise on university entrance and post-16 options can be difficult to access – leaving students and their families uninformed. Socially underserved families are unable to navigate the cultural and financial obstacles of application processes.

4. **Underchallenged pupils are not identified or treated as having different needs.** Inclusion departments in schools tend to be completely devoted to SEN/EAL needs. Teachers are given a one-size-fits-all list of top scorers in a cognitive ability test, or nothing at all. Schools lack a teaching and learning lead in charge of 'more-able' provision (what I would refer to as challenge for all and enrichment). Student progress is difficult to establish in schools without effective assessment, tracking and targeting. Slippage not

caught at the beginning of secondary school means late or non-existent interventions.

5. **Inequalities between student groups are not tackled.** The attainment of underachieving students who are eligible for free school meals, especially the most able boys, lags behind that of other groups. Few schools use the Pupil Premium funding to support the most able students from the most economically under-resourced backgrounds. Interestingly, it is class that is the key barrier – data indicates that non-white students had roughly the same (or slightly better) outcomes as their white peers (Ofsted, 2013).

Note again that while class is highlighted as a barrier in the English system, race and first/second generation immigration are still key components in the marginalisation of ethnic minority students. Similarly, in the US, Canada and other countries, class and race are intertwined and many equity-seeking groups face injustice.

Each school in England is expected to create their own policy for the management of 'more-able' students. Conceptually, this enables schools to identify individual needs and consider the context of their community. The policy can then be reflective of each school's development plan. Stakeholders such as teachers, school leaders, parents and governors are ideally involved in the creation of the policy. This includes clear guidelines on the identification of more-able pupils and best practice. However, in reality, the incentives encourage a cookie-cutter approach to passing muster in inspections and place top-line exam results at the forefront. There can be a default to traditional conceptions of giftedness, setting and low expectations for certain groups of students.

I would go further and look at the structural guidance. There are contradictions in the national policy, with gifted and talented language couched in expectations of enrichment. Poorly aligned requirements of certain policies create practical limitations to the provision of more inclusive programmes. Take a national policy requirement to use a percentage-based identification strategy, for example, which requests that schools place 5% to 10% of their students on a gifted and talented student register. Predictably, this appears to have been taken as encouragement to utilise test-based, quantitative measurements for creating gifted and talented cohorts (Smith, 2006).

These policies have had unintended or inverse consequences. As Heuser, Wang and Shahid (2017) write: 'Although the education system of the

United Kingdom appears more aligned with the concept that giftedness incorporates both academic and nonacademic excellence, *due to poor policy design, gifted and talented programs currently do not reflect what the majority of people believe is giftedness and, instead, tend to promote scholarly success only.'* [Emphasis added.] There is all the intention of promoting enrichment, but the implementation often ends up as a fig leaf G&T register.

When approaching challenge, we must implement strategies *and* structure. There are many exciting techniques and ideas, and they work best when deployed within a clear structure. It is necessary to have systems for challenge, a reliable place to go for extension and built-in routines for challenge that are easily accessible for students.

## Making Challenge Routine

Let's go back to Jenny. I shadowed her through four lessons the next day to get a taste of her experience. There were three things I observed – waiting time, straight-line lessons and lack of autonomy. Jenny spent a lot of time waiting. While material was being modelled or explained her eyes glazed over. During think-pair-share and group discussions she bullet-pointed her answers but didn't expand on them with her peers. Occasionally she would correct a misconception but often she stayed silent. She waited for her peers to come to the conclusion. Halfway through an online quiz game she stopped answering questions; she had gotten every answer correct thus far and decided to opt-out, waiting for the game to conclude. When Jenny was given a research task, she opened three extra tabs on her laptop and went off on a tangent. She was directed to go back on task.

What I found fascinating is that the teaching had amazing scaffolding. However, it completely missed the mark for Jenny. When teachers used retrieval practice to activate prior knowledge in a starter, this tended to be wasted time for Jenny. Explicit instruction and worked examples had her looking out the window. Chunking information into small steps, one at a time, had her tapping her foot. She appreciated being able to go ahead with a full checklist. When learning paused for the teacher to check for understanding with the whole class, she sighed impatiently. The purpose of scaffolding is to empower students and remove dependence on the teacher. Scaffolds are slowly removed in phases as the student internalises the information and becomes more independent and self-motivated (InnerDrive, n.d.). Scaffolds help learners reach higher levels of comprehension and skill acquisition, but this was not the result in Jenny's case. Three of the main challenges of scaffolding are: 1) correctly identifying students' zone of proximal development; 2) knowing when to taper off so as to allow students to work independently; and 3) releasing more responsibility to students (Mulvahill, 2022). The pitch point for students is different, and navigating differentiated scaffolding is a minefield. Too often the temptation is to scaffold 'down' instead of 'up'. Scaffolding down is simplifying activities, bringing content down to what students currently do and limiting progress. The emphasis tends to be about revisiting old material and 'catching up'. Scaffolding up focuses on having students master key practices, principles and concepts that enable learner autonomy. What I discovered over the course of the day was that Jenny was constrained to the curriculum, restrained by the pace and inhibited by her role as a student.

Engagement is a key aspect of preventing underachievement for learners. What does engagement look like? We could use a continuum model with a linear view of the cognitive stages a student reaches on the way to a desired outcome. Researchers Ronksley-Pavia and Neumann (2020) go beyond this to conceptualise a cyclical model with four interrelated dimensions:

- Behavioural engagement (e.g. presence, participation in activities and discussion, perseverance when challenged, on-task involvement).

- Affective engagement – emotions during learning that are closely related to behavioural engagement (e.g. student attitude, drive, interest, enjoyment, pride, enthusiasm).

- Social engagement (e.g. cooperative learning, collaboration, sense of belonging at school, connections with peers and teachers, inclusion).

- Cognitive engagement (e.g. focus on mastery, deep thinking, agency, self-regulation, goal setting, higher-order processes).

Identifying students who are underchallenged or who have disengaged can be problematic. Ronksley-Pavia and Neumann (2020) acknowledge how tricky it is to catch disengagement: 'These students frequently appear to be behaviourally engaged (e.g., on task), affectively engaged (e.g., positive reactions to teachers), and socially engaged (e.g., involved in their learning) and there may even be some signs of cognitive engagement (e.g., goal setting). Yet, their classwork or assessment results may not provide positive outcomes of this apparent engagement.' So how do we make disengagement visible? How do we capture these students and what strategies work best to meaningfully engage them?

I can easily see how pupils can be lost along the way. In my first year teaching in a non-selective state school I remember having a Year 7 class of 29 pupils, 21 of whom had specific learning differences/EAL requirements. On top of this, behaviour management issues seemed to take up all my energy as a classroom teacher. I was grateful for the reprieve of those students who just got on with the work, and it was easy to appreciate the ease they brought to the classroom. They were often ones I didn't need to worry about and as such didn't make my list of priorities. I remember having a discussion with my first head of department and mentor about how to handle these diverse classes. I argued that prioritising a classroom environment with set behaviour expectations was how to ensure progress; I pitched low and rewarded obedience. She advocated engagement for the more-able students should always be integrated. It immediately raises the bar – when all kids are challenged, then good habits, conduct and progress follow. When we looked at the data for my classes it was clear – my 'easy' students were not making progress. What's more, the underperformance went under my radar. The longer I've taught, the more I have come to wholeheartedly agree with my mentor. Progress is made when pupils are interested and stimulated. Enthusiasm is contagious; a positive action-packed environment captures students from the get-go.

One of the most useful schematics I have found has emerged from the field of gifted education. It explicitly highlights the impact enrichment can have on underachievement, specifically in relation to the achievement gap. Underachieving students may not be motivated because interventions have used a traditional teacher-directed approach to focus the problem, as opposed to using enrichment as a vehicle to drive positive outcomes (Renzulli, 2013).

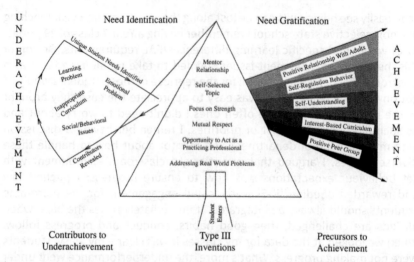

Figure 9.1 The prism metaphor for reversing underachievement[15] (Baum, Renzulli and Hébert, 1995). This figure has been reproduced with the permission of The National Research Center on the Gifted and Talented.

Students may be overwhelmed by learning and emotional problems, social-emotional problems, behavioural issues or simply an inappropriate curriculum. I'd like to use another gifted framework to address students and some of the reasons they are unable to engage or perhaps underchallenged.

# Profiles of Underachieving Pupils

Disengagement and underachievement are complex issues with no one root cause. However, it is well established that when students are actively engaged in their learning, they learn more effectively (Ronksley-Pavia and Neumann, 2020). There is an interesting pocket of research that identifies types of underachievement in high-ability pupils (Betts and Neihart, 1988). I would like to note these observations can be applied to all pupils. Betts and Neihart developed six profiles as a useful way to understand the feelings, behaviours

---

15 Note that Type III enrichment interventions feature self-selected investigative and creative projects, where students become investigators of real-world problems and target their work for real-life audiences. They are tasked with producing creative products through the collection of raw data, the use of advanced problem-solving techniques and the application of research strategies or artistic innovations that are employed by front-line people in various fields, albeit at a more junior level than adult investigators.

and needs of learners. Unmasking students' motives and uncovering the reasons for underachievement can be illuminating, helping us to put strategies in place. It can be reductive to place students into these neat categories, and I'm betting that you can see your students flitting between these types. I would add that these profiles were also developed from research in 1988, when teachers did not have the same awareness of trauma-informed practice. As Kate Bachtel commented, 'Behaviours associated with some of the profiles are actually indicators of trauma and need to be named as such to orient towards fixing programming and adult behaviours rather than fixing children' (Bachtel, 2023). As teachers, we see every day that behaviour is a form of communication. There are different causes, and any underachievement requires different interventions and approaches. Here is an adapted breakdown of the profiles, using Betts and Neihart's insight with added observations. These archetypes can inform adaptive teaching, discern why students underachieve, and highlight the interventions that can help them.

## 1. The 'Successful' Student

This child sits at the front of the class and clamours for the teacher's approval. 'Successful' students are easy to spot as they tend to be disciplined high attainers. They crave order, structure and clear instruction. The students who strain their arms to answer a question first or quietly sit in the front row. However, their motivation 'may be directed mainly towards teacher acceptance, rather than the full development of their abilities' (Betts and Neihart, 1988). Depending on circumstances, they can be dependent, complacent, conformist, perfectionist, risk-averse and define themselves by their academic success. They may get great grades, but don't stretch themselves outside the syllabus. They are duteous students but may not be fully stretched and challenged beyond the exam results. Obedience can lead to these learners becoming mere consumers of knowledge. Dependent learners can be 'overly reliant on the teacher to carry the load of cognitive tasks and are unsure of how to tackle new tasks because they aren't given opportunities to learn *how* to be expert learners' (Novak, 2021). If their effort is extrinsically motivated or they are sensitive to criticism, they can fall into a trap of low self-esteem.

Emotionally, perfectionism and 'mattering' are often associated with high-attaining students. Mattering is a feeling of self-worth that comes from being important to others, possessing a sense of belonging and being worthy of special attention. Joan Freeman observes that an identification of 'giftedness', or having one's identity entangled with academic success, often makes children feel pressure to always live up to the label and race to be 'ahead' (Freeman, 2010). Hill and Madigan (2022) point out that students' stress can build up through harsh self-evaluation, doubts, fears and feelings of inadequacy. They also found that this was exacerbated during the COVID-19 lockdowns. While students with tendencies of perfectionism were better at self-regulation, this correlated to higher academic stress.

## Developing and Supporting the Successful Student

- Challenge students by assigning open-ended work designed to foster creativity, imagination and enterprise.

- Embed independent learning through enquiry study or project-based learning. Furnish students with choice in their endeavours. Learning and mastery goals are linked with intrinsic motivation (Blumenfeld, 1992).

- Build assertiveness skills – give these students leadership roles in group tasks.

- Provide opportunities to take small risks and provide the psychological safety net – this could include low-stakes drafts, exercises in thinking outside the box and messy brainstorming.

- Socratic seminars and debating.

- Affirmation of their ability to cope with obstacles and stretch themselves.

- Wellbeing support and counselling to combat stress or imposter syndrome.

## 2. The Uninspired Student

This type of underachieving student is best recognised as 'bored' or apathetic in the classroom. As one of my colleagues noted, 'Is this student a trouble-making loudmouth? Or are they simply asking for more challenge?' A child can easily be mislabelled as having behaviour issues – they distract others in lessons and will openly question authority (e.g. asking 'why are we doing this miss?' or stating, 'I can't be asked.') They can get quite frustrated at the pace of lessons or the level of the material. They express their impulses and may have poor self-control. They can be arrogant in their abilities, racing ahead with sloppy half-done work, calling it a day and making fun of how slow other students are. They may be the class clown, using punch lines and sarcasm to gain popularity, or they may be argumentative in lessons, a constant devil's advocate, leading peers to roll their eyes at the continued disturbance. We may need to reorientate our thinking from labelling them an 'attention-seeking' student to a 'challenge-seeking' student. Betts and Neihart titled this student 'the creative' because this is how they seek to flourish.

### Developing and Supporting the Uninspired Student

- Allow students to set their own goals, and set time aside for them to propose ideas for project outcomes and delivery. Make sure you have a clear system to make them accountable.

- Give students the stage – have them plan a teacher takeover lesson, create a podcast or become a resident expert in a topic where their peers interrogate them.

- Host debates and assign speech topics that allow the student to play devil's advocate within the structure of the exercise.

- Provide opportunities for creative productivity – gaming platforms (e.g. Minecraft), design platforms, 3D printing design, coding programs, drawing, painting or animation apps (Neumann and Ronksley-Pavia, 2020).

- Build rapport, model polite behaviour, and give positive reinforcement (e.g. 'I was impressed with your decorum and wit during the debate. It was a particularly clever point of information.').

## 3. The Underground Student

This is the student who desperately wants to fit in with their friend group, to the point of concealing their knowledge or capacity. The underground student has a strong need to belong. Betts and Neihart write that these students 'have responded to the "forced-choice dilemma"—the choice between excelling academically and being accepted by the peer group—by choosing peer acceptance. Unfortunately, they may then become afraid that they will lose this acceptance if they drop their camouflage' (Betts and Neihart, 1988). It is difficult to bring a child out of their shell; this hiding tactic is self-protective. Going underground can be a sign of insecurity, on top of which the student may feel guilty and unfulfilled academically.

Going underground is also wrapped up in identity. There can be issues in cultural identity or the expectation that a student can and should code-switch. Cultural code-switching (depending on social context) can be exhausting and places the responsibility on learners to navigate two (or more) distinct communities (Morton, 2014). Assimilation tactics can also be wrapped up in masking gender identity or sexual orientation. Students may purposely fail to be placed in classes or groups with their friends or to avoid social isolation and/or bullying.

## Developing and Supporting the Underground Student

- Rearrange seating, thoughtfully assign students new groups for tasks, expose students to new friendship circles and pair the student with a mentor they can relate to and admire.

- Use mixed-ability grouping – friendship groups tend to form along ability lines, so this can be calcified and exacerbated by setting students by ability. When classes are mixed then high-achieving students have opportunity to collaborate and share with low-achieving students, blurring or erasing these lines and reorganising friendship groups. Research by Flashman (2012) concludes that adolescents respond to changes in academic achievement by changing their friendship ties.

- Provide cultural icons, role models and mentors who reflect the students' backgrounds.

- Build confidence in their identity and create safe spaces for all identities such as wellbeing programmes and celebrations of different cultures, genders and orientations.

- Take small steps for students to engage with new material outside of the classroom. Create a low-stakes entry point and invite students to 'read around' a topic that interests them. Provide them with articles, documentaries, books and games that ignite their curiosity.

- Change the false dilemma (grades versus friends) through career counselling – ask students to evaluate the cost-benefit of buying into their learning. Use goal-setting exercises and short-term/long-term framing.

- Use online engagement for alternative routes to engagement – online breakout rooms for friendship and socialisation, virtual tours of museums or science centres, collaborative discussion platforms and Padlets as a blank wall for sharing ideas (Neumann and Ronksley-Pavia, 2020).

Friendship dynamics are tricky to navigate, and literature underlines how positive relationships can have a great impact on performance. Researchers cite peer motivation as a driving factor: 'Motivation is the reasoning behind the actions of an individual. This shows that students help each other improve their academic performance and encourage each other' (EduBirdie, 2022).

## 4. The Student in Crisis

These students are underachieving because, although they may be physically present in the classroom, they are emotionally and intellectually divested. These students can be fragile learners who are close to conceding defeat to circumstances that threaten their education. In Dr David Matthew's PhD dissertation, he observes that fragile learners 'might experience anxieties that are internal and complex but which appear to be attacks from other people. Alternatively, Fragile Learning might be a consequence of learners having suffered illness or indisposition' (Matthew, 2016).

Academic underachievement can be a symptom of a larger problem. Safeguarding the student is the first and highest priority. The system needs to meet the needs of students in crisis. It is only after this problem is resolved, and a student is in a safe space, that they can enter an academic environment ready to learn. Trauma-informed teaching starts with an understanding of how trauma can impact learning and behaviour. It is important that we don't exacerbate traumatic experiences for students. With this approach, educators think about what student behaviour may be telling them and adjust their teaching practices to support students who may be experiencing trauma. This includes being culturally responsive. The correlation between low self-esteem and low performance is clear. Depression, resentment and anger are the defining feelings. The inner worlds of these students are varied. However, the outward response can be apathy, distress, recklessness, defiance or anti-social behaviour. For these students to thrive, the underlying trauma must be addressed first in the form of a safe and structured environment and professional counselling. 'Social and emotional wellbeing is essential for effective learning, yet there will always be students who lack confidence in their learning and who don't always feel connected with school and their teachers' (GL Education, 2023). There are wellbeing assessments that can show how a student feels about themselves, their engagement with the curriculum and their feelings about school. When students are ready to engage and we have established the non-negotiables, there are teaching and learning strategies we can implement to support their emotional and academic growth.

### Developing and Supporting the Student in Crisis

- Individualised programme with high expectations but short-term goals for easy wins. Creating this programme should be a collaboration where agency is prioritised and students have choice.

271

- Depth studies on a topic of particular interest can help a student become an expert and build confidence. Focusing on a learner's strengths and building on those while they develop a foundation of coping skills is powerful in constructing a sense of self.

- Establish a routine of checking in. Students should be held accountable, and this requires frequent follow-up and feedback. Learners are provided with clear messages about their rights and responsibilities. One-on-one interviews can build rapport and trust, and demonstrate a tangible investment in students' learning. It is important that interpersonal boundaries are maintained while students are validated.

- Apply principles of trauma-informed practice – safety, choice, collaboration, trustworthiness and empowerment. This applies not only to individual teachers, but to systems. Administrators can provide staff with training, and change policies, procedures and practices to minimise barriers to services and care (Buffalo Center for Social Research, 2023).

- Coaching and mentorships can be powerful, but they must be long-term and stable to build rapport and trust. Mentors should be trained and trauma-informed: 'mentors are uniquely positioned to help young people process these experiences by providing a space to express their emotions, ask for help, and channel uncertain feelings into positive, constructive action. However, mentors may need strategies for supporting these discussions and actions' (Mentor National, 2023). There are guides and resources available, and schools can take advantage of mental health training.

## 5. The Autonomous Student

Autonomous learners are confident, optimistic, resilient and enthusiastic about learning. They tend to be skilled at socially navigating school, with both their teachers and peers. They are autonomous in that they are intrinsically motivated – they self-regulate to reach goals and care little about approval as they are preoccupied with following their own passions. Their independence goes beyond their work ethic and can touch on their ability to stand up for their convictions; they are active in extracurriculars that extend their learning.

Autonomous learners can be underachieving because they have reached the learning ceiling, where educators believe that these students have met the year-level learning outcomes, and therefore, their learning and achievement are sufficient. Neumann and Ronksley-Pavia observe that the journey of autonomous learners is not straightforward and that they may require intervention: 'Because learning and achievement tends to come naturally to these learners, they may underachieve and disengage from learning. In the primary years they can often cruise along, but as the work becomes more challenging in middle school, this disengagement can worsen as they may have missed foundational skills' (Neumann and Ronksley-Pavia, 2020, p. 28). If learning is 'too easy' it may hinder the enhancement of their academic growth and cognitive engagement.

Learners with this profile may not view learning in class as their highest priority. They may want to do *their work*, not the teacher's work. Some subjects may take a hit – I'm sure we have all had students enamoured with one focus. For instance, if their passion is science, they don't see the point in studying English or drama.

### Developing and Supporting the Autonomous Student

- Give them space and opportunity to self-direct tasks – empower them with choice whenever possible.

- Find and present them with opportunities to interact with extracurricular activities and competitions outside of the school on a local, regional, national and international level. Allow them to specialise in an area they particularly wish to grow in.

- Autonomous learners may disengage when they are not particularly passionate or challenged in subjects or topics, so ensure that there is an entry point of interest to maintain sustained challenge.

- Roles such as peer mentors provide purposeful and collaborative opportunities in the classroom.

- Provide acceleration with above-year-level content in subjects where the student has shown mastery.

- Track effort and attitude to ensure a speedy intervention before there is a loss in learning or disengagement becomes entrenched.

## 6. The Multi-Exceptional Student

Twice exceptionality can be characterised by major domain differences. This could be disparities in completing complex tasks in one domain and struggling with easier, simpler tasks in another domain (Postma, 2022).

Twice- or multi-exceptional students are underchallenged students who have other learning needs – characterised, for instance, as 'gifted *and* dyslexic'. The capability of twice (or multi) exceptional youth is great but can be hard to recognise and cultivate. Often, the focus is on one primary identification rather than the whole child (Postma, 2022). There are academic, social and emotional repercussions when one characteristic overshadows all others. When a student is defined by 'another star on the register' their strengths tend to be cloaked. For example, there is obviously justifiable frustration for a student to enter a classroom and be primarily defined by their wheelchair. Twice-exceptional students can be broadly grouped into four subcategories: specific learning differences (SpLD),[16] additional or second language learners, emotional and behavioural, and pupils of determination (physical differences).

Note that some educators have shifted to use 'learning differences' while others use 'learning difficulties/disability'. This can change depending on the context and purpose of use. Redefining language around accommodations as differences embraces a broader perspective for inclusivity without coding any divergence as 'disability'. This also frames 'thinking differently' as an advantage and strength. On the other hand, some pragmatic advocates make the point that the language of 'difficulties' and 'disabilities' can stress the vital need to change or aid in navigating policies and procedures in institutions, with these terms legitimising the need for accommodation. In certain institutions the term 'disability' holds a justification that forces a system to be accountable.

Neurodiversity describes the infinite variation in human minds and does not seek to define what is, and is not, 'normal'. This emerged as a concept in the 1990s to celebrate variation in human thinking as both natural and beneficial. Neurodiversity encompasses all specific learning differences. While the term emerged from a dialogue regarding common neurotypes, such as autism and ADHD, it is not restricted to diagnostic categories (Bulluss and Sesterka, 2023). The movement promotes the view that all neurological differences are to be recognised and respected. It is used to counter negative social connotations that exist and to make it easier for people of all neurotypes to contribute to the world as they are, rather than attempting to think or appear more 'typically'.

---

16  Language around SpLD is varied and evolving, with usage including specific learning disability/difficulty/difference. For purposes here I am using specific learning difference.

In all cases of exceptionality, it is a good idea to understand how a student views their own identity and how they reference it. Autism identity is a common example – how do we describe autism and autistic people? There exists degrading, but still commonly used, ableist language in autism such as 'high functioning' or 'low functioning'. Terms such as 'special interests' and 'special needs' can be patronising; these terms could be replaced with 'focused interests' and descriptions of autistic people's specific needs (Bottema-Beutel et al., 2021). There is 'person-first' language, such as calling someone a 'person with autism' – describing what a person has, not what a person is. Individuals may be against the use of 'person-first' language, instead preferring 'disability-first' language, such as he/she/they are an 'autistic person'. This is because 'Many autistic activists argue that person-first language is dehumanising, as if they can somehow be separated from their autism, that there is a "typical" person affected by autism, rather than a person whose life is in part defined by being autistic' (Pellicano, 2015). As educators, we can understand what ableism is, reflect on the identifiers we use in our written and spoken work, and use non-ableist language alternatives. The best path, however, is an open conversation with a student and taking cues from them.

A teacher may go out of their way to provide accommodations for learners with dyslexia or additional language learners, but then forget that the level of challenge may need similar adjustment. There can be confusion about a pupil's capacity to perform when they are neurodiverse – strengths can be overlooked or there can be low expectations. Learners can have high performance in some domains, but struggle with other aspects of learning, making for uneven development (Brody and Mills, 1997). This can be detrimental to a student's self-efficacy. Such learners may have a negative self-concept and may need support to recognise and value their advantages. It is tempting to lump all learning differences together or assume a uniform experience. For instance, dyslexia manifests in myriad ways, meaning that some students are never identified. Methods and measures for diagnosing dyslexia change from country to country. Dr Martin Bloomfield points out that:

> 'Dyslexia does not "belong" to the Anglo-American world; yet almost all research and perspectives are focused on the Anglosphere, and carry with them Anglo-American "white" cultural biases and preconceptions. This risks marginalising BAME dyslexics, and the different impacts dyslexia has on cultures whose language is non-alphabetic, or whose cultures involve interactions which will be differently affected by dyslexia.' (Millin, 2020)

Along these lines, the term 'neurodivergent', as opposed to neurodiversity, describes a single mind that diverges significantly from socioculturally constructed norms in some way. This doesn't mean that someone must meet certain diagnostic criteria or identify as belonging to a discrete neurotype (Bulluss and Sesterka, 2023).

In terms of multi-exceptional students there are a few issues at hand:

1. When students are underchallenged or underachieving, educators must thoughtfully devise for domain differences and recognise when the exceptionalities co-occur and overlap.

2. Hidden exceptionalities may prevent learners with advanced capacity from realising high academic results. Traditional methods of gifted identification have not accurately picked up the cognitive ability of neurodivergent learners. As discussed in previous chapters, these learners can score 'average' in standardised achievement tests. However, average scores often mask peaks and troughs in performance (i.e. both aptitudes and gaps). What we can note are significant discrepancies across test categories. These often indicate an SpLD, such as the scores from oral responses being much higher than scores from written responses.

3. There can be conflation, where elements of one identification are attributed to another. Dr James T. Webb points to how this can lead to misdiagnosis. A common example is level of intensity, intellectual or emotional. Webb points to one mother who described this as 'my child's life motto is that anything worth doing is worth doing to excess' (Webb, 2000). A child can live and breathe dinosaurs as a devoted and single-minded pursuit to the exclusion of other learning. Containing this or redirecting their interest can lead to frustration. Webb then goes on to say some students can be 'extremely intense, whether in their emotional response, intellectual pursuits, sibling rivalry, or power struggles with an authority figure. ... [the] drive to understand, to question, and to search for consistency is likewise intense, as is the inherent ability to see possibilities and alternatives. All of these characteristics together result in an intense idealism and concern with social and moral issues, which can create anxiety, depression, and a sharp challenging of others who do not share their concerns' (Webb, 2000). We can see this intensity as obsessive-compulsive disorder or oppositional defiance disorder. Intensity can also manifest as heightened motor activity, sensory sensitivity (being overstimulated by sound or light) and physical restlessness.

These can overlap with a diagnosis of attention deficit hyperactivity disorder (ADHD). Intensity is an absorption that can be read as giftedness, neurodiversity or a psychological issue. It can be seen as a symptom to be managed or an aptitude to be fostered.

4.  We as educators don't know the individual circumstances, preferred language and/or identity that a student enters the classroom with. As such we should not make assumptions but let the student's voice lead. Nor should we expect unlimited perseverance from students but listen with a recognition that we should design better systems. Here is an excerpt from disability advocate Lauren Berglund's blog:

    *'I don't just "happen to be" a student with a disability, I am a disabled student plain and simple. Being disabled greatly impacts my ability to be a college student. It means I have to advocate for myself daily. It means I have to plan ahead and be prepared for any situation. It means I have to work twice as hard as my peers to read the same article. It means preparing weeks in advance for the start of a semester and it means that sometimes I just can't make it to class that day.*

    *When you tell me not to let my disability define me you are telling me not to embrace a huge part of my existence. You are asking me to ignore the part of me that has greatly shaped who I am today. You are indirectly telling me that part of my identity isn't important. When you treat my disabilities as something separate from me and say they don't define me, you are denying the overwhelming significance disability has had on my life.' (Berglund, 2017)*

    There is a responsibility we bear to recognise the additional labour these students face and anticipate how we can make their journey easier.

## Developing and Supporting the Multi-Exceptional Student

Susan Winebrenner has written extensively on multi-exceptional students and advises that we should go beyond accommodations and give students an understanding on *how* they learn best: 'While planning and teaching compensation strategies, educators must acknowledge the need for teaching the same concepts in many different ways: If students are not learning the way we teach them, *teach them the way they learn*' (Winebrenner, 2003, p. 132). This could mean providing specific instruction in organisational techniques, self-monitoring, structuring their environment, using self-consequences/rewards and recognising when to seek support. Winebrenner asserts that the term 'disability' doesn't fit: 'Such students would better be labelled as "learning strategy disabled" because their academic outcomes can improve dramatically when they learn to use appropriate compensation techniques' (Winebrenner, 2003, p. 132). Tactics for educators include the following:

- Develop a clear understanding of SpLD. The most serious challenge is that the aptitudes will go unnoticed and unaccommodated in favour of attending to learning deficits. Engage in CPD, listen to student needs and advocate. Value and follow individual education plans. Don't put the onus on students to do the hard work of constantly advocating for themselves.

- Create a culture of safe space where differences are celebrated in the classroom. Be aware of peer interaction, social circles and language. Teach students to appreciate neurodiversity, individual differences and differentiated opportunities.

- Stay out of the way of multi-exceptional students when they approach tasks differently.

- Create a wide variety of acceleration and compacting options. Moon and Reis (2004) note that there is a general consensus that multi-exceptional students benefit from acceleration, especially when accelerative strategies are geared to students' interests and are provided in a positive learning environment that combines challenge and support.

- Provide challenge in an area of strength first. Create individualised curricula and curate these through diagnostic assessments that test knowledge before and after learning units.

- Recognising and nurturing learners may require the involvement of specialist teachers and assistive technologies. Search out and use any assistive technology that will improve a student's productivity (Te Tāhuhu o te Mātauranga, n.d.). This could include using recording devices, typing rather than writing, learning apps and multimedia resources (such as video lessons over direct instruction). Where appropriate, extend time given on assessments and assignments.

- Ensure that school policy has methods to identify aptitudes within and alongside other designations – SpLD, EAL or pupils of determination. This includes procedures for things like a friendly testing environment so that sensory stimuli do not interfere with concentration. Multi-exceptional students tend to have significantly different scores across assessment batteries. This means we should interpret inconsistencies in standardised assessments using discrepancy scoring.

- Give students the words and space to build social-emotional intelligence. This area is one of the biggest hurdles for multi-exceptional students. Help students expand their emotional vocabulary to better express their needs or use visual aids.

- Teach self-regulation and metacognitive strategies that allow students to reflect and use their preferred strategies.

- Transition planning from one stage of education to another is key, with collaboration and case management handover.

- Investment in adaptive software: 'These innovative platforms provide customized learning experiences that cater to individual student's needs, progress, and preferences, ensuring that each learner receives the optimal level of support and challenge. The importance of personalization in education cannot be overstated, as it allows for more effective learning experiences that accommodate the unique learning styles and abilities of each student' (Silicon Valley Innovation Center, 2023).

- Adopt the principles of Universal Design for Learning.

There are entire books dedicated to multi-exceptional students and neurodiversity. I can't do complete justice to all identification and intervention of all SpLD, so I highly recommend further reading. Research is now much better at prioritising neurodivergent and disability advocates and their student experience, changing the vocabulary and approaches educators use. There is an ethical obligation to champion exceptional students, a sub-population that historically has been neglected (Leggett, Shea and Wilson, 2010). We can keep abreast of the best practices for inclusion. In a review of implications for multi-exceptional students in inclusive education, Gierczyk and Hornby (2021, p. 9) write:

*'Schools need to provide organisational structures that support teachers in implementing strategies such as Universal Design for Learning, Individual Education Programs, curriculum differentiation, and various other accommodations for twice-exceptional students. Most importantly, schools need to focus on providing favourable learning environments and supportive school contexts in which positive attitudes towards inclusion embrace the celebration of diversity,*

*so that twice-exceptional students feel supported and can achieve optimally at school.'*

While these six profiles are generalised and broad, they do provide some initial starting points for teachers to ascertain the needs of individual students and develop opportunities to capture those who might otherwise go under the radar. Students are unique – their characteristics, personalities and needs vary and fluctuate throughout their education. We have the opportunity to further understand them and personalise our approach with curated support strategies. We can also embed these in our curriculum by implementing Universal Design for Learning.

## Universal Design for Learning and Equity

Universal Design for Learning (UDL) is a framework for designing learning experiences so that students have options for how they learn. As Kate Novak explains, 'It may not be our intent to exclude our learners, but the reality is that many students do not have opportunities to learn at high levels or to access curriculum and instruction that is accessible, engaging, culturally sustaining, and linguistically appropriate' (Novak, 2021). The goal of UDL is to accommodate for a wide variety of needs and eliminate unnecessary hurdles in the learning process (Center for Teaching Innovation, 2023). One inflexible pathway for all learners, where they work at the same pace, from the same resource, and are assigned the same task ignores cultural, social, emotional or neurodivergent differences. So how do we reach students who have been historically marginalised? UDL guides educators in diversifying how information is presented, providing options for how students engage, and creating inclusive assessments and evaluations. One of the most powerful ways we can provide challenge is to give students choice while holding high standards and expectations for all learners. UDL can maximise learning opportunities, close opportunity gaps and put students in the driver's seat. The emphasis is on learners' autonomy and empowerment.

Traditional differentiated instruction (DI) is usually teacher-directed, done by changing content, process, product and learning environment. Just like UDL, DI adjusts teaching practice, modifies and accommodates for students, and uses multiple media to help students learn effectively. There is a clear overlap between DI and UDL – so how are they different? DI is responsive, with adjustments made based on individual student needs. This can be problematic as the differentiation is typically done after data is collated and trends are noticed. DI may capture targeted individuals who have already been diagnosed but miss unidentified needs or marginalised groups. UDL is anticipatory of the full range of learner needs from the outset and looks for universal supports. It is proactively designed so students self-differentiate, as opposed to being teacher-directed (Choudhury, 2021). UDL prescribes a careful audit of the curriculum. The focus is on removing barriers to student-centred learning, with the aim of creating expert learners. UDL asks that we be flexible, proactive and purposeful in our planning by using the Universal Design for Learning principles. Adaptive teaching (as opposed to traditional differentiated instruction) is responsive to in-the-moment student needs and complements the environment UDL creates.

## Universal Design for Learning Principles

**Principle I.** Provide multiple means of representation – present information and content in different ways.

**Principle II.** Provide multiple means of action and expression – differentiate the ways that students can express what they know.

**Principle III.** Provide multiple means of engagement – stimulate interest and motivation for learning.

# Universal Design for Learning Guidelines

| Provide Multiple Means of **Engagement** *Purposeful, motivated learners* | Provide Multiple Means of **Representation** *Resourceful, knowledgeable learners* | Provide Multiple Means of **Action & Expression** *Strategic, goal-directed learners* |
| --- | --- | --- |
| **Provide options for self-regulation** + Promote expectations and beliefs that optimize motivation + Facilitate personal coping skills and strategies + Develop self-assessment and reflection | **Provide options for comprehension** + Activate or supply background knowledge + Highlight patterns, critical features, big ideas, and relationships + Guide information processing, visualization, and manipulation + Maximize transfer and generalization | **Provide options for executive functions** + Guide appropriate goal-setting + Support planning and strategy development + Enhance capacity for monitoring progress |
| **Provide options for sustaining effort and persistence** + Heighten salience of goals and objectives + Vary demands and resources to optimize challenge + Foster collaboration and community + Increase mastery-oriented feedback | **Provide options for language, mathematical expressions, and symbols** + Clarify vocabulary and symbols + Clarify syntax and structure + Support decoding of text, mathematical notation, and symbols + Promote understanding across languages + Illustrate through multiple media | **Provide options for expression and communication** + Use multiple media for communication + Use multiple tools for construction and composition + Build fluencies with graduated levels of support for practice and performance |
| **Provide options for recruiting interest** + Optimize individual choice and autonomy + Optimize relevance, value, and authenticity + Minimize threats and distractions | **Provide options for perception** + Offer ways of customizing the display of information + Offer alternatives for auditory information + Offer alternatives for visual information | **Provide options for physical action** + Vary the methods for response and navigation + Optimize access to tools and assistive technologies |

**Figure 9.2 Framework for Universal Design for Learning (CAST, 2018).**

Presenting our students with alternatives in a learning episode varies their diet within the curriculum. Redesigning all your lessons to follow the principles of UDL can be overwhelming, and it takes time. A great way to start is with the 'plus one' strategy. Choose one topic or area in your curriculum, then either add one new way to present the content, add one new activity for students to complete or add one new way to assess understanding. When you've added this one new option to your course and feel comfortable with it, pick another area and use the plus one strategy (Office of Disability Resources, 2023). In relation to UDL there is much more that will be addressed on culturally responsive teaching in coming chapters.

## Celebrate the Journey

Students' accomplishments are to be lauded. We love to see our students' brilliance celebrated, parents proud and stakeholders in the community impressed. Incentivising challenge by making the outcome visible is stimulating. There is a temptation to assert that students are all 'gifted' in their own special way. This doesn't celebrate students who take on extension and feels like a hollow platitude. We don't wish to strip individual strengths away or devalue effort. I don't recommend the 'everybody gets a trophy' tactic – when students stand out, they should get a trophy. At the same time, achievements should not be diluted when they can be divaricated – we can create different routes or categories for success. Recognition should have weight and be specific. Reward the journey at each step as a way to map the efforts and successes of highflyers, all-rounders and those who are taking tentative first steps. Small wins and big wins should be marked. Students should feel seen, acknowledged and encouraged.

External competition and venues can place accomplishments in real-world contexts and give students authentic audiences. In educational structures, there is an emphasis on accountability and testing, which distances student achievement from students' motivation.

## Conclusion: Build the Safety Net to Catch Disengagement and Underachievement

An ethos of high expectations at a school can be a driver of change. However, it is important to recognise that challenge can be lacking in schools that garner incredible exam results. On a macro level, when we design programming we can pay attention to barriers that exist for equity-seeking groups. On a micro level, within our classrooms every day, we can consider the inner worlds of our students. I would not make the argument that there is an epidemic of 'busywork'. In fact, it seems that teachers are pressured to ensure that every lesson must be differentiated to death. The heart of the issue is that we have straight-line curricula, driven to cover the content for standardised tests and exams. This constrains the classroom. Within Gagné's Differentiated Model of Giftedness and Talent both environmental and intrapersonal catalysts impact capacity to engage, with a direct effect on student learning outcomes. Actualising potential is possible when we approach with empathy. We can guide teaching and learning for all students using engagement dimensions, learner profiles and personalised pedagogical approaches. Jenny is one example of disengagement, one that we caught and were able to re-engage. Once we recognise students, we can deploy strategies to animate and illuminate our learners.

# Reference List

Bachtel, K. (2023) *Gifted and Talented Program Teachers group*, [Facebook comment], 16 January 2023.

Barton, G. (2013) 'Pass the G&T', *Geoff Barton's Pick 'n' Mix*, 13 June. Available at: http://blog.geoffbarton.co.uk/site/Blog/Entries/2013/6/13_Pass_the_G&T.html (Accessed: 27 February 2023).

Baum, S. M., Renzulli, J. S. and Hébert, T. (1995) 'The prism metaphor: A new paradigm for reversing underachievement.' Storrs: University of Connecticut, The National Research Center on the Gifted and Talented.

Berglund, L. (2017) 'My disability defines me and that's okay', *But You Don't Look Blind*, 31 July. Available at: https://lifethelaurenway.wordpress.com/2017/07/31/my-disability-define-me-and-thats-okay/ (Accessed: 27 February 2023).

Betts, G. and Neihart, M. (1988) 'Profiles of the gifted and talented.' *Gifted Child Quarterly*, 32(2): pp. 248–253.

Blumenfeld, P. C. (1992) 'Classroom learning and motivation: Clarifying and expanding goal theory.' *Journal of Educational Psychology*, 84(3): pp. 272–281.

Borra, K. (2020) *Don't Coast: Accelerate Your Personal and Professional Growth*. Chennai, India: Notion Press.

Bottema-Beutel, K., Kapp, S. K., Lester, J. N., Sasson, N. J. and Hand, B. N. (2021) 'Avoiding ableist language: Suggestions for autism researchers.' *Autism in Adulthood*, 3(1): pp. 18–29.

Brody, L. E. and Mills, C. J. (1997) 'Gifted children with learning disabilities: A review of the issues.' *Journal of Learning Disabilities*, 30(3): pp. 282–296.

Buffalo Center for Social Research. (2023) *What is trauma-informed care?* Available at: https://socialwork.buffalo.edu/social-research/institutes-centers/institute-on-trauma-and-trauma-informed-care/what-is-trauma-informed-care.html (Accessed: 27 March 2023).

Bulluss, E. and Sesterka, A. (2023) '5 things everyone should understand about neurodiversity', *Psychology Today*, 5 October, [Online]. Available at: www-psychologytoday-com.cdn.ampproject.org/c/s/www.psychologytoday.com/au/blog/insights-about-autism/202310/5-things-we-should-all-know-about-neurodiversity?amp (Accessed: 19 December 2023).

CAST. (2018) *Universal Design for Learning guidelines version 2.2*. Available at: https://udlguidelines.cast.org/ (Accessed: 13 March 2023).

Center for Teaching Innovation. (2023) *Universal design for learning*. Available at: https://teaching.cornell.edu/teaching-resources/designing-your-course/universal-design-learning (Accessed: 13 March 2023).

Choudhury, S. (2021) 'Differentiating between UDL and differentiated instruction', *Novak Education*, 6 December. Available at: www.novakeducation.com/blog/udl-vs-differentiated-instruction-a-new-perspective (Accessed: 13 March 2023).

Didau, D. (2012) 'How effective learning hinges on good questioning', *Learning Spy*, 4 February. Available at: https://learningspy.co.uk/assessment/how-effective-learning-hinges-on-good-questioning/ (Accessed: 27 February 2023).

EduBirdie. (2022) *Relationship between friends and academic performance*. Available at: https://edubirdie.com/examples/relationship-between-friends-and-academic-performance/ (Accessed: 27 February 2023).

Eyre, D. (2011) *Room at the top: Inclusive education for high performance*. Available at: https://policyexchange.org.uk/publication/room-at-the-top-inclusive-education-for-high-performance/ (Accessed: 18 December 2023).

Flashman, J. (2012) 'Academic achievement and its impact on friend dynamics.' *Sociology of Education*, 85(1): pp. 61–80.

Freeman, J. (2010) *Gifted Lives*. London: Routledge.

Freire, P. (1993) *Pedagogy of the Oppressed*. New York, NY: Continuum Books.

Gierczyk, M. and Hornby, G. (2021) 'Twice-exceptional students: Review of implications for special and inclusive education.' *Education Sciences,* 11(2), p. 85.

GL Education. (2023) *PASS: A tool that supports students' wellbeing in learning and offers practical next steps*. Available at: www.gl-education.com/assessments/products/pass/ (Accessed: 27 February 2023).

Heuser, B. L., Wang, K. and Shahid, S. (2017) 'Global dimensions of gifted and talented education: The influence of national perceptions on policies and practices.' *Global Education Review,* 4(1): pp. 4–21.

Hill, A. P. and Madigan, D. J. (2022) 'Perfectionism, mattering, stress, and self-regulation of home learning of UK gifted and talented students during the COVID-19 pandemic.' *Gifted and Talented International*, 37(1): pp. 56–63.

InnerDrive. (n.d.) 'How to use scaffolding in your lessons', *InnerDrive*. Available at: https://blog.innerdrive.co.uk/scaffolding-in-lessons (Accessed: 27 February 2023).

Leggett, D. G., Shea, I. and Wilson, J. A. (2010) 'Advocating for twice-exceptional students: An ethical obligation.' *Research in the Schools*, 17(2): pp. 1–10.

Matthew, D. (2016) *Fragile learning*. Abstract in PhD by publication thesis. University of Bedfordshire. Available at: https://uobrep.openrepository.com/handle/10547/622106 (Accessed: 27 February 2023).

Mentor National. (2023) *Supporting youth in the wake of trauma*. Available at: www.mentoring.org/resource/supporting-youth-in-the-wake-of-trauma/ (Accessed: 27 February 2023).

Millin, S. (2020) *Dyslexia bytes – Q&A with Martin Bloomfield*. Available at: https://sandymillin.wordpress.com/2020/08/03/dyslexia-bytes-qa-with-martin-bloomfield/ (Accessed: 18 December 2023).

Moon, S. M. and Reis, S. M. (2004) 'Acceleration and twice-exceptional students.' In: Colangelo, N., Assouline, S. G. and Gross, M. U. M. (eds.) *A Nation Deceived: How Schools Hold Back America's Brightest Students, Volume II*. Iowa City, Iowa: Blank International Center for Gifted Education and Talent Development, pp. 109–120.

Morton, J. M. (2014) 'Cultural code-switching: Straddling the achievement gap.' *Journal of Political Philosophy*, 22(3): pp. 259–281.

Mulvahill, E. (2022) '18 effective ways to scaffold learning in the classroom', *We Are Teachers*, 17 October. Available at: www.weareteachers.com/ways-to-scaffold-learning/ (Accessed: 27 February 2023).

Neumann, M. M. and Ronksley-Pavia, M. (2020) 'Leveraging digital technologies for (re)engaging gifted and talented students in the middle years.' *Australian Journal of Middle Schooling*, 20(1): pp. 22–34.

Novak, K. (2021) 'If equity is a priority, UDL is a must', *Cult of Pedagogy*, 21 March. Available at: www.cultofpedagogy.com/udl-equity/ (Accessed: 27 February 2023).

Office of Disability Resources. (2023) *Universal Design for Learning*. Available at: www.rochester.edu/college/disability/faculty/universal-design.html (Accessed: 13 March 2023).

Ofsted. (2013) *The most able students: Are they doing as well as they should in our non-selective secondary schools?* Available at: https://assets.publishing.service.gov.uk/government/uploads/system/uploads/attachment_data/file/405518/The_most_able_students.pdf (Accessed: 27 February 2023).

Pellicano, L. (2015) *Watch your language when talking about autism*. Available at: https://theconversation.com/watch-your-language-when-talking-about-autism-44531 (Accessed: 27 February 2023).

Postma, M. (2022) *What does twice exceptional mean? Identifying and nurturing gifted children with ADHD*. Available at: www.additudemag.com/twice-exceptional-adhd-signs/ (Accessed: 27 February 2023).

Reis, S. and Renzulli, J. (1995) *Curriculum compacting: A systematic procedure for modifying the curriculum for above average ability students*. Available at: https://renzullilearning.com/wp-content/uploads/2019/08/4.-Curriculum-compacting-A-systematic-procedure-for-modifying-the-curriculum-for-above-average-ability-students.pdf (Accessed: 27 February 2023).

Renzulli, J. S. (2013) 'The achievement gap and the education conspiracy against low income children.' *International Journal for Talent Development and Creativity*, 1(1): pp. 45–55.

Ronksley-Pavia, M. and Neumann, M. M. (2020) 'Conceptualising gifted student (dis) engagement through the lens of learner (re) engagement.' *Education Sciences*, 10(10): p. 274.

Sherrington, T. (2012) 'Gifted and talented provision: A total philosophy', *Teacherhead*, 12 September. Available at: https://teacherhead.com/2012/09/12/gifted-and-talented-provision-a-total-philosophy/ (Accessed: 22 May 2024).

Sherrington, T. (2019) 'The #1 problem/weakness in teaching and how to address it', *Teacherhead,* 4 October. Available at: https://teacherhead.com/2019/10/04/the-1-problem-weakness-in-teaching-and-how-to-address-it/ (Accessed: 27 February 2023)

Silicon Valley Innovation Center. (2023) *Revolutionizing education: The power of adaptive learning platforms.* Available at: https://siliconvalley.center/blog/revolutionizing-education-the-power-of-adaptive-learning-platforms (Accessed: 15 January 2024).

Smith, A. (2006) 'Minister unveils national register for gifted pupils', *The Guardian,* 11 July, [Online]. Available at: www.theguardian.com/education/2006/jul/11/schools.uk3 (Accessed: 27 February 2023).

Te Tāhuhu o te Mātauranga (Ministry of Education). (n.d.) *Twice-multi exceptional learners.* Available at: https://gifted.tki.org.nz/define-and-identify/identification/twice-multi-exceptional-learners/ (Accessed: 27 February 2023).

Webb, J. T. (2000) 'Mis-diagnosis and dual diagnosis of gifted children: Gifted and LD, ADHD, OCD, Oppositional Defiant Disorder.' *The Annual Conference of the American Psychological Association*, Washington, DC, USA, August 7. Available at: https://files.eric.ed.gov/fulltext/ED448382.pdf (Accessed: 27 February 2023).

Winebrenner, S. (2003) 'Teaching strategies for twice-exceptional students.' *Intervention in School and Clinic,* 38(3): pp. 131–137.

# PART 3:
# EQUITY

# 10. TOSSING YOUR HAT IN THE RING

*Some of the brightest minds in the country can be found on the last benches of the classroom.*

**Dr A. P. J. Abdul Kalam, aerospace scientist and 11th president of India, The Tribune India, 2022**

A school has decided to invite everyone to the big top by embracing enrichment – excellent! Opening up programmes to all is the first step in creating a thriving enrichment environment, but there is more to entry than altering the selection process. I wish to explore what happens when we have the best intentions, but students still miss out. What are the larger barriers to enrichment?

Let's begin by pointing to a historic example of talent development: Mozart. No, not Wolfgang. I refer to Maria Anna Mozart, nicknamed Nannerl. She was considered the shining star in her musical family, and as a child, she overshadowed her brother. In 1763, the *Augsburger Intelligenz* pictured her thusly: 'Imagine an eleven-year-old girl, performing the most difficult sonatas and concertos of the greatest composers, on the harpsichord or fortepiano, with precision, with incredible lightness, with impeccable taste. It was a source of wonder to many.'

She received top billing (it was Wolfgang who toured *with her*) as she wowed audiences across Europe on the fortepiano and harpsichord (Hall, 2022). Nannerl's father, Leopold, surrounded his children with instruments and drilled them in intense and rigorous lessons. She practised for hours daily and performed constantly. Leopold observed that she played 'with incredible precision and so excellently. What it all amounts to is this, that my little girl, although she is only 12 years old, is one of the most skilful players in Europe' (Classic FM, 2021).

Nannerl was not only a performer; she also wrote music. Dr Martin Jarvis, a conductor and professor, spent a decade forensically analysing Wolfgang's scores and found evidence that three of his five violin concertos could have been composed or modified by Nannerl (Hall, 2022). In addition to the stylistic differences, Jarvis notes the different handwriting used on the original sheet music and the fact that Wolfgang compliments Nannerl's compositions in letters, writing in 1770, 'My dear sister! I am in awe that you can compose so well, in a word, the song you wrote is beautiful' (Classic FM, 2021). He frequently encouraged her to write more.

This brings us to ask: where did all the talent go? Nannerl's public career came to an abrupt end at 18 years old. When she reached adulthood, her place on the stage was gone. Her father stopped taking her on the road. Nannerl was left in Salzburg while Wolfgang continued to perform. Playwright Sylvia Milo, who penned *The Other Mozart*, notes that 'women had to play for nothing. If they made money off their music, they were thought of as prostitutes' (Classic FM, 2021). Nannerl apparently stopped composing after her marriage, and her early work was lost. Like so many female composers of the time, it was not preserved or given the equivalent value.[17] Biographers relegated her to a footnote – an inspiration to her brother's greatness, as opposed to a musician in her own right. Her story is not one of a single villain thwarting her success and legacy; it is simply one example of how a person's gifts can be both repressed and overlooked (Milo, 2015). Nannerl was lucky to be born to a determined father who taught and nurtured her talent. She was unlucky to be born in the wrong era and have her career truncated by her gender.

Gifted education has become the face of unequal academic opportunities. This is a shame because special programmes can nurture talent and develop the next generation of leaders. Is gender a significant barrier when it comes to gifted programming? Depressingly and historically, the answer is yes. Since gifted programmes have been introduced, there have been studies tracking the participation and identification gaps between girls and boys. There has been overall discrimination in gifted programmes in favour of boys, and one of the contributors is teacher referrals and recommendations. The Petersen meta-analysis of 130 studies published between 1975 and 2011 found that boys were 1.19 times more likely than girls to be identified as gifted and included in gifted programmes. This was especially evident among pre-adolescents, within gifted summer programmes and for students who were

---

17  It is only recently that her virtuosity and musical contributions have been recognised. There is now an annual symposium dedicated to Nannerl Mozart at the Mozarteum University in Salzburg.

identified as gifted using IQ scores and standardised tests (Petersen, 2013). Of the American system, Winner (1996) found that at the start of school, girls and boys are identified in equal proportions for gifted programmes, but as they get older there is a striking loss in the proportion of girls selected. In addition, parents appear to hold gender-differentiated beliefs about their children's abilities, even when objective indicators find that competence in girls and boys is similar (Jacobs and Weisz, 1994). In gifted education, gender stereotypes affect children's self-perception. There is a 'stereotype threat' for women and minorities; when these students are subjected to constant negative stereotyping based on their academic proficiency and ability, there is an actual decrease in performance (Aronson, Quinn and Spencer, 1998). Research has also shown that these perceptions in gifted programmes have impacted the identification, guidance and mentoring of girls (Jacobs and Weisz, 1994). Long-standing controversies concerning gender relations and definitions of giftedness continue to have an impact on the educational and career development of girls and women. Moderate differences favouring boys in batteries of cognitive abilities, like spatial rotation, continue to be highly publicised and are often interpreted to mean that gifted girls are less able than men to achieve in science, technology, engineering and mathematics (STEM) fields (Kerr and Malmsten, 2020).

As Dr Sally Reis writes: 'Gifted and talented females face conflicts between their own abilities and the social structure of their world. They confront both external barriers (lack of support from families, stereotyping, and acculturation in home, school, and the rest of society) and internal barriers (self-doubt, self-criticism, lowered expectations, and the attribution of success to effort rather than ability)' (Reis, n.d.). I felt it in my own experience as a student. I have female friends who have been vastly outnumbered in their fields, finding themselves isolated among a sea of men in their university engineering classes. I've witnessed the extra pressure they have internalised to prove themselves. A sense of belonging is important. For instance, the message that maths ability is a fixed trait and that women are less able has eroded women's sense of belonging in maths and their desire to pursue the subject (Good, Rattan and Dweck, 2012).

The lack of girls in STEM-related gifted programmes has been well publicised. A 1992 study reported that fewer females are labelled as mathematically gifted than males. The study also stated that females labelled as gifted are less likely to take demanding high school maths and science courses, major in maths or science in college (40% versus 72%), or pursue a career in a maths or science-related field (24% versus 56%) (Rose, 1999). Fortunately, in the past few years, we have observed a massive course correction to get girls into STEM subjects – there is progress, if not parity. More women in the US are majoring in STEM. The Integrated Postsecondary Education Data System found that in 2020, 45% of students majoring in STEM fields were women, up from 40% in 2010 and 34% in 1994 (Kantrowitz, 2022). However, engineering and computer science – two of the most lucrative STEM fields – remain heavily male-dominated. Only 21% of engineering majors and 19% of computer science majors are women (American Association of University Women, n.d.).

In the UK, there has been a 31% increase in entries from women and girls to STEM A-levels between 2010 and 2019 (Mediaofficer, 2021). Boys are still far more likely to study STEM A-level subjects despite the fact that girls outperform boys in most STEM subjects at both GCSE and A-level. There has been a correlating modest increase of female entrants to engineering and technology courses at university, running at 21% in 2019, but this needs to be contextualised by the fact that women made up 57% of the student population overall. Encouragingly, there have been recent increases in girls studying physics A-level, taking this to 25% overall, but this is still strikingly low given that data shows girls are more likely than boys to pass A-level physics and maths (Raraty, n.d.). A lack of female professors and role models in the workforce contributes to fewer women feeling encouraged, mentored and supported in labs.

In the long run, academic self-concept is one of the main predictors for academic achievement, motivational variables associated with learning like academic interest, and academic emotions like test anxiety and enjoyment (Precke and Brüll, 2008). In addition, academic self-perceptions influence educational and vocational choices, like lower participation rates of females in the maths/science domain. Recommendations to reduce gender bias include encouraging pre-adolescent girls to apply for gifted programmes and using multiple assessment criteria to identify gifted students, but these are yet to be widely implemented.

Unfortunately, gender is not the only aspect of gifted education where we find larger cultural barriers. We have seen that advanced learning programmes tend to benefit children who are already advantaged, taking resources away from those who can't participate (Callahan and Plucker, 2020). As researchers Worrell and Dixson write: 'The disproportionality in the ethnic-racial and socioeconomic make-up of students in gifted and talented education programs has been identified by many scholars as the most critical and most intractable issue facing the field of gifted education' (Worrell and

Dixson, 2022, p. 79). Despite the efforts of educators and policymakers, this disproportionality has not been remedied. Social justice and civil rights are now being addressed with urgency, with *Gifted Child Quarterly* devoting an entire special issue to equity in gifted education in 2022, but there remains a low gifted enrolment for economically under-resourced students. There are gender stereotypes still prevalent in STEM subjects. There are weaknesses in how we treat twice-exceptional students. There is institutional racism facing students of colour.

A nationwide 2019 study by Yaluma and Tyner found that Black and Latin American students are consistently underrepresented in US gifted education, especially those in high-poverty schools. In fact, from 2012 to 2016, the percentage of Black students in gifted programmes fell by 4.2% in high-poverty schools and 5.1% overall, to make up less than 10% of all gifted students and less than 5% of gifted students in high-poverty schools. Students from equity-seeking groups across the board are missing from gifted programmes. South Dakota and Alaska, for instance, have a combined 46,000 Indigenous American children, but fewer than 300 (0.6%) were considered gifted in 2015–16 (Gentry et al., 2019). The field of gifted education has much work to do to mitigate the inequity and lack of opportunity.

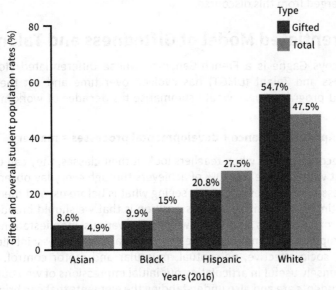

Figure 10.1 Racial/ethnic breakdowns of students in gifted programmes compared to population share (Yaluma and Tyner, 2021).

As teachers we see individual students suffer from lack of access to gifted programming. However, the long view can be seen through the lens of social reproduction theory, whereby generational inequity is reinforced. Gifted education is seen by some as an instrument of social reproduction and one of the means whereby schools perpetuate racism and economic injustice – by denying enhanced educational opportunities to the poor and non-white students and extending special privileges to the more affluent (Borland, 2004). By not identifying students, the field of gifted education contributes to and fuels achievement gaps.

It is against this background that enrichment programmes and whole-child development are overtaking and replacing gifted and talented programmes. Even if programmes are 'open' to all, we cannot make assumptions that everyone can then take part. Opportunities can be presented to students, but still remain out of reach. There are barriers that enrichment programmes face and that we should consider in our design. I'd like to evaluate these obstacles and how to overcome them. It is impossible to discuss the gifted paradigm without looking at one of the most influential models in the field. Let's unpack this important framing of giftedness and how it considers the specific conditions necessary for gifts to flourish, and competing theories that emerged from this discourse.

## Differentiated Model of Giftedness and Talent

Dr Françoys Gagné is a French-Canadian whose Differentiated Model of Giftedness and Talent (DMGT) has evolved over time and set the stage for gifted programming. I would summarise his decades of work into this formula:

**Aptitude + chance + developmental processes = mastery**

Gagné recognises that when teachers look at their classes, they can usually point out who is in the top 10% of achievers through everyday observation and assessment. However, there is seeing what is before us, and then there is activating this potential. Gagné's position is that we should broaden the concept of giftedness and acknowledge its various manifestations. The DMGT proposes six domains for the raw material of giftedness: intellectual, creative, socio-affective, perceptual, muscular and motor control. These are immensely useful in articulating our initial impressions of who our high-ability students are and also understanding the elements that can bring gifts forward in all (Gagné, 2013).

In Gagné's view, the distinction between gifted and talented is that one can turn into the other. Gifts are developed into talents, and talents have competencies across disciplines. There are factors and processes that transform natural ability into mastery. Gagné created these definitions:

## Gagné's Definitions

**'Gifted' is not academic. 'Talented' is not athletic.**

**Giftedness** designates the possession and use of untrained and spontaneously expressed superior natural abilities (called aptitudes or gifts) in at least one ability domain to a degree that places an individual at least among the top 10% of his or her age peers.

**Talent** designates the superior mastery of systematically developed abilities (or skills) and knowledge in at least one field of human activity to a degree that places an individual within at least the upper 10% of age peers who are or have been active in that field or fields (Gagné, 2000).

Gagné's model sees a gift as being brought forth by catalysts. The catalysts for activating giftedness are environmental and intrapersonal. He also postulates an environment of gifts within the individual, which can then be developed into talents due to the environment surrounding the individual. Gagné's *intrapersonal* factors are familiar – I see a resemblance to Renzulli's model with dispositional traits like task commitment and self-regulation. *Environmental* factors can be macro (e.g. cultural or demographic) and micro (e.g. family, teachers, events). These catalysts can have positive or negative impacts. The *developmental process* is talent development through engagement with systematic learning and deep practice. Schools can create these opportunities through valuable activities, investment in programmes and expertise. Gagné points to school provision as part of the environment – both a school's explicit programming and its overall structure. What I would draw attention to are the hidden factors that require us to adapt our provisions.

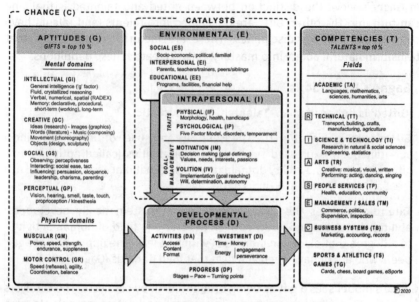

Figure 10.2 Differentiated Model of Giftedness and Talent (Gagné, 2013).

Gagné has written controversially that 'one cannot be talented without first being gifted' (Gagné, 2000, p. 2), and this determines the flow of the DMGT. Before making assumptions, Gagné is abundantly clear that the construct of 'natural abilities' in no way subscribes to the innate view of giftedness. He writes that 'in every presentation of the theory I insist that gifts are not innate, that they develop during the course of childhood, and sometimes continue to do so during adulthood' (Gagné, 2013, p. 12). Gagné has vigorously discussed and debated the research. One fantastic paper that he has written is 'The pronat vs. antinat', where he engages head-on in the debate of whether 'giftedness' exists (Gagné, 2009). We may say that a child is a 'born pianist' to convey that she progressed rapidly through the grades of piano, but no one is born 'innately' knowing how to play the piano. No 3-year-old sits down and plays a concerto. A child will experiment by plunking the keys and teasing out tunes, then study notes and encode sheet music; she will practise routinely and hit the wrong keys. Eventually, her finger movements become autonomous, she matures, she evolves, she learns and she creates. Natural abilities are not immutable, nor do they 'suddenly appear'; they are fostered by the environment and subsequently matured by skill development.[18] A student's metacognitive abilities can be awakened, retrieval fluency honed or creative artistry granted the space to flourish. The DMGT recognises that abilities in any domain can be progressively transformed and realised as achievements. The model emphasises the systematic development of knowledge and skills. Note that other theories don't place the same emphasis on the 'nature' component.

## Evolving Complexity Theory

In Dai's Evolving Complexity Theory (ECT), talent is not a fixed genetic constant waiting to be 'unleashed' based on resources. Instead, 'Talent emerges contextually and temporarily through maturation and adaptive transactions with relevant social-cultural environments' (Dai, 2021, p. 102). There has been much debate over Gagné's role in perpetuating a 'nature-first' argument, with gifts to be developed. On the other hand, we see Anders Ericsson's work on deliberate practice, which places 'nurture' at the forefront. ECT doesn't stake a claim in the nature versus nurture dichotomy, but attempts to transcend it. Evolving Complexity Theory is a developmental theory that views talent as 'a prolonged process of human adaptation resulting in outstanding human accomplishment' (Dai, 2021, p. 101). Human potential is organismic, holistic and non-reductionist. A person is an open dynamic system that can produce novelty, is constantly in transition, intrinsically robust and extrinsically adaptive to the environment. The model also emphasises the role of feedback loops and self-organisation in shaping the evolution of complex systems. As the system becomes more complex and interconnected, it may develop feedback loops that reinforce certain patterns or behaviours, leading to further organisation and complexity. A feature of ECT is that education offers both pedagogical tools and social-cultural support for human development. Both Dai's ECT and Gagné's DMGT attempt to explain why some students' gifts appear more easily, and more profoundly, than others. Both allude to stochastic processes – that the behaviour of the 'system' or individual learner's progress is not completely predictable due to the presence of random elements. The process is defined by a set of variables that represent the system's state at different points in time. Behind all gifts is chance.

---

[18] One could make an argument that savantism is an exception – where peoples with developmental differences exhibit abilities like hyperlexia or exceptional memory. I do not address savantism in this book because it is a marginal phenomenon, but those spectacular cases are fascinating to investigate. They too are part of 'chance'.

# 'Chance' and Enrichment

'Chance' is compelling as a catch-all phrase. However, it should not imply that success is a roll of the dice. We should not frame educational structures as passive inheritors as opposed to perpetrators. Chance is often a benign way of whitewashing structural inequity. Chance encompasses the 'where, what and when' that presents some individuals with more opportunities than others. The chance of living near a school with an enrichment programme, the chance of being born with hyperextended joints for swimming and the chance of having an enthusiastic mathematics teacher as a mother are all ways a child could be lucky. There is also the chance of being thwarted and having barriers that block the progression of gifts into reaching fruition as talents.

Purdue University's Gifted Education Research and Resource Institute concluded in a shattering and extensive 2019 publication that wealthy schools identified more children as gifted than underfunded ones, with students of colour being underrepresented across the board (Gentry et al., 2019). The Purdue study determined that whether a child is identified with gifts and talents is largely determined by three structural forces in the United States:

1. Access: a child must attend a school that actually identifies students, and in 2019, more than one third of children in the US did not attend such schools. In the 2015–16 school year, 42% of schools did not identify a single student with gifts or talents.

2. Class: children who attend non-wealthy (Title I) schools are identified at only 58% of the rate of those who attend wealthier (non-Title I) schools.

3. Race: children who are Asian or white are two to more than 10 times more likely to be identified with gifts and talents than students who are Indigenous American, Indigenous Hawaiian/Pacific Islander, Black or Latin American.

Chance is the lived experience of structural inequality. It is our environment – part of the larger geographic, demographic and sociological picture. This is where class, race, ethnicity and gender bias come into play. I would point to studies that look more specifically at the socio-economic context. Gymnastics is often cited as a prohibitively expensive sport. Parents must be able to afford the uniforms, camps, gym fees, coaching fees, transportation and hotel costs for competitions, and have access to great medical care. This is on top of having the time to transport their child to early morning practices and commit to weekend travel. Parents' ability to support their children may be constrained by work or familial commitments.

This is one example of why aptitude is not a guarantee of success. Gagné explains that 'no causal component stands alone. They all interact with each other and with the learning process in very complex ways, and these interactions will differ significantly from one person to the next' (Gagné, 2004, p. 123). Chance can have a strong role in physical domains. These physical gifts can be easily cancelled out by sociological biases. The world of ballet is a prime example – height and the shape of a ballerina's feet are genetic traits that may allow a dancer to excel. At the same time, dance is plagued by sizeism, racism and colourism. The lack of people of colour in ballet could first be explained by the financial barriers. There are structural inequities that result in an unequal distribution of educational resources. People of colour live disproportionately in areas lacking access to studios, specialised equipment and one-on-one training in many sports. However, even students with genetic advantages and financial means come up against ballet's rigid white beauty ideal. This is not unusual. It was only in 2018 that Berlin's prestigious Staatsballett removed the requirement for people of colour to wear white makeup when performing on stage (Suliman, 2021).

We see slow changes but at a cost to people of colour. In 2015, Misty Copeland became the first Black woman promoted to a principal dancer in the American Ballet Theatre, the pre-eminent ballet company in the United States. She was born with the 'right feet' and trained to reach the elite level, but as a Black woman, she had to overcome racial roadblocks. Copeland has been quite vocal in calling out the barriers she faced in the world of ballet. Her pathway to success was one where she was required to pancake her skin white. In one instance, she was dropped from a filmed performance because she did not 'match' the other dancers in the corps. Copeland had the emotional isolation of being a person of colour in a white space. As Copeland writes: 'It could be a very lonely experience, at times. I was already different, already being judged. But deep down, what kept me going was that I believed that if I could keep working on my craft, and just be the best, then eventually the colour of my skin wouldn't matter' (Copeland, 2020). While her determination is admirable, she had the burden of proving herself above and beyond for her talent to be seen before her race. Copeland's journey is not unique. As researcher Emma D. Golden writes: 'As long as the predominantly white audience of ballet continues to place a premium on

Euro-centric identities and standards of beauty, ballet institutions will not be competitively incentivized to diversify and to render ballet accessible to marginalized communities' (Golden, 2018).

Dr James Borland points out that one misconception tangled in the underrepresentation of low-income children in gifted programmes is that underachievement results from a lack of motivation to achieve, especially among those from equity-seeking racial and ethnic groups. This fallacy places blame on individual students as opposed to systems. He goes on to point out that this is part of a larger issue: 'the failure of our educational system to educate economically disadvantaged and minority students that is the product of persistent structural inequities in our society' (Borland, 2004, p. 11).

These are the larger barriers. We can't fix the element of chance, but we can see the inequity it creates and adapt. Understanding racial barriers, class differences or gender bias is part of making education inclusive. On the surface, it can look like school enrichment is open to all – this may stem from the fact that there is no explicitly selective gifted programming, or that programming is done through student self-selection. In my introduction, I gave the example of Luka, where an intervention could be a referral to Model United Nations – but there could be a lack of financial ability to pay for trips and conferences or a lack of time for Luka to participate because he works a part-time job after school. A bully could impact his wellbeing, or an injury could derail his participation. Teachers, siblings and peers can exert a positive or negative influence. If a school does not have a Model UN provision due to a lack of funding, lack of student interest or lack of experienced teachers to lead, there is little opportunity for skills development. Access to programmes and guidance from experts is key. Out-of-school programming is one of the most common ways to implement enrichment. Students benefit from exposure to new activities, mentorship from adults, exploration outside the curriculum, opportunities to practise new skills and roles, and develop independence.

Students don't all leave the starting line when the gun fires. Let's take a look at the variable of 'when'. Children born at the start of the year may have an advantage in size and experience in athletics. Boucher and Mutimer (1994) conducted a famous study that showed this cumulative effect, with December-born children falling short of their January-born peers in the national hockey leagues. This cumulative effect on early-born students can exist in schools. I have a son born in June. He will start school nine months earlier than my October-born daughter. My daughter will have had more time to practise and develop skills. This comes into play in the identification of gifted students where typically that precocity matters, whether in accessing extension in the classroom or enrichment outside of it. Early-born children will be 'ahead' in their year group. This can be an accrued advantage with some building on this head start. There are simple ways to address this – for instance, schools frequently track students who are later born, factoring this into early childhood education. We should question whether recruiting for gifted programmes at a very young age is a good idea. The approach is problematic and illustrates the need for schools to audit their policies and implement change. Pre-school identification is not unusual, with experts writing about qualities that students can be assessed for in the first year of life (Ruf, 2009). For the most part, any early leads will dissipate over time, but early identification for special gifted programmes creates an uneven playing field. Worrell and Dixson have commented that we should focus less on early identification for gifted programming and more on providing quality educational opportunities to as many students as resources allow before societal inequalities start to compound (Worrell and Dixson, 2022). The structures of our schools and the decisions we make in creating programmes have a tremendous impact. Borland makes the argument that gifted programmes are often held back from the students with lowest household incomes who, if they had access, the programmes could have the largest impact on. He writes:

> 'As a society, we have made a collective decision to provide a significantly richer public education to children from more affluent suburban families and an often shockingly inadequate one to poorer urban children, children who are much more likely to be children of color. Moreover, those children to whom we have deigned to give the crumbs of our public educational system are also those who depend on it the most, those whose parents cannot afford supplementary classes, private tutoring, academically oriented camps, and so forth.

> 'The implications for gifted education are obvious. Giftedness, however it is defined, is more likely to emerge in schools in which the prevailing assumption is that children have talents, not deficits, in schools in which the teachers have the professional skills to recognize and nurture these talents, in schools in which there are adequate materials to allow children to learn, and in schools in which the curriculum has not been picked clean of such "frills" as music and art, areas of human experience that enrich the mind and the spirit. And these are more likely to be schools attended by White middle- and upper-middle-class children.' (Borland, 2004, pp. 12–13)

There has been a large movement towards universal screening as a strategy to shrink the achievement gap for underrepresented groups (Margot and Melin, 2020). In theory, universal testing should allow all students to qualify for special programmes as it casts a wide net and eliminates teacher referral bias. However, as previously outlined, while the intention is there to identify students from diverse backgrounds, the results can perpetuate social immobility. Plucker and Peters (2018) have written about how universal screening using local norms is a way to close poverty-based excellence gaps. One recommendation to combat this is to shift the purpose of universal testing from a process of selection to a process of support. It is through early intervention that we can intentionally seek students from low-income households or underserved populations and in the early years provide psychosocial and academic support (Margot and Melin, 2020). There is also the matter of which type of data is used – a qualitative approach can be much more useful, as Kate A. Bachtel wrote in her doctoral dissertation:

> 'Changing how schools measure success holds tremendous potential to positively impact educational practices and subsequently student outcomes. Associating children with numerical scores can dehumanize and blind educators to individual student developmental intricacies, to understanding how they are experiencing the world which is the key to facilitating growth. To this end, I recommend an increased emphasis on the collection and communication of qualitative data.' (Bachtel, 2017, p. 227)

Offering enrichment programming to everyone makes complete sense when considering how arbitrary and artificial conceptions of giftedness are. Dr Albert Ziegler is another key player in gifted education and has made the powerful argument that gifts are not personal attributes, even though we have largely conceptualised gifts as the properties of individuals (Ziegler, 2005). It is we as observers who determine what a gift is, and our perception can change. Rules and definitions are fleeting. Ziegler gives examples of basketball players and theoretical physicists. Imagine basketball rules were altered so that the basket now hangs 20cm lower than previously dictated. This would seriously reduce the significance of height for success in this game, and all of a sudden, players who were previously gifted would be joined by a much larger pool – they would no longer be special and would in essence 'lose' their gift. Then consider physicists who a few decades ago found themselves redundant when computer-based simulations replaced the complex processing functions that once made them excellent in their domain. The abilities of basketball players and theoretical physicists have not changed; our 'rules' have. As Ziegler writes: 'Let us make clear: Talents and gifts are not personal attributes, but attributions made by scientists' (Ziegler, 2005, p. 414).

There are also several effects that we should consider:

- The big-fish-little-pond effect – it is not the level a student plays at but who they play against that is measured.

- The Aldrin effect – Neil Armstrong made history as the first human being to set foot on the moon. The action was 'copied' by Buzz Aldrin moments later. Armstrong is the groundbreaker; Aldrin is the second fiddle.

- The echo effect – the orientation of norms changes. For instance, Johannes Kepler was an astronomer who conceived the three laws of planetary motion in 1609 through 10 years of study – college students using Kepler's data set are easily able to recognise the mathematical relationships in an hour. Does this mean that these university students should all be considered geniuses?

Given how mutable a 'gift' is, enrichment programming starts with the premise that anyone can toss their hat in the ring. We have seen the disadvantage a student can have when throwing their hat from the back benches. It is a daunting task to overcome barriers. So, let's explore how we can place every child in a favourable position.

## Action Over Traits: The Actiotope Model

In Albert Ziegler's Actiotope Model of Giftedness, the focus is not on the properties a person possesses, but on actions and their development within a complex system. *Action* is how learners can consciously progress over time by interacting with their environment.

My favourite Ziegler article uses the following scenarios to bring the Actiotope Model to life: we are asked to imagine a boy playing cards in a favela of Rio de Janeiro, a girl in suburbia deciding whether to study for a mathematics test or watch TV after school and a boy in an underserved community in Harlem playing basketball. Each represents a different opportunity for personal development – but how could they become experts? What conditions would lead to becoming a professional card player, a brilliant mathematician or an NBA all-star (Ziegler, Vialle, and Wimmer, 2013)? The argument 'emphasizes the dynamic interaction of individuals with the environment. The focus of interest under the Actiotope Model, then, is action not traits.' This in turn asks educators to create an environment of action.

In the Actiotope Model of Giftedness, excellence is also considered a result of self-organisation and adaptation. While the above-mentioned learners may show a propensity for their field for their age, they can in no way be classified as experts. This work echoes the studies done by Anders Ericsson on deliberate practice. People become experts through effective action repertoires. Action repertoires mean that we can create experts in a specialised field in a number of ways:

- *Create automated cognitive action steps.* Automated cognitive action steps refer to the mental processes or actions that become habitual and ingrained through repetition and practice. These are cognitive tasks or behaviours that individuals perform with little conscious effort or thought because they have become routine. For example, when someone learns to ride a bike, initially they have to consciously think about balancing, pedalling and steering. However, with practice, these actions become automatic, and the individual can ride the bike without actively thinking about each movement. Similarly, in academic or professional contexts, tasks such as reading, writing, problem solving or decision making can become automated cognitive action steps through repeated experience. After students automate foundational cognitive skills, such as basic maths operations or reading comprehension strategies, they can the focus their cognitive resources on more complex tasks and learning goals.

- *Develop strategies based on experience.* This means having more approaches to draw from and a rich basis to link those strategies. For instance, in a science class, a specific example of an automated cognitive action step could be the process of making observations and forming hypotheses during an experiment. Initially, students may need explicit instruction and guidance on observing carefully, recording their observations accurately and using evidence to formulate hypotheses. They can then move on to drawing inferences, making connections between observed phenomena and scientific principles, and forming hypotheses about the outcomes of experiments without extensive prompting.

- *Use introspection to find more elegant strategies when problem solving.* This would include applying prior knowledge and using existing knowledge and concepts to interpret observations, generate explanations and anticipate outcomes when problem solving.

- *Refining for mastery.* The learning cycle continues with students building on past successful strategies and honing them to sophistication.

Together these characteristics explain how one arrives at mastery.[19] Ziegler positions the Actiotope Model in opposition to Gagné's Differentiated Model of Giftedness and Talent when it comes to developmental potential. As he states, 'Let us make clear: Talents and gifts are not personal attributes, but attributions made by scientists' (Ziegler, 2005, p. 414). In this view, traditional conceptions of giftedness have an overemphasis on personality traits and insufficient consideration of environmental aspects. Albert Ziegler has noted that, with exceptions, we see gifts as personal attributes, which can be immediately refuted when gifts emerge or disappear when there are changes in a person's environment.

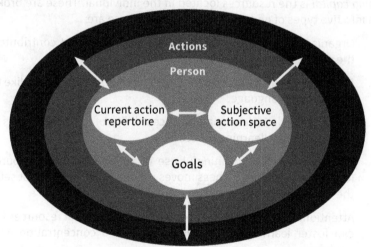

Figure 10.3 The Actiotope Model (Ziegler et al., 2006).

This chasm between individual responsibility and systemic structures captures the thought process behind the Actiotope Model. The model begins with the simple fact that living systems develop and evolve alongside their environment. In the natural world, we would call this environment a biotope,

---

19 There are also the physical adaptations that one can make to meet the requirements of a particular domain – for instance, the different muscular structures of weightlifters.

so the action system that encompasses an individual's environment is therefore referred to as an 'actiotope'. Listing traits we should look out for in identifying giftedness is useful. Identifying behaviours we can develop is constructive. Within this model is the concept of educational and learning capital – simply put, the former is external capital and the latter is internal capital. These are key factors in the pursuit of excellence. *Educational capital* is in the environment. It refers to all external resources that build up effective action repertoires. We have already covered some of these at length, like economic and infrastructure capital (e.g. amount of funding a government provides for education per student, a school's facilities or a family's economic status), cultural capital (e.g. stereotype threat for girls in STEM) and social capital (e.g. having an older sibling at home to help with homework). Another crucial external factor is didactic education capital, which is the design and implementation of pedagogical approaches (e.g. teachers' efforts to continually improve their practice).

*Learning capital* is the resources located in the individual. These are broken down into five types of endogenous resources. These are:

1. Organismic – a person's health and constitution that contribute to the success of the learning process.

2. Actional – cognitive actions that a person is able to perform, like the ability to use language.

3. Telic – attitude to learning and accessibility of functional goals for improving one's learning processes.

4. Episodic – making meaningful use of actional learning resources (e.g. knowing different chess moves is not enough – one must select the strongest move).

5. Attentional – quantitative and qualitative attentional resources that can foster learning (e.g. sufficient time and concentration when studying).

What is important is the co-evolution of educational and learning capital. A student's motivation in mathematics (telic learning capital) may be affected if all their friends are mathletes (social educational capital). A fencer may not develop their full episodic capital unless they have access to expert competitors to practise against in the form of didactic capital. The lesson here is that when we design enrichment programming, we must do so with the view that learning and educational capital together facilitate mastery.

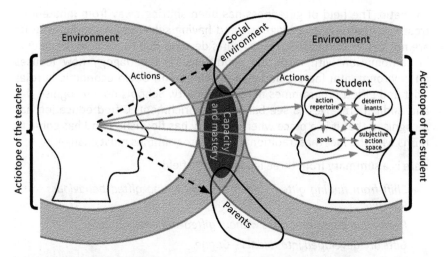

Figure 10.4 Actiotope environment (adapted from Ziegler and Stoeger, 2007).

So how do we build effective repertoires of action? It requires a thoughtful evaluation of all educational and learning capital. As Ziegler notes, the chain breaks at its weakest link. In planning individual learning pathways for students, it is vital that we understand how interconnected and possibly fragile these links are: 'Otherwise, the long chain of learning episodes, which is necessary to achieve excellence in a card game, in a basketball game, or in mathematics, would be damaged at some point' (Ziegler, Vialle and Wimmer 2013). Learners can be seen as 'actiotope units' that interact with their environment to create a specific behavioural outcome. This outcome is determined by the individual's goals, motives and abilities, as well as the affordances and constraints of the environment. Overall, the Actiotope Model provides a useful framework for understanding how human behaviour is influenced by a complex interplay of personal and environmental factors. It helps us to better understand how to design spaces that support positive outcomes for individuals and communities. We create enriching environments that empower, motivate and challenge students to achieve excellence.

## Design with Diversity, Equity and Inclusion

Inclusion is the foundation of enrichment, with the transformational power to reframe giftedness and move it from a label to a state of mind. 'Gifted and talented' has a loaded history, and any change in nomenclature is cosmetic. The field of giftedness has been shifting away from innateness, treating giftedness as a diagnosis and having selective programmes. Gifts are not the result of static traits – gifts develop due to a set of behaviours in combination with nurturing conditions. The pedagogy now focuses on environmental factors and skill development. Socio-economic hurdles exist and gifted programmes magnify inequity. Schools now recognise this and audit themselves to see barriers to enrichment. Gifted education has recognised that it is a place where inequity has flourished and has come to terms with the fact that traditional gifted programmes must change.

Here is a summary from three leaders in the field:

*Shift from finding gifted students to cultivating gifted behaviours – Renzulli.*

*Reimagine gifted programs without gifted students – Borland.*

*Gifts are developed into talents – Gagné.*

The traditional divide between 'gifted' and 'talented' is artificial. Creativity and task commitment are evident across all disciplines. Identifying our high-aptitude pupils is important – it allows teachers to effectively differentiate in the classroom, plan tiered learning experiences and question with intention. Education is moving away from old-fashioned identification. Single-criterion identification is giving way to triangulation through multifaceted subject and/or skill-specific identification. Targeted extension recognises that some students need different learning opportunities and support in their education. Targeted extension does not mean we offer the same uniform set of differentiated work to a prescribed group – these are not a set category of students with identical interests and needs. We should be responsive to them and use adaptive teaching to view them as individuals. In addition, extension in the classroom can target high-ability students due to the level of challenge it presents. However, it should be open and visible to all students.

All children have potential; some aptitudes appear more easily and profoundly than others. These aptitudes can be developed and transformed into mastery, intrinsic motivation, self-esteem, accomplishment and even virtuosity. There is an element of luck in a student's environment, but as educators, we influence that environment. We can recognise these elements of chance to help determine how we can open opportunities to more students. Self-selection and the creation of student profiles are examples of processes that invest students in their own growth. Educators and school structures are capable of shaping the environmental catalysts and intrapersonal traits that lead to achievement and mastery.

# Reference List

American Association of University Women. (n.d.) *The STEM gap: Women and girls in science, technology, engineering and mathematics.* Available at: www.aauw.org/resources/research/the-stem-gap/ (Accessed: 3 May 2024).

Aronson, J., Quinn, D. M. and Spencer, S. J. (1998) 'Stereotype threat and the academic underperformance of minorities and women.' In: Swim, J. K. and Stangor, C. (eds.) *Prejudice.* Cambridge: Academic Press, pp. 83–103.

Bachtel, K. A. (2017) *Seeing the unseen: An educational criticism of a gifted school.* PhD dissertation. University of Denver.

Borland, J. H. (2004) *Issues and practices in the identification and education of gifted students from under-represented groups.* New York, NY: Teachers College, Columbia University.

Boucher, J. L. and Mutimer, B. T. (1994) 'The relative age phenomenon in sport: A replication and extension with ice-hockey players.' *Research Quarterly for Exercise and Sport,* 65(4): pp. 377–381.

Callahan, C. M. and Plucker, J. A. (2020) *The evidence base for advanced learning programs.* Available at: https://kappanonline.org/evidence-base-advanced-learning-programs-gifted-plucker-callahan/ (Accessed: 16 September 2022).

Classic FM. (2021) *Was Mozart's sister actually the most talented musician in the family?* Available at: www.classicfm.com/composers/mozart/nannerl-mozarts-sister-better-musician/ (Accessed: 16 September 2022).

Copeland, M. (2020) *Technique has no color.* Available at: www.theplayerstribune.com/posts/misty-copeland-ballet-racism (Accessed: 16 September 2022).

Dai, D. Y. (2021) 'Evolving Complexity Theory (ECT) of talent development: A new vision for gifted and talented education.' In: Sternberg, R. J. and Ambrose, D. (eds.). *Conceptions of Giftedness and Talent.* New York, NY: Palgrave, pp. 99–121.

Gagné, F. (2000) *A differentiated model of giftedness and talent, year 2000 update.* U.S. Department of Education: Educational Resources Information Center (ERIC).

Gagné, F. (2004) 'Transforming gifts into talents: The DMGT as a developmental theory.' *High Ability Studies,* 15(2): pp. 119–147.

Gagné, F. (2009) 'Debating giftedness: Pronat vs. antinat.' In: Shavinina, L. V. (ed.) *International Handbook on Giftedness*, Springer, pp. 155–205.

Gagné, F. (2013) 'The DMGT: Changes within, beneath, and beyond.' *Talent Development and Excellence,* 5(1): pp. 5–19.

Gentry, M., Gray, A. M., Whiting, G. W., Maeda, Y. and Pereira, N. (2019) *System failure: access denied gifted education in the United States: Laws, access, equity, and missingness across the country by locale, Title I school status, and race.* United States of America: Purdue University.

Golden, E. D. (2018) *From tropes to troupes: Misty Copeland and the hyper-whiteness of ballet*. Available at: https://cupola.gettysburg.edu/student_scholarship/700 (Accessed: 16 September 2022).

Good, C., Rattan, A. and Dweck, C. S. (2012) 'Why do women opt out? Sense of belonging and women's representation in mathematics.' *Journal of Personality and Social Psychology,* 102(4): pp. 700–717.

Hall, S. A. (2022) *Mozart claimed credit for his sister's compositions, says former conductor turned professor*. Available at: www.classicfm.com/composers/mozart/claimed-credit-sister-compositions/ (Accessed: 16 September 2022).

Jacobs, J. E. and Weisz, V. (1994) 'Gender stereotypes: Implications for gifted education.' *Roeper Review,* 16(3): pp. 152–155.

Kantrowitz, M. (2022) 'Women achieve gains in STEM fields', *Forbes,* 7 April, [Online]. Available at: www.forbes.com/sites/markkantrowitz/2022/04/07/women-achieve-gains-in-stem-fields/ (Accessed: 3 May 2024).

Kerr, B. A. and Malmsten, R. N. (2020) 'Gifted girls and women.' *Oxford Research Encyclopedia of Education,* 27 Aug.

Margot, K. C. and Melin, J. (2020) *Gifted Education and Gifted Students: A Guide for Inservice and Preservice Teachers*. New York, NY: Prufrock Press Inc.

Mediaofficer. (2021) 'Women in STEM week 2021: How we're empowering the next generation', *Department of Education: The Education Hub,* 11 February. Available at: https://educationhub.blog.gov.uk/2021/02/11/women-in-stem-week-2021-how-were-empowering-the-next-generation/ (Accessed: 3 May 2024).

Milo, S. (2015) 'The lost genius of Mozart's sister', *The Guardian,* 8 September, [Online]. Available at: www.theguardian.com/music/2015/sep/08/lost-genius-the-other-mozart-sister-nannerl (Accessed: 16 September 2022).

Petersen, J. (2013) 'Gender differences in identification of gifted youth and in gifted program participation: A meta-analysis.' *Contemporary Educational Psychology,* 38(4): pp. 342–348.

Plucker, J. A. and Peters, S. J. (2018) 'Closing poverty-based excellence gaps: Conceptual, measurement, and educational issues.' *Gifted Child Quarterly,* 62(1): pp. 56–67.

Precke, F. and Brüll, M. (2008) 'Grouping the gifted and talented: Are gifted girls most likely to suffer the consequences?' *Journal for the Education of the Gifted,* 32(1): pp. 54–85.

Raraty, O. (n.d.) *Girls and engineering and other STEAM subjects*. Available at: https://serviceschools.co.uk/girls-engineering-stem-subjects/ (Accessed: 3 May 2024).

Reis, S. M. (n.d.) *External barriers experienced by gifted and talented girls and women.* Available at: https://gifted.uconn.edu/schoolwide-enrichment-model/external_barriers/# (Accessed: 16 September 2022).

Rose, L. (1999) *Gender issues in gifted education.* Available at: https://nrcgt.uconn. edu/newsletters/spring994/ (Accessed: 10 March 2023).

Ruf, D. L. (2009) *Preschool behaviours in gifted children.* Available at: https://mcgt.net/ preschool-behaviors-in-gifted-children (Accessed: 16 September 2022).

Suliman, A. (2021) *Black dancer calls out racism in 'elitist' European ballet world.* Available at: www.nbcnews.com/news/world/black-dancer-calls-out-racism-elitist-european-ballet-world-n1257141 (Accessed: 16 September 2022).

The Tribune India. (2022) *Thought for the day.* Available at: www.tribuneindia. com/news/thought-for-the-day/some-of-the-brightest-minds-in-the-country-can-be-found-on-the-last-benches-of-the-classroom--–-dr-apj-abdul-kalam-415626 (Accessed: 17 September 2022).

Winner, E. (1996) *Gifted Children: Myths and Realities.* New York, NY: Basic Books.

Worrell, F. C. and Dixson, D. D. (2022) 'Achieving equity in gifted education: Ideas and issues.' *Gifted Child Quarterly,* 66(2): pp. 79–81.

Yaluma, C. B. and Tyner, A. (2021) 'Are U.S. schools closing the "gifted gap"? Analyzing elementary and middle schools' gifted participation and representation trends (2012–2016).' *Journal of Advanced Academics,* 32(1): pp. 28–53.

Ziegler, A. (2005) 'The Actiotope Model of Giftedness.' In: Sternberg, R. J. and Davidson, J. E. (eds.) *Conceptions of Giftedness.* Cambridge: Cambridge University Press, pp. 411–436.

Ziegler, A., Heller, K. A., Schober, B. and Dresel, M. (2006) 'The actiotope.' In: Frey, D., Mandl, H. and von Rosenstiel, L. (eds.) *Knowledge and Action.* Munich: Hogrefe, pp. 143–175.

Ziegler, A. and Stoeger, H. (2007) 'The role of counseling in the development of gifted students' actiotopes: Theoretical background and exemplary application of the 11-SCC.' In: Mendaglio, S. and Peterson, J. S. (eds.) *Models of Counseling Gifted Children, Adolescents, and Young Adults.* New York, NY: Prufrock Press, pp. 253–283.

Ziegler, A., Vialle, W. and Wimmer, B. (2013) 'The actiotope model of giftedness: an introduction to some central theoretical assumptions.' In: Phillipson, S. N., Stoeger, H. and Ziegler, A. (eds.) *Exceptionality in East Asia.* London: Routledge, pp. 1–17.

# 11. THE TRAVELLING CIRCUS

*The proper education of any people includes the sympathetic touch between teacher and pupil; knowledge on the part of the teacher, not simply of the individual taught, but of his surroundings and background, and the history of his class and group; such contact between pupils, and between teacher and pupil, on the basis of perfect social equality, as will increase this sympathy and knowledge; facilities for education in equipment and housing, and the promotion of such extra-curricular activities as will tend to induct the child into life.*

**W. E. B. Du Bois, 1935, p. 328**

*Education either functions as an instrument which is used to facilitate integration of the younger generation into the logic of the present system and bring about conformity or it becomes the practice of freedom.*

**Paulo Freire, 1970**

Welcoming students in means recognising differences. These differences have not traditionally been acknowledged within our educational structures, leaving students to navigate difficult terrain. Here is a poem written by an Apache child in Arizona that illustrates this sentiment:

Have you ever hurt about baskets?

I have, seeing my grandmother weaving
    for a long time.

Have you ever hurt about work?

I have, because my father works too hard
    and he tells how he works.

Have you ever hurt about cattle?

I have because my grandfather has been working
    on the cattle for a long time.

Have you ever hurt about school?

I have, because I learned a lot of words
    from school,

And they are not my words.

(Cazden, 2001, p. 67)

Education holds up a mirror to our larger societal systems, and gifted education has magnified the inequities. We must design our enrichment with this in mind, as we are building on a polluted site. Gifted programmes have been systemically racist and have marginalised groups who were already disenfranchised. Enrichment has the responsibility to put these communities at the centre. We can work to minimise careless damage, examine our thinking and cease to perpetuate inequity in the smaller systems we create in our schools. We can also seek shields to protect our students from the structural harm of systemic inequality. There is a moral imperative for teaching-and-learning policies to be created and implemented with careful thought to how they may impact equity-seeking groups. Good intentions are not enough.

Even in enrichment settings that seem open and accessible, the practical and emotional needs of particular groups go unaddressed. A true understanding of intersectionality builds empathy, understanding and coalition. This can include neurodiversity, gender identity and sexual orientation, second language learners, class, race, ethnicity, religion and physical differences (people of determination, sizeism). These groups are not necessarily separate and identities overlap. Intersectionality is not additive, with every identity being a single-issue struggle. Nuance is missed when we assume that each new 'ism' compounds a person's suffering, setting up an 'Oppression Olympics' (Maxfield, 2021). We can acknowledge and investigate the differences in lived experiences. In addition, each person uniquely inhabits these identities and their narratives are not uniform. Historically feminist movements have been monopolised by the white experience. As a cis white woman, I cannot fully grasp or understand all these barriers. There are many voices for deeper reading in the field of diversity, equity and inclusive education that I am still learning from.[20]

With this in mind – why doesn't every school have an enrichment-for-all model? With challenge-for-all teaching? Why do conceptions of giftedness persist? Why do we see programmes still limited to a particular profile of students? Why is there debate when surely challenge and enrichment for everyone is sensible? Does an ideal and inclusive model for enrichment exist that can be replicated?

## Around the World and Back in Time

It is useful to look at the wide breadth of philosophies and programming that exist across the landscape of pedagogy, gifted programming and enrichment services. Depending on the type of intervention and how it is implemented, we can gain insight into how impactful specific enrichment strategies can be. However, given all the variables, there is no empirical way to compare which approaches enhance the all-round success of students in life. Raw comparisons between the achievements of equally able students who have attended a particular 'gifted' scheme do not provide reliable evidence of which aspects of that intervention are the most impactful. In meta-analyses, messy collections of gifted programming deliver a confusing and often contradictory mixed bag for us to explore. Borland points out that in multicultural societies, conceptions of excellence and giftedness are likely to be shaped by the values of the dominant culture, which can overlook minorities and outliers (Borland, 2004, p. 15). The cut-off points for giftedness in each place differ – what is considered gifted in Toronto may not be near the standard in Tashkent. However, whatever the implementation

---

20  Great reading to start: *All About Love* by bell hooks; *Race, Equity, and Education: Sixty Years from Brown* edited by Pedro A. Noguera, Jill C. Pierce and Roey Ahram; *A Little Guide for Teachers: Diversity in School* by Bennie Kara; *The Wake Up* by Michelle Mijung Kim; *Becoming a Totally Inclusive School: A Guide for Teachers and School Leaders* by Angeline Aow, Sadie Hollins and Stephen Whitehead; *Against White Feminism: Notes on Disruption* by Rafia Zakaria. I'd recommend any work by Sonya Douglass Horsford – this includes *Learning in a Burning House* and *The Politics of Educational Policy in an Era of Inequality*. *Reading, Writing and Racism* by Bree Picower is pivotal in understanding the curricular tools of whiteness, and I also recommend the groundbreaking work *Pedagogy of the Oppressed* by Paulo Freire.

method for special provision, the outcome is most likely to be positive, although measuring that impact is difficult. It is not surprising that children who have experienced extra programmes of any kind will benefit when given the extra opportunity (Freeman, 2005).

It is worth highlighting that meta-analyses, like Dr John Hattie's *Visible Learning*, can be insightful but not completely illuminating. As Hattie himself noted, 'The problem is: we are hopeless at identifying successful teaching and scaling it up; that's one of the most frustrating things in our business' (Parker, 2023). The variation that exists within the label of 'gifted programming' is vast. Averaging the outcome of studies done on students of different ages, with different starting points, evaluated with different tools, in different places, with different kinds of interventions and different measures of outcomes, will inevitably have misleading and confusing results. I like to hold two contradictory ideas: educational research into the effectiveness of gifted programming is both vital and useless. Dylan Wiliam summarises this so much more elegantly in his presentations on why education is not a research-based profession, where he has asserted that 'I think, that those who call for "evidence-based education" are missing the point. Evidence is important, of course, but what is more important is that we need to build teacher expertise and professionalism so that teachers can make better judgments about when, and how, to use research' (Wiliam, 2019). Research doesn't tell you what might be, it only tells you what was. This is why our profession is best described as 'evidence informed' as opposed to 'evidence based'. I hope I can do justice to this sentiment. We build our programmes not based on what works in someone else's school, but by being responsive to the students in our school. Hattie makes a similar case when citing his meta-analysis *Visible Learning* – it is the impact we see *in our own classes* that is empowering; the research is a lens (Waack, n.d.). For now, let's stick to the big picture and look at the state of gifted provision across education. I believe in the shift to enrichment, but the reality is that gifted programming has a weird history and is solidly entrenched as a norm. There are systems changing in interesting ways, and they are responsive to attitudes in the zeitgeist.

As a construct, giftedness is inevitably tied to notions of excellence and potential. The idea of giftedness can easily be conflated with 'genius' and 'prodigy', regardless of the fact that these have originated from theological and metaphysical traditions (Ziegler, 2005). The myths surrounding wunderkinder and savants perpetuate gifted designations. Every country has its own approach to high-ability programming; it is fascinating to see how the experience for students varies. There are international bodies on giftedness to support students, teachers and parents, but there is no unified agreement on the identification and intervention methods. Many systems do not explicitly distinguish between aptitude and achievement in their definitions of giftedness – some rely on IQ type tests while others use more triangulated measurements. Many policymakers wrestle with the tension between the promotion of gifted education, against the perception and reality that this exacerbates inequality. As renowned British researcher Dr Joan Freeman notes, 'There is no general agreement on either side of the Atlantic, so provision is inconsistent, geographically biased, and associated with both the reality and the fear of elitism' (Freeman, 2005, p. 88). The ethical debate surrounding giftedness has pushed some countries to develop value systems in direct opposition, with an explicit denial of giftedness and pointed refusal to pursue any gifted ventures.

On the other hand, some governments have promoted giftedness on a national level. There is the 'cure for cancer' argument: the best students will improve society for us all. Then there is a 'self-actualisation argument': through gifted programming students will have maximum cognitive growth and fulfilment in their education (Freeman, 2002). There are manifold ways we can discover gifts and challenge students. Why is giftedness still so prevalent in education? The evolution and proliferation of giftedness throughout the world is fascinating. The origins of large-scale gifted programming were rooted in nationalism. American pedagogy has dominated the gifted field from its inception. As a result, its gifted programmes are older and more numerous. The United States has made the existence of 'gifted and talented' students a settled concept. The launch of Sputnik in 1957 rocketed giftedness into the American imagination. The race to find the best and brightest was fuelled by Cold War anxiety. The USSR had begun to seek out and promote its highly able students into advanced classes and early university placement, especially in the sciences. The Soviet Union instituted huge Olympiads and elite competitions to uncover every talent, with bright students being deployed to push technological advancement for the nation.

Finding the mathematicians and scientists to compete on the international stage then became a matter of paramount importance for American politicians. Money poured in from government grants and philanthropic organisations. Throughout the 1970s individual states determined school districts' funding by the number of gifted pupils. By the 1980s, all 50 states had gifted and talented legislation. While enthusiasm for gifted education has waned, even the 1990s saw national funding increases with numerous gifted education acts, advocated by the National Research Center on the

Gifted and Talented. The problems have long been recognised – in the US, the 1972 Marland Report purposely underlined that: 'Outstanding talents are present in children and youth from all cultural groups, across all economic strata, and in all areas of human endeavour' (US Commissioner of Education, 1972). Serious effort has been devoted to the passage of the Jacob K. Javits Gifted and Talented Students Education Act, which funds local programmes directed at marginalised groups. America has been fertile ground – welcome to the land of the gifted.

### United States Education Code Definition of Gifted and Talented

'Students, children, or youth who give evidence of high achievement capability in areas such as intellectual, creative, artistic, or leadership capacity, or in specific academic fields, and who need services or activities not ordinarily provided by the school in order to fully develop those capabilities'* (Cornell Law School, n.d.).

*Note that this puts the onus on separate development for those with a gifted designation. This is outside of the regular school services and classroom differentiation.

In the United States, giftedness as an entity is an established norm. An example of this is Mensa. Mensa International is an organisation devoted to IQ, with members in the top 2% of IQ tests administered worldwide. It encourages special-interest groups that focus on sharing specific fields of interest, from biochemistry to Egyptology to heraldry. The composition of MENSA International by nationality is notable. For instance, Brazil boasts around 520 members, Canada 2000, Hong Kong 200, China 400, India 1500 and the UK 19,000. The US trumps all, with over 50,000 members (Mensa International, 2023). This is not to say Americans perform better in IQ tests, but rather this reflects that IQ is more culturally significant – more Americans take the test and apply for Mensa. This membership holds a cachet.

While America was explicit in its 'gifted' labelling, other countries had similar intentions and goals and had long been setting and streaming children. The British system has long identified and 'set' children into ability groups. In addition, there is a clear divide in state versus independent and/or grammar schools. The selective versus non-selective arrangement has created a tiered system with de facto 'high ability' schools. British education has always politely hesitated and danced around using gifted labels.

Countries are by no means uniform in their national approaches. There are also ongoing debates as education systems evolve. The United States is considered the home of gifted education. However, there are pockets of heated debate. In 2021, Seattle Public Schools moved to phase out its 'highly capable cohort schools'. The district had 11 gifted schools devoted to teaching students at an accelerated pace. The current plan is to phase out these specialised schools by the 2027–28 school year. The reasons behind the change are rooted in racial inequity. Replacing the current system is a whole-classroom model where all students are in the same classroom and the teacher individualises learning plans for each student. However, detractors argue that will only exacerbate the problem:

> 'When school districts get rid of advanced offerings in a bid to reduce racial inequality, they end up doing to opposite of what they claim to intend. While wealthier families can move to better school districts or enroll their children in private schools, smart—yet poor—kids end up getting stuck in "equitable" classrooms that leave them under-stimulated and ignored.' (Camp, 2024)

In British Columbia, Canada, there are recent headlines that include 'B.C. parents of gifted children decry pause in accelerated learning program' (Ryan, 2024). The Transition Program for Gifted Students, to accelerate 'profoundly gifted' children, has been paused pending external review. In 2021, the Vancouver School Board began to phase out its multi-age cluster classes designed for children with high IQs and said in a report that 'segregating learners with a gifted designation amongst themselves does not develop a well-rounded student'. This was a move towards a policy of inclusion and away from 'segregating' students of different abilities (Ryan 2024). Now 1600 parents, students and alumnae of the transition program have signed a petition, asking the Vancouver School Board to restart the admissions process. They cite a 2006 B.C. Supreme Court judgement (Hewko vs. British Columbia) that the education system must make meaningful accommodations for special needs students on the basis that children are neurodivergent and must have equitable participation in special education (Ryan, 2024).

In Australia it was announced in March of 2024 that every public school in New South Wales will offer gifted education programmes to 'high potential' students under a new plan to challenge those who are not reaching their full potential (White and Carroll, 2024). The reasoning emerged after fresh data showed an increasing disparity in outcomes between low- and high-income students. Selected streams and opportunity classes are currently only available to half the state's public schools. Federal Education Minister Jason Clare justified this decision by pointing to the New South Wales Department of Education research review. He commented, 'What I'm trying to do is help build a country where your chances in life don't depend upon who your parents are or where you grow up or the colour of your skin' (Lock, 2024).

As laid out throughout this book, using gifted programmes as a vehicle for equity doesn't guarantee an equitable outcome. These examples are not meant to erase good intentions.

Behind all pedagogy is an ethos and value system. This determines the blueprint of our education systems, and there is a divide in how giftedness is framed in different places. There can be school-driven philosophy, but as the rider on an elephant, it is hard to change direction when in the middle of a giant herd. Cultural context and government policies drive ethos. The dialogue surrounding giftedness has nudged educators to experiment with tactics in the classroom and programmes outside it. Funnily enough, it is the diverse and heterogenous field of giftedness that has led to enrichment. International approaches to gifted education and enrichment make for intriguing comparisons. Conceptions of giftedness can be found across the globe. What we have is an abundance of philosophies and strategies to explore.

# Gifted Approaches in Broad Strokes

| Region/ Country | Ethos | Implementation |
|---|---|---|
| China | • We are all born with potential.<br>• Work ethic determines success.<br>• Abilities are developed as opposed to fixed.<br>• When cultivating talents, the earlier the better (Freeman, 2002).<br>• Egalitarian admission and self-selection.<br>• Respect those experts who guide you. | Application for any gifted provisions begins with a child self-selecting and working their way through testing. Based on results students may 'skip' forwards, attend extension classes, participate in weekend programmes or take individual instruction. China also has widespread enrichment schools known as Children's Palaces. The emphasis is on effort and working up to a high standard.<br><br>Children can rapidly accelerate and enrol in university whenever they qualify for early admission. Universities have special classes for advanced adolescents. |

| | | |
|---|---|---|
| Japan | • Equal access to opportunities.<br>• Effort and hard work trumps innate ability.<br>• Moral education is embedded in curriculum.<br>• Cooperative collaboration or 'han'. | In Japan the conception of giftedness is associated with elitism, as traditionally only the children of a higher class had access to education. In response to this, equal opportunity has become a core value of modern Japanese education.<br><br>Primary education prescribes multi-ability classes with diverse small groups, known as 'han'. Fast learners are expected to help slower ones. Children do not 'skip' grades and there is no separate gifted provision. Instead, the emphasis is on differentiation in the classroom.<br><br>In secondary school, there is streaming into academic and vocational curricula. Enrichment is provided through abundant extracurriculars and after-school education.<br><br>Traditionally Japan has avoided any explicit policies and programming for gifted students. However, there is an emerging tension between egalitarian principles and ensuring that high-ability achievers are given a platform to compete on the perceived need to remain internationally competitive, especially in STEM. Recently Japan has established super science high schools and the selection of students for special learning opportunities (Heuser, Wang and Shahid, 2017). |
| South Korea | • Gifted education is a tool for promoting equality. | Gifted programmes were introduced in 2005 to identify and educate gifted children from low-income backgrounds. These students were selected through tests that assessed their critical thinking, rather than through curriculum-based, subject-orientated tests, which historically had demonstrated a bias towards students of higher socio-economic status (Heuser, Wang and Shahid, 2017). |

| India | • All students have potential and unlimited capacity.<br>• As an incredibly diverse country, ensuring learning outcomes for all children means focusing on outreach for underserved children.<br>• Giftedness is manifested through creativity (Roy, Güçyeter and Zhang, 2017).<br>• Students have a responsibility to work hard.<br>• STEM subjects are the future and students should be at the forefront of innovation. | Outreach to marginalised students is a driving focus of gifted education. This is most evident in the creation of gifted schools. In 1986 there was the introduction of Jawahar Navodaya Vidyalaya schools for the gifted and talented students predominantly from rural backgrounds, without regard to their family's socio-economic conditions. These autonomous schools are funded by the Ministry of Education – they are fully residential, free and located in almost every district of India.<br><br>India's first national project on gifted education was launched in 2012 with the identification of gifted children aged 3–15 years (with a focus on maths and science). The National Institute of Advanced Studies (NIAS) has since expanded to support children gifted in diverse fields of social sciences, arts, etc. They offer resources and curriculum development to educators. NIAS has also initiated different programmes to support gifted and talented students belonging to different age and social groups in both urban and rural areas. There are summer programmes for students identified through testing and the Gifted India Network is growing with residential gifted camps.<br><br>There is a notable government scholarship scheme for the STEM subjects by the NIAS national programme of identification and mentoring of gifted children. These scholarships are awarded after widespread testing, interviews and submission of an engineering or science project supervised by experts in the field. |

| South Africa | • Giftedness is an important component of a nation's intellectual capital.<br>• Gifted students possess the qualities needed to find innovative solutions for many scientific and social challenges (Oswald and Rabie, 2017). | Schmerenbeck Educational Centre for Gifted and Talented Children, an organisation based in Johannesburg, promotes the education of gifted children within South Africa without regard to race (Eriksson, 1987). Focus is on acceleration, enrichment and self-study courses. |
|---|---|---|
| Sub-Saharan Africa | • Giftedness has a spiritual foundation. The Bantu view is that individuals can be blessed with special gifts.<br>• The Shona and Ndebele cultures consider gifts to be 'blessed through ancestry' and transmitted through family. These gifts are not necessarily academic but dispositional attributes.<br>• Giftedness can be characterised as the capacity to showcase resilience and thrive despite hardship.<br>• Provision for gifted education has elitist history associated with colonialism. | In some cultures, gifts are considered to be developed through family heritage and have a cultural significance.<br>On the other hand, gifted education is associated with elitist education (Freeman, 2002). This is partly a vestige from colonial oppression when the finest education was reserved for a few and the vast majority of the population received almost none. Hence, specialised schools for the gifted are not in favour. The essential first aim is universal primary education, as there are areas in the region with a lack of access to primary education and a prevalence of low literacy. Giftedness is not explicitly included or prioritised in government policy.<br>International development organisations have implemented some gifted programming. For example, Africa Gifted is an organisation devoted to promoting girls in STEM. Their primary project is the African Science Academy, which seeks out academically gifted young women with a passion for maths and science from across Africa and provides them with a world-class STEM education – all on full scholarships (Chakamba, 2017). |

| The United States | <ul><li>Giftedness can be discovered and diagnosed.</li><li>Gifted education is a part of the American dream, and gifted provision is an opportunity for social mobility.</li><li>Students identified as gifted are entitled to educational accommodations.</li><li>Abilities must be fostered by the correct environment and opportunities.</li><li>Gifted and talented children should be sought out and given specialised education.</li></ul> | The states are decentralised with separate programming. A 'diagnosis' of giftedness through testing is key.<br><br>Gifted programmes vary with acceleration, streaming, after-school initiatives, Advanced Placement classes, specialised schools and pull-out classes. There is competition for entrance into elite schools.<br><br>There is an emphasis on extracurriculars in conjunction with academics. There is a private industry of university summer schools and distance education. Giftedness is a key component in the larger competition for prestige education.<br><br>Gifted education and its impact on equity is becoming a growing debate, with school districts taking varied approaches in addressing specialised provision. |
| Nordic countries<br><br>Sweden<br>Norway<br>Finland<br>Iceland<br>Denmark | <ul><li>Giftedness is not innate; instead, it is a false social construct.</li><li>Cooperation and social-emotional development are key.</li><li>There is no race to win; students grow and develop on their own terms.</li></ul> | No specific government provision for gifted children. Student-led pacing is integrated into classroom practice.<br><br>Denmark has private Mentiqa schools for high-ability pupils that focus on the development of emotional intelligence and ethical responsibility. The pedagogy is meant to create conditions that build self-esteem, internal motivation, and belonging. The school's task is preparing students to be community builders and good citizens (Mentiqa, n.d.). |
| Austria | <ul><li>All children are educated according to their individual development and learning needs.</li><li>Gifted instruction is couched in individualised instruction for all.</li></ul> | Austria has had strong reservations about applying the label 'gifted' due to the negative associations with elitism. However, schemes for high-ability students have been introduced in recent decades. This is justified as part of the drive for differentiation and has an egalitarian emphasis on delivering instruction catering to each individual's specific learning needs (Heuser, Wang and Shahid, 2017). |

| The United Kingdom | • Teaching to the top and focusing on more-able learners will embed a culture of high expectations and lead to progress for all.<br><br>• Every school is different and given the freedom to choose how they identify and support more-able pupils as context matters.<br><br>• High-ability pupils should be identified for extension. Enrichment is the emerging pedagogical approach to capture students in and out of the classroom.<br><br>• There remains structural vestiges of a gifted and talented paradigm despite the unpopularity of the term and its elitist connotations.<br><br>• There is a legacy of 'setting' students by ability. | England:<br>Schools know their students and communities best and should tailor their approach with differentiation and co-curricular programming. Past government policy asked schools to place 5–10% of students on a gifted register and that legacy remains prevalent. Giftedness was academic, while talented referred to the arts and physical education. More-able pupil identification emphasises standardised testing as a key indicator. Traits like leadership are emerging in some schools as part of multifaceted identification.<br><br>The National Association for Able Children in Education (NACE) works with schools to improve the quality of teaching and curriculum modification. There is guidance in identifying abilities and talent. Extracurricular activities and enrichment are important, but the emphasis is on increasing challenge for all in classrooms. Ability is seen to develop through opportunity and self-belief. There is the Challenge Development Award accreditation to schools who go through the framework to embed policies for teaching to the top and extension for all learners (NACE, 2023).<br><br>Schools are beholden to national inspectors (Ofsted). Success of a school is derived from progress tests in key subjects and standardised exams at 16 and 18 years of age driven by independent exam boards. Stretch and challenge-for-all students has been a focus of Ofsted inspectors. Implementation should include academic challenge, alongside a co-curricular programme of enrichment activities.<br><br>Setting and streaming are still common within schools. The state versus non-state divide has created a de facto selective school system. |
| --- | --- | --- |

| | | |
|---|---|---|
| | | Wales:<br><br>The Welsh Assembly has adopted the term 'more able and talented' to describe pupils who require opportunities for enrichment and extension that go beyond those provided for the general cohort of pupils. These students make up approximately 20% of the total school population. In every school, there will be a group of pupils who require greater breadth and depth of learning activities. Schools are expected to work towards the Quality Standards for More Able and Talented Pupils.<br><br>Scotland:<br><br>The term G&T is not used and deeply unpopular. The system places greater emphasis on equity and raising attainment among pupils from low-income backgrounds (tracked by the Scottish index of multiple deprivations). Setting students has decreased, with many schools moving to mixed ability in English and maths. The Broad General Education (ages 3–14) has no ceiling and uses benchmarks, so a 10-year-old can work at the same level as a 14-year-old.<br><br>Upward mobility is a priority up to and including access to higher education, with university being free.<br><br>Northern Ireland:<br><br>No database exists in Northern Ireland along the lines of the G&T register in England. In addition, schools within Northern Ireland do not record or maintain records of G&T pupils. There was a branch of the National Association for Gifted Children (NAGC). However, it folded due to a lack of support (Ryan, 2012). |

| Australia | • Giftedness exists and there should be equality of opportunity in accessing gifted programming.<br><br>• Gifted programmes are a strategy that caters for individuals. It can solve problems related to student underachievement and disengagement.<br><br>• It is important to engage historically marginalised groups in gifted programming. | Gifted education has grown into a prominent educational movement with special programmes, competitions, organisations, schools and accelerated pathways (Schulz, 2005). Programming is decentralised with variation among states. Widespread testing, alongside self-selection, is designed to ensure equality of opportunity to enter gifted programmes. This is viewed as the fairest way to identify gifted students as it ensures a lack of bias in identification. There is outreach to Indigenous people and Pacific Islanders.<br><br>Most secondary schools in Australia choose to group students into classes based on ability. There are multi-ability classrooms, alongside a mixture of 'opportunity classes', after-school programmes, acceleration and selective high schools for the academically gifted. Some states, like New South Wales, are expanding their gifted provision on the basis that it will open up more opportunities to low-income and marginalised families. |
| --- | --- | --- |
| Canada | • Embed opportunities to explore in the curriculum.<br><br>• Each child has unique needs that educators should be responsive to. | Each province in Canada differs – for example, secondary schools in Ontario include project-based learning in the curriculum through independent study projects, which are designed to extend learners and create space for student-centred extension.<br><br>Individual education plans are curated for students and may include acceleration. Decisions are left to individual school boards.<br><br>Specific gifted programmes that are devoted to identified groups are rare but do exist in some school boards. |

| | | |
|---|---|---|
| **Russia** | • Students prove themselves gifted through competition.<br>• Support and resources are devoted to those who win.<br>• Accelerate the best and the brightest.<br>• Involve youth in productive activities (Karp, 2011). | Identification of gifted students is carried out through knowledge, understanding and problem-solving ability. This is based on performance-based competitions called Olympiads (Grigorenko, Park and Csilla, 2017).<br><br>Once identified, children are placed into specialised schools. These are buttressed by summer programmes and distance learning.<br><br>Students are accelerated into early university entrance where they are given the opportunity to contribute through meaningful research alongside their advanced classes (Evered and Nayer, 2000). Gifted students are to be productive through their learning and then deployed as part of national human capital. |
| **Brazil** | • Gifted children should be sought out. Their personal interests and emotional needs should be supported.<br>• Youth should be stimulated to develop specific abilities and talents to reach their potential. | Gifted education in Brazil is considered a need as formulated in the governmental regulations for specialised education since 1971. Although several centres for educating the gifted have been established, there are still socio-economic barriers to overcome.<br><br>Educational policies have called attention to the gifted. However, the number of students who are identified and given access to programmes is low (Wechsler et al., 2017). |
| **Gulf Cooperation Council**<br><br>Saudi Arabia<br><br>United Arab Emirates | • Giftedness is the future and by investing in gifted students a country will innovate.<br>• Giftedness is part of the strategic vision and a point of national pride. | Saudi Arabia:<br><br>Mawhiba is a national system for giftedness and creativity. It is part of a strategic plan to foster giftedness, creativity and innovation to actively contribute to the Kingdom's 2030 Vision.<br><br>Students are identified through Mawhiba Multiple Cognitive Aptitude Test (MMCAT), which has a STEM focus. A large part of the programme is training for science and maths Olympiads through after-school classes. Performance in international competition is a key driver. There is an emphasis on promoting students to the international stage, such as research opportunities for patent projects. |

| | | United Arab Emirates: |
|---|---|---|
| | | 'School for all' is a government initiative that guarantees equal education opportunities for all students, including provision for gifted students. Most gifted programmes are in Dubai, where pilots in primary schools have been developed. The Emirates Association for the Talented works mostly with identified gifted students in the school breaks and offers them summer programmes. |
| | | There is a push for gifted centres in the UAE. The government has many scholarship initiatives for high-achieving Emirati youth, which provide tutoring, career guidance and leadership training. The government has teamed up with universities in Emirati Ambassador Programs, which prepare secondary students for application to elite universities. Private companies like Educational Initiatives (Ei) Asset Talent Search have partnered with the UAE government to identify potentially gifted students in the UAE with mandatory external benchmarking assessments identifying the top 15% of students and then a further 'talent search' to identify the top 2% of academically gifted students and give them access to programmes like the Northwestern University for Talent Development, Johns Hopkins Centre for Talented Youth, Purdue University and GENWISE that are specifically designed to challenge the cognitive abilities of gifted students (Gulf News, 2024). |
| | | Schools in the UAE are expected to devise their own gifted and talented provision. UAE inspectors expect schools to create a G&T register and demonstrate these students are challenged and progressing. |

There are so many nations missing here, but hopefully this gives you a flavour of the different approaches. In each of these places, there are rebelling schools, subversive leaders and innovative teachers who take the preconceptions of giftedness and turn them upside down. Many educators buck the trends. This synopsis misses the nuance. However, it is intended to capture the varying cultural and political contexts that schools live in. Part of the difficulty in measuring the impacts of these programmes is that giftedness exists in a confusing cultural place, measured and reacted to in a completely unique context.

A seminal 2009 report, written by Dr Robin Attfield, articulated solutions for schools in the UK. The report, entitled 'Developing a gifted and talented strategy: Lessons from the UK experience', was published by the CfBT Education Trust[21] and offered common sense remedies to break the G&T rut. While the outdated language and framing of giftedness is used, some substantive points are in line with enrichment arguments made throughout this book. He promotes extension within the mainstream classroom by embedding challenge and using additional enrichment experiences outside the classroom. He recommends a whole-school approach and policy, and encourages an enrichment lead to coordinate, provide resources and deliver CPD. He underlines that it is important to unpack myths about giftedness and disassemble stereotypical views about gifted and talented provision (Attfield, 2009). Attfield evaluates various interventions and then completes the picture by noting that they must work in conjunction with each other as an integrated continuum of special services. His conclusion is in line with my own beliefs that 'enrichment and extension need not be mutually exclusive and perhaps the best strategy is to do both: create a mainstream classroom environment that meets the needs of gifted and talented students, while also providing additional targeted opportunities'. Developing a whole-school approach means collaboration with a school's policies on teaching and learning, assessment and wellbeing support. By making such links there is less danger of 'giftedness' standing alone as a selective provision for some, and it is more likely that enrichment will be integrated into all aspects of school life.

This brings me back to inclusive design – a great school will begin with a holistic overview, understand its unique context and then look for the barriers to entry. Environmental factors can shape the success of enrichment programming, and how we respond to them will empower our students to take action.

---

21  CfBT Education Trust is a leading charity providing education services for public benefit in the UK and internationally.

# Reference List

Attfield, R. (2009) *Developing a gifted and talented strategy: Lessons from the UK experience*. Available at: www.edt.org/research-and-insights/developing-a-gifted-and-talented-strategy-lessons-from-the-uk-experience/ (Accessed: 7 March 2023).

Borland, J. H. (2004) *Issues and practices in the identification and education of gifted students from under-represented groups*. New York, NY: National Research Center on the Gifted and Talented. Available at: https://nrcgt.uconn.edu/wp-content/uploads/sites/953/2015/04/rm04186.pdf (Accessed: 7 March 2023).

Camp, E. (2024) 'Seattle is getting rid of gifted schools in a bid to increase equity', *Reason*, 4 April, [Online]. Available at: https://reason.com/2024/04/04/seattle-is-getting-rid-of-gifted-schools-in-a-bid-to-increase-equity/ (Accessed: 23 May 2024).

Cazden, C. (2001) *Classroom Discourse: The Language of Teaching and Learning*, 2nd edn. Portsmouth: Heinemann.

Chakamba, R. (2017) *Pan-African academy helps gifted girls get into science and tech*. Available at: https://deeply.thenewhumanitarian.org/womenandgirls/community/2017/05/12/pan-african-academy-helps-gifted-girls-get-into-science-and-tech (Accessed: 18 May 2023).

Cornell Law School. (n.d.) *20 U.S. Code § 7801 – Definitions*. Available at: www.law.cornell.edu/uscode/text/20/7801#27 (Accessed: 22 May 2024).

Du Bois, W. E. B. (1935) 'Does the negro need separate schools?' *Journal of Negro Education*, 4(3): pp. 328–335.

Eriksson, G. I. (1987) 'An educational centre for growth.' *Gifted Child Today*, 10(4): pp. 25–28.

Evered, L. J. and Nayer, S. (2000) 'Novosibirsk's school for the gifted – changing emphases in the new Russia.' *Roeper Review*, 23(1): pp. 22–24.

Freeman, J. (2002) *Out-of-school educational provision for gifted and talented around the world*. London: Department of Education and Skills.

Freeman, J. (2005) 'Permission to be gifted: How conceptions of giftedness can change lives.' In: Sternberg, R. J. and Davidson, J. E. (eds.) *Conceptions of Giftedness*, 2nd edn. New York, NY: Cambridge University Press, pp. 80–97.

Freire, P. (1970) *Pedagogy of the Oppressed*. Translated by Ramos, M. B. New York, NY: Continuum.

Grigorenko, E. L., Park, K. (ed.) and Csilla, F. (ed.) (2017) 'Gifted education in Russia: Developing, threshold, or developed.' *Cogent Education*, 4(1).

Gulf News. (2024) 'Identifying gifted students in the UAE: Registration opens for UAE Ei ASSET Talent Search', *Gulf News*, 11 March, [Online]. Available at: https://gulfnews.com/business/corporate-news/identifying-gifted-students-in-the-uae-registration-opens-for-uae-ei-asset-talent-search-1.1710153871536 (Accessed: 15 May 2024).

Heuser, B. L., Wang, K. and Shahid, S. (2017) 'Global dimensions of gifted and talented education: The influence of national perceptions on policies and practices.' *Global Education Review,* 4(1): pp. 4–21.

Karp, A. (2011) 'Gifted education in Russia and the United States: Personal notes.' In: Sriraman, B. and Lee, K. H. (eds.) *The Elements of Creativity and Giftedness in Mathematics: Advances in Creativity and Giftedness, vol 1.* Rotterdam, NL: SensePublishers, pp. 131–143.

Lock, S. (2024) 'Gifted education program to roll out in all NSW schools', *The Canberra Times,* 14 March. Available at: www.canberratimes.com.au/story/8555877/gifted-education-program-to-roll-out-in-all-nsw-schools/ (Accessed: 15 May 2024).

Maxfield, M. (2021) 'On intersectionality', *Mary Maxfield Writing,* 17 March. Available at: www.marymaxfield.com/writing (Accessed: 12 February 2023).

Mensa International. (2023) *Welcome to Mensa.* Available at: www.mensa.org/ (Accessed: 7 March 2023).

Mentiqa. (n.d.) *Our pedagogy.* Available at: https://mentiqa-com.translate.goog/vores-paedagogik?_x_tr_sl=da&_x_tr_tl=en&_x_tr_hl=en&_x_tr_pto=sc (Accessed: 7 March 2023).

NACE. (2023) *About National Association for Able Children in Education.* Available at: www.nace.co.uk/page/about (Accessed: 12 May 2023).

Oswald, M. and Rabie, E. (2017) 'Rethinking gifted education in South Africa: The voices of gifted grade 11 students.' *Gifted Education International,* 33(3): pp. 273–285.

Parker, K. (2023) 'John Hattie: Why teaching strategies don't make you an expert teacher', *tes Magazine,* 11 January, [Online]. Available at: www.tes.com/magazine/teaching-learning/general/john-hattie-visible-learning-teaching-strategies-dont-make-you-expert (Accessed: 7 March 2023).

Roy, P., Güçyeter, S. (ed.) and Zhang, S. Z. (ed.) (2017) 'Gifted education in India.' *Cogent Education,* 4(1).

Ryan, D. (2012) *Gifted and talented in Northern Ireland.* Available at: www.teachingexpertise.com/articles/gifted-and-talented-in-northern-ireland/ (Accessed: 7 March 2023).

Ryan, D. (2024) 'B.C. parents of gifted children decry pause in accelerated learning program' *Times Colonist,* 6 May, [Online]. Available at: www.timescolonist.com/local-news/bc-parents-of-gifted-children-decry-pause-in-accelerated-learning-program-8701143# (Accessed: 15 May 2024).

Schulz, S. (2005) 'The gifted: Identity construction through the practice of gifted education.' *International Education Journal,* 5(5): pp. 117–128.

US Commissioner of Education. (1972) *Education of the gifted and talented: Report to the Congress of the United States.* Washington, DC: US Government Printing Office.

Available at: www.valdosta.edu/colleges/education/human-services/document%20/marland-report.pdf (Accessed: 7 March 2023).

Waack, S. (n.d.) 'Hattie ranking: 252 influences and effect sizes related to student achievement', *Visible Learning*. Available at: https://visible-learning.org/hattie-ranking-influences-effect-sizes-learning-achievement/ (Accessed: 7 March 2023).

Wechsler, S. M., de Souza Fleith, D., Gomez-Arizaga, M. P. (ed.) and Roncoroni, A. M. (ed.). (2017) 'The scenario of gifted education in Brazil.' *Cogent Education*, 4(1).

White, D. and Carroll, L. (2024) 'Every school in NSW to offer gifted education programs', *The Sydney Morning Herald*, 14 March, [Online]. Available at: www.smh.com.au/national/nsw/every-school-in-nsw-to-offer-gifted-education-programs-20240313-p5fc94.html (Accessed: 15 May 2024).

Wiliam, D. (2019) 'Dylan Wiliam: Teaching not a research-based profession,' *tes Magazine*, 30 May, [Online]. Available at: www.tes.com/magazine/archive/dylan-wiliam-teaching-not-research-based-profession (Accessed: 7 March 2023).

Ziegler, A. (2005) 'The Actiotope Model of Giftedness.' In: Sternberg, R. J. and Davidson, J. E. (eds.) *Conceptions of Giftedness,* 2nd edn. New York, NY: Cambridge University Press, pp. 411–436.

# 12. WELCOME TO THE BIG TOP

*Education must be increasingly concerned about the fullest development of all children and youth, and it will be the responsibility of the schools to seek learning conditions which will enable each individual to reach the highest level of learning possible.*

**Benjamin Bloom, 1956**

To enrich is to enhance, deepen, complement and elevate student learning. Students benefit from enrichment, and these effects can be realised in school and later in life. A holistic plan encompasses strategies for extension inside the classroom, which echoes the structures for enrichment throughout the school. **Diversity, equity and inclusion are at the heart of challenge for all and enrichment.** How do we begin a pedagogical overhaul from giftedness to enrichment? What design scheme will work best for our school and students? How can we be thoughtful and intentional in the construction of enrichment programmes? As educator and author Tom Sherrington notes, 'In order to fully cater for the most able students – and create that aspirational achievement-raising effect for all – it needs to be embraced as a total philosophy' (Sherrington, 2012). Comprehensive provision inside and outside the classroom has a broad range of choices open to diverse groups of students. This should take into account many types of aptitudes (academic, athletic, artistic, leadership, etc.) and a spectrum of development (latent, emerging, manifest, actualised) (Reis and Gubbins, 2017). This chapter will look at the purpose of enrichment as a school ethos, examine how we can foster skills development and discuss the lessons we can learn from the equity programmes.

When we design, we begin with a purpose. There is consensus that we want to amplify and accelerate learning. What are we trying to achieve when we reflect on enrichment? The goal is simple: **we want to challenge those who would otherwise go underchallenged.** The activities offered outside lesson instruction allow students to grow, create and learn without pressure or limits. There are demonstrated benefits in performance that result from extracurricular activities that are based on a pedagogy that is the polar opposite of drill and practice (Kaufman and Gabler, 2004). There are opportunities for independent research, real-world application and collaboration. Understanding needs and the existing gaps is key, which is why we ask questions. The goals of a school's enrichment offering are unique to its students and milieu. Schools may also have different priorities that will shape their objectives.

# Purposes of Enrichment

- To see each child through the lens of their strengths (Bachtel, 2017).

- To challenge students and guide them in developing talents and mastery. To hone skills through deep practice and expert feedback.

- To provide opportunities for personal growth, self-actualisation and intrinsic motivation.

- To explore topics with greater depth, breadth and complexity. To give space and time for interests that students have outside of the prescribed curriculum.

- To develop independence and instil rigour. To give opportunity for students to take initiative, have autonomy and ownership over their projects, and engage meaningfully.

- To give a platform for innovation. To encourage high-level thinking skills through problem solving, inventiveness and experimentation. To instil creative behaviours and provide access to tools and supplies to innovate.

- To have students reflect on learning and develop metacognition. To embrace new learning strategies and support self-regulation.

- To encourage curiosity. To present contradictions and grey areas for students to evaluate. To promote agility and capacity for navigating complexity.

- To showcase achievement, growth and effort. To instil confidence, pride and self-esteem.

- To champion empathy and emotional intelligence.

- To impart character, and civic and ethical responsibility.

- To give a safe space for practising resilience, adaptability, grit, persistence and growth mindset.

- To develop a sense of belonging, foster friendships and collaboration, and create new peer groups. To promote social and cultural awareness. To involve a diverse range of students to display and celebrate different cultures.

- To extend real-world application of knowledge and leadership experience.

- To build and hone 21st century literacies, competencies and character qualities necessary for lifelong learning (Soffel, 2016).

- To expand communicative capacity through the integration of strands like oracy.

- To buttress everyday classroom learning, receive academic support or build on core skills.

- To build résumés, prepare for higher education and enhance university applications.

- To give exposure to new fields of study. To try a future career on for size.

Many of these aims focus on how individual students benefit from enrichment. I've heard so many students describe their extracurriculars as key formative experiences that changed their life trajectory. This is a valuable perspective. However, I suggest enrichment go one step further and aim for community actualisation. Enrichment can create strong communities, systems of support and legacy. But let's not design our programming for some; let's build our programmes for all.

# Case Study: Alexandra Park School, Haringey, London, UK

Alexandra Park School is an unassuming mix of brown, low-rise brick buildings, with a more recently built sixth form centre (The Good Schools Guide, 2022). Hedged in with smaller grounds, the school makes the most of its limited space. Originally a technical college, then relaunched as a comprehensive school in 1990, the school is a non-selective academy with about 1850 boys and girls aged between 11 and 18. About 13% of its students are eligible for free school meals (UK Government, 2023). A large majority of the student body is from minority ethnic backgrounds, with one third of the students speaking English as an additional language (McGill, 2016). The proportion of students identified with inclusion needs is well above average. While the facilities look modest, the school is hugely oversubscribed with 1847 applicants for 232 Year 7 places in 2019. This is with good reason. The school may be the best in the world.

Why may it be the best in the world? Or perhaps the best in the UK? The opinions of students, parents, and current and former staff certainly carry weight. However, the best school in the world moniker seemed to stick after the 2015 Programme for International Student Assessment (PISA) scores were released (McGill, 2016). The BBC touted the results with an article on 'London school's towering performance in Pisa tests' (Burns, 2016). How did this school quietly secure a world-topping ranking? The secret is in plain sight – the school logo is inscribed with the motto 'Success for all'.

Educational leaders across the UK see this as key, and many influential figures in the field worked at Alexandra Park embedding 'for all' as a virtue. Ross Morrison McGill, of the *Teacher Toolkit* blog, writes that when he worked at the school from 2000 to 2007, the headteacher Mrs Rossyln Hudson 'was canny, scrupulous and unrelenting in her vision for "success for all"' (McGill, 2016). This dictum was continued under the next head, Mike McKenzie. Tom Sherrington writes fondly of being a part of this culture at Alexandra Park School when he was a deputy head. The school embraces teaching to the top, unwaveringly rigorous standards and pitching every lesson high. Sherrington highlights that teaching for the most able is pivotal in lifting the lid of learning for all.

A rising tide lifts all boats. This was evident in the school's performance in that reputation-forming 2015 PISA, which tests 15-year-olds from 75 developed countries in maths, science and reading (Organisation for Economic Co-operation and Development, 2018). The cohort from Alexandra Park who sat the tests topped the world charts with an average score of 564, higher than the top country rankings of Singapore, Hong Kong, Finland and Canada (Burns, 2016). This one-off test is not a standalone anomaly. By the value-added measures using Alps (a performance analysis that measures progress against UK benchmarks), Alexandra Park School's 2022 A-level results put it in the top 5% of the UK nationally (Alexandra Park School, 2023).

In its last Ofsted inspection (Office of Standards in Education, Children's Services and Skills, the UK body for school inspection), the school was graded as 'outstanding' in 24 of the 27 inspection indicators. The sixth form, at the highest end of the school, achieved 'outstanding' in every criterion (Ofsted, 2023a). The quality of teaching across the school was also judged to be 'outstanding' – an accolade that is given to just 3% of schools nationally (World Class Schools, 2019). Alexandra Park is a National Teaching School – an exceptional school that provides high-quality training and development to new and experienced school staff. Ofsted highlighted that 'staff at the school are very thoughtful and build on each individual's capabilities, so allowing them to blossom' (Ofsted, 2023b). I find this attention to individual capabilities fascinating, and it speaks uniquely to the school's values.

The 'success for all' motto is a powerful driver. When reading the value statement of the school I was struck with a particular passage:

> 'One of the goals of education is to give students **independence** so that they can flourish on their own. The first step on this road is to take responsibility for your own learning and, rather than waiting to be shown something, take the initiative and find out for yourself. The best learners show **drive**; they are independent and motivated, with high ambitions for their work. Longer-term ambitions usually begin with the spark of interest in something. Finding this spark is part of the school experience.' (Alexandra Park School, 2017)

Alexandra Park School has an all-encompassing approach that transcends any gifted and talented register. The school starts with expectations of excellence and at the same time provides every opportunity for students to find that 'spark'. These sparks ignite when students take part in the school's dynamic extracurricular programme. We have probably seen this effect in action, where enrichment activities outside the classroom drive engagement inside it. Motivationally rich environments promote a genuine enthusiasm for learning. As Renzulli notes:

> 'How many unengaged students have you seen on the school newspaper staff, the basketball team, the chess club, the debate team, or the concert choir? Their engagement occurs because these students have some choice in the area in which they will participate; they interact in a real-world goal oriented environment with other likeminded students interested in developing expertise in their chosen area.' (Renzulli, 2013, p. 8)

Enrichment and challenge work in unison to the benefit of all students. Teaching to the top in a diverse, multi-ability setting is key. In the case of Alexandra Park School, there is a recognition in its mission that 'whilst some people are naturally curious, others must make an effort. However, it is its own reward. Learning new things opens up new worlds and our curiosity grows' (Alexandra Park School, 2017). Sherrington expands on the reasoning: 'The school gains a reputation for being a place that delivers rigour, challenge and high standards. This rewards the staff for their efforts and secures their buy-in. At the same time as this, the learning environment in each lesson is characterised by high expectations. This raises aspirations and, through differentiation and support, all students are pulled along in the wake of the most able' (Sherrington, 2012). I heartily agree with Sherrington's assessment that a whole-school culture of challenge is essential. To extend that, I would add that there are structural and environmental barriers to enrichment that exist outside the classroom that absolutely must be taken into account. Creating success involves stakeholders moving in the same direction when designing programming and pushing challenge for all in every classroom.

Gifted and talented education has exacerbated and cemented cyclical inequality. The gifted field has excluded marginalised groups, so we must actively promote equality of opportunity and uncover the hidden barriers that hold back participation. Diverse voices are vital, and allies have a duty to work alongside them. Enrichment programming lifts students up but the power resides in how truly accessible it is.

# Uncovering Barriers to Enrichment

Enrichment is providing opportunities for extension that enhance, deepen, complement and elevate learning for all students. Schools can have incredible 'enrichment' – performing arts, student leadership and award-winning science fairs – but these opportunities should be linked in thoughtful ways and designed accessibly. Why are some students doing the state-wide debating competitions while others aren't? Why are some students in after-school prep classes and others missing? Why are there 'invite-only' extracurricular activities? To exclude pupils can exacerbate attainment gaps. We can easily aim high and give all students equal opportunity to benefit from extra time or support with a maths or science teacher. Scaffolding is good practice to allow students who express interest and wish to improve their time and attention outside of regular lessons. Curriculum in the classroom should be thoughtfully extended with opportunities outside the classroom.

A school's enrichment may be 'a rose by any other name' – a rebranded gifted programme to avoid falling over the 'G&T' tripwire. Schools may have vague 'enrichment' programmes that are a mixed bag of STEAM activities or interschool competitions. Enrichment may just be a school's regular after-school extracurricular offering renamed – this can be a haphazard offering. I've seen incredible diploma programmes that schools have used to structure and reward enrichment activities. Schools may have a programme that focuses on community service or independent projects that they have labelled 'enrichment'. This catch-all term makes it difficult to measure the effectiveness of enrichment. When is enrichment impactful and inclusive?

For our purposes now, let's frame enrichment as a thoughtful multifaceted programme that ensures that all the components of a busy school are working together and reinforcing student engagement in and out of the classroom. Whether we are looking at extracurricular activities, pull-out sessions, Advanced Placement classes, project-based learning or individual education plans, let's concentrate on the many variables that block participation in enrichment activities.

## Barriers to an Enriching Environment

| Structural barriers | Barriers for students |
|---|---|
| • Preparation gap – unequal access to early childhood opportunities<br><br>• Allocation gap – lack of funding, equipment or facilities<br><br>• Oversubscribed programmes<br><br>• Restrictive policies and procedures e.g. invite-only, flawed selective process or identification for admittance<br><br>• Lack of tracking participation to make visible equity-seeking groups of students who are not represented<br><br>• Lack of exploration time in curriculum<br><br>• Lack of diverse range of voices and representation in curriculum and canon<br><br>• Timetabling constraints<br><br>• Limitations for EAL, learning support and inclusion departments<br><br>• Top-down school development<br><br>• Beholden to government frameworks<br><br>• Information flow – disrupted or convoluted. Parents and schools unaware of how to navigate bureaucracy for funding (e.g. Pupil Premium in UK), transitions (e.g. university applications), and/ or diagnosis and application for accommodations and programming | • Lack of information about and access to enrichment opportunities<br><br>• Lack of time due to outside factors – e.g. part-time jobs, familial obligations, sibling carers or long commutes to school<br><br>• Practical and emotional needs for particular groups not addressed – this can include religious practice, neurodiversity, gender identity and sexual orientation, second language learners, physical differences (sizeism, health challenges and students of determination), and racial and ethnic discrimination<br><br>• Internal and external pressures and/or motivations to succeed<br><br>• Lack of wellbeing support structures to build emotional skill sets and self-esteem<br><br>• Peer influence, stereotyping and bullying<br><br>• Lack of meaningful student consultation and voice<br><br>• Passive or superficial inclusion<br><br>• Lack of culturally relevant curriculum |

| Staff barriers to delivering enrichment | Societal barriers |
|---|---|
| • Inspection or results-based culture<br><br>• Overburdened with administrative work, extended school days and/or large teaching loads<br><br>• Lack of staff buy-in, enrichment seen as a 'checklist' item e.g. apathy, burnout or 'hero' culture that divests staff<br><br>• Lack of meaningful consultation with staff as stakeholders<br><br>• Lack of training or expertise to guide students in high-level skill development (e.g. staff who have high level experience in a field to effectively help students 'master' a competency)<br><br>• Staff expertise overlooked and underutilised<br><br>• Limited teacher autonomy<br><br>• Beholden to priorities of senior leadership, board of governors or government management<br><br>• CPD for enrichment programming not a priority | • Economic deprivation and the 'family gap' – differences in the amount of support affluent families can provide as compared to low-income families, whether this be financial (money to pay for extracurricular activities) or time (flexibility to be able to drive to early morning practice)<br><br>• Cultural mismatch/cultural reproduction<br><br>• Representation and role model gap – racial/ethnic/gender gaps between teachers and the students they instruct<br><br>• Inequality between public and private schools or between school districts<br><br>• Lottery of geography and catchment areas<br><br>• Enclaves or divides within school and community<br><br>• School safety and fear of violence<br><br>• Communication barriers – language, internet access, etc.<br><br>• Constructs of giftedness |

There is a lot to unpack here. Naming these barriers is powerful. Some of these problems are outside of our control, but all are within our influence. These barriers can be applied to many schools and programmes. The social context can be overwhelming. Disproportionally, studies in the US have found that students of colour (Black, Latin American and Indigenous Americans particularly) are over-represented in categories associated with risk and failure, and underrepresented in categories associated with academic success (Skiba et al., 2008). Recent research asserts that ability grouping resegregates students within schools and has the effect of denying students of colour access to opportunities like college preparatory courses (Noguera, 2015). A lack of representation in the staffing and curriculum offering of a school is demotivating for students. The first step we can take is to look at who is not taking advantage of the opportunities offered. Tracking enrichment participation in the same way we track academic progress can help us see trends. Which groups are underrepresented? When a school begins to focus on enrichment there are fundamental questions that can quantify the issues and unearth the barriers.

Inclusive design begins with the goals of diversity, equity and inclusion, so let's review their meaning. These definitions are adapted from the Cooperative Extension (2022) of Tuskegee University:

**Diversity:** the presence of differences that may include race, gender identity, religion, sexual orientation, ethnicity, nationality, socio-economic status, language, neurodiversity, pupils of determination/ (dis)ability, age, religious commitment or political perspective. There are groups that have been, and remain, underrepresented in the field of gifted education and marginalised in the broader society.

**Equity:** promoting justice, impartiality and fairness within the procedures, processes and distribution of resources by institutions or systems. Tackling equity issues requires an understanding of the root causes of outcome disparities within our societies and in our school programming, instructive practices and curriculum.

**Inclusion:** an outcome to ensure that equity-seeking groups actually feel, and are, welcomed. Inclusion outcomes are met when stakeholders, the institution and programmes are truly inviting to all. When diverse individuals are able to participate fully in the decision-making processes and development opportunities.

It is important to note that while an inclusive group is by definition diverse, a diverse group is not always inclusive. We need to articulate the current school culture and be honest about the ways various student populations may be marginalised.

## Fostering an Enriching Environment

| Structural change | Addressing student needs |
| --- | --- |
| • Diversity, equity and inclusion (DEI) lens in school self-evaluations and development plans | • Culturally responsive instruction |
| | • Student voice present in school decisions |
| • Auditing structures and policies with inclusion and equity in mind | • Actively inviting underrepresented groups to enrichment and student leadership |
| • Procedure audits and reform (often it is logistics, not policy, that can be a barrier) | • Empowered and active student leadership |
| • Space and time for students to explore in and out of the classroom | • Flexibility and choice in how students access enrichment – embrace the metaverse with independent learning, flipped learning, online learning, etc. |
| • Opportunities that extend and go beyond the curriculum | |
| • Decolonising the curriculum, dismantling the curricular tools of whiteness | • Strong wellbeing programming and accessible counselling |
| • Curated extracurricular programmes | • Diversity programmes – anti-racism, mental health awareness, anti-bullying, etc. |
| • Multifaceted identification of high-ability pupils within subjects | • Collaborative environment and safe spaces |
| • Allowing students to self-select and put themselves forward for extension and enrichment programming | • Peer support |
| | • Constant feedback loops |
| • Considered groupings – multi-ability, interest-based clusters, social friend groups, etc. | • Celebration and recognition of student accomplishments |
| • Abolishing (or creating open processes for) setting or streaming of students (a move to mixed-ability classes) | |
| • Use of local norms and context | |
| • Early intervention to support underrepresented groups | |
| • Strong learning support departments (that include accommodations for high-ability pupils) | |
| • Tracking and analysing participation in enrichment programming | |
| • Scholarship and funding support to make enrichment financially accessible to all families | |

| Empowering staff | Changing the social context |
|---|---|
| • Establish a head of DEI position | • Diversity in our stakeholders and leaders that reflects the diversity of our student population |
| • Effective CPD on DEI, enrichment pedagogy, adaptive teaching, teaching to the top, action research on challenge strategies and shared best practice | |
| | • Advocating for reform in government policies, laws and funding |
| • Drive and enthusiasm of senior leadership to promote whole-school enrichment models | • Pedagogical shift from giftedness to enrichment for all stakeholders |
| • Establish a head of enrichment position | • Building a shared vision, vocabulary and ethos |
| • Utilise the expertise and interests of teachers in creating enrichment opportunities | |
| • Collective teacher efficacy – e.g. enrichment focus groups or committees | |
| • Create and/or elevate inclusion programmes | |
| • Take away 'scarcity mentality' and give staff time to embed – change does not happen overnight and must be managed thoughtfully to gain staff buy-in | |

There is no complete fix that ensures a perfect barrier-free environment for enrichment programming to flourish. I would recommend a change in process and procedures – this sounds prosaic but involves a lot of creative problem solving. This is codifying equity, empathy and kindness.

Codifying is the keyword. Equity is a key value at many schools, with leadership and staff who truly wish to embrace this ethos. The trick is embedding these intentions in policy, language, structures and systems. To foster an inclusive school culture for students and staff there is a need to go beyond a blanket declaration of compassion. I was recently discussing facile 'kindness' statements with two women colleagues of colour and felt them immediately tense with frustration. Diversity, equity and inclusion requires changing systems, evaluating policies and institutional reflection. As one of my colleagues has commented:

> 'As a woman of colour in leadership, who has had to work extremely hard to get to where I am, a response to cultivating diversity amongst staff and pupils of "be kind to everyone" is unacceptable and offensive … I am curious to know how aware the leaders may be of their unconscious bias, and how this translates to cultivating a truly

*inclusive teaching and learning environment. Has the concept of having individuals that pupils can see themselves in, as far as success or leadership roles, or the impact this has on wellbeing and pupil self-perception of what their future holds, truly been explored? Or how this may impact their academic engagement and achievement? I worry that if sentiment alone is an accepted/acceptable response to such an important issue, we may be regressing in diversity and inclusion.'*

The onus should not be on a few individuals to advocate for change – it is a lot of energy for one person in an organisation to constantly confront the established norms. Social capital is burned when you are the person repeatedly pushing an agenda to move inclusion forwards. Real change begins with organisational shifts as opposed to tokenistic superficial gestures. This requires the real work of policy audits, equitable hiring practices and updated terms of reference. All school leaders should be wearing a new lens and promoting a holistic change in procedures, ethos and values. Women and people of colour are often given the responsibility to fight for equity. This is exhausting. There is an emphasis on changing yourself as opposed to structures, processes and institutional culture. We shouldn't have to lean in. It's 2024 and we are preparing increasingly diverse students for a better world – schools should be leaning in.

So where to begin? When we looked at Alexandra Park School at the start of this chapter there was a clear values statement and mission that permeated the school culture. Diversity, equity and inclusion are often not expressed school priorities even though they are inherent to challenge for all. This is key. An effective mission statement guides design, crafts a vision and fosters values that recognise community culture. The mission is a short written passage that clarifies the intention, nature, needs and goals of a school (Eckert, 2006).

## Mission Statement

There are several points to consider when writing a mission statement:

- How are diversity, equity and inclusion highlighted in the broad goals and vision of your institution?
- Where does capacity come from? How do we ensure stretch and challenge for all?
- How do educators foster creativity, excellence and mastery?
- Why should enrichment and extension be accessible to all?

There is a hesitancy to place DEI at the centre of a school's philosophy, but this is gradually changing. The Pew Research Center did a content analysis of 1314 mission statements from US public school district websites, collected 16–28th November 2022. Overall, 34% of school districts highlighted the importance of diversity, equity and inclusion efforts in their mission statements. For comparison, this is much lower than the share of districts that mention topics like future readiness (80%). Digging a little deeper in how school districts discuss diversity, equity and inclusion, Pew Research Center found that 'diversity' and 'culture' were mentioned in a quarter of all mission statements, but 'equity' and 'inclusion' were each used in roughly one in 10 mission statements. There were larger discrepancies in the demographic make-up of districts in terms of DEI – most notably, urban and suburban school districts are at least twice as likely as those in rural areas to mention this issue. Diversity-related topics were also more common in school district mission statements from areas with relatively high median incomes, as well as areas with a lower proportion of white residents (Odabaş and Aragão, 2023). While DEI is coming into sharp focus in some areas, others do not see it as a priority at all. The 'for all' part of enrichment and challenge for all hinges on DEI, so let's look at how to embed it into the foundations of a school.

## Guiding Principles for Crafting an Inclusive Mission Statement

### Clarity

- Decide on a vocabulary and define these keywords. What words are key but need clarification? Enrichment? Equity? Inclusion? Diversity? Challenge? Having definitions understood by all is a crucial starting place. Avoid jargon and write in a manner that is easily understood by teachers, administrators, parents and students (Eckert, 2006). If you are hesitant to use a word like 'gifted' or 'ability', then interrogate why and look to language that articulates your philosophy.

A great example of this can be found in Illinois. After defining diversity, equity and inclusion, the statement goes further into what this looks like by highlighting keywords:

## Northbrook District 28 (Illinois, US): diversity equity and inclusion statement excerpt

'In support of diversity, inclusion and equity in District 28, all members of our community commit to:

**Respect** every individual

**Trust** each other to engage in difficult conversations

**Share** our unique stories and listen to others' stories

**Learn** from different perspectives and experiences

**Examine** our biases and endeavor to overcome them

**Foster** belonging, connectedness and safety

**Invest** in the personal growth of children and adults alike

**Forgive** each other as we make mistakes, learn and grow in this work.' (Northbrook District 28, n.d.)

There is no need to be restrictive in language. There are great mission statements that turn conceptions of 'gifts' and 'talents' on their heads. Here is a vision for learning from Malaysia that does just that:

## Garden International School (Kuala Lumpur, Malaysia): vision for learning

'We believe that every learner is gifted with boundless potential and that our role as educators must be to awaken the various forms of intelligence and spark curiosity about everything in the real and abstract world. Rich and authentic learning experiences are used to cultivate innate talents, provide opportunities to pursue interests and passions, both inside and outside of the classroom, and strive for excellence; all in the spirit of respect, integrity, and well-being.' (Garden International School, 2023a)

Garden International School head Simon Mann underlines his school's mission to enrichment: 'It is the quality and range of learning and enrichment opportunities we offer that helps to ensure every student has the opportunity to reach their greatest potential.' (Garden International School, 2023b)

### Rationale

- Point to gaps, analyse who is missing, highlight evidence and reflect on how your mission will address these issues.

- Provide justification for challenge for all and a larger vision of enrichment.

These excerpts from Phillips Exeter Academy's DEI statement and Village School's diversity mission statement are comprehensive and name the groups they aim to include.

---

**Phillips Exeter Academy: excerpt from diversity, equity and inclusion vision statement**

'Fostering an experience where all participants feel they can bring their full selves forward is not merely aspirational, it is fundamental to our educational mission and method. Our commitment to our community is to do more than assemble a diverse population of students and adults: our commitment is to teach the skills, model the behaviors, provide the resources, and cultivate the environment of inclusion that is required to unlock the richness of that diversity. Only through inclusion can diversity act as a catalyst to dispel ignorance and fear, and create space to achieve equity and excellence ... Only when we skillfully engage our differences - whether they are grounded in race; ethnicity; national or geographic origin; religious, philosophical or political beliefs; gender or gender identity; sexual orientation; age; physical ability; family structure, socioeconomic status or life experience - will we find a path to that greater understanding of the world and how we can be of service to it.' (The Trustees of Phillips Exeter Academy, 2023)

---

## Village School (Pacific Palisades, California, US): diversity mission statement

'Village School is committed to fostering a community that honors the diversity of the human experience. We believe race, ethnicity, religion, gender identity and expression, sexual orientation, age, ability, family dynamic and socioeconomic status to be examples of what constitutes diversity in our community. We are devoted to cultivating and sustaining a safe environment that empowers individuals and groups to celebrate their culture, heritage and identity. Through affirmation and education, we strive to build and support an open and inclusive community dedicated to the principle of respect. Village School is deeply committed to enriching all of its programs through a meaningful and actionable lens of equity and inclusion and ensuring that every member of the Village community feels an authentic and equal sense of belonging. The value and importance of this work is integral to the health and wellness of any community.' (Village School, 2022)

Our next example, the Ontario Government's vision of ensuring equity, differs in that it is specifically targeting groups that are marginalised, while not limiting its commitment of equity for all.

## Ontario Achieving Excellence: a renewed vision for education in Ontario (Ontario, Canada): excerpt from Ensuring Equity

'Ontario schools need to be places where everyone can succeed in a culture of high expectations. They need to be places where educators and students value diversity, respect each other, and see themselves reflected in their learning. It is particularly important to provide the best possible learning opportunities and supports for students who may be at risk of not succeeding. **This often includes, but is not limited to, some of our Aboriginal students, children and youth in care, children and students with special education needs, recent immigrants and children from families experiencing poverty.**' [Emphasis added.] (Ministry of Education, 2014, p. 8)

### Comprehensiveness
- Ground the statement in theory and research. Thoughtfulness in approach and design is key as myriad strategies and approaches can change depending on your local context.

- Be outcome focused – specify long-term overarching outcomes that involve stakeholders. This could mean intentionally setting language around attainment gaps.

- Address the issue of responsibility – how will accountability be brought into your provision and who will be responsible?

- Be specific with inclusion – which groups will be invited? How will policies and actions address equity?

Harbor Day School does this well by outlining the steering committee and identifying clear action points.

## Harbor Day School (Corona del Mar, California, US): DEI mission statement

'Harbor Day School promotes a culture of understanding where we value the unique qualities of our community constituents. Instilling a sense of ownership as we strive to increase awareness and influence actions, we take a stand against prejudice, and we celebrate inclusivity. Within the Harbor Day curriculum, we aim to recognize, appreciate, and share each person's experiences, thereby enhancing the lens through which we all view the world. The steering committee, consisting of 9 faculty and staff members, meets regularly to work toward specific goals:

- Diversify curriculum

- Evolve the language and be more conscientious

- Understand the changing needs of our community

- Create an inclusive and safe environment

- Educate faculty on how to reach all of our students

- Celebrate differences in our community

- Develop empathy and advocate for self and others' (Harbor Day School, n.d.)

Swafia Ames recommends that a DEI statement should be an extension of your organisation's mission. It defines why your school is pursuing its DEI journey. The institution should know and describe underrepresented groups – each school will be different, depending on its geography and demographics (Ames, 2020). We must have interlocking systems. Equity statements exist in many schools as a statement of non-discrimination, but this can be a passive stance and one that is introduced as a requirement by law. A statement that reflects your school's commitment to inclusion should be embedded in all policies. I suggest full readings and research on equity frameworks, of which there are many examples. Defining what we are talking about before we start talking about it ensures that a team has a shared understanding of terms like 'culture', 'equity', 'diversity' and 'anti-racism' and the difference between them. An inclusive enrichment policy can only work in the context of a larger organisational commitment to DEI. Frameworks generally include six elements:

- DEI strategic plan
- Leadership commitment
- Recruitment and hiring of diverse talent
- Inclusive professional development
- Equitable and inclusive culture
- Stakeholder feedback for impact. (Ames, 2020)

We should embrace diversity because it drives innovation and better outcomes. Studies have found that gender (Hansen and Quintero, 2018a) and racial diversity (Hansen and Quintero, 2018b) in the teaching workforce impact student outcomes. This is not in isolation. Analysis by McKinsey and Company found a statistically significant relationship between a more diverse leadership team and better performance. The companies in the top quartile of gender diversity were 15% more likely to have returns that were above their national industry median. Companies in the top quartile of racial/ethnic diversity were 35% more likely to have returns above their national industry median (Hunt, Layton and Prince, 2015). All school leaders should be wearing a new lens and promoting a holistic change. The onus should not be on individuals to advocate for change – it is a lot of energy for one person in an organisation to constantly confront the established norms. Diversity drives innovation and better outcomes. DEI creates better learning and progress. Here is the justification laid out in the New York State Schools Diversity, Equity and Inclusion Policy:

*'A growing body of research finds that all students benefit when their schools implement strong Diversity, Equity and Inclusion (DEI) policies and practices – including academic, cognitive, civic, social-emotional, and economic benefits. Strong DEI policies, in partnership with parents*

*and families, empower students from all backgrounds to visualize successful futures for themselves and provide them with a sense of belonging and self-worth. These benefits can lead to improved student achievement, which in turn can lead to better outcomes in other areas of their lives, including work and civic engagement.' (New York State Board of Regents, 2021)*

We should not put sole responsibility on women and marginalised groups to take on the labour of being heard. They should simply be heard because they are always invited into the room. Larger institutional shifts such as tracking for diversity, feedback loops and transparency are vital. They remove barriers to those in the room, cultivate trust and build psychological safety that can excel performance and foster a happy workplace. We should not be going for diversity 'tick boxes'. Diversity is multifaceted and intersectional. Implementing better systems is not a simple quota; it is building a culture of support. Being an outstanding school means having an organisational audit.

## Analyse Outcome, Not Intent

Policies should not be evaluated on their benign intent. Instead, we should concentrate on the outcome. It is powerful to recognise that many barriers are not intentionally erected but tend to be products of bureaucratic systems. The outcomes of these systems can be hostile. Audits on outcomes can aid in identifying implicit and unconscious bias. Establishing metrics to gauge progress is powerful. When groups are negatively impacted or excluded this means unpicking policies and processes that unwittingly cause hurt. We can do this by looking at data to see who and what is missing. Creating great feedback loops is key. If certain students are less involved in after-school programmes, let's investigate the root cause and adapt.

For example, a simple policy barrier might be the way parents register for extracurricular programmes. Let's say that a school has a first-come-first-serve registration policy. This means that a working parent who only checks their emails at the end of the day may miss the chance to secure their child a place in the robotics club. The procedure seems fair, but it unwittingly excludes students whose parents can't easily acquire or act on the information. A simple solution for this barrier is a registration window and a lottery system for more equitable access. Remember there can be multiple reasons and fixes – there could be language barriers for parents (send out emails in preferred language), or a lack of internet access at home (students sign themselves up during school hours). It is important to understand the context of the school community. For many immigrant students, language barriers are as significant as racial barriers in terms of access to critical resources (e.g. college prep classes) (Noguera, 2015).

Policies also give power, and we shouldn't be afraid to change decision-making structures and remits. Social context is often seen as immovable, but it can be changed on a small and large scale by empowering new voices. One reform that I lived through in Ontario, Canada was to have student trustees on local school boards. These student trustees then campaigned for voting rights. Even non-binding votes allowed for student voices to be amplified on a political platform. Student trustees directly represented thousands of students and could impact school board decisions. It made so much sense to give the most important stakeholder in education a place in the room and on the record. Allies can question structures and work to implement DEI across different segments of a school community. We can examine current school systems, policies and practices with an eye towards equity and how they impact both teachers and students.

These statements should inform strategic goals. You can see the alignment and values threaded throughout specific actions. I'd point to an excerpt of two of the current strategic goals of the Ontario School Board I grew up in:

**Hastings Prince Edward District School Board (Ontario, Canada): excerpt from Strategic Priorities 2020–25**

### Foster a Culture of Excellence and High Expectations

- Decisions will be made from a student-centered approach considering the impact on students and connected to this plan
- Improve the student experience as informed and evidenced by the annual completion of secondary school exit surveys
- Provide universally designed learning opportunities and supports based on each student's learner profile
- Enhance staff potential and professional development experiences through the utilization of employee growth plans, performance appraisals and recognition opportunities
- Recognize and celebrate innovation and excellence on an annual basis ...

## Strengthen Community through Equity and Social Justice

- Provide intentional resources and opportunities to create a culture of acceptance, adopting principles of equity which reflect the diversity of our students, their families and staff

- Create inclusive environments by increasing the visibility and recognition of diversity, including the celebration of Black History Month, Pride Month and Indigenous History Month

- Ensure greater inclusion and diversity of student representation at all levels of Board and school leadership

- Identify and reduce discrimination through enhanced tracking, monitoring and education

- Support and implement necessary actions to incorporate Recommendation #10 of the Calls to Action from the Truth and Reconciliation Commission:

  - Closing identified educational achievement gaps to within one generation

  - Improving education attainment levels and success rates

  - Developing culturally appropriate curricula

  - Asserting and teaching aboriginal languages as credit courses

  - Enabling parental and community responsibility, control and accountability for what all parents enjoy in public school systems

  - Enable Aboriginal parents to fully participate in the education of their children

  - Collect voluntary self-identification Indigenous student data to intentionally make program and resource decisions

  - Ensure recruiting, hiring, and retention practices reflect diversity and inclusion

  - Utilize gender-neutral language in all Board documents and practices. (Hastings and Prince Edward District School Board, 2021)

# Culturally Responsive Instruction

Culturally responsive instruction supports high levels of learning. The curriculum we teach is the everyday interaction that builds student schemas. Our instruction needs to reflect the world, meet students where they are and celebrate different cultural identities. Incorporating DEI into our curriculum design is incredibly important, if for no other reason than the demographic shifts that are creating more ethnically diverse classrooms. When evaluating the US public school population, de los Ríos, López and Morrell (2015, p. 85) write that 'while a growing non-White student population should bring forward important conversations about diversifying curriculum for all students, what we have instead are hypersegregated non-White educational spaces where students are still provided a curriculum and a set of pedagogical practices representative of an ethnically homogenous America that never existed'. Some professional programmes still equivocate about including multicultural education despite the growing numbers of and disproportionately lower performance of equity-seeking groups. Teachers' education as a whole has inadequately them prepared to teach ethnically diverse students (Gay, 2002). Other programmes are trying to decide what is the most appropriate place and 'face' for it. Fortunately, more and more teaching programmes are incorporating cultural lenses into their syllabus for curriculum, pedagogy and educational leadership. The profession as a whole has reached a place where there is a recognised need for courses within BEds, MEd programmes or 'specialisms' that include critical studies, anti-oppression in education, pedagogies of solidarity, sociocultural theories of learning and identity construction.

Culturally responsive teaching (CRT) 'acknowledges and infuses the culture of such students into the school curriculum and makes meaningful connections with community cultures... CRT is best understood as a response to traditional curricular and instructional methods that have often been ineffective for students of colour, immigrant children, and students from lower socioeconomic families' (Vavrus, 2008, p. 49). This instruction can incorporate cultural values, traditions, communication styles, contributions and relational patterns.

A culturally relevant curriculum is paramount. We cannot discuss the state of educational inequity without reference to the underrepresented voices. Studies show that non-inclusive behaviours in learning environments create stereotype threats. For instance, the evidence has been mounting for quite some time that the departure of underrepresented students from

STEM majors results from reduced social belonging more than academic preparedness to handle the material (Dewsbury and Brame, 2019b). The delivery of content, actively or didactically, is only one part of teaching. Progressive pedagogy strives to promote deep learning in students and a climate of respect. Constructing deep learning means connecting the material to students' lives. 'Inclusive teaching similarly requires deep teaching. This is a pedagogy that is reflective and built on authentic relationships and dialoguing between key stakeholders. ... deep teaching relies on instructors examining their own position and working to hear and understand their students as the basis for teaching and learning decisions' (Dewsbury and Brame, 2019a). Educational philosopher Paulo Freire argued that instructors should build pedagogy around the voices and lives of their students, 'If the structure does not permit dialogue then the structure must change' (Freire, 1970). Dewsbury and Brame (2019b) write that 'in this context, inclusion is built on the quality of the social relationship, which in turn relies on a knowledge of its participants'. Culturally responsive instruction is a student-centred approach that creates dialogue, inclusive space and curriculum representation.

It is difficult to introduce culturally responsive teaching without asking staff for a lot of introspection and self-awareness. I taught in Canada and the UK before moving to the Middle East, and I needed a crash course with each new school I've taught in. I must admit to being wholly unprepared to teach the Polish immigrants I had in my classes in Birmingham. I learned to be more responsive 10 years later when teaching at a school with a large Korean community in Abu Dhabi. It is hard work to interrogate the cultural interactions we have with students.

I'd recommend reading the work of Dr Geneva Gay, who has shaped the field of multicultural education and its essential role in an increasingly diverse and interconnected world. In telling the story of her 30-year career, Dr Gay reflected that as her doctoral studies progressed, she dug deeper into why she had been more successful in bonding with her Black students than other more experienced teachers – even though it wasn't an intentional strategy on her part. 'That ultimately led to what I do these days,' Gay said. 'I stumbled into what would eventually become multicultural education [and] culturally responsive teaching' (Wunderlich, 2020). Expecting students to master academic tasks while functioning under cultural conditions unnatural (and often unfamiliar) to them is arduous. Removing this second burden is a significant contribution to improving academic achievement.

This can be done by all teachers' being culturally responsive to ethnically diverse students throughout their instructional processes. Dr Gay's insightful direction for building culturally responsive instruction begins with these precepts:

1. Awareness of, respect for and engagement with cultural diversity is simply teachers learning about the students they teach. Being curious about culture leads us to explore heritage, habits and customs in our classrooms. Developing a knowledge base for culturally responsive teaching means acquiring detailed factual information about the cultural particularities of specific groups (e.g. African, Asian, Latin American and Indigenous). There are many examples of how this informs our instruction. Teachers can familiarise themselves with groups that give priority to communal living and cooperative problem solving, as these preferences affect educational motivation, aspiration and task performance. Gender role socialisation can vary, and this has implications for grouping, collaboration or equity initiatives in classroom instruction. Understanding holidays, commemorations or observances allows us to honour and celebrate alongside our students. This can make schooling more stimulating for, representative of and responsive to our students.

2. All subjects can be taught in a culturally responsive manner, as Gay notes:

   *'Too many teachers and teacher educators think that their subjects (particularly math and science) and cultural diversity are incompatible, or that combining them is too much of a conceptual and substantive stretch for their subjects to maintain disciplinary integrity. This is simply not true. There is a place for cultural diversity in every subject taught in schools. Furthermore, culturally responsive teaching deals as much with using multicultural instructional strategies as with adding multicultural content to the curriculum. Misconceptions like these stem, in part, from the fact that many teachers do not know enough about the contributions that different ethnic groups have made to their subject areas and are unfamiliar with multicultural education.' (Gay, 2002, p. 107)*

3. Educators can design culturally relevant curricula in a way that reverses the trends and narratives of the dominant culture. What does this look like? Course materials may include works that are

written or produced by scientists from dominant groups and leave out resources by scientists from underrepresented groups. We are quite often handed a curriculum that avoids or downplays racism as a 'controversial issue' or focuses on the same few high-profile individuals, ignoring hegemony or the actions of groups. This can be rectified by dealing directly with controversy, contextualising issues within race, class, ethnicity and gender, and studying a wide range of ethnic individuals and groups.

4. Educators can diversify communication styles. Communication styles of different ethnic groups reflect cultural values and shape learning behaviours. Didactic teaching has a passive-recipient role for students (they listen while teachers speak). Communication styles in the classroom can be diversified to be 'more active, participatory, dialectic, and multimodal. Speakers expect listeners to engage with them as they speak by providing prompts, feedback, and commentary. The roles of speaker and listener are fluid and interchangeable. Among African Americans, this interactive communicative style is referred to as "call-response"; for Native Hawaiians, it is called "talk-story". Among White American females, the somewhat similar practice of "talking along with the speaker" to show involvement, support, and confirmation is described as "rapport talk"' (Gay, 2002, p. 111). There are differences in how children interact with adults in an instructional setting.

5. Use cultural scaffolding in teaching students – that is, use their own cultures and experiences to expand their intellectual horizons and academic achievement.

6. Modify resources and instructional strategies. For example, cooperative group learning arrangements and peer coaching fit well with the communal cultural systems of African, Asian, Indigenous and Latin American groups. Autobiographical case studies and fiction can crystallise ethnic identity. Research has cited that incorporating motion and movement, music, frequent variability in tasks and formats, novelty, and dramatic elements in teaching improves the academic performance of African American students.

We do not necessarily recognise how our identities shape the way we interact with others or the way others interact with us. Representation is an important part of an enriched curriculum.

*'Learning environments should foster a sense of belonging and make all students feel welcome, valued, and respected. The instructional design process should avoid negative stereotypes and unconscious bias, encourage respect, representation, access, and communication, and recognize students with varying abilities. To achieve these goals, a more comprehensive, inclusive instructional design model is needed.'* (Gamrat, Tiwari and Bekiroglu, 2022)

With inclusive teaching in mind Gamrat, Tiwari and Bekiroglu created the Inclusive ADDIE Model,[22] an extension of previous work on inclusive teaching and course design:

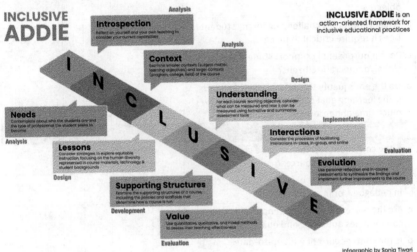

Figure 12.1 The Inclusive ADDIE Model for instructional design and implementation. Infographic by Sonia Tiwari (Gamrat, Tiwari and Bekiroglu, 2022).

There are massive movements to decolonise and diversify curricula. It is amazing that this debate is ongoing – of course, we need diverse curricula. There has been an increased call to action and a heated backlash to expanding or changing the voices and books given prominence. As teachers, we can push for reform and help each other. In terms of evaluating and sharing our resources, we can use tools like the Pinning with Pause Checklist to think critically about our resources. Teachers are empowered to decide

---

22  An incredible resource for staff is the EDUCAUSE Workbook utilising the ADDIE instructional design model using the INCLUSIVE acronym for inclusive design considerations that can be downloaded here: https://teaching.ist.psu.edu/teaching-students/inclusive

whether or not a resource, activity or idea supports learning goals, is reliable and promotes equity-orientated learning for the purposes of social justice and inclusion. This can also be adapted for students to use – the questions are organised by critical media literacy skills, challenging problematic narratives, considering the hidden curriculum and promoting inclusive counter stories (Gallagher, Swalwell and Bellows, 2019).

| | Yes | Maybe | No | Notes: |
|---|---|---|---|---|
| **Section 1: Attributing a Purpose** | | | | |
| a. Does the activity, resource, or idea support my inquiry question, standards, or learning objectives? | | | | |
| b. Is it appropriately challenging for my students? Does it require critical thinking? | | | | |
| c. Does it purposefully support students becoming global, democratic citizens? | | | | |
| d. Do the ends justify the means? In other words, is the learning goal commensurate with how much time and resources it requires? | | | | |
| **Section 2: Reliability Assessment** | | | | |
| a. Is the content accurate? Can it be corroborated with other credible sources? | | | | |
| b. Does the author have expertise in the discipline, in pedagogy, or in my context? | | | | |
| c. Are the representations of people and communities authentic and nuanced? | | | | |
| d. Is the content current with up-to-date information? | | | | |
| **Section 3: Judging the Perspective** | | | | |
| a. Does the content reflect my students' cultures or contexts? | | | | |
| b. Does the content give my students windows into new cultures or contexts? | | | | |
| c. Does it help my students question dominant ideas about what is normal or good? | | | | |
| d. Am I sure that this activity, resource, or idea will not harm students—especially those with marginalized identities and/or backgrounds? | | | | |
| **Total** | | | | |

| Scrap It! | Modify It! | Keep It! |
|---|---|---|
| 0-1 Questions in Each Section Answered Yes | 2-3 Questions in Each Section Answered Yes | 4 Questions in Each Section Answered Yes |
| This curriculum resource might be beyond redemption. Scrap it! Consider searching for resources from national professional organizations dedicated to your subject. | Your source met some of the criteria but you may want to modify or supplement it with other materials to be sure your curriculum counts in appropriate and meaningful ways. Consider sharing your edited version onto a site of curriculum sharing. | It seems like you have found a great resource, activity, or idea to use! Pin that gem! |

Figure 12.2 Pinning with Pause Checklist – supporting teacher's critical consumption on sites of curriculum sharing (Gallagher, Swalwell and Bellows, 2019).

# Representation and Diversity at the Top

If schools want better leadership, they need diverse teams. Dissenting voices matter – that is how we make better collective decisions. If schools want excellent structures, processes, culture, wellbeing and ethos, they need empowered women and marginalised voices. When educational leadership is not representative of the diversity of teachers or students in the system, it results in barriers and missed opportunities.

Diversity in our leadership and staff is important. One study found that 80% of students from underrepresented groups chose not to participate in gifted courses because they felt that they would be a minority within a minority group (Margot and Melin, 2020). Recruiting a group, as opposed to an individual student, with purposefully thoughtful enrichment that speaks to their culture is a great tactic. Worrell and Dixson have written extensively on motivating capable students who underperform and have cited how important it is that educators consider ethnic background (Worrell and Dixson, 2018). Providing role models from underrepresented groups and intentionally staffing programmes to mirror our student populations is powerful. Seeing academically successful persons from similar backgrounds can serve as a crucial motivator for students. A student's ethnic identity does not always correspond to their academic identity. Students of colour often resort to code-switching – changing the way they speak, dress and present themselves – for white audiences. Culturally relevant pedagogy is a valuable tool. We can celebrate cultural heritage through enrichment opportunities to help students feel more comfortable and directly addressed in these environments. Worrell and Dixson also found that programmes for diverse student groups were more successful when schools intentionally developed students' psychosocial skills (Worrell and Dixson, 2018).

Diverse teams are better teams. There is an intersection between leadership and strategic diversity plans. Buy-in is crucial, as leaders and middle managers are pivotal in carrying out diversity initiatives. It is documented that a staff's negative diversity beliefs can lead to diminished group cohesiveness, absenteeism and turnover (Young, Madsen and Young, 2010). When teachers are not equipped to address diversity, the results can be low student expectations, unfair discipline practices and less equity for students.

Hierarchical and vertical leadership structures also impede diversity – having one teacher of colour at the very top does not mean that DEI is achieved. Distributed leadership models are more flat and horizontal – these delegate decision making and empower more voices. With this sharing of power comes increased collaboration, trust and autonomy among team members (Bachtel, 2017). Distributed leadership gives space for dissenting voices and is increasingly status blind. This empowers staff to become experts and approach initiatives in a nuanced manner. Alma Harris has linked distributed leadership to capacity building and school improvement (Harris, 2003).

As Fonati Abrokwa writes, 'Start with the premise that bias is normal' (Abrokwa, 2022). Appointing a diversity, equity and inclusion point person to captain the boat, promote awareness, deliver staff training and evaluate policies is invaluable. The person in this role having involvement in deeper decision making is necessary for systemic change. Again, it is important to note that people from equity-seeking groups should not have to do the hard work and heavy lifting. The school's policies, structures, processes and institutional culture should. One-size-fits-all or 'diversity quotas' do not make for a complete overhaul. Nor should educators simply be 'unpacking the invisible backpack of privilege', as this tends to focus on our own experience as opposed to institutional structures (Margolin, 2015). Unpacking my white privilege is not the same as understanding another person's lived experience. True diversity halts groupthink and uniformity. While the work may be harder, the outcomes are better. Homogenous teams feel easier but have been found to have poorer performance. Carnegie Mellon, MIT and Union College Studies have found that individual intelligence doesn't have a direct impact on how each team performed. What was important was how team members treated each other. Unsuccessful teams were dominated by one or two people, while successful teams were characterised by an 'equality of distribution' and social sensibility (Jackson, 2023). Our students should see the diversity in their classrooms reflected in school leadership.

## Feedback for Empathy and Diversity

Hearing the needs of students, parents, staff and stakeholders is key because it creates empathy. Ideally, we want to have a diversity of voices that can be heard through a variety of channels. This means creating many methods of feedback. Surveys are a place to start but can be a cursory approach. Evaluating the number of people who answer a survey does not reveal the 'why', and there is a danger of surveys resulting in a tyranny of the majority. In the same way, a focus group can include those from underrepresented groups, but they may not feel comfortable speaking up. Participants may be speaking in a second language or feel isolated because they are the only person of their gender or ethnicity. It is difficult to be burdened with the weight of representing a collective group identity. It is also common to be outnumbered – the power dynamics in the room should be considered. There is a temptation to get every single stakeholder in one room and expect results. This can be useful, but large groups can be intimidating and cumbersome. Tokenism and round-robins are not enough – concerns are not necessarily amplified or given credence, nor is there a guarantee of some accountability. Large groups are also easily dominated by one or two charismatic voices. This relegates diversity to a tick box of superficial participation. I highly recommend the podcast *Nice White Parents*, which looks at how parents with the best of intentions shape school reforms designed to help children of colour, but instead fail them by not listening to those voices (Snyder, 2022).

There is pressure for marginalised groups to assimilate without accommodation, and the cost of 'culturally passing' is high and exhausting for many students and parents. It is important to begin by establishing group norms of respect, understanding and safe spaces. There is more space for voices in smaller meetings, so make focus groups that are small and targeted in scope. Create and empower single-issue groups to make recommendations and do deep dives – they can take the time to do rigorous interviews with stakeholders. This is a way to gather more nuanced feedback. There are better collective decisions with a diversity of voices heard. Ensure dissenting voices matter, as it is through listening to critics that real concerns are acknowledged and addressed. Ignore status with invitations – for instance, teaching assistants are staff members who are rarely given the opportunity to speak, even though they are the staff who spend the most one-on-one time with SEN children. Hold student forums – they can be focused on a specific topic like curriculum reform or extracurricular offerings. Do the same for parents.

What I have enjoyed is working on projects with small teams who bring back recommendations to a larger committee. This was one of my most formative experiences when first becoming a senior leader. I remember being part of a three-person team on data and reporting – we spent 30 hours interviewing over 25 staff and used survey data from parents to get a full picture of our school's needs. We drew up a reporting plan and the recommendations were then presented to an action group of representatives from different areas of the school. This flat horizontal structure of leadership allowed us to be slow, thoughtful, deliberate and empowered when we embarked on programmes. This is in line with research on leadership and change management.

Taylor Cox Jr writes about how institutions can meet the challenge of managing diversity and points to diversity as a value-added activity that improves performance (Cox, 2001). His model is a standard operating guide for an organisational culture shift. Cox and Blake (1991) defined the essence of cultural diversity management through committed leadership, organisational evaluation and research, conscious training, change in management styles (recruitment, orientation, appraisal, compensation, etc.) and follow-up with continuous improvement. McKinsey and Company have done incredible work investigating how organisations can innovate and stress that the first step in designing and implementing an innovation network is to connect (Barsh, Capozzi and Davidson, 2008). The recommendations for connection to occur are:

1. Find pockets of people with a mindset to innovate.

2. Combine people with different approaches and skills (e.g. idea generators, researchers, experts and producers). Bring together a diversity of people – this includes different stakeholders and varying levels of seniority.

3. Define the group's role and include subgroups devoted to specific tasks and objectives.

This requires effective leadership, ongoing continuous professional development and a diverse staff reflective of students who can establish safe and engaging learning environments and a sense of belonging. Feedback is not an end point or a start point; it is a circle for continuous improvement. Creating benchmarks and tracking progress to measure success is how feelings of inclusion and belonging can grow (Abrokwa, 2022). Gifted programmes have traditionally been a place of selection and elitism. Enrichment requires a new mindset of inclusivity that begs for a diversity of voices and expanded methods of feedback.

**Enrichment Focus Group Starter Questions**

DEI statements and mission statements should be embedded in enrichment programming. We need to ask questions in order to identify the gaps. How do different groups of families perceive the school culture? Do we have a clear system for helping us identify and act on inequities? Are teachers and staff properly trained and equipped to overcome these challenges? Can we use an equity lens when making budget decisions? Are we effectively communicating DEI policies and decisions (RocketPD, 2021)?

**Gathering data is a great place to start – we are then working from an informed place.**

- Which students are participating in enrichment activities? Which students are not?
  - What is the proportion of participating students who receive free-school meals or are from underserved and under-resourced backgrounds?
  - What proportion of SEN identified students are participating?
  - What proportion of EAL identified students are participating?
  - Which marginalised/equity-seeking groups are not partaking?
  - What age/cohort groups are not partaking?
- What is the demographic breakdown of students in higher sets or Advanced Placement classes?
- When is participation highest and lowest? What time of year? What time in the day (i.e. before, during or after school)?
- What are the participation rates of:
  - After-school activities
  - Activities, competitions or conferences with associated costs
  - Programming during summer/winter breaks
  - Weekend programming.
- What are the differences in participation across the types of extracurriculars offered?
  - Breakdown of sports/performing arts/academic societies
  - Academic extension and/or foundational tutoring in a subject

- Exploration of a topic or skill outside the curriculum – e.g. robotics, archery
- Recreation or mindfulness – e.g. meditation, yoga, gaming
- Service and contribution to the school or larger community
- Student leadership
- Preparation for competition or conferences
- CV building for university/higher education.

- Are there differences in how particular activities are staffed or funded?
- Is there a separation or segregation of groups in certain fields? (e.g. More boys in STEM clubs? More girls in performing arts?)
- Is there cultural representation in the activities offered?
- Which enrichment activities are flourishing?

Then we can ask the most pertinent question – why? Surveys to students, staff and parents are an easy way to take the temperature and find out why we are seeing particular trends. This can go further than participation. Every part of enrichment can be improved by polling students, from skills they would like to hone, to topics outside of the curriculum they would like to explore, to the extension activities that challenge them. We should also look at whether enrichment is fulfilling and valuable to students. We can enquire about skills they wish to hone, perhaps by tagging the World Economic Forum's 21st Century Skills to activities. We live in the age of online surveys, and it is fairly easy to ask students what they want, how they want it and why it challenges them. Enrichment is a place where we can further build skills, embed the hidden curriculum, extend beyond the syllabus and boost student wellbeing. The next step for a focus group is to make thoughtful enquiries.

## Quality of Enrichment

- Are the activities and programmes offered of interest to students?
- How engaging are activities?
- Do students feel challenged?
- Are staff knowledgeable and experts in the activities they are delivering?

- Is planning evident and purposeful?

- How do activities reinforce in-class learning?

- How do activities extend and explore outside of the curriculum?

- What incentives would promote meaningful participation?

- How effective are activities? How is effectiveness measured?

- What skills are being developed? Are skills in activities identified and tracked?

- Are students assessed and targeted for development? Do students see tangible growth? Is there a final goal or output?

- Do students practise and hone skills outside of the activity?

- Are students given specific and immediate feedback on how to improve?

- What are students' career aspirations and do the activities offer guidance to reach those goals?

## Structure of Enrichment

- Are the timings of activities or programmes conducive to learning?

- What is the current work–life balance of students?

- Are activities financially accessible to all families?

- Do activities require too much or too little social capital and time from families?

- Is there a need for introductory boot camp or novice preparation? Are there levels of development and scaffolding built in?

- Are applications, auditions or sports try-outs inhibitive?

- Do students and staff have the energy and commitment to meaningfully embrace enrichment?

- What facilities or equipment need improving?

- Do students engage with each other? Is there any opportunity to go beyond the school and engage at a local, regional, national and international level?

- Which stakeholders are involved?

**Student Outlook**

- How can students' needs and preferences be better addressed?
- What are the barriers that stop participation? What are the reasons students 'lean out'?
- Are activities safe spaces for marginalised groups?
- Would students like the option of gender-segregated opportunities?
- How are friendship groups or cliques influencing the selection of activities?
- Are activities celebratory of different cultures and belief systems?
- Do students have wellbeing support?
- Are activities accessible? How could flexibility be offered to enhance participation and experience?
- Are student accomplishments and achievements recognised and celebrated?

Here are a few options beyond surveys:

*Fishbowls*

A small group of participants get together in a circle while those outside the 'fishbowl' listen to what they are discussing. When those on the outside have something to contribute, they can replace someone in the fishbowl. You can also include the audience virtually through technology or shared questions using technology like Mentimeter to engage participants with live polls or word clouds.

*Notes days*

Pixar regularly organises a 'notes day' – an internal reflection day on which participants gather in small groups. At first, they start in their own trusted teams, but after that people from different areas and groups are brought together to think about the most relevant issues or challenges. This is a human-focused approach that raises involvement and energy.

*Dare to ask sessions*

This format asks for engagement and conveys to the audience that their questions are important. Dare to ask sessions are a forum to ask questions of leaders. At the beginning, topics can be brainstormed. Questions can be asked in an open session for parents and students or internally with staff. With a tech set-up there are many apps participants can use to pose questions anonymously or for questions to be 'liked' and voted upon. Results can then be made available in real-time for a crowdsourced discussion.

### Focus groups

Once feedback is acquired it must be presented effectively. We've probably all seen schools with vertical structures, where three or four leaders at the top have to approve and make all decisions. These leaders are in the unenviable position of being stretched very thin and are expected to be experts in everything. They aren't given the time to properly consider, or hear from, all stakeholders. This breeds a scarcity mentality and decision fatigue, with judgements made quickly in rushed meetings with packed agendas. Leaders are also then very separate and distant from the staff who are implementing these policies and initiatives. Distributed leadership models make the argument for better decision making.

So often a focus group will spend weeks interviewing stakeholders and researching. Then when it comes time to present a nuanced report to leadership, decision makers are presented with a truncated and simplified presentation. Amazon has moved away from abbreviated analysis or a short slide presentation – instead, it writes narratively structured memos. This is a great way to identify experts and empower them. Agenda-driven meetings favour those who speak the most confidently, not necessarily those who know the most. Former CEO Jeff Bezos explained that these memos take days or weeks to produce (Carmichael, 2021). Memos are never circulated in advance so they can't be skimmed, people can't bluff and stances are not established before the meeting. The devil is in the details, so let's know the details.

## Staff Empowerment

The number one resource in any school is time. It is tempting to build an enrichment programme by adding more extracurriculars, more training, more curriculum planning and more hours. Teachers can best embrace enrichment programmes when they are given the time and energy to do so. So let's not add more – let's simplify so that any initiative makes a teacher's life easier. Bachtel recommends the same: 'I suggest increased trust in teaching professionals and simplification of policies, standards and procedures so more time can be invested in educating and caring for children. Each educator I know has experienced times where policy and/or a high volume of administrative tasks negatively impacted the quality of care provided [to] students' (Bachtel, 2017, p. 229). A rule of enrichment should be not to add more, but instead to take away unnecessary burdens from teachers. The best enrichment programmes should be streamlined and create systems of efficiency. The mantra should always be 'not more, but interesting'.

This means asking staff to do less – one extracurricular instead of two and giving flexibility in how an activity is offered: online, through flipped learning, during lunchtime or weekend sessions. Good enrichment design should be labour-saving and time-saving. Having staff share a club can halve the work and allow more time for each teacher to plan high-quality sessions. Teacher autonomy is also important. We all have passions and a desire for what and how to deliver enrichment. I have seen teachers who speak Japanese and wish to teach the language sighing with exasperation when they are assigned to run ping-pong. Part of gaining staff buy-in is to appreciate the unique talents they can offer. Surveys of staff and students can determine the interests and priorities of our extracurricular programmes. Instead of a school offering 200+ clubs we should recognise first that teachers and students are meant to enjoy enrichment. If a teacher is burnt out and students are overburdened, then there is no energy at the end of a long day to run an effective STEM club. In designing an enrichment programme, we will be exploring the many strategies to overcome these challenges for staff. In this case, cluster grouping can really help streamline extracurricular commitments. On the other end of the spectrum, an enrichment club should not be determined by popularity or headcount – there can be incredible opportunities where a two-student club can take the lid off learning. I had a club of three students publish research papers on astrobiology.

We can run pilots, float balloons, tweak existing programmes or just change the promotion on an existing programme to modify recruitment. There is no perfect solution. As Renzulli and Delcourt have written, 'It is far better to have imprecise answers to the right questions than precise answers to the wrong questions' (Renzulli and Delcourt, 2013, p. 42).

Inclusivity begins with placing the student experience at the centre. We should not stop at surveys – focus groups and student forums are perfect places to create in-depth feedback loops. Auditing our school to explicitly evaluate our policies, structures and stakeholders is powerful because it helps us discover barriers and begin to put plans in place for more inclusive enrichment.

Diversity, equity and inclusion are at the very heart of challenge for all. If we want to increase joy, close achievement gaps and reverse cycles of social immobility, then inviting and empowering all students and stakeholders is the silver bullet.

Everyone is welcome to the big top.

# Reference List

Abrokwa, F. (2022) '6 strategies for promoting diversity and inclusion at your school', *Education Week,* 27 January. Available at: www.edweek.org/leadership/opinion-6-strategies-for-promoting-diversity-and-inclusion-at-your-school/2022/01 (Accessed: 16 September 2022).

Alexandra Park School. (2017) *Alexandra Park School's values.* Available at: www.alexandrapark.school/images/pdf/parents_guides/APS_Values_Reporting.pdf (Accessed: 7 March 2023).

Alexandra Park School. (2023) *Sixth form results.* Available at: www.alexandrapark.school/about-us/performance/sixthform-results (Accessed: 7 March 2023).

Ames, S. (2020) 'Diversity, equity & inclusion: A framework to make it happen', *Brighter Strategies,* 4 August. Available at: www.brighterstrategies.com/blog/diversity-equity-inclusion-framework/ (Accessed: 2 March 2023).

Bachtel, K. A. (2017) 'Seeing the unseen: An educational criticism of a gifted school.' *Teaching and Learning Sciences: Doctoral Research Projects,* 7.

Barsh, J., Capozzi, M. M. and Davidson, J. (2008) 'Leadership and innovation', *McKinsey Quarterly,* 1 January, [Online]. Available at: www.mckinsey.com/business-functions/strategy-and-corporate-finance/our-insights/leadership-and-innovation (Accessed: 16 September 2022).

Bloom, B. S. (1956) *Taxonomy of Educational Objectives, Handbook I: The Cognitive Domain.* New York, NY: David McKay Co Inc.

Burns, J. (2016) *London school's towering performance in Pisa tests.* Available at: www.bbc.com/news/education-38262047 (Accessed: 7 March 2023).

Carmichael, S. G. (2021) *New CEO Andy Jassy's scary 'chop' meetings and what goes on.* Available at: www.ndtv.com/opinion/new-ceo-andy-jassys-scary-chop-meetings-and-what-goes-on-2365484 (Accessed: 16 September 2022).

Cooperative Extension. (2022) *Diversity, equity, and inclusion.* Available at: https://dei.extension.org/ (Accessed: 27 November 2022).

Cox, T. and Blake, S. (1991) 'Managing cultural diversity: Implications for organizational competitiveness.' *Academy of Management Perspectives,* 5(3): pp. 45–56.

Cox, T. Jr. (2001) *Creating the Multicultural Organization: A Strategy for Capturing the Power of Diversity.* San Francisco, CA: Jossey-Bass.

de los Ríos, C. V., López, J. and Morrell, E. (2015) 'Toward a critical pedagogy of race: Ethnic studies and literacies of power in high school classrooms.' *Race and Social Problems,* 7(1): pp. 84–96.

Dewsbury, B. and Brame, C. J. (2019a) 'Evidence-based teaching guide: Inclusive teaching.' Available at: https://lse.ascb.org/evidence-based-teaching-guides/inclusive-teaching/philosophy/ (Accessed: 16 May 2024).

Dewsbury, B. and Brame, C. J. (2019b) 'Inclusive teaching.' *CBE Life Sciences Education,* 18(2): pp. 1–5.

Eckert, R. D. (2006) 'Developing a mission statement on the educational needs of gifted and talented students.' In: Purcell, J. H. and Eckert, R. D. (eds.) *Designing Services and Programs for High-ability Learners: A Guidebook for Gifted Education.* California, USA: Corwin Press, pp. 15–22.

Freire, P. (1970) *Pedagogy of the Oppressed.* Translated by Ramos, M. B. New York, NY: Continuum.

Gallagher, J. L., Swalwell, K. M. and Bellows, M. E. (2019) '"Pinning" with pause: Supporting teachers' critical consumption on sites of curriculum sharing.' *Elementary Education,* 83(4): pp. 217–224.

Gamrat, C., Tiwari, S. and Bekiroglu, S. O. (2022) *INCLUSIVE ADDIE: Initial considerations for DEI pedagogy.* Available at: https://er.educause.edu/articles/2022/3/inclusive-addie-initial-considerations-for-dei-pedagogy#fn4 (Accessed: 1 January 2024).

Garden International School. (2023a) *GIS Learning culture.* Available at: www.gardenschool.edu.my/learning/gis-learning-culture/ (Accessed: 1 January 2023).

Garden International School. (2023b) *Principal's welcome.* Available at: www.gardenschool.edu.my/ (Accessed: 1 January 2023).

Gay, G. (2002) 'Preparing for culturally responsive teaching.' *Journal of Teacher Education,* 53(2): pp. 106–116.

Grady, C. (2020) *Why the term 'BIPOC' is so complicated, explained by linguists.* Available at: www.vox.com/2020/6/30/21300294/bipoc-what-does-it-mean-critical-race-linguistics-jonathan-rosa-deandra-miles-hercules (Accessed: 1 March 2023).

Hansen, M. and Quintero, D. (2018a) *How gender diversity among the teacher workforce affects student learning.* Available at: www.brookings.edu/blog/brown-center-chalkboard/2018/07/10/how-gender-diversity-among-the-teacher-workforce-affects-student-learning/ (Accessed: 16 May 2024).

Hansen, M. and Quintero, D. (2018b) *School leadership: An untapped opportunity to draw young people of color into teaching.* Available at: www.brookings.edu/blog/brown-center-chalkboard/2018/11/26/school-leadership-an-untapped-opportunity-to-draw-young-people-of-color-into-teaching/ (Accessed: 16 May 2024).

Harbor Day School. (n.d.) *Student life: Diversity, equity, and inclusion.* Available at: www.harborday.org/student-life/diversity-equity-and-inclusion (Accessed: 1 January 2024).

Harris, A. (2003) 'Distributed leadership in schools: Leading or misleading?' *Management in Education,* 16(5): pp. 10–13.

Hastings and Prince Edward District School Board. (2021) *2020-2025 strategic plan*. Available at: www.hpeschools.ca/board/connection_pieces/newsroom/2021/board_meeting_update_october_25_2021/2020_2025_strategic_plan (Accessed: 1 January 2024).

Hunt, V., Layton, D. and Prince, S. (2015) *Diversity matters*. Available at: www.mckinsey.com/capabilities/people-and-organizational-performance/our-insights/why-diversity-matters (Accessed: 12 March 2023).

Jackson, F. (2023) *How to build and develop high-performing teams*. Available at: www.cultureamp.com/blog/how-to-enable-high-performing-teams (Accessed: 22 May 2024).

Kaufman, J. and Gabler, J. (2004) 'Cultural capital and the extracurricular activities of girls and boys in the college attainment process.' *Poetics*, 32(2): pp. 145–168.

Margolin, L. (2015) 'Unpacking the invisible knapsack: The invention of white privilege pedagogy.' *Cogent Social Sciences*, 1(1): 1053183.

Margot, K. C. and Melin, J. (2020) *Gifted Education and Gifted Students: A Guide for Inservice and Preservice Teachers*. New York, NY: Prufrock Press Inc.

McGill, R. M. (2016) 'The best school in the world!', *Teacher Toolkit*, 19 December. Available at: www.teachertoolkit.co.uk/2016/12/19/pisa-2015/ (Accessed: 7 March 2023).

Ministry of Education. (2014) *Achieving excellence: A renewed vision for education in Ontario*. Ontario Government: Queen's Printer for Ontario.

New York State Board of Regents. (2021) *Policy on diversity, equity and inclusion*. Available at: www.regents.nysed.gov/common/regents/files/521bra7.pdf (Accessed: 1 March 2023).

Noguera, P. A. (2015) 'Race, education, and the pursuit of equity in the twenty-first century.' In: Noguera, P. A., Pierce, J. C., and Ahram, R. (eds.) *Race, Equity, and Education: Sixty Years from Brown*. Switzerland: Springer Cham, pp. 3–23.

Northbrook District 28. (n.d.) *Diversity equity and inclusion statement*. Available at: www.northbrook28.net/about-us/diversity-equity-and-inclusion-statement (Accessed: 1 January 2024).

Odabaş, M. and Aragão, C. (2023) *School district mission statements highlight a partisan divide over diversity, equity and inclusion in K-12 education*. Available at: www.pewresearch.org/social-trends/2023/04/04/school-district-mission-statements-highlight-a-partisan-divide-over-diversity-equity-and-inclusion-in-k-12-education/ (Accessed: 28 December 2023).

Ofsted. (2023a) *Alexandra Park School: Rating and reports*. Available at: https://reports.ofsted.gov.uk/provider/23/137531 (Accessed: 7 March 2023).

Ofsted. (2023b) *Alexandra Park School*. Available at: www.alexandrapark.school/about-us/our-values (Accessed: 7 March 2023).

Organisation for Economic Co-operation and Development (OECD). (2018) *PISA 2015: Results in focus*. Available at: www.oecd.org/pisa/pisa-2015-results-in-focus.pdf (Accessed: 7 March 2023).

Reis, S. M. and Gubbins, E. J. (2017) 'Comprehensive program design.' In: Eckert, R. D. and Robins, J. H. (eds.) *Designing Services and Programs for High-Ability Learners: A Guidebook for Gifted Education*, 2nd edn. California, USA: Corwin, pp. 58–76.

Renzulli, J. S. (2013) *The achievement gap: Using strength-based pedagogy to increase the achievement of all students*. Available at: https://renzullilearning.com/wp-content/uploads/2018/07/AchievementGapPaper.pdf (Accessed: 22 May 2024).

Renzulli, J. S. and Delcourt, M. A. B. (2013) 'Gifted behaviours versus gifted individuals.' In: Callahan, C. M. and Hertberg-Davis, H. L. (eds.) *Fundamentals of Gifted Education: Considering Multiple Perspectives*. New York, NY: Routledge, pp. 36–48.

RocketPD. (2021) *A framework to make diversity, equity and inclusion (DEI) part of your school culture*. Available at: https://rocketpd.com/a-framework-to-make-diversity-equity-and-inclusion-dei-part-of-your-school-culture/ (Accessed: 1 March 2023).

Sherrington, T. (2012) 'Gifted and talented provision: A total philosophy', *Teacherhead*, 12 September. Available at: https://teacherhead.com/2012/09/12/gifted-and-talented-provision-a-total-philosophy/ (Accessed: 7 March 2023).

Skiba, R. J., Simmons, A. B., Ritter, S., Gibb, A. C., Rausch, M. K., Cuadrado, J. and Chung, C. (2008) 'Achieving equity in special education: History, status, and current challenges.' *Exceptional Children*, 74(3): pp. 264–288.

Snyder, J. (2022) *Nice white parents*. 30 July, [Podcast]. Available at: www.nytimes.com/2020/07/23/podcasts/nice-white-parents-serial.html (Accessed: 16 September 2022).

Soffel, J. (2016) 'Ten 21st-century skills every student needs', *World Economic Forum*, 10 March. Available at: www.weforum.org/agenda/2016/03/21st-century-skills-future-jobs-students/ (Accessed: 7 March 2023).

The Good Schools Guide. (2022) *Alexandra Park School*. Available at: www.goodschoolsguide.co.uk/schools/alexandra-park-school-london#tab_review (Accessed: 7 March 2023).

The Trustees of Phillips Exeter Academy. (2023) *Diversity, equity and inclusion vision statement*. Available at: www.exeter.edu/community/inclusive-community/diversity-equity-and-inclusion-vision-statement (Accessed: 1 January 2024).

UK Government. (2023) *Alexandra Park School*. Available at: www.get-information-schools.service.gov.uk/Establishments/Establishment/Details/137531 (Accessed: 7 March 2023).

Vavrus, M. (2008) 'Culturally responsive teaching.' In: Good, T. L. (ed.) *21st Century Education: A Reference Handbook,* Thousand Oaks, CA: SAGE Publications, pp. 49–57.

Village School. (2022) *Equity and inclusion: Diversity mission statement.* Available at: www.village-school.org/about-us/equity-and-inclusion (Accessed: 1 January 2024).

World Class Schools. (2019) *Alexandra Park School.* Available at: www.worldclass-schools.org/our-schools/alexandra-park-school/ (Accessed: 7 March 2023).

Worrell, F. C. and Dixson, D. D. (2018) 'Recruiting and retaining underrepresented gifted students.' In: Pfeiffer, S. I. (ed.) *Handbook of Giftedness in Children: Psychoeducational Theory, Research, and Best Practices.* 2nd edn. New York, NY: Springer, pp. 209–226.

Wunderlich, D. (2020) *Geneva Gay: A legacy of elevating multicultural education to prominence.* Available at: https://education.uw.edu/news/feature/geneva-gay-legacy-elevating-multicultural-education-prominence (Accessed: 17 May 2024).

Young, B. L., Madsen, J. and Young, M. A. (2010) 'Implementing diversity plans: Principals' perception of their ability to address diversity in their schools.' *NASSP Bulletin,* 94(2): pp. 135–157.

# ACKNOWLEDGEMENTS

This book was written on Friday afternoons, with my husband John taking all three little ones so I could escape for a few hours each week. Every step of the way he has been such an encouraging and kind partner. He is always a wonderful dad. Thank you, sweetie.

My thoughts on enrichment were formed over my years of teaching in Abu Dhabi. Huge thanks to Brendan Law who shared his vision of whole-child development and gave me every opportunity to build the enrichment programme of my dreams.

I've been so lucky to work at outstanding schools with extraordinary people. I could not have been a mum and a school leader without the words of wisdom from the dazzling Helen Board. Colleagues have become dear friends – I am in awe of Rosemarie Lewis, Laura Oliver, Colette Bruton, Sophia DeLee, Rich Hay, Lewis Baille, Stephen Daly, Luzardi Fischer, Thom Faulkner and the lovely Tara-Lyn and David Gibson. David Slade is a marvel, one year is not enough. I'm so grateful for the support from the irrepressible Helen Currie and warm-hearted Linda Law. Simon and Phoebe Kenworthy, your smiles always made my day and I hope to work with you both again one day soon!

Thank you Nigel Davis for your passion for teaching and learning; you ignited a whole city with your enthusiasm! There are a group of T&L nerds who have shaped so much of my thinking, including the superb Rizwana Shaikh, Amit Patel, Guy Schooley, Dean Williams and Matt McNaught. There are those who read my early chapters and shared their expertise. Cat Chowdhary is modest and magnificent in everything she does, a remarkable educator, author and mum. Tod Brennan is the most insightful person I've ever had the pleasure of debating with and no one knows their pedagogy better. Stephen Moffatt is one of the best leaders I've ever worked with; his relentless positivity and restorative lattes got me through the last two years of writing. Olly Lewis, you are a superhero and I don't know how you do it all – I can't wait to read your book. Leisa Grace Wilson, thank you for reading my final draft – your words and support have been invaluable.

Kate Jones was the one who said 'you should write a book' and her advice is everything! She is my feminist ally, good friend and an incredible author. Thank you, Kate! I'm grateful to everyone at John Catt and Hodder Education, especially the phenomenal Natasha Gladwell for all her guidance and expertise. I'm so appreciative of Hillary Fry for being my first sounding board. Thank you to Alex Sharratt and Jonathan Barnes for supporting my work. I was hugely influenced by the writings of Tom Sherrington, Deborah Eyre, Geneva Gay, James Borland, Andy Tharby, Shaun Allison, Dante D. Dixson, Frank C. Worrell, Sally Reis and Joseph Renzulli.

My sisters Laura and Kyly are simply the best; my mom and dad are exceptional. Hugs to my delightful Iona, sweet Stafford and adorable Fraser.

And of course, many thanks to my students who have left me astonished, awestruck and amazed.